INTRODUCTION TO PROFESSIONAL NEWSWRITING

Reporting for the Modern Media

INTRODUCTION *To* PROFESSIONAL NEWSWRITING

Reporting for the Modern Media

Conrad C. Fink

University of Georgia

Longman

Introduction to Professional Newswriting

Longman, 95 Church Street, White Plains, N.Y. 10601

Associated companies:
Longman Group Ltd., London
Longman Cheshire Pty., Melbourne
Longman Paul Pty., Auckland
Copp Clark Pitman, Toronto

Acquiring editor: Kathleen Schurawich
Development editor: Elsa van Bergen
Production editor: Dee Amir Josephson
Text design: Kevin Kall
Cover design: Kevin Kall
Cover photo: Anthony Alberts

Library of Congress Cataloging-in-Publication Data

Fink, Conrad C.
    Introduction to professional newswriting : reporting for the
modern media / Conrad C. Fink.
        p.   cm.
    Includes bibliographical references and index.
    ISBN 0-8013-0691-4
    1. Journalism—Authorship—Handbooks, manuals, etc.
2. Journalism—Style manuals.   3. Journalism—Language.
4. Technical writing—Handbooks, manuals, etc.   I. Title.
PN4783.F56   1991
808′.06607–dc20   91–18968
                                                              CIP

1 2 3 4 5 6 7 8 9 10-MU-9594939291

This book is dedicated to
Bud, Kathryn and Midge,
scattered but close.

Contents

Part 2   Your Newswriter Tools   37

Chapter Two   Language: The Newswriter's Basic Tool   39

Chapter Five   Leads That Hook Readers   125

Part 4 The Art of Reporting, Legal Traps and Ethical Questions — 223

Chapter Ten   A Personal Code of Ethics   275

Chapter Thirteen Writing Science News 351

Chapter Fourteen Sports Writing: More Than Fun and Games 369

List of Sidebars:

Contributions by Professionals

Preface

This book is designed to lead you through a process that will help you become an effective newswriter. You will learn to look discerningly at the clamorous, ever-shifting world of news, select those elements most crucial, and convey their meaning and importance in simple and direct language that communicates clearly.

Even after more than 25 years as a media professional and nearly a decade in teaching, I feel kinship with you as you start the process. That kinship guided my writing of *Introduction to Professional Newswriting*. I structured the book to acquaint you first with basic definitions of news, then to lead you with careful pacing toward more sophisticated newswriting techniques in later chapters.

Learning effective newswriting is a fascinating journey of discovery. Many of us who already have made it could envy you the adventures and accomplishments that lie ahead and, yes, even the frustrations you surely will encounter along the way.

Your journey won't be easy. Even for highly talented professionals, effective newswriting can be an agonizing (if wondrous) process. Red Smith, one of the greatest ever and a Pulitzer Prize winner for *The New York Times,* said near the end of his long career that even for him writing was like sitting down, opening a vein, and bleeding.

But, oh, the rewards for those who persist! Imagine a career on the cutting edge of news, being there when it happens, charged not only with watching and understanding what it all means, but, also, communicating that to those poor souls unfortunate enough not to be there. Wes Gallagher, an Associated Press war correspondent and executive, likened the task (he would call it an honor) to having a ringside seat to the unfolding of history.

And always, beneath the glamor and adventure, there is the central and very serious mission of *communicating*—gathering facts, yes; understanding them, yes; but then going that essential step further and translating into understandable terms, through clear and concise writing, the human condition in all its joy and misery, its positives and negatives, its creative and destructive dimensions.

Newswriting is work that often is fun, frequently creative, sometimes thrilling, but *always* important. It is socially responsible work with meaning, work that can shine light in dark corners and change things, work that can make the world just a little bit better place to live. Don't be overawed by the challenge of reaching for such distant journalistic horizons. Those who took this journey before you—and

I've made the trek—started where you are starting. Even the greatest of the professionals learned, as you will learn, to take it step by step.

At journey's end, whatever your career interest, you should be a better *communicator.*

If newspapers or magazines attract you, *Introduction to Professional Newswriting* will show you how to sense what is news, where to find it, then how to report and write it to real-world specifications. This should position you to do well in later and more advanced specialty newswriting in public affairs, business and economics, sports, science or other important topics you see in print every day.

If your goal is television or radio, your basic—and essential—tools must be discerning news judgment and effective newswriting skills, just as in print journalism. *Introduction to Professional Newswriting* should equip you with those tools and prepare you for later concentration in your chosen specialty.

Some of you undoubtedly will be attracted to careers in alternate methods of communication—newsletters, book publishing, electronic delivery of information to homes, or other and yet unknown techniques that future technology almost certainly will open. For you this book has real pertinence because whatever the techniques or technologies in years ahead, the core of effective communication will remain your ability to sort through facts, discarding the nonessential and presenting the essential in clear, concise terms.

Those of you inclined toward public relations should note that effective communication—particularly *written* communication—is the heartbeat of your chosen industry. PR firms repeatedly say, "Send us people who can write." *Introduction to Professional Newswriting* will help you meet that request. In advertising, where careers stand or fall on ability to communicate, effective writing skills are supremely important. Great ad campaigns that sell products and services—or slogans that push ideas and causes or build fame for personalities and ideologies—all begin in a writer's mind and find expression on a keyboard.

Avoid locking yourself in too early to a set career path. The discovery process of learning basic newswriting could well open to you new and yet unimagined options. American media history is filled with examples of men and women who built successful careers by crossing from one medium to another. Michael Gartner rose from a newspaper reporter's typewriter to important executive jobs with the *Wall Street Journal, Des Moines Register* and other newspapers and then became president of NBC News. A dean of television news anchors, Walter Cronkite, started as a newspaper and news service reporter. America's PR and advertising industries are filled with ex-reporters from newspapers, magazines and broadcast. All began by learning basic newswriting.

ORGANIZATION OF THIS BOOK

A news story *must communicate news,* and if it doesn't, even the most superbly crafted, beautifully written story will fail. Obviously, then, your first step in developing newswriting skills must be to understand what news is and, importantly, learn how the various types of media define news. This we cover in Part 1, Chapter One, "The Professional Context."

In Part 2, "Your Newswriter Tools," I devote Chapter Two to discussing writing techniques used by professional journalists. The techniques include writing simple sentences, using present tense, and translating terms your readers might not understand. Chapter Three introduces the fundamentals of newspaper style and the constant battle in newswriting against bloated, abstract language. Your ability to write in correct style and to avoid redundancies and cliches will be a major test of your professionalism.

Part 3 is designed to help you build your personal newswriting style. Chapter Four provides hints on organizing a news story. The actual writing of your first paragraph, or "lead," cannot proceed until you have the story structure firmly outlined in your mind. Chapter Five, "Leads That Hook Readers," starts you on the search for ways to grab readers and pull them into your story. Chapter Six provides ideas on how, once you have hooked readers, you can pull them through your story so they experience minimum reading difficulty—yet obtain maximum reading enjoyment and information. Accomplishing that requires you to construct a "bridge of confidence" with your readers by quoting authoritative sources and relaying facts, and that's the subject of Chapter Seven.

Effective newswriting flows, of course, out of effective reporting, and Part 4, Chapter Eight, discusses how newsrooms are organized to find and bring in news. Of particular importance to beginning newswriters is the discussion on "care and feeding" of news sources and how to extract news from them in interviews.

We then turn to press law and ethics. Both are essential subjects if you are launching into a news career. You *must* understand basics of libel law before you publish one word, and I discuss that in Chapter Nine. In Chapter Ten, we look at how you can start developing a personal code of ethics. Doing the *ethically right* thing in newswriting is as important as being *legally correct*.

In Part 5, Chapter Eleven, I provide hints on specific kinds of stories a beginner will cover—speeches, meetings, news conferences and so forth. We continue this approach in subsequent chapters with beginner's hints for newswriting categories particularly "hot" in journalism today: economic, business and financial news, in Chapter Twelve; news about science, the environment and health, in Chapter Thirteen; sports, in Chapter Fourteen. In Chapter Fifteen, I discuss "Devices for Focusing the News." They include newsfeatures, sidebars (stories written to illuminate another story), personality profiles and obituaries (they are being written these days in new, interesting ways).

Part 6, Chapter Sixteen, turns to broadcast writing. I provide a few hints on how to write for the ear, not the eye, to weave your words into a mosaic that includes pictures and sound.

Public relations writing is *advocacy writing* and sometimes ranges far from the newswriting ideal of dispassionate and balanced reporting. Thoroughly legitimate careers are open in the commercial marketplace of ideas for those who openly wear the label "advocate." In Part 7, Chapter Seventeen, I pass along guidance on PR writing skills.

Finally, in Part 8, Chapter Eighteen, I suggest how to write your résumé, contact professionals in your chosen field and get started, while still in school, with a serious effort to ensure you have a job upon graduation. Now is the time to launch your career.

I've included in this book many examples of newswriting drawn from newspapers nationwide, included in text, or as "sidebars." In a few cases, where there are legal or ethical reasons to not identify persons named in news stories, I've substituted fictitious names in brackets: [Fred Smith], for example. All other names and facts in examples are as published.

Throughout the book, I've positioned notes in the margins to signal a discussion of a key concept in the adjacent text. These should be particularly useful when you need to quickly search for guidance on how to solve a writing problem or when you are reviewing for a test.

The standard for this textbook in style, punctuation and usage is *The Associated Press Stylebook and Libel Manual.* Excerpts from it are published in the appendix for handy reference. Most American newspapers use AP style, although many have their own approach to some usages. For example, some papers use *yesterday* or *today* time elements when AP style calls for *Monday* or *Tuesday.* In news stories reproduced as examples, I have left intact the usage and style published in the original version, even if they conflict with AP style.

ACKNOWLEDGMENTS

The wonderful students I've had the pleasure of teaching over nearly a decade gave me the idea for this book. Their enthusiasm for learning about news and newswriting transported me back to days when I wrote for The Associated Press under datelines from Chicago to Kabul. I resolved to try to capture for my students the excitement of reporting and writing the news, and to pass along a few newswriting techniques.

Fortunately, Gordon T. R. Anderson, executive editor of the College and Professional Book Division of Longman, immediately sensed what I had in mind, and we agreed to develop this book. Tragically, "Tren" Anderson died before the project was completed. His death was a grave loss to me and to anyone who loves books. I owe Tren much for his guidance in structuring this book and an earlier one, *Inside the Media,* also published by Longman.

To my good fortune, Elsa van Bergen, Longman developmental editing supervisor who helped plan this book, has continued to give me excellent guidance. To Elsa, a superb editor, I owe gratitude.

I also am indebted to the talented people who worked on the production of this book: Joanne Jay, director of production; Dee Josephson, managing editor; Walter Norfleet, art director; and Kevin Kall, senior designer.

David Fox, assistant editor in Longman's college division and a man of uncommon good cheer, has my thanks for his alert, responsive help throughout.

Special thanks go to scores of writing instructors at colleges and universities throughout the nation who helped plan this book: They responded in helpful detail to an extensive survey Tren Anderson and I conducted to determine how newswriting text should be structured. Their ideas are incorporated throughout this book.

Many of my colleagues at the University of Georgia's Henry W. Grady College of Journalism and Mass Communication deserve special thanks for their helpful advice. Kent Middleton, who has taught newswriting for years, devoted countless hours to reading and (without pulling punches) critiquing the manuscript. His suggestions were very important to me. Dan Kitchens, for 30 years a newswriting teacher and our "house expert" on grammar and style, provided excellent guidance. Melinda Hawley and Laura Sweep, both experienced newspaper reporters and editors, labored over my manuscript while working on graduate degrees at the Grady College. Both proved to be tough and, thus, helpful critics.

David Hazinski, a former NBC correspondent who now teaches broadcast newswriting in our Grady College, read my chapter on broadcast writing and was very helpful. Scott Cutlip, one of the nation's leading scholars in public relations history and practice, critiqued my chapter on PR writing. So did Roland Page, a former newspaper correspondent in Washington who now teaches public relations at the Grady College. My thanks to both. Dean Tom Russell of the Grady College provided marvelous support in this project, as he has in all my teaching and writing efforts.

My special thanks to others in academia who reviewed the manuscript and helped shape its final form: Peter Gross, California State College, Chico; John Zelezny, California State College, Fresno; Freda McVay, Texas Tech University; Don Guimary, San Jose State College; Thomas Dickson, Southwest Missouri State University; William Utter, Miami University of Ohio; Len Sellers, San Francisco State College; Jon Willis, Ball State University; Dan Harper, Cabrillo College; Pat Robertson,

Southern University; Laurie O'Brien, University of West Florida; Kent Middleton, University of Georgia; and Dan Kitchens, Emeritus, University of Georgia.

In all my writing projects, I have received wonderful support from professional colleagues. This book was no exception. Thanks to all of you, particularly to Gene Roberts, then executive editor of *The Philadelphia Inquirer,* for contributing a thoughtful essay on news definition; Lou Boccardi, president of The Associated Press, for providing photos and permission to reproduce portions of *The Associated Press Stylebook and Libel Manual,* and Ben Bradlee, executive editor of *The Washington Post,* for permission to reproduce portions of the ethics statement he wrote for his newspaper. For many newspaper colleagues whose work strengthens this book, I've accorded the best accolade of all—a byline.

Finally, deep thanks to Nicki Parham, a woman of enormous enthusiasm, who typed this manuscript and did much to help keep my writing project moving.

Conrad C. Fink
Athens, Georgia

INTRODUCTION To PROFESSIONAL NEWSWRITING

Reporting for the Modern Media

Part 1

The Professional Context

The Chinese have an old saying that goes something like this: Even the longest journey starts with the first step.

It's the same in learning newswriting. We—you and I—must take the first step. *But in which direction?*

Well, to move toward effective newswriting our first step must be to understand our basic commodity: news. We must understand where it comes from, how it is defined by professionals, and, importantly, how they shape it for use in the various media for which you might work one day.

The core of this is understanding the fundamental news missions adopted by newspapers, magazines, and TV and radio stations to meet their own business and competitive goals. Professionals define and use news within that context. True understanding of how and why they do that will help you bound—not merely step—toward the effective newswriting skills of a professional.

In Chapter 1, we will study two major concepts:

- What is news?

- How is news used?

You will learn that different news strategies are pursued by newspapers, magazines, radio and TV stations, and news services. Consequently, the media often define news differently. You will learn, however, that whatever their strategies may be, all the media seek news stories that are *timely,* that deal with *conflict* and *prominent people,* and that have *impact* on large audiences.

You will discuss these concepts in class and write about them. Outside class you should begin immersing yourself in news. It's vital that you read newspapers and magazines, listen to radio news and watch TV newscasts. If successful media professionals demonstrate any single trait it is that they are news freaks—they share something akin to a compulsion to know what is happening in the world about them, and they search, probe, ask to find out.

However, don't read, listen and watch only to find out what is happening. Note also the types of stories professionals select for front pages and newscasts, which facts or "angles" they emphasize, and which they relegate to secondary position. Note their writing, their language, and their style.

If you want to move into the pro leagues watch—very carefully—how the pros play the game.

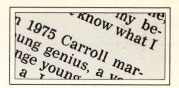

Chapter One

News and How It Is Used

Picture this scenario:

You are in a Chicago newsroom, assigned not to an outside news "beat" reporting news firsthand but, rather, to "rewrite"—an inside newswriting job.

It's 2 p.m., and your editor shouts, "We've got a big one! Get line one."

You take notes via telephone from a breathless colleague: "Fire sweeping through Chicago Board of Trade . . . no injuries . . . heavy smoke forcing commodities brokers into streets . . . trading halted . . . firemen dragging hoses across streets . . . traffic gridlocked for 10 blocks in all directions."

Now what?

Well, if you're in the *Chicago Tribune*'s newsroom you won't start writing. The *Trib* is a morning paper and you have hours until "deadline," when your copy must be in so presses can roll on time. But this is a very big local story, so you and your editor immediately begin coordinating coverage by many reporters and photographers. You'll hit front page with this one, and your eventual writing approach for your general audience of metropolitan Chicago readers will be straightforward: fire guts Chicago landmark, thousands watch, traffic snarled, trading halted—in that order.

If you're in the Chicago bureau of *The Wall Street Journal,* also a morning paper, you too, like your *Trib* colleague, have plenty of time to collect more facts. But your eventual newswriting angle will be quite different. For your business readers worldwide you will take this approach: trading halted at world's largest commodities exchange; deals worth millions fall through; international markets in disarray; trading will resume in 24 hours. And, maybe a few—but just a few—details will be included on the fire itself and traffic snarl.

If you're in the newsroom of a leading Chicago radio station, WGN-AM, you, unlike your morning newspaper colleagues, start writing quickly—*very* quickly. First, you do two terse, fact-filled paragraphs emphasizing (in order) location, no injuries, traffic snarl, trading halted. The disk jockey on duty airs the story immediately. WGN's commuter listeners rely on radio to avoid traffic problems. Besides, smoke can be seen for miles and people turn quickly to radio for details on such "breaking" stories. With two "grafs" (paragraphs) out, you turn to gathering and writing additional details that will be broadcast throughout the afternoon.

If you work for WGN-TV, you know the station manager won't permit interrupt-

Associated Press cartoonist Atchison
catches both the original meaning of
"deadline"—and what it can mean to
you in a newsroom today.

WORD FOR WORD

(Used with permission)

ing the afternoon soaps (with their lucrative commercials) for extended coverage of
a fire with no deaths. So, you write a one-liner for hurried insertion between commercials at the next break: "Fire strikes Board of Trade in downtown Chicago.
Details at 6." And, because it is a great *picture story,* the newsroom assignment
editor immediately sends camera crews and reporters ("on-air talent") racing to the
scene. You'll need a "stand-up"—a live report—for the 6 p.m. newscast. Otherwise,
you won't be competitive with other Chicago stations in the contest for best rating
in the important evening news slot.

If you're in *Time* magazine's Chicago bureau you add the fire to other Midwest
stories to watch over the next few days until the weekend "close," when your magazine goes to press. Your base, Chicago, is only part of your news beat and you
cannot put aside the cover story you are doing on regional economic trends in the
Midwest. But you make a mental note to discuss with your New York editors
whether to schedule the fire story for the "Nation" section, which would require a
general, human-interest newswriting angle. Or, maybe the story should be a
"brief"—just a couple of tight paragraphs—for "American Notes," a weekly review
of stories of secondary importance from around the nation. Of course, New York
might want a "business" section story, so you'd better consider, like your *Wall Street
Journal* colleagues, the fire's impact on commodities trading.

If you work for The Associated Press in Chicago, you do several things, in a great
hurry: For Illinois newspapers receiving the news service's wires, you do a story
angled toward "fire strikes landmark in state's largest city." The story is transmitted
urgently, probably as a "bulletin," which alerts editors that major news is coming.
You also transmit a version to New York, AP's headquarters, for relay throughout
the nation and world. Angle for that wider audience: "commodities trading halted."
You also write, in "broadcast language," a version for AP's radio and TV news

wires. And, you help coordinate AP's photo coverage. For AP, there is no "deadline." Somewhere in the world, right now, an AP newspaper is going to press; AP broadcast stations are on the air. In AP, you get it *now,* you write it *now,* you transmit it *now*—24 hours daily, seven days weekly.

As the scenario above demonstrates, your first step in learning effective newswriting is *not* simply to sit down and start writing. (If you did, *which direction would you take?*) Rather, aspiring newswriters first must understand the media's journalistic dynamic and their news-handling systems. They differ dramatically.[1]

First Understand the Media

THE INFLUENCE OF THE MEDIUM

News and Newspapers
Like most media in the American free enterprise system, the *business* of newspapers is delivering attractive audiences to advertisers, who pay about 80 percent of the bills (the readers' 20 percent contribution doesn't even cover the cost of the newsprint on which the paper is printed). Toward that end, newspapers define news and construct news and editorial content designed to serve different "markets."[2] Think, for example, of newspaper markets on two dimensions:

• Horizontal or geographic

• Vertical or interest

Horizontal or geographic markets include cities, or cities plus nearby counties, regions, the nation, even huge areas of the world. To help advertisers reach readers within those markets, newspapers define and collect news with what might be called "geographic coherence." That is, the *Chicago Tribune* serves mostly Chicago-area advertisers and readers and thus emphasizes news that either originates in metropolitan Chicago or, if it originates elsewhere, is of particular interest there. Note that doesn't mean news from Afghanistan or other distant places is ignored. It is published *if* editors consider it pertinent to Chicago readers. But a fire in downtown Chicago—local news—often is relatively more important. National newspapers serve much larger geographic markets—for example, *The New York Times,* the nation; *USA Today,* the nation as well as Europe and Asia. Some weekly newspapers serve only small neighborhoods. Whatever the case, editors serving horizontal markets mostly select news with direct relevance to their turf and to the wide-ranging *general* interests of their readers.

Local News Is Important

Vertical or "interest" markets often have little to do with geography. Rather, they are made up of readers with specific and specialized information needs. *The Wall Street Journal,* for example, serves readers with common interests in news that affects business, finance, industry. Thus, in our scenario above, the *Journal's* Chicago bureau defines news not so much as the *fire* at the Board of Trade but rather as the *effect* of the fire on business. Where in the United States their readers live is irrelevant to *Journal* editors, as long as the readers have income and spending habits attractive to the *Journal's* national advertisers. Specialty newspapers covering, say, sports or farming also seek "interest" markets.

Four other factors bear directly on how newspapers define "news" and thus on how you write for them.

1. In response to competition from magazines with specialized news content, newspapers use "internal zoning." That is, the large daily package is broken into separate sections for readers with narrow interests—business, sports, the arts, and so forth. That means, for example, that although you might work for a general-circulation newspaper such as the *Chicago Tribune,* you could be assigned to write

Newspaper "Internal Zoning"

for the business section's highly specialized audience—and thus need business news-writing skills fully as expert as those of your *Wall Street Journal* colleague.

2. Except for a few that publish editions in both "cycles" (morning and after-noon), most newspapers publish only once in 24 hours. That means your judgment of what is news and how to write it must take into account competitors who can break stories faster than you can. In our fire scenario, you don't start writing imme-diately at the *Chicago Tribune* because your deadline is hours away. Meantime, both radio and TV are breaking the story, airing colorful, dramatic details as they develop. By the time your version flops on doorsteps at dawn tomorrow much of metropolitan Chicago will know at least that the fire occurred. Your newswriting

Write to Move Story Ahead

angle must *move the story ahead* so the *Tribune* gives readers something they al-ready don't know. We'll discuss this later in detail, but if you want to write news you must learn to keep tabs on what competing media are doing.

3. Newspaper production and delivery are so cumbersome that you must develop newswriting techniques to overcome the competitive disadvantages they inflict on you. For example, if you work for the morning *Tribune* you will write the fire story this evening—and no later than about midnight—for a presstime of about 1 a.m. and doorstep delivery at about 6 a.m. tomorrow (see Fig. 1–1). And, how can you, at, say, 10 p.m. today, put an angle on a still-developing story that will "stand" (be journalistically valid) and fresh at breakfast tables at 6 a.m. to 8 a.m. tomorrow? It's a challenge. For afternoon papers you will write in the morning for a presstime of noon or earlier, for doorstep delivery at about 4 p.m., and, very likely, for read-ing not until 6 p.m. or later, when people arrive home from work. Radio announces *now* that a fire is under way: Television shows pictures *tonight*—and newspapers

Explain *How* and *What*

tomorrow morning must go behind the scene to report *how* the fire broke out, full details of the damage, and *what* it all means.

4. Whether you work for a morning or afternoon paper has another crucial im-pact on how you define news and write it. Note again in Figure 1–1 the four-hour "fresh news window" for afternoon newspapers. Relatively little fresh news develops

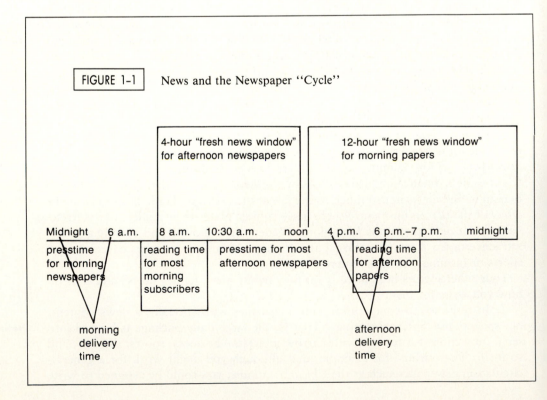

FIGURE 1–1   News and the Newspaper "Cycle"

in the United States in the period 8 a.m. to noon, when afternoon papers generally go to press. That is because officials and groups schedule few meetings, news conferences or other events to break news before noon. Consequently, many afternoon newspaper writers develop "soft" approaches to the news, emphasizing analysis, indepth explanation, and timeless features. Conversely, most fresh news in the United States breaks for morning papers. Afternoon and evening events yield news for morning, not afternoon papers. Morning papers thus generally take on a "hard" news character. For example, if you write the Chicago fire on, say, a Tuesday night

Newspapers use big headlines to signal readers on the day's top news story. Magazines feature cover stories on their top items. Radio and TV interrupt regular programming with news bulletins.

(Gannett photo used with permission)

for *Wednesday morning's* paper, your angle will be straightforward and "hard." Something like this.

> Fire raged through the Chicago Board of Trade Tuesday, forcing commodities brokers into the streets and snarling downtown traffic for hours.
>
> Cause of the fire was not known. . . .

Write Second-day Angles

If you cover the fire for *Wednesday afternoon's* paper, the whole town knows of the fire even before you sit down to write. So you must take what we call a "second-day" newswriting angle, one that *advances* the story and emphasizes not so much the fire itself but, rather, why it occurred and its impact. For example:

> A faulty $5 electrical wiring connection was blamed Wednesday for a multimillion dollar fire that gutted the Chicago Board of Trade and disrupted international commodities trading.
>
> Fire Chief Fred Smith said the fire erupted at about 2 p.m. Tuesday because the connection short-circuited, causing sparks that set the flooring on fire.

The *time imperative* in newswriting often forces you to rush into print or on air with an initial version that rather simply states in broad strokes the few known facts. When time permits, as in the afternoon newspaper example above, strive for an explanatory dimension.

You'll need to develop many newswriting techniques that compensate for the cumbersome production of newspapers and their slow delivery—and to compete against the speed of radio and the visual impact of television. For example (and we'll return to this later), if you want to succeed in newspaper writing you must go deep into stories for detail and meaning that radio and TV don't have time to explore. Go beyond superficialities. Write not just *who* won. Tell *how* they won, *why* and *what* likely comes next. (See A Professional's View on p. 9.)

Magazine Newswriting

Profound changes in magazines are affecting the news sense and newswriting skills you must develop to succeed in that industry.

Most important, specialty or "niche" magazines are flourishing by serving narrowly defined groups of readers seeking specialized information. More than 11,000 magazines tailor their content for well-defined reader groups attractive to advertisers—business executives, aviation industry managers, antique collectors and so forth.

General circulation magazines with wide-ranging, unfocused content are not doing so well. Advertisers get cheaper, more efficient access to general audiences by using television or newspapers. Competition from TV, starting in the 1950s, helped kill *Look* and forced *Life* and *Saturday Evening Post*—both national institutions—to halt regular weekly publication.

In developing magazine writing skills, strive for broad education and writing experience, but, with those many niche publications in mind, also obtain experience in specialty news sectors that interest you—science, economics or sports, perhaps. Specialty magazines hire writers to cover those subjects and many others.

Even newsweeklies that succeed with general audiences—*Time, Newsweek, U.S. News & World Report*—seek writers with deep, specialized background as well as general reporting and writing skills. Flip through one of those magazines and you'll note why: They have many "back-of-the-book" sections carrying specialized information for niche readers interested in subjects such as business, arts and entertainment, travel and so forth.

A Professional's View:
News Broadly Defined

As executive editor and president of The Philadelphia Inquirer, *1972–1990, Gene Roberts created one of the nation's outstanding newspapers—and an unprecedented record of 17 Pulitzer Prizes in 18 years. Here is how one of the great editors of our time defines news.*

At *The Philadelphia Inquirer,* we took the broadest possible definition of news. This means that while we must be diligent in reporting on every form of government, we must never fall into the trap of thinking that government news is the be-all and end-all of newspaper reporting.

A newspaper is negligent if it is filled only with pro forma announcements from public officials, or press releases from anyone who can afford a publicist.

News is what people do, what they say, what they think, what they wear, what they eat. News is art and music and books and comedy and pathos. News is sports and television and business and politics.

What does news look like? News looks odd. "When a dog bites a man, that is not news," goes the famous quote from John B. Bogart, the city editor of the *New York Sun.* "When a man bites a dog, that is news."

Astonishing things are news. A grand slam home run is news. Toppling the Berlin wall is news. A homicide is news.

Things that affect peoples' lives are news. A 10-percent tax increase is news. Five hundred new jobs coming to your hometown is news. Crime statistics, stock tables, television listings and unemployment rates are news.

Sometimes the news is breaking and immediate—like an explosion or a train wreck. The story is obvious, the news coverage spontaneous.

Sometimes the news is hidden by people who have an interest in suppressing the story—like the Watergate scandal during the Nixon presidency or the Iran-Contra scandal during the Reagan administration. News of this nature is revealed only after painstaking research, hours of digging and hundreds of interviews.

Sometimes the news is not pretty. Often, the news is tragic. And sometimes people get hurt—even ruined—by what a newspaper prints.

So whenever we find news, we must be very careful with the stories we publish. Careful with our facts. Careful of the sensitivities of our readers. And we must be always mindful of the private lives and public reputations of the people on whom we report and write.

A newspaper can, and should, be both aggressive and honorable. Reporters can, and should, be both tenacious and accountable. Editors can, and should, be both skeptical and sensitive.

We insist that our reporters dig and dig and dig to seek the truth in all matters of public interest and importance.

And when the truth is found, our newspaper devotes as much space and as many resources as we can muster to unflinchingly explain the story.

Gene Roberts

Consider other realities in shaping your definition of news for magazines and how to write it:

Magazines Are Slower Than Competitors

1. By their very nature, magazines are slow to reach readers. After the time-consuming production at central printing plants, magazines are sent across the nation by plane, truck, bus and U.S. Postal Service. An article written just hours before *Time*'s "close" at headquarters in Manhattan might not be read in Idaho for three days. Hard, timely story angles won't stand up that long.

2. Competing media are faster. Certainly radio and TV—both broadcast and cable—are much quicker in breaking news. Even national newspapers and huge regional dailies—*Los Angeles Times, Dallas News, Boston Globe,* and others—beat magazines to the punch. They also carry highly detailed lifestyle, entertainment, business and other types of specialized news—once a selling point for newsweeklies.

Magazine newswriting, then, requires understanding how to compensate for the magazine's inherent slowness and its competitors' speed plus their in-depth strength. For newsmagazine writers, this generally requires taking one of three directions:

Magazine Writers "Pitch" Ahead

1. *Writing that sums up developments of last week but quickly—very quickly—pitches ahead to what will probably develop next week.* For years, *Time* and *Newsweek* thrived by essentially summing up the past week's news events. The magazines became concise, readable, single stopping points for busy readers who did not have time to keep pace with news each day. Today, however, breaking news inundates us from newspapers, newsletters, radio, TV, and other sources. So, a newsweekly story on, say, U.S.-Soviet relations now must use events last week as a "peg"—or starting point—but deal primarily with in-depth exploration of their *meaning* and what likely comes next.

Magazines Features Specialty Coverage

2. *Writing highly expert stories on specialty areas that readers might not find adequately covered in their daily media.* *Time,* for example, offers strong reporting on other media; *U.S. News* features "how-to-cope" information on living costs, tuition bills, income tax—"news you can use," the magazine says.

Newsweeklies Emphasize Human Interest

3. *Writing offbeat or "human interest" stories the newsweeklies can develop exclusively.* Not many major, breaking "hard" news stories are exclusive to newsweeklies. Newspapers and television normally cover them well before magazines reach readers. But both *Time* and *Newsweek* can be exclusive—be different—with those little anecdotal pieces that make you laugh or maybe cry a bit.

"Trend" Writing Looks Ahead

Much magazine writing concentrates on "trend" pieces that survey a subject and pull other significant bits and pieces into a single, comprehensive article. Recall in our Chicago fire scenario that *Time*'s bureau is working on a roundup of Midwest regional economic trends. The writing pitch in trend pieces often is ahead, taking readers toward understanding what the future might bring. Something like this:

> Economic bad times may be ahead for parts of the Midwest.
> A *Time* survey last week of Midwest business leaders and economists at Big Ten universities indicates the future will be. . . .

Much magazine writing is similar to in-depth writing in major newspapers, particularly in Sunday editions where larger "newshole"—space devoted to news, not ads—permits more detailed reporting. Both writing styles often pitch ahead.[3]

Broadcast News

We'll cover broadcast writing later in the book. But here, as we strive to define news and understand its use, note these factors:

Radio News Is Fast

1. Radio newswriters must be fast. Live sounds of laughter, screams, gunfire—

"actualities," they are called—add drama to radio news. But, above all, radio's competitive strength is its speed in reaching news consumers.

2. Broadcast newswriters must adapt to the voice, delivery style and pace of the anchor. And, importantly, the TV newswriter writes for pictures. Television newswriters package word *and* picture news. It takes special skills.

Write for Voice and Pictures

3. Broadcast newswriters work under cruel time constraints. Many radio stations devote just a minute or so to headlines "at the top of the hour." As for TV, use a stopwatch next time you view Dan Rather, Tom Brokaw, or Peter Jennings. They give just *seconds* to major, complex stories as they rush to jam world and national news into less than 30 minutes (half an hour with eight minutes or so out for commercials).

Write Short Stories

What is the bottom line, then, in broadcast newswriting?

Develop a keen sense of news priorities. Your precious minutes must be devoted to only the top, most significant news stories. Learn to ruthlessly discard news that, even if interesting, is of secondary importance.

In writing, learn to focus on only those most vital elements within each story. You must learn to digest and understand a lengthy news story in its full complexity, then deal it back out via the keyboard in just a few sentences.

Learn to write for the ear, not the eye. What reads well on paper may cause an anchor to choke on air and confuse listeners. Read your copy aloud. If *you* choke midway through or become breathless, your anchor will too.

New Technology and the News

New "hybrid" media are developing rapidly, combining elements of print journalism, broadcast, and exciting new technology. Two factors spur this development:

1. Consumers increasingly are demanding new information options. They want specialized information not always provided by traditional mass media. They want it in special formats—computer-compatible, for example—and perhaps not on newsprint or jammed into an evening TV newscast. Most importantly, news consumers demand information at *time of their choosing,* not when a newspaper decides to roll its presses or when CBS decides it's time for Dan Rather to go on air.

Media Consumers Demand Options

2. New technology makes it possible to meet these new consumer demands. Cable TV—particularly Cable News Network (CNN)—illustrates how technology met the American public's demand for more news, information and entertainment (and at different times) than the three principal networks provided. In the case of the Gulf War in early 1991, CNN in fact provided the world's political leaders as well as its networks with live, continuous coverage. And there is real space-age stuff on drawing boards. Satellites and other high-tech devices will give consumers even greater choices in news and information they receive, as well as when and in what format.

Technology Gives Consumers Choices

It's unclear what form all this eventually will take. However, one thing is clear: At the center of any new mass communication systems will be news professionals with a keen sense of what news is and isn't, men and women who know how information is collected, collated *and written* for quick, full comprehension.

Hardware is changing; your needs for professional news sense and newswriting skills aren't.

THE INFLUENCE OF AUDIENCE NEEDS

In another time, when newspapering was perhaps less genteel than today, most newsrooms maintained at the absolute bottom of their hierarchical pecking order a group of young reporters called "cubs." They drew all the lousy assignments, worked nights, weekends and holidays—and, for the privilege, were paid very little indeed.

Two things united cubs: The fellowship of common financial misery and overwhelming desire to win assignment to a Big Story. To do well on a Big Story was a ticket up the ladder, into acceptance among your elders and betters, the *real* reporters. You might even get a raise.

I was a cub in the Chicago AP bureau when my Big Story arrived one night under less than flattering circumstances: The "real" reporters were busy and I alone could be spared to look into reports of a brutal crime southwest of Chicago.

My ensuing education in how news is defined is valid for you today. You might not be called "cub" in your first newswriting job. But unless you are extremely lucky, you'll labor under remarkably similar conditions, writing about minor accidents (fender benders) and kindly old gardeners who grow huge vegetables (it's called the "Big Pumpkin Story") while awaiting your truly Big Story.

When mine broke, I borrowed $50 from city desk colleagues, rented a car, and sped through the wintry night toward what was to become the "Starved Rock State Park Murder Case." A Big Story, indeed.

Three wealthy women, socially prominent and with names known nationally, were bludgeoned to death while out for a holiday stroll in a snowy park wood. Their mutilated bodies were left sprawled in a cave. Their killer was on the loose.

Not much else was in the news that night, and by next morning the Starved Rock State Park Murder Case was running on front pages and dominating newscasts. In the minds of editors across the United States it was, simply, a helluva story that would maintain reader and viewer interest for days. It did.

Lessons:

Psych-up for Your Big Story

• Do well during your apprenticeship on those routine fender benders and Big Pumpkin stories. But news is unpredictable; expect the unexpected. And when *your* Big Story arrives, as it will, "psych" yourself up to go for it.

• A good story for you often is bad news for someone else. Bad news frequently is defined by editors and (research shows) also by readers and viewers as more important than good news.

News Is Timely

• The murder story was fresh—"newsy"—and timely. Editors strive for fresh copy, sometimes to a fault, by, for example, shoving aside important but "old" stories in favor of "new news." For such editors, "news" by definition is "new." But readers and viewers also tire quickly of "old" stories, which is why editors constantly search for timely, breaking stories.

• News isn't defined in a vacuum; rather, it is judged in relation to other news developing. The triple murder occurred in one of those news lulls that drive editors to search frantically for a story that will strengthen the front-page appeal to readers or make TV viewers sit up and pay attention.

For three days and nights, reporters "worked" the murder story (I without a change of clothing or much sleep) and the "play"—the prominence given it by editors—was enormous. In Chicago and throughout Illinois, the story dominated front pages. Across the country, it was played less prominently but still was front page. Overseas, the story was played "inside" but, nevertheless, was being read by hundreds of thousands, maybe millions. It was a cub's dream.

Lessons:

• News stories can achieve their own momentum, a continuity that builds editor, reader and viewer interest. This is true particularly if stories are open-ended—

ongoing mysteries without solutions; confrontations building toward climax; intriguing questions without answers.

• The *closer* to home the story breaks, the greater the interest of readers and viewers. There's a joke about this: Oldtimers used to say, "A kitten stranded in a tree on Main Street is bigger news than a revolution in China." In the 20th century, American journalists lived to regret the flippance of that old joke when they witnessed distant world events drag America into wars, both hot and cold. But you get the picture of how the *distance factor* influences definition of news.

In my murder case, authorities came under enormous pressure from media attention and threw huge resources into solving it. A special state police sex crime squad set up headquarters in a park lodge. But the murders went unsolved. The story trailed off into, "Police pursued scanty leads today . . . police continued the hunt. . . ."

Then, new disaster: An airliner shed a wing over neighboring Indiana. Wreckage and bodies rained from the sky.

"Well, kid," a veteran Chicago reporter said, "that's it for the Starved Rock State Park Murder Case."

And it was. New horror had arrived. Close by, too. The world shifted its interest to new directions; the parade of reporters moved on.

Lessons:

• The media, in part, can *create* news merely by zeroing in on a story. Sad to say, a triple murder in a Chicago slum, whose victims' only claim to fame is their brutal demise, would not draw intense sustained media coverage. But murdered society matrons were news, and reporters piled on the story. You'll learn, early in your career, that merely by arriving on the scene with reporter's pad and pen in hand you not only help define what is news by your presence but also *change what happens around you*. People say and do things differently when reporters are around.

• Even the most dramatic story won't sustain public attention for long. In arriving at your own personal definition of news, remember that the public, and thus editors, have short attention spans. You'll agonize over this when "working" a story you *know* is important, crucial even, but which won't interest readers (or editors).

News, obviously, is a highly complex commodity defying simple definition. Thus, your newswriter approach to it must consider many nuances and subtleties in ways the American media handle it.

Nevertheless, we can isolate and summarize fundamental factors influencing the media's definition of news.

Audience (or "Market")

The audience's own perception of its interests and information needs is the strongest single influence on news definition in the media.

The Wall Street Journal's specialized package of in-depth economic, business, and financial news is put together daily in careful response to hugely expensive reader research. *USA Today* spent millions in the 1980s determining news interests of its selected audience—young, "hip" men and women on the go who want their news fast and snappy. Quickly, the colorful national paper's circulation zoomed to No. 2 position (behind only the *Journal*).

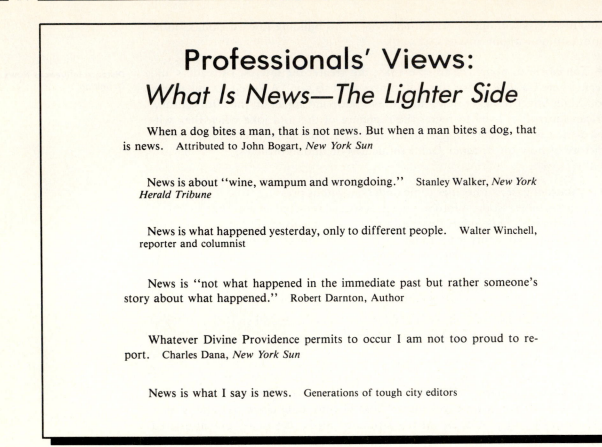

Professionals' Views:
What Is News—The Lighter Side

When a dog bites a man, that is not news. But when a man bites a dog, that is news.   Attributed to John Bogart, *New York Sun*

News is about "wine, wampum and wrongdoing."   Stanley Walker, *New York Herald Tribune*

News is what happened yesterday, only to different people.   Walter Winchell, reporter and columnist

News is "not what happened in the immediate past but rather someone's story about what happened."   Robert Darnton, Author

Whatever Divine Providence permits to occur I am not too proud to report.   Charles Dana, *New York Sun*

News is what I say is news.   Generations of tough city editors

Know Your Readers

For beginning newswriters, caution on two points:

1. It's essential you *know your readers' demographics*—their age, income, education. *Understand their psychographics*—their thinking habits, lifestyle, interests. Events you define as news, the structure of your writing, even the language you choose—all these must be in tune with your readers' interests and capabilities. It's obvious, isn't it: A steady diet of stories for affluent college graduates about travel to European cathedrals, great books and ballet won't do for readers who seek entertainment at county fairs and movies.

Cover News Readers Need

2. However, don't concentrate so intently on responding to what readers *say they want* that you neglect to give them what you know, as a trained journalist, they *need*. Some news, frankly, is uninteresting to many—unpalatable, even—but extremely important. It's your journalistic responsibility to shape important news, write it interestingly and make it readable, then place it before readers in understandable terms that will help them be informed participants in our democratic society.

Impact

Impact flows directly from audience and is measurable in two ways: the *number* of people affected by an event and *how deeply* people are affected.

Research breakthroughs in, say, growing roses may warrant mention, but only far back in Sunday's Home & Garden section. They affect relatively few people who are fanatical rose growers. Research breakthroughs in cancer, the nightmare of millions, obviously are front-page news.

In terms of how deeply events affect people, two illustrations suffice: A drought that sets back Ghana's cocoa crop immediately affects only the profits of commodities brokers who trade in the stuff. A drought in Ethiopia can kill tens of thousands. Which has deeper impact? Which is bigger news?

The *immediacy* of impact also enters news definition. We're told the earth will cool in billions of years from now, and every living thing remaining will die. In the competition for top billing on tonight's 6 p.m. newscast or in tomorrow's headlines, that doesn't quite match news that a hurricane will crash ashore in 24 hours.

Immediacy Helps Define News

Caution: The media can define the impact of events. A fistfight during an untelevised high school football game might not warrant mention in the story you write; a fistfight at midfield during Super Bowl, watched by a national TV audience of millions, *must* be explained in your story. (See the sidebar on p. 16, Wordsmiths at Work, for examples of news definitions at work.)

Proximity

Nothing in news definition is as complex as deciding whether an event is news simply because it breaks nearby but not news if it develops beyond the horizon.

No longer completely trusting editor instincts, which for years generally regarded nearby events and people as more newsworthy, the media today spend millions to determine what *readers* think is most important. The most frequent answer—"local news"—is confusing, however, because the definition of "local" often is incomplete.

For example, a war in China indeed is "local" news for Main Street USA if youngsters in town will be drafted for it, or if U.S. taxes will be raised to help one side or the other fight it.

The bottom line: Regardless of where it occurs, an event is local news if it affects local people and local life. That presents a major challenge for newswriters, of course. They must watch carefully the rivers of news flowing by each day, plucking out those items that indeed have local impact and then writing in a manner that connects the distant event to Main Street in terms that local readers understand.

Important news can flow from one or more of several wellsprings. Three of them are:

• *People.* What they do, what is done to them, what is done that affects them. (See sidebar for a professional's view of this.)

People, Money, Power Are News

• *Money.* It has its own stand-alone fascination, of course. But its important news value is in how it affects, again, people.

• *Power.* Political power, economic, military, psychological—any kind of power that people wield over other people is news. Move upstream to people, money, and power and you'll find news.

Timeliness

Of all elements in modern news definition, none is changing as rapidly as the importance of *timeliness*.

Speed is ingrained in the American journalistic fiber because generations of readers, listeners and viewers demanded quick word on what was happening. Newspapers published "extras"—special editions designed to quickly get a breaking story onto the streets. Radio and, to some extent, TV flourished by being fast. However, in today's complex world, fast word of an event falls short unless surrounded by analysis of *why* it is occurring and *what* it means. The media, particularly newspapers and magazines, increasingly concentrate on in-depth explanation and less on being fast.

Explain the *Why* of News

As you develop newswriting skills, remember it's good to be first; it's mandatory that you be accurate and that you adequately explain.

Wordsmiths at Work

Here are examples of newswriters who successfully tied stories to traditional definitions of news. Note how their writing reverses the expected (man bites dog), sharpens the sense of conflict (Amish), and stresses the unusual and odd (shooting).

Man Bites Dog

Cradled in a white plastic casket lined with silky orange cloth and attended by his grieving owners, Skippy, the dog allegedly shot to death by an annoyed postman, was buried Wednesday in a Calabasas pet cemetery, surrounded by TV cameras, reporters and the graves of other famous animals.   Psyche Pascual, *Los Angeles Times,* Jan. 4, 1990, p. B-1

Conflict

LANCASTER, Pa.—In the heart of the Pennsylvania Dutch country, the 18th-century lifestyle of the Amish is on a collision course with 20th-century America.   Joe Simnacher, *Dallas Morning News,* published Feb. 17, 1990, in the *Seattle Times,* p. A-3

Impact on Reader Audience

It's time to pull out the heavy blankets and the thermal underwear.
At 4:22 p.m. Thursday, winter officially began. And it announced its arrival by ushering in a string of bitter cold days. . . .   Gayla R. Moore, *Augusta* (Ga.) *Herald,* Dec. 22, 1989, p. A-1

The Unusual and Odd

VINCENT, Ala.—A Shelby County man was charged with manslaughter after he shot at a truck carrying two rocking chairs he believed were stolen from his home and fatally wounded the alleged burglar's 3-year-old son, authorities said.   Associated Press dispatch for Dec. 29, 1990

Proximity: Localizing the Distant

WASHINGTON—The president of the National Urban League proposed Tuesday that the defense budget be cut by half, and that some of this "peace dividend" be used to fund a $50 billion "urban Marshall Plan" to educate and employ the nation's minorities.
John Jacob characterized the idea as a way to help American businesses become more competitive and forestall a developing labor shortage. In Minnesota, for example, the labor force is expected to grow by less than one percent a year in this decade. In the 1970s, it grew by three percent a year.   Alexis Moore, *St. Paul Pioneer Press Dispatch,* Jan. 10, 1990, p. A-1

Prominence

See Ted look suave and debonair. See Jane admire Ted. See Ted hold Jane's hand. See Jane talk Ted into working out—which he rarely does. This thing may be getting serious.   Norman Arey, *Atlanta Constitution,* revealing on Page One, March 28, 1990, that TV entrepreneur Ted Turner and Jane Fonda were seeing each other.

A Professional's View:
Write News of Record

John Morton, a newspaper analyst and former reporter, advises newswriters to stay close to local news in their communities.

I remember an iron-clad rule in my police-reporting days in the early 1960s at a newspaper in upstate New York: A story must be written about any automobile accident in which there was an injury, however slight. After all, the injured person had friends, neighbors and relatives who would want to know what had happened and how.

This newspaper tried to be a "paper of record," with a vacuum-cleaner approach to gathering news. By staying so close to the daily life and events of the community, stories of greater significance often were discovered. All newsmen should remember that the Watergate scandal began with a routine breaking-and-entering note on a police blotter.

Moreover, paper-of-record journalism provides a newspaper's reader with the warp and woof of the town's social fabric. This is the kind of information that keeps people connected to one another and, not incidentally, to the local newspaper.[4]

John Morton

Conflict

Conflict often dominates our front pages and newscasts. Armies battling, politicians shouting, ideologies clashing all rank high in news priority with American media.

News *does* come out of conflict. Death and injury, victory and surrender, laughter and tears—all come from conflict and all can be news. But not automatically *important* news.

The Starved Rock State Park Murder Case was conflict between innocent good and incredible evil, between pursuing detectives and elusive killer (he was caught years later). However, in terms of wide-ranging, long-lasting impact on the human condition, the story wasn't very important.

Therein lies the trap for us newswriters. We get drawn to the clash of swords or words, sometimes automatically assuming noise is news. Learn to see the news in a quiet discussion of environmental hazards or, perhaps, the lonely pursuit by an unassuming scientist of a cure for AIDS. (See Issues and Challenges.)

Noise Isn't Always News

Prominence

That President Bush goes public to say he hates broccoli is news; your dietary habits and mine aren't news. Few quarrel with covering in elaborate and sometimes highly personal detail the President of the United States and leader of the western world. What he does every day is of compelling—and legitimate—interest to hundreds of millions around the globe. Many do quarrel, however, with our occasional tendency to plunge headlong into what might be called "personality voyeurism," a

Issues and Challenges

Things to remember when you define what is news and what isn't:

Objectivity—No reporter is truly dispassionate about news; we all have likes and dislikes, prejudices and special interests. But strive for objectivity. And, when you define an event as news, ask yourself whether you did so because the event fits your *personal* preconceptions of what is important or whether it meets *professional standards* of what is news—audience, impact, proximity and so forth. For example, do you instinctively see more news value in a pro-life than a pro-abortion rally because you are pro-life? If so, you're distorting the definition of news.

Conflict of interest—If you own General Motors stock, beware if you suddenly begin discovering news favorable to GM. And don't suggest to your editor that you do stories on GM. Whatever your professionalism, the *perception* will be that you are in conflict of interest. *Question:* If you are a deeply committed fan of your university's football team can you cover a game truly free of conflict of interest?

Privacy—Gary Hart's sex life was defined as news by many newspapers because he wanted to be president of the United States. But many media critics said reporters revealed Hart's relationship with a young woman to "sell newspapers." Ask yourself whether you truly are serving the public interest in revealing personal and intimate details of someone's life, or whether you are pandering to base instincts.

The herd effect—Some great newspapers—*The New York Times, Washington Post, The Wall Street Journal* among them—are watched closely by editors nationwide for how they define and cover news. Successful reporters and columnists are watched for how they "angle" stories. Sometimes, a "herd effect" sets in, with newspapers, editors and reporters rushing to follow the leaders. Make your own decisions on what is news for your newspaper and your readers.

Negativism vs. journalism of hope—Yes, conflict yields news; bad news indeed is well read. But isn't anything *good* happening out there? It is, of course, and every readership survey shows us newspaper subscribers want more news about it and less drumfire coverage of depressing news. Obviously you can't select only happy news and thus distort your newspaper's picture of the world. But when defining news, throw into the mix a few good things. Al Neuharth, founder of *USA Today,* calls it the journalism of hope—finding time to cover good people doing nice things.

Timing and context—If you decide street crime in your town is news and do a hard-hitting series in an election off-year, that's one thing. It's quite something else to run the series two weeks before the mayor is up for reelection. When defining news, remember that timing and context can change dramatically the impact of the very same reporting and readers' perception of your motives.

News and the daily miracle—Sometimes the sheer physical effort of getting the newspaper out can be overwhelming. Often it leads to short-sighted news definition and handling: Grab the visible spot news stories that broke last night, throw 'em in—and we'll try again tomorrow. Search out hidden nuances and piece them together to reveal the underlying importance of news truly critical to your readers.

You, news and marketing—The newspaper and broadcast industries are multibillion dollar enterprises increasingly managed by non-journalist business experts employing the latest marketing techniques. Sometimes, business-oriented executives feel success comes from simply researching what readers say they *want* and giving it to them. Use your journalism training to insert the news readers *need* into the marketing equation. The manager must keep the paper profitable; you must define and select news that ensures its journalistic quality and integrity.

Your gatekeeper function—Remember that as a reporter you help determine which news reaches thousands, perhaps millions, of readers, viewers, listeners. As such a "gatekeeper," you help set the national agenda for what is discussed in government and in private life. It's an enormous responsibility. Make sure you establish professional standards for defining news and handling it.[5]

Pushing in close to get a story earned Associated Press reporter Laurinda Keys a police "escort" away from the scene. She was trying to cover the release of a political prisoner in Johannesburg when a South African plainclothes security officer grabbed her.

(AP photo
used with permission)

nearly compulsive desire to find and tell the most intimate details about people who are prominent merely because they appear in films, hit baseballs extremely well, or enjoy great wealth. As a newswriter you must balance legitimate interest in true public figures against gossipy interest in the rich and famous. The entire news process can be distorted by undue pursuit of "people in the news."

The Novel, Unusual and Humorous

People who run faster or jump higher than other people are news. So are people in Topeka who sing fisherman's chanteys from the Maldives. And darned if that Big Pumpkin story doesn't sell every year. So, if you draw the assignment, write the best Big Pumpkin story ever written—complete with the gardener's secrets in watering, fertilizing, and selecting seeds. Incidentally, if you run across something humorous, write it. The whole world, including your editor, needs a laugh.

Now you can spot elements that signal "news" to professionals. What's next?

Writing Your Story Idea

You must learn to write a story idea in convincing form. Pages 20 and 21 show two examples of ways to highlight the value of a story idea and "sell" it to your editor.

Story Idea

_____

Your name

_____

Date

_____

Story for (newspaper, afternoon/*morning*)

Wall Street Journal reported this morning college tuition rates nationwide will rise about six percent next year. I will interview admissions officials at local university on expected tuition hikes here; also will interview local bankers, student loan officials on expected loan availability next year. To personalize story, will interview students already forced to work part-time to help pay education costs. Will aim for 400–450 words and submit by 4 p.m., Tuesday for Wednesday AMS publication.

Tie Distant News to Local Interests

Note that the story idea above "ties in" a national story with its impact on a local campus. It offers *proximity*. The local audience for the story is huge, of course, and your idea flows from both the people and money news streams. Note the reference

Entertainment personalities such as Zsa Zsa Gabor periodically surface in the news, posing a dilemma for principled journalists: Does writing about these individuals serve legitimate news interests or merely pander to gossipy public interest in the rich and famous?

(AP photo used with permission)

to interviewing *authoritative* sources, essential on a technically complex story such as this. Note particularly the impact on *people.* The story won't really be a story about tuition increases; it will be about *impact* on people.

Another sample story idea:

Story Idea

_____

Your name

_____

Date

_____

Story for (newspaper, *afternoon* / morning)

School board last night fired high school football coach Fred Smith without explanation, as reported in today's AMS edition. For PM edition today, I'll pitch story ahead and interview board president, coach, football players, high school students, faculty on *why* he was fired. I hear rumors of grade-changing scandal that permitted academically ineligible athletes to play, but we can't go with that unless I can pin it down. Will submit by 11 a.m.; length uncertain but will be longish.

Note that both story ideas are "contracts" with your editor, promising copy in approximate wordage by a definite time. Your editor has many such contracts with other reporters, and only if all of you meet your deadlines will the presses run on time. If anything delays submission of your story *notify your editor immediately.*

Part 2 of the text contains a detailed discussion of the tools you'll need as a newswriter. We'll first look at using language that communicates effectively, and then study ways to polish your writing with professional care.

SUMMARY CHECKLIST

☐ News definitions relate to the chosen mission of your medium. Radio is fast but sketchy; TV's strength is visual coverage; newspapers and magazines, though relatively slow to reach information users, compete strongly by explaining, analyzing, and interpreting in detail.

☐ Newspapers define news for "markets," which are *horizontal,* or a piece of geography in which chosen readers live; or *vertical,* meaning groups of readers with similar, specialized news interests. For a general-interest audience in a geographic market, your newswriting angle might be a fire itself; for a vertical market interested in specialized news, the fire's impact on, say, business could be the most important angle for you to pursue.

☐ Much of the news that develops in the United States breaks for morning papers; thus they tend to have a "hard" news character. Because relatively little hard news breaks for afternoon papers they often emphasize "soft" news—features, in-depth analysis, interpretation.

☐ Magazines, like newspapers, are disadvantaged because other media reach news consumers much faster. But magazines achieve competitive success with "trend" stories that deal not primarily in "spot" news but, rather, in behind-the-scenes, in-depth exploration of the *meaning* of news.

☐ Media definition of news is influenced by the *audience* and its own perception of its news and information needs; by the *impact* of news, or the number of people affected by it and how deeply they are affected; by the *prominence* of people involved; by *proximity,* or how close an event occurs to readers; by *timeliness,* or how quickly news reaches readers; and by *conflict,* or the clash of people, factions, ideologies.

☐ In arriving at your own professional definition of news, strive for *objectivity,* a worthwhile if probably unattainable goal; avoid *conflict of interest;* stop and think before invading someone's *privacy;* do your own thinking on what is news and avoid the *herd effect* of following the lead of other newswriters; look for *good news* once in a while; remember *timing and context* of your story can change its meaning and impact; be sobered by your *gatekeeper* responsibilities and your duty to strive for journalistic *quality and integrity* in your newspaper.

RECOMMENDED READING

News and its handling are discussed in *Washington Journalism Review, Columbia Journalism Review, presstime, Gannett Center Journal* and, for radio and TV, *Broadcasting.* Also note the "American Society of Newspaper Editor's Bulletin."

For a look at media evolution and the handling of news see Michael Emery and Edwin Emery, *The Press and America: An Interpretive History of the Mass Media,* 6th ed. (Englewood Cliffs, N.J.: Prentice-Hall, 1988) For current research, see *Journalism Quarterly.*

To see professionals demonstrate keen news judgment day in, day out, note *The Wall Street Journal*'s front-page feature, "What's News." Both discerning judgment and tight writing are displayed. Also, the *Journal* and *The New York Times* feature daily media coverage, much of it pertinent to young newswriters.

Folio and *Advertising Age* report regularly on magazines. Also see Theodore Peterson, *Magazines in the Twentieth Century,* 2d ed. (Urbana: University of Illinois Press, 1964) and Betsy Graham, *Writing Magazine Articles With Style* (New York: Holt, Rinehart, & Winston, 1980).

NOTES

1. For more detailed examination of major media, their strategies and news procedures, see Ray Eldon Hiebert, Donald F. Ungurait, and Thomas W. Bohn, *Mass Media VI* (White Plains, N.Y.: Longman, 1991); Warren K. Agee, Phillip H. Ault, and Edwin Emery, *Introduction to Mass Communication,* 10th ed. (New York: Harper & Row, 1989); Conrad Fink, *Inside the Media* (White Plains, N.Y.: Longman, 1990).
2. Newspaper economic and marketing concepts are discussed in Herbert Lee Williams and Frank W. Rucker, *Newspaper Organization and Management* (Ames: Iowa State University Press, 1978); D. Earl Newsom, ed., *The Newspaper* (Englewood Cliffs, N.J.: Prentice-Hall, 1981); Ardyth B. Sohn, Christine L. Ogan, and John E. Polich, *Newspaper Leadership* (Englewood Cliffs, N.J.: Prentice-Hall, 1986); Conrad Fink, *Strategic Newspaper Management* (New York: Random House, 1988).
3. More information on types and missions of magazines is available from Magazine Publishers Association, 575 Lexington Ave., New York, NY 10020.
4. John Morton, "Back to Basics: Smalltown Coverage," *Washington Journalism Review,* October 1989, p. 10.
5. For more detailed discussion of ethical issues in news definition and selection see William L. Rivers, Wilbur Schramm, and Clifford G. Christians, *Responsibility in Mass Communica-*

tion (New York: Harper & Row, 1980); John L. Hulteng, *The Messenger's Motives: Ethical Problems of the News Media* (Englewood Cliffs, N.J.: Prentice-Hall, 1985); Edmund B. Lambeth, *Committed Journalism: An Ethic for the Profession* (Bloomington: Indiana University Press, 1986); Conrad Fink, *Media Ethics: In the Newsroom and Beyond* (New York: McGraw-Hill, 1988).

Exercise 1–1   Local vs. National News

Because they seek different reader audiences, editors of national and local newspapers use different news judgments in planning their front pages. National newspapers generally strive for high-income, well-educated audiences throughout the country. Local newspapers most often try for broader audiences, in terms of education and income, and feature local news, of course, for local readers.

Read today's front pages of your local daily and the national edition of The New York Times *(or another major daily your instructor selects) and address, in about 200 words, these points: How is front-page content of the two papers similar? How is it dissimilar? Did both papers carry any of the same stories? If so, what were they and why do you think editors of such different papers decided to cover the same news? Which front page appealed most to you? Why?*

Exercise 1–2　Newsmagazines and the News

One of the hottest competitive fights in American journalism is among Time, Newsweek, *and* U. S. News & World Report. *Weekly, each tries to outdo the others by selecting a cover story that will grab reader interest and spark newsstand sales. Highly professional news judgment is applied to this contest.*

　Read this week's cover stories in all three magazines, and, in about 200 words, address these questions: Were the cover stories "hard" or "soft" news? Which seemed more attuned to the general flow of news in the past week, as reported in newspapers and on television? Which cover story probably had the greatest newsstand sales appeal? Why?

Exercise 1–3 Packaging TV News

Like any news medium, television must cover major news stories to be competitive. Events, that is, dictate most of what evening network news covers. However, TV news directors also make a great effort to "package" news shows by selecting a little human interest, some entertainment, perhaps humor—"offbeat" stories that will create broadest possible viewer interest.

Watch tonight's principal newscast by ABC, NBC, or CBS (or any other newscast your instructor selects) and list each news item in the appropriate category below:

News of politics/government: _____

_____

Foreign news: _____

_____

Economic news: _____

_____

Weather/environment: _____

_____

Tragedy/natural disaster/accident: _____

_____

Human interest or "people" news: _____

_____

Other: _____

_____

_____

_____

_____

_____

_____

_____

In about 150–200 words, describe the program's news "mix." Did you agree with the appropriate news items for airing? Was each given time and emphasis consistent with its importance? Did you feel fully informed on the compellingly important issues of the day?

_____
_____
_____
_____
_____
_____
_____
_____
_____
_____
_____
_____
_____
_____
_____
_____
_____
_____
_____
_____
_____
_____
_____

Exercise 1—4 Public Perceptions of What Is News

To stay in business, media companies must cover news that interests you, me, and millions like us (as well as editors). Therefore, any real-world definition of news must include what the public—readers, viewers and listeners—think is news. To gain insight into public perceptions of what news is ahead in the 1990s, the Hearst Corp., owner of newspapers and many magazines, conducted a nationwide survey.

Below are five broad news categories plus some issues that survey respondents thought would be important news stories in the 1990s. For each category, write one idea outlining how you can develop a similar news story with a local angle. Use no more than 50 words. Describe how you can tie in your local story to national news perceptions revealed in the Hearst survey. For example, the survey revealed that Americans thought any major war in the decade ahead would develop in the Middle East. Which local—or campus—authoritative sources can you interview? Political science professors? Economists familiar with Middle East oil politics?

Survey findings:

1. *International affairs.* Among respondents, 56 percent expected the 1990s to be a decade of peace interrupted occasionally by regional military conflict; 57 percent didn't believe a major war would erupt. Regional conventional war was feared by 58 percent, and nuclear war by 22 percent of respondents. The Middle East was considered by 55 percent to be a likely hotspot if a major war erupted; 36 percent said Britain would be the major U.S. political ally in the 1990s.

Your story idea localizing one of these issues:

_____

_____

_____

_____

2. *Science, technology and the environment.* Among respondents, 65 percent said U.S. leadership in scientific research would increase, 35 percent believed the U.S. standard of living would improve. Ocean pollution will continue to increase, 72 percent of respondents said; 69 percent indicated air pollution would worsen. Will intelligent life from other planets contact us? The response: yes, 20 percent; no, 76 percent; don't know, 4 percent.

Your local story angle:

_____

_____

_____

_____

3. *The economy.* Just 41 percent or respondents said that, in general, their life in America in the year 2000 would be better; 31 percent said it would be the same; 23 percent expected it to worsen. The greatest financial burden for the typical American family in the 1990s was expected to be medical costs, 43 percent; housing, 26 percent; education, 13 percent.

Your local story idea:

_____

_____

4. *Social issues.* Problems expected to have most significant impact on the typical family in the 1990s: drug abuse, 52 percent; alcohol abuse, 15 percent; divorce, 13 percent. Many people—35 percent—feared their own family would be affected by long-term disability; 29 percent feared drug abuse, 11 percent divorce. Many—47 percent—said teenagers in the 1990s would be about as sexually active as today; 32 percent expected them to be more active; 20 percent said less active.

A local news angle:

_____

_____

_____

_____

_____

5. *Lifestyle.* Asked what probably would happen to their own living standard in the 1990s, 49 percent of respondents said it would improve; 46 percent believed it would stay about the same, and 5 percent expected a decline. Just 38 percent said they expected children to be better off than their parents; 36 percent expected them to be worse off; 25 percent thought it would be about said about the same, and 84 percent expected rising tuition to prohibit the average American family from sending children to the college of their choice in the 1990s.

A localized angle:

_____

_____

_____

_____

_____

This exercise is drawn from "The American Public's Hopes & Fears for the Decade of the 1990s," The Hearst Corp., 959 Eighth Ave., New York, NY 10019.

Exercise 1–5   News and Impact on People

News is defined in part as events with dramatic impact on large numbers of people.

Below are enumerated the top five stories of 1989 as selected by American newspaper editors using Associated Press (AP) coverage and by news directors of AP broadcast stations. Rounding out the list of top 10 were:

6. *International drug war.*
7. *Hurricane Hugo hits Caribbean.*
8. *Scandals and criminal trials shake confidence in federal government.*
9. *Federal government attempts rescue of savings and loan industry.*
10. *Lt. Col. Oliver North convicted; Iran-Contra investigation continues.*

For each of the top five stories, write a one-paragraph summary of why you think it caught the attention of professional editors and warranted widespread coverage by newspapers, magazines, TV and radio stations. Why did editors, acting on behalf of their readers, viewers, and listeners, react so strongly to these events?

Be certain to write in complete sentences, using concise and clear language. And, watch your spelling and grammar!

1. Communism crumbles in Eastern Europe; Mikhail Gorbachev leads Soviet Union in new direction.

_____

_____

_____

_____

_____

_____

_____

2. Military crushes student-led pro-democracy movement in China.

_____

_____

_____

_____

_____

_____

_____

_____

3. *Exxon Valdez* oil spill contaminates Alaska coastline.

_____

_____

_____

_____

_____

_____

4. Earthquake hits California.

_____

_____

_____

_____

_____

_____

_____

5. Abortion debate shifts to state legislatures and elections.

_____

_____

_____

_____

_____

_____

_____

_____

Exercise 1–6 Proximity in News

Most news definitions include proximity—*simply, how close an event occurred to readers, viewers and listeners.*

With that in mind, examine the list below of the top 10 stories of 1989 compiled by Reuters, an international news agency with headquarters in London, in a poll of 16 news organizations in Asia, Africa, Europe, and North America.

In about 200 words, write why you think professional editors polled by Reuters selected stories somewhat at variance with stories picked in The Associated Press poll of American editors, listed in Exercise 1–5. What different elements entered the news judgment expressed by the two groups?

Strive for simple, clear sentences. Check your copy carefully for spelling and grammar.

Reuters' top 10 news stories for 1989:

1. Communist parties fall in Eastern Europe; Berlin Wall, and other parts of Iron Curtain are breached.
2. Mikhail Gorbachev assumes new power in Soviet Union, introduces *glasnost* and *perestroika*.
3. Democratic movement crushed in China.
4. Cold War draws near end, with Intermediate-Range Nuclear Forces Treaty, and other reductions in super-power tension.
5. Iran and Iraq agree to stop fighting.
6. Soviet forces withdraw from Afghanistan.
7. Chernobyl nuclear accident spreads radiation in Europe; global concern grows for environment.
8. AIDS epidemic spreads worldwide.
9. Lebanon civil war, hostage crisis.
10. Anti-apartheid movement grows in South Africa.

Exercise 1–7   Heroes, Villains, and Others Make News

Editors at the Dallas Times Herald *define news broadly. This became clear in a special section* Times Herald *editors published reviewing events and people the newspaper covered in the tumultuous 1980s.*

Below is a partial list of news stories—and newsmakers—mentioned. For each category, list current *news events and newsmakers you think might warrant similar look-back coverage in a special section reviewing the 1990s.*

1. "Heroes" of the 1980s included Lech Walesa, Poland's Solidarity leader; Ronald Reagan; Mikhail Gorbachev; Dallas Cowboy coach Tom Landry; Tom Cruise, star of the film *Top Gun;* John Bankston, a 17–year-old Texan who saved bus passengers in a flood before being swept away to his death.

     Your picks for today's heroes in the news:

_____

_____

_____

_____

_____

2. "Villains" included serial killer Ted Bundy; Libya's leader, Mu'ammar Qaddafi; Panamanian dictator Manuel Noriega; Jack Nicholson, "mean-spirited menace" in the film *Batman.*

     Today's "villains" in the news:

_____

_____

_____

_____

_____

3. "Comings" included Ted Koppel's debut with "Nightline" and Sandra Day O'Connor as first woman Supreme Court justice; Pope John Paul II visits San Antonio; Exxon announces it will move headquarters "to Big D from the Big Apple."

     "Comings" in today's news:

_____

_____

_____

_____

_____

4. "Goings" included the deaths of film stars Mae West, Cary Grant, and Jimmy Cagney; Gary Hart withdraws from presidential race in sex scandal; Vietnamese invaders leave Cambodia; Dallas Civic Ballet folds; an 86–year-old building in Dallas is demolished despite environmentalists' protests.

"Goings in today's news:

_____

_____

_____

_____

_____

_____

5. "Crazes and Phrases." Crazes included gourmet foods, Sony Walkmans, Cabbage Patch dolls, New Age music, dry beer, safe sex, Elvis sightings, and the film *Lonesome Dove*. Phrases included, "You know what comes between me and my Calvins? Nothing" (Brooke Shields); "Go ahead, make my day" (Clint Eastwood); "I think greed is healthy" (Ivan Boesky); "I think we have a little problem here" (radio message from *Exxon Valdez* captain after his tanker struck an Alaskan reef).

"Crazes and phrases" currently in the news:

_____

_____

_____

_____

_____

_____

6. Editors at the *Times Herald* defined three other news categories: "Living in America" (Elizabeth Taylor checks into drug clinic, for example); "Takeovers & Turnovers" (Walter Cronkite turns over CBS Evening News to Dan Rather; Jimmy Johnson replaces Tom Landry as Dallas Cowboy coach); "What Made Us Cry" (space shuttle Challenger explodes; John Lennon slain); "Lasting Impressions" (Shi'ite terrorists hijack TWA airliner; earthquake in Soviet Armenia kills 25,000).

Other important news categories covered by the media today:

_____

_____

_____

_____

_____

_____

_____ 35 ☐

Exercise 1–8   Localizing Stories

*Examine the front pages of two newspapers (*The Wall Street Journal *and a large metropolitan daily published near your campus, or other papers your instructor selects). Below, write two ideas on how you can localize stories that the two papers published on international, national, or state news developments.*

    Write no more than 70 to 80 words for each, and remember to tie in the distant story with your campus or local newspaper audience's interest. Go for a story with true local *impact. Mention the* authoritative sources *you will interview. Estimate wordage you will need, and state when the stories will be submitted.*

Part 2

Your Newswriter Tools

Conductors must use more than a baton to draw beautiful music from an orchestra. They must employ keen understanding of the composer's intent and mechanics of the music, its style and beauty, its flow. They must understand the musicians, their instruments—and the audience.

Similarly, newswriters use many tools to fashion the ultimate beauty of written journalism: clear, precise communication of important, meaningful news to people who, though hurried and preoccupied with life's many challenges, need desperately to understand it.

You began assembling your newswriter tools in Chapter 1, which provided an understanding of what news is and how it develops.

We turn now in Part 2 to two areas that are essential parts of your journey toward professionalism.

Chapter 2 discusses the language of the newswriter. This language tool is a gift that took centuries to develop. Treat it lovingly.

Chapter 3 takes you into the fundamentals of style, editing, and how to prepare clean copy. These are the "house rules" in newsrooms everywhere. Without knowing them you cannot get through most front doors, or, certainly, hold a job for long.

Before we start, a final point: Do you have, within easy reach, (1) *The Associated Press Stylebook and Libel Manual,* (2) *Webster's New World Dictionary,* Third College Edition, published by Prentice-Hall (or a dictionary recommended by your instructor) and (3) a hand calculator? All three are mandatory for a reporter in the 1990s. Don't be without them.

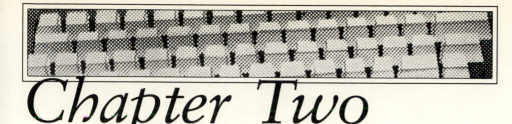 

Chapter Two

Language: The Newswriter's Basic Tool

Beautiful writing, like beautiful music, can be admired all day long.

But we're journalists and we have many things to do, often hurriedly and in circumstances not conducive to rapture. We cannot devote much time simply to admiring the language, as enjoyable as that might be.

For us, language is a tool, a device for catching reader attention and communicating. If we must, we'll even sacrifice beauty in language in exchange for effective communication. I hope you don't have to make that sacrifice too often, though. In fact, I hope you learn to use the beauty of our language as one way of *facilitating* communication.

In keeping with this book's step-by-step march toward professional newswriting, we'll concentrate first on the essentials of lean, direct, precise language. Our immediate goal is active, positive, colorful writing that uses simple language to communicate even the most complex thoughts and issues.

In the pages ahead, concentrate on *accurate* newswriting. Inaccuracy in journalism is mortal sin. It hurts and offends people in the news; it misleads readers, viewers, listeners; it seriously harms media credibility, and damages newspapers, magazines, and broadcast stations in their marketplaces. *Inaccuracy also destroys careers.*

Now onward to effective newswriting—simple, direct newswriting with accuracy and all the grace and beauty we can muster!

The first essential is to refresh your memory on a few fundamental rules of *grammar* and *writing structures*—the building blocks of precise communication. We'll then turn to *sentence structure,* the use of *colorful and vibrant language, writing with rhythm, using present tense* and other techniques professional newswriters use to write with impact.

A QUICK REFRESHER ON GRAMMAR

Does a mysterious process, perhaps genetic, pass from generation to generation certain problems that ruin effective newswriting? Some veteran editors wonder because the same problems pop up time after time among young newswriters.

With basic reference books close by, a reporter at *U.S. News & World Report* fine-tunes copy as "close" or final deadline approaches.

(Photo by Bill Author, *U.S. News & World Report*)

We'll now examine basic techniques you can use to handle those problems. For starters, you should read carefully the following basic rules of grammar and writing structure. Whatever else the pros bring to newswriting, the good ones bring a firm grasp of those fundamentals.

Parts of Speech

Nouns, Pronouns, Verbs

Nouns name or denote persons, places, things, qualities, ideas (Gorbachev, Soviet Union, army, house, fear, communism).

Pronouns assume functions of nouns and take their place (his, they, it, us).

Verbs express action and tell what nouns or pronouns are doing (Gorbachev *threatens*. The army *attacks*).

Adjectives, Adverbs

Adjectives limit, qualify, or modify nouns and pronouns and thus describe them (*stocky* Gorbachev, *strong* army).

Adverbs modify verbs, adjectives, or other adverbs by degree, time, manner, and so forth (threatens *quickly,* attacks *slowly*).

Interjections are exclamations (dang! whee!).

Prepositions link nouns and pronouns to another element in the sentence (*in* the attack, *after* attacking).

Conjunctions connect sentences, phrases, clauses, words (Gorbachev *and* Bush, attack *or* retreat, negotiate *but* demand).

Sentence Parts

A *subject* is the noun or noun substitute about which something is said. Or, to put it another way, the noun or pronoun is doing, acting or being something: The *army* attacked the hill.

Subject, Verb, Object

The *verb* expresses action: The army *attacked* the hill.

The *direct object* receives the action of the verb and, thus, the sentence: The army attacked the *hill.* An *indirect object* is the indirect recipient of the action: Give *me* the AP *Stylebook.*

The simplest, most direct and often most easily understood sentence structure keeps the sentence parts in this order: subject + verb + direct object. Because such sentence structure generally is comprehended easily, it is used often by professional newswriters. However, if used exclusively, that sentence structure gets dull. So, other approaches are used to vary things a bit.

Vary Your Sentence Structure

For example, something other than a direct object can follow the verb:

> The army fled south.
> The hill was attacked by the army.

Often, clarity and impact can be achieved in newswriting if you vary how you arrange sentence elements. Experiment as you develop your own style. For example, effective newswriting emphasizes "who" and "what" and that can inspire sentences that open with the subject:

> Regiments attacked the hill all night.
> Wounded screamed for help.

For special emphasis, you can use an adjective to open a sentence:

> Rare was the man who gave ground
> that night.
> Determined were the defenders that
> night.

Phrases are two or more related words conveying a thought but lacking subject or verb or both: The army, *firing as it went,* attacked the hill.

Phrases, Clauses

Clauses are related words with a subject and verb and come in two types. *Independent clauses* form complete thoughts: The general wants the hill. *Dependent clauses* are not complete thoughts: The general attacks the hill *because he wants it.*

Sentences have one or more independent clauses or dependent clauses. Sentences *must* express complete thoughts.

Nouns and Pronouns

Nouns and pronouns are *singular* (I, he, she) and *plural* (they, us).

They have *gender*—*masculine* (actor), *feminine* (actress), or are considered *neuter* (persons, children).

Nouns and pronouns come in *person: first person* (I, we); *second* (you); *third* (they, he, she, it, one).

And pronouns have *case:*

- *nominative,* when they are the subject of a sentence (*He* is leading the attack)

- *objective,* when they are either the direct object (Assist *him* in the attack) or indirect object (They helped *him* attack)

- *possessive,* to show ownership (The general's army)

All about Verbs

Verb Person, Number, Tense

Verbs have *person* appropriate for each personal pronoun: first-person singular (I *attack*); second-person singular (you *attack*); third-person singular (she, he, it, one *attacks*); first person plural (we *attack*); second-person plural (you *attack*); third-person plural (they *attack*).

Verbs have *number*—singular or plural appropriate to the subject's number. *Make certain the subject and verb agree.* (The army [singular] *attacks* the hill. Soldiers [plural] *attack* the hill.)

Verbs have *tense*:

- *present tense* (I attack, you attack, she/he attacks)

- *past tense* (I attacked, you attacked)

- *future tense* (I shall attack, you will attack)

- *present perfect tense* (I have attacked, you have attacked.)

- *past perfect tense* (I had attacked, you had attacked)

- *future perfect tense* (I shall have attacked, you will have attacked)

Verb Tone, Voice, Mood

Verbs have *tone* in each tense: normal (I attack, you attack, etc); emphatic (I *do* attack, she *does* attack, etc.); progressive (I *am* attacking, you *are* attacking, and so forth); progressive-emphatic (I *am* attacking, I *was* attacking, I *will* be attacking, I *have been* attacking and so forth).

Verbs have voice:

- *active voice,* when the subject of the sentence is the doer of action (The general attacked the hill)

- *passive voice,* when the sentence's subject is receiver of action (The hill *was attacked* by the general)

Verbs have *mood.* For our purposes, two are most important:

- *indicative mood,* to state a fact or ask a question (They *attack* the hill. *Are* they *attacking* the hill?)

- *imperative mood,* to issue instructions or command (*Attack* the hill. *Defeat* the enemy)

Use Strong Verbs, Active Voice

To create newswriting that sparkles, here are a few hints: Use strong verbs in the active voice and present tense, whenever you can. In most news stories, *pick a tense and stay with it throughout.* Be certain that subject and verb agree (They attack the hill. *Not:* They attacks the hill).

Some forms of verbs—called *verbals*—are used as parts of speech other than verbs. There are three types.

Gerunds are verbs used as nouns in the present participial form (with *-ing* ending) or sometimes in the past participial form (with *-ed, -t,* or other ending). (*Fighting* is a terrible way to spend a day. He was one of the *overlooked.*) Inexperienced newswriters sometimes violate a basic rule: If a pronoun or noun directly precedes a gerund, the pronoun or noun *must* be in the possessive case. Thus: She's concerned about her friends' complaining.

Participles are verbs in present or past participial forms used as adjectives. They usually end in *-ed, -ing, -t* or *-en:* Marching, they arrived at their goal (*Marching* describes *they*). The exhausted soldiers arrived unhurt (*exhausted* and *unhurt* describe soldiers).

Infinitives are created most often when *to* precedes a verb: He would like *to attack*. You'll get complaints from many editors if you split infinitives: He would like *to soon attack*.

Using Adjectives

In modifying nouns and pronouns, adjectives have three *degrees* of comparison in telling what kind, how many, and so forth:

- *positive* (The *fierce* general)

- *comparative* (The *fiercer* general)

- *superlative* (The fiercest general)

Beware of adjectives in newswriting. Linking too many in one sentence can lead you toward meaningless froth: The *fierce, determined, stocky, angry* general attacked the hill.

To vary your impact, move adjectives around in a sentence. For example, they can follow nouns: The general, *fierce* and *determined,* attacked the hill.

Usually, however, your newswriting is much more effective if, rather than *tell* your readers the general is fierce, you describe his actions that *show* he is fierce: The general ordered his men to attack the hill *despite their heavy losses and to show no mercy for the fallen enemy.*

Use Adjecctives Sparingly

More on Adverbs

Next to verbs and nouns, adverbs can have the most importance in a sentence. But use them gently, with care.

Most adverbs are formed by adding *-ly* to positive-form adjectives: easy–easily; careful–carefully. In the comparative form, construct adverbs by using *more* or *less* in front of adjectives: more or less care, more or less carefully. The superlative form is made with *most* or *least:* most easily, least carefully.

There are four types of adverbs:

- *simple,* tightly tied to the word they modify: The general dressed *beautifully* (modifying the verb dressed). The *beautifully* dressed general (modifying the adjective dressed).

- *interrogative,* asking a question: *When* is the general coming (modifying the verb *is coming*).

- *conjunctive,* linking dependent clause to sentence or previous clause: The general was planning his attack *though* he feared it might be too late.

- *parenthetical adverbs,* which don't change the sentence meaning but, rather, modify a sentence or link it to another: *Nevertheless,* aides told the general there was time to launch an attack. (Also: still, yet, accordingly, etc.).

Four Types of Adverbs

As for Interjections

Interjections—dang! whee!—shouldn't appear in your newswriting except under rare circumstances: when one occurs in a direct quote that is essential to your story; in the occasional light feature you write.

For certain, interjections that are profane have no place in your newswriting unless in direct quotes you (and your editor) feel are essential to your story.

Interjections and Profanity

Pointers on Prepositions

These are connecting words that relate a noun or pronoun to another word or that illustrate the relation between two words: The dugout *in* the valley was the temporary home *of* the general.

There are two classes of prepositions:

- *simple,* such as *in, at, to, up, beside, within*

- *compound,* containing more than one word: *in front of, along with, because of*

Use Prepositions with Care

Many editors will give you trouble on two usages of prepositions:

First, if you end a sentence with a preposition, expect an argument (although this is not objectionable to some editors).

Second, some editors require you to repeat the preposition in parallel prepositional phrases: The general said the meeting would be *on* training and *on* maneuvers. Usually, however, you can get along without that second preposition.

Finally, Conjunctions

Like prepositions, conjunctions are linking words. Two broad groups:

- *coordinate,* which link words, phrases or clauses of equal rank. They are of two types: simple, which add, enumerate or show contrast (The general *and* his aides arrived. The general arrived *but* his aides did not).

- *subordinate,* which introduce subordinate clauses in a sentence and join subordinate with independent clauses (The general could not order the attack *because* he wasn't ready. *Because* he wasn't ready, the general could not order the attack).[1]

WRITING TECHNIQUES THE PROS USE

Technique 1: Using Simple vs. Complex Structures

Successful newswriters can properly handle the foundation of effective writing, the sentence. Young newswriters often make two errors.

First, they write in fragments. Not complete sentences. That don't properly hang together. Like this. It drives editors wild. Readers, too. Because it ignores the proper order for sentence parts: subject + verb + direct object.

Subject + Verb + Direct Object Works Well

That order can be extremely effective in newswriting, particularly when you're on deadline and rushing to complete a story. A good guideline: When hurried, fall back on subject + verb + direct object, in that order. You at least will communicate clearly, even if your writing isn't beautiful.

Avoid "Run-on" Sentences

A second problem young newswriters have is a tendency to get carried away and write "run-on" sentences, those that go on and on, detouring here, stretching over there, but never seeming to get where the writer wants to go and, of course, completely confusing the poor reader whose child is crying and whose dog is barking and who doesn't have enough time to sit down and sort out the meaning of a sentence that—like this one—is so poorly written that it defies understanding.

Read Your Writing Aloud

Another guideline the pros follow: Read your sentences aloud. If you run out of breath midway through, start throwing in periods. Periods are the most underrated punctuation device in the English language. We have plenty, and they are free.

Use language to penetrate barriers to understanding. Don't let it become a barrier itself. It's crucial to remember that a news story often will *tell itself best* if you relate the facts and get out of the way. Don't overwrite.

Make no mistake, though. Writing in simple language is not simple. Imagine the writing and rewriting that went into this story about a woman suing her former lover:

[Jane Smith] wanted lasting love from her former boyfriend. Instead, she says, she got herpes.

"He looked me in the eyes and told me that he loved me," said [Ms. Smith], 28, who discovered a year ago that she has the incurable disease. "But he didn't love me enough to tell me that he had this." *Elizabeth Coady, "Lovers File Suits Over Spread of Sexually Transmitted Disease,"* Atlanta Journal and Constitution, *Jan. 21, 1990, p. C-1*

Let Quotes Express Emotion

Note below the impact a writer achieves by using short, strong sentences and by getting out of the way of a story that is terribly complex in legalities and human emotion:

SACRAMENTO—A Pennsylvania woman plans to legally adopt the daughter she gave up 30 years ago.

"I guess some people might think it's ridiculous, but this is what we are going to do," [Jane Smith], 49, a school crossing guard, said of her decision to legally adopt [Alice Doe], 30, of Sacramento. "It's important to her and it's important to me."

It's also an unusual move, a representative of the Adoptees Liberty Movement Association says. *Steve Gibson, McClatchy News Service dispatch for Jan. 7, 1990.*

A few years back, many editors became enamored of "formula" writing, with rules dictating use of words of few syllables and short, almost truncated sentences. (For example, they would have rewritten the sentence you just read: "Years ago, many editors fell in love with writing by 'formula.' They ordered writers to use short words that are easy to understand. They also insisted on short sentences.")

The idea was to create newspapers for people with something like eighth-grade reading skills. Unfortunately, the rules were followed excessively, almost down to, "See Jane run. See Spot. See Dick." Short, punchy stuff like that started boring readers across the nation. Before long, even "formula" editors became bored, and good writers went back to doing what good writers always do: writing with a sense of creativity even if it involves using big words and long sentences.

Nevertheless, research proves short words and punchy sentences *do* communicate more effectively than do long words and convoluted sentences. Note that sentence length averages 16.2 words in the *Atlanta Journal and Constitution* and McClatchy News Service examples above.

Short Sentences Communicate Effectively

A steady diet of short, staccato sentences can numb the mind—yours and your readers'. But they do have impact if used with care. Look how everybody remembers, "See Jane run"!

Technique 2: Using the Living Language

In the news business we're not writing the Dead Sea Scrolls. Too many young newswriters think we are and write in dull, emotionless language. The pros, however, know we're writing minute by minute and for busy people who need to know about life and death, joy and misery—about action, color, movement, vibrancy. (See the sidebar A Professional's View on p. 46.)

Pros use language that is alive. On Jan. 16, 1990, the *Los Angeles Times* "fronted"—displayed on page one—nine stories. Note how *Times* writers use the living language in six of them to capture excitement and drama:

A Professional's View:
Good Writing Is Good Reading

Question: What makes great writing?

Answer: "I know great writing when I start reading a story and I find myself at the end of the story and I haven't had time to think about how the story's written. I just read it naturally. It flows; it has great transition; it is cleanly written. Good choice of words. Colorful writing. Descriptive writing."

Keith Moyer, executive editor,
Fort Myers (Fla.) *News-Press* and Gannett Co. Editor of the Year in 1989[2]

MOSCOW—As fighting between heavily armed Armenians and Azerbaijanis *flared into open warfare,* the Soviet Union on Monday *declared* a state of emergency in the disputed region of Nagorno-Karabakh and adjacent areas and *sent* troops there to *quell* what it called efforts to overthrow the government by force. *Michael Parks*

NEW YORK—Campeau Corp.'s vast department store empire, overburdened by $7.5 billion in takeover debts, *came thundering down* Monday in one of the biggest bankruptcy cases in U.S. history. *Stuart Silverstein*

BONN—Thousands of angry demonstrators *stormed the headquarters* of the state security police in East Berlin on Monday after officials disclosed the extent of the agency's spying on the people. *William Tuohy*

SOFIA, Bulgaria—In a move that virtually ends communism's ascendancy in the former Soviet satellites of Eastern Europe, Bulgaria's Parliament on Monday *voted overwhelmingly to abolish* the leading role of the Communist Party. *Tyler Marshall*

EVERETT, Wash.—*Facing furious deadlines,* [Jane Smith] worked 34 out of every 35 days on the Boeing Co.'s aircraft assembly line. Mandatory overtime, 12-hour days. She *gained* a pile of money. She *lost* a disgruntled husband. Then her teenage daughter *suffered* an unrelated psychological breakdown. *Bob Baker*

> As early morning commuters *streamed along* the Santa Ana Freeway in Anaheim, one man *was shot* to death and another *critically* *wounded* Monday when gunmen in two vehicles pulled *to the shoulder, jumped out* and *exchanged fire,* authorities said. *Matt Lait and Jim Carlton*

Strong, colorful writing entices readers into exploring the depths of your story—and getting them started to read is the first step in effective communication.

Note what a pro does with one of those business stories that can be so deadly dull:

Colorful Writing Entices Readers

> NEW YORK—A group of European central banks *launched a surprise attack* on the dollar yesterday that sent the U.S. currency *tumbling* around the world. *AP dispatch for Jan. 5, 1990*

Even a single word, if alive and vibrant, can make a difference:

> . . . a man is arrested for *stalking* a woman (not following, annoying, pestering). *San Francisco Chronicle*

> . . . a long-promised *war* on illegal drugs begins in the Georgia General Assembly with *skirmishes* (not debate, hot words, discussion) breaking out on the floor. *Atlanta Journal and Constitution*

> . . . India ends its "*ill-fated* three-year involvement" in Sri Lanka's civil war. *New York Times*

> "President Bush *passionately* denied Thursday that he was involved . . ." *Miami Herald*

See the sidebar on page 48 for issues that can rise in colorful writing.

Technique 3: Using Language with Rhythm

Ever hear music that started you humming and tapping your toe? Its rhythm *carried you along,* didn't it? Good newswriting establishes rhythm that *engages* readers and carries them along. It is melodious (but not lulling) and can make even the most difficult information palatable for the reader.

Once you have your readers hooked on the rhythm, you can do many things to make your central point with impact. For example, to continue the music analogy, you can play *counterpoint:* You can interrupt sharply or halt the rhythm, and the contrast jars readers into paying particularly close attention.

Counterpoint Catches Readers' Attention

Issues and Challenges

When developing your personal newswriting style, keep these crucial points in mind:

Color vs. accuracy. Writing *accurately* is your No. 1 priority. Don't try so hard for colorful, dramatic writing that you sacrifice accuracy. Writing that politicians *screamed* at each other is colorful. It's also inaccurate unless they actually did scream. Color writing can sketch lies in brilliant hues. But they're still lies.

Writing vs. facts. Not even the most skillful writing will cover lack of factual substance in your story. A pound of adjectives and only an ounce of facts yield thin soup. Precise, informative writing that nourishes readers' minds is your goal. Strive to blend facts, statistics, figures into the mix. Then write fact-filled stories to be *palatable.*

Exaggeration. It lurks near inaccuracy, hidden in clever disguise—and can ambush you. It sets traps, for example, when you interview five students on the library's front steps and write that "university students believe . . ." *Note:* Those interviews reveal what five (not all) students *say* (not believe; who knows what they truly believe?). To determine what all or most university students say (let alone believe) would take skilled pollsters using scientific research methodology. Exaggeration is a danger when these words appear in your writing: *every, all, most, always, totally, completely.* Even pros get trapped. A veteran *New York Times* foreign correspondent writes that a Chinese intellectual ". . . has written more than a dozen books on every conceivable subject." *Every* conceivable subject? With about *12* books?

Fact vs. opinion. Effectively writing with expertise about complex subjects for non-expert readers requires you to *translate,* to explain and interpret. However, don't cross the boundary between writing news and writing opinion. You help readers if you explain the mayor proposes "a one-year spending increase of 20 percent, the *largest ever.*" You've crossed the boundary if you write "a one-year spending increase of 20 percent, *which he cannot justify.*" Insert essential background to help readers form their own opinions; keep your opinions out.

Color writing and good taste. In a journalism career you will see things that turn your stomach. Does writing with color and drama require you to also turn your readers' stomachs at their breakfast tables? It depends somewhat on which publication you write for. Readers *seek* a little stomach churning when they buy one of those supermarket magazines. (The headline in one, "Chocoholic Mom Gives Birth to Sugar-Coated Baby," gave 'em their money's worth.) But in major part the decision is yours. Start considering now how far you will take "color" writing.

Hemingway and you. There was only one Ernest Hemingway. So don't try to write like he did. (An earlier generation of journalists tried to emulate Hemingway, even growing moustaches and running before the bulls in Spain, as he did. There still was only one Hemingway.) Read the pros carefully. Note their styles and techniques. But don't mimic. Develop your own personal style. It eventually could become as distinctively yours as Hemingway's was his. And, don't rush it. Don't try to force your style overnight. Truly distinctive writing style takes years to develop. Let yours build naturally and flow of itself. The way to do that? Start writing. Now.

Note how the following pros start toes tapping with rhythm; then—bang—they stop the music.

First, a story about plans to fix up and paint the Statue of Liberty:

NEW YORK—A century after she crossed the Atlantic in 85 wooden packing crates, 59 years after she was declared a national monument, six years after Vietnam veterans occupied her overnight, three years after Iranian students chained themselves to her base, two years after a man clambered onto her crown to launch his campaign for mayor, one year after French feminists demanded she be returned because the ERA had failed—the Statue of Liberty needs a new dress.

Small wonder.

She's been wearing the same one for 97 years. *Nancy Shulins, AP dispatch for May 29, 1983*

Second, rhythm—and counterpoint—are used to tell a business story with flair and impact:

NEW YORK—Once a shy, insecure number cruncher and workaholic, Peter Cohen became a surprising star in Wall Street's glittering orbit. Through sheer tenacity, the chairman and chief executive of Shearson Lehman Hutton Inc. made his firm a rival to Merrill Lynch & Co. as the nation's biggest brokerage house. He seemed determined to make everybody else on the Street stop and take notice, and if he hadn't succeeded before, he did yesterday—by resigning. *William Power, Matthew Winkler, Bryan Burrough, "How Grand Ambitions Proved the Undoing of Shearson Chairman," The Wall Street Journal, Jan. 31, 1990, p. A-1*

Technique 4: Reaching for Something Different

Successful newswriters aren't afraid to reach for more effective ways of getting impact. A danger in "stretching" for something unusual, of course, is that you can reach too far and your writing effort—and you—fall flat. Don't worry too much about it. With experience you'll develop judgment.

First, successful efforts:

An infamous murder in Boston catches national attention. *Los Angeles Times* editors assign Bettijane Levine to do a wrap-up. Note her bang-bang, staccato style that reaches for—and catches—the horror of violence.

About 20,000 times each year in the United States, murderers shoot, stab, strangle, mangle and perform other unthinkable acts. *Bettijane Levine, "Who You Know Can Be Deadly," Los Angeles Times, Jan. 11, 1990, p. E-1*

It's election year in Georgia and the *Atlanta Journal and Constitution* begins looking at the state's political power brokers (thus fulfilling *timeliness* in our definition of news). One politician is particularly powerful, and staff writer Gary Pomerantz stretches to convey that power—and unmistakably catches it for his readers:

BREMEN Ga.—It's going on 17 years now that Tom Murphy has been Speaker of the Georgia House of Representatives, and the sound of his gavel still sends a mean clap of thunder across the state.

The 65-year-old Mr. Murphy is a holdover from the political Meso- zoic: the powerful Southern rural Democrat who rewards loyalty, never forgets, and is blunt as an on- coming cannonball. *Gary Pomerantz, "Iron-Fisted Murphy Keeps Capitol Friends, Foes Marching to His Tune,"* Atlanta Journal and Constitution, *Jan. 21, 1990, p. A-1*

Translate Unfamiliar Terms

Question: Can you precisely define "Mesozoic"? (It is a geologic era of at least 65 million years ago.) Should the writer expect Georgia readers to know?

December sales are under way in Portland, Oregon, and *Sunday Oregonian* editors want a business page piece on how local retailers are doing. Staff writer Ken Hamburg reaches for the flavor of sales hype:

Ten-hour sale! 15-hour sale!! One-day sale!!! Three-day sale!!!! Four-day sale!!!!!

Local retailers, who are beset by increasing competition, cash crunches and predictions of a so-so season, offered them all last week in hopes of luring customers into their stores during the most important shopping period of the year. *Ken Hamburg,* The Sunday Oregonian, *Dec. 10, 1989, p. D-1*

Below, a *Los Angeles Times* reporter enthusiastically stretches in writing about election of the nation's first black governor. You make the call: Does the writer reach too far?

RICHMOND, Va.—Making history is a roll of the dice and Virginia's new governor, Lawrence Douglas Wilder, knows it. This elemental lesson rises like vapor from the swampy, treacherous waters of the Old Dominion's politics, where the bones of losers are picked clean and dumped in the murky depths of oblivion.

Now, an obvious example of reaching too far:

In an aria from an early Bach cantata, the goddess of agriculture sings that sheep graze safely when a conscientious shepherd is watching.

The wolves take many forms: grief, depression, job stress, mental illness, terminal disease, marital problems . . . etc.

To arm themselves with current information from the field of psychiatry, Texas law and the hospice movement, members of the clergy and laity met with specialists in a non-pastoral setting (Fort Worth's Hilton Inn) last week for a skill-sharpening conference called "Tending the Flock."

Lesson: In general, the best rule in newswriting is that if it works, do it. If you come up with an approach—even one far out—that grabs reader attention and communicates accurately and effectively, your approach is a good one. But if you stretch so far that you see sheep grazing on hillsides, stroll to the water fountain and cool off for a few minutes. Then ask yourself: Do those sheep still look as good as they did originally? (See sidebar for other examples of writing that reaches for clarity and succeeds.)

Wordsmiths at Work

Short, punchy sentences sometimes are best for writing with clarity, imagery, and impact. Some writers, however, can let their sentences wander a bit and still maintain disciplined control. Note below the examples of both approaches.

WASHINGTON—U.S. and allied forces poured into Kuwait last night, launching the first wave of their long-awaited ground offensive.   Andrew Miga and Joe Battenfeld, ''Allies Launch Ground War,'' *Boston Sunday Herald,* Feb. 24, 1991, p. 2

MUTLAA, Kuwait—As far as the eye can see along this road to Iraq is a tangled sea of scorched, twisted metal littered with bodies of Iraqi soldiers apparently caught in reteat after seven months of occupying Kuwait.

The carnage and destruction, resembling a great martial demolition derby, is the gruesome remnant of a mile-long Iraqi convoy that once had been a battalion-sized column of more than 1,000 vehicles.

Early Tuesday morning, U.S. warplanes swooped down on the convoy as it fled Kuwait's capital. Now, all that's left are the burned and bombed metal skeletons of tanks, towed cannons, buses, trucks and stolen civilian vehicles scattered bumper to bumper along the bomb-cratered road.   William Claiborne and Caryle Murphy, ''Retreat Down Highway of Death,'' *Washington Post,* March 2, 1991, p. 1

TONGZHI, China—This remote village in south central China, five miles by muddy path from any road with pretensions to pavement, is populated by diligent mud-between-the-toes peasants, joyful mud-all-over children, well-fed pigs oblivious to the cleavers hanging nearby—and a clan of rice farmers who sought to make their fortune by selling stuffed pandas to American children.   Nicholas D. Kristof, ''Of Paddies, Toy Pandas and Unraveled Dreams,'' *The New York Times,* national edition, Feb. 12, 1990, p. A-4

The F-117 slid through warning radar in predawn darkness . . .   George C. Wilson, '''Stealth' Plane Used In Panama,'' *Washington Post,* Dec. 24, 1989, p. A-1

Roofs were leaking. Homeless shelters were jammed to capacity. Firewood sales were up, ice cream sales were down. Drivers on bald tires were finally shelling out for new ones. The flu bug and the ski bug were out in force.

All over Los Angeles, the signs of winter were apparent on Wednesday, as jarring, in their way, as a four-lane road closure.   David Ferrell and Jocelyn Stewart, ''How Cold Was It? If You Say Plenty, You're Warm,'' *Los Angeles Times* Jan. 18, 1990, p. A-3

Confirming again that weather forecasting is not a precise business backed by guarantees, the cold-air mass that was supposed to bring up to 4 inches of snow into Seattle has refused to make the trip.   ''Snow Job?,'' *Seattle Times,* Feb. 15, 1990, p. A-1

A faraway siren hinted at a news story for the next morning's paper as first the rifles and then a bugle saluted Col. Maynard R. Ashworth Sr. a final time.   Richard Hyatt, reporting burial of a former army officer and newspaper editor, ''Tribute Paid to Newsman,'' *Columbus* (Ga.) *Ledger-Enquirer,* Dec. 22, 1989, p. D-11

Technique 5: Drawing Word Pictures

Words are like a painter's oils. They can draw beautiful pictures. Do you *see* pictures a pro painted with the following?

Astronomers already facing a crisis in theories of how the universe formed are in for another shock—clusters of galaxies apparently lined up like regularly spaced street lamps—as far as they can see. *Charles Petit, science writer,* San Francisco Chronicle, *Feb. 22, 1990, p. A-6*

Listen as a newswriter describes a tour guide leading visitors through Georgia's capitol building. Can you *hear* it?

The click-clack of high heels on the marble floor bounces between the walls in the long corridor and mixes with the sounds of a bell from a nearby elevator, jingling keys and the electronic beeps of newly installed metal detectors. *Linda Day, "Capitol Readies for Fun,"* The Augusta Chronicle, *Jan. 7, 1990, p. A-1*

Read—but also *watch* and *feel*—as a reporter describes a 23–year-old woman arriving one night at her New York City apartment and meeting death.

Detail Takes Readers to Scene

Beyond the dimly lighted, 15–foot lobby, with its faded yellow walls and dirty tile floor, behind the black door of a 4-foot-square self-service elevator sheathed in imitation-wood Formica and lighted with a single dim bulb, the killer was waiting. He had a knife . . . *Robert D. McFadden, "Drama Student Is Stabbed to Death in New York,"* The New York Times, *Dec. 3, 1984, p. A-1*

Sometimes, word pictures flow from a single sentence. For example, *The Wall Street Journal* follows up on a major retailer's optimistic claim that it can head off bankruptcy and:

Six months later, the only sound inside its cavernous main store was the low hiss of adhesive tape being unwound by workmen readying goods for auction. *Jeffrey A. Trachtenberg, "Lessons for Campeau: It's Not Easy Being a Chapter 11 Retailer,"* The Wall Street Journal, *Jan. 30, 1990, p. A-1*

Even a short phrase can draw a picture that aids reader comprehension:

Reagan's written responses plus exhibits—combined *in a telephone-book-size document*—were given to the federal grand jury in answer to questions posed by Iran-Contra prosecutors. *Pete Yost, AP dispatch for Sunday papers, Feb. 25, 1990*

Technique 6: Using Present Tense to Make Writing Come Alive

Use of the present tense can make a story jump off a page, figuratively grab readers and hold them.

Examples:

KUALA LUMPUR, Malaysia—It is still dark. The moon, partially obscured by clouds, offers little light. Stars flicker vaguely in the sky. Street lights cast long, thin shadows on the streets. Swallows flit by, seeking food.

Kuala Lumpur has begun to stir.
Jennifer Rodrigo, "New Days, Old Ways," Los Angeles Times, Feb. 25, 1990, p. L-1

Investigators are still looking for a motive in the case of a Bangor submarine-base sailor who apparently killed himself after fatally shooting two sailors and a Bremerton pawnshop clerk. *Michael Arrieta-Walden, "Officials Seek Motive in Shooting Rampage," Seattle Times, Jan. 19, 1990, p. C-1*

BETHPAGE, N.Y.—Teams of engineers and scientists at two of the nation's largest aerospace companies sit before consoles in rooms that resemble the flight deck of the starship Enterprise.

The rooms are free of dust. The frigid cold of space is simulated. Much of what goes on is hush-hush.

It all sounds very sci-fi, but we're not talking fiction here. The scientists and engineers are from Grumman and Lockheed, and next month they are scheduled to . . . *James Bernstein, "Racing to Win Big Spy Satellite Deal," Newsday dispatch for Feb. 21, 1990*

Phoenix police start going after not only drug dealers but also casual users, and *The Wall Street Journal*'s Paul M. Barrett decides to focus on a single arrested user. Barrett uses the present tense effectively:

Personalize Stories in Present Tense

PHOENIX, Ariz.—It is 10:30 a.m. on a warm evening at the Maricopa County Jail. Two policemen hustle [Fred Smith], handcuffed, disheveled and looking scared, through the intake door.

Guards search the 25-year-old retail stock worker, take fingerprints and a mug shot, and put him in a cell with 19 other men. The cell is 14 feet by seven feet. Soon a fight erupts in an adjoining cell; onlookers whoop and cheer until guards wrestle the brawlers to the concrete floor.

"There's guys in here who are real criminals," says a disconcerted [Smith] in an interview outside his cell. He has never been behind bars before, he says. Lowering his voice, he confides, "this freaks me out."
Paul M. Barrett, "Program to Prosecute the Casual Drug User Is Casting Wider Net," The Wall Street Journal, Jan. 31, 1990, p. A-1

In the last example above, the writer could not have achieved such dramatic impact with a story of sweeping generalities written in the past tense. Compare that version with this example that makes no effort to personalize the drug arrests:

PHOENIX, Ariz.—Police in Phoenix arrested 29 persons during the past week in a crackdown on drug users as well as dealers. Users, many of whom never had been behind bars before, were thrown into jail with habitual criminals. . . .

Active Voice Often Preferable

Pros inject extra sparkle in their writing by using the active voice in sentence construction.

All verbs are in either the active or the passive voice. Sentences in the active voice aid reader comprehension because they emphasize the doer of the deed by making it the subject. Examples:

ACTIVE VOICE
A Royston woman *pleaded* innocent Friday to a charge of murdering her lover.

PASSIVE VOICE
A plea of innocent *was entered* Friday by a Royston woman charged with murdering her lover.

In the example above, the passive voice weakness is twofold: It increases wordage (16 words to 13 in the active voice version) and, second, it is flabby and indirect and thus loses punch.

Note how this rewrite of a passive-voice sentence uses the punch delivered by the active voice:

ACTIVE REWRITE
A judge sentenced an Athens man to life in prison Friday after he was convicted on three counts of selling cocaine to an undercover police officer.

PASSIVE
A sentence of life in prison was handed out Friday to an Athens man after he was convicted on three counts of selling cocaine to an undercover police office.

Note the active-voice example above is shorter (26 words vs. 29) than the passive-voice version. More importantly, it places the "action" on the Athens man by making him the subject of the sentence. In the passive-voice version, life sentence is the subject.

Passive Voice Sometimes Best

Sometimes writers deliberately choose passive-voice construction to emphasize certain elements by placing them at or close to the beginning of sentences. Example:

ACTIVE
The County Board of Education fired Green High School Principal Fred Smith Friday on charges he changed football players' grades to keep them eligible to play.

PASSIVE
Green High School Principal Fred Smith was fired Friday by the County Board of Education on charges he changed football players' grades to keep them eligible to play.

Numerous situations exist where passive-voice construction works best. Presidents of the United States and what they do are news. So too what is told to them. Note how passive-voice construction emphasizes that in the following example:

ACTIVE
Soviet military and economic power is weakening, CIA analysts told President Bush today.

PASSIVE
President Bush was told today by CIA analysts that Soviet military and economic power is weakening.

Two other devices pros use:

1. They rewrite if a first attempt opens a sentence with *there is, there are, there were*. For example:

NO
There are more than 60 officers assigned to the narcotics squad that arrested the Athens man.

YES
More than 60 officers are assigned to the narcotics squad that arrested the Athens man.

2. They rewrite to express even a negative in positive form:

NO
The police did not make any arrest that night.

YES
The police made no arrests that night.

Technique 7: Taking the Extra Step

Sometimes a short phrase, even a word or two, drives your newswriting closer to the magic of immediate reader comprehension. Let's see how professionals take an extra step to accomplish that.

President Bush says there is too much criticism of secrecy in his administration. He smiles. But he is angry. How to catch that for the distant reader? Jack Nelson, *Los Angeles Times* Washington bureau chief, writes this:

Declaring he "hates to be secretive, to say nothing of deceptive," Bush, *flashing a tight smile,* said he plans a "whole new relationship" with the news media. . . .   *Jack Nelson, "Upset at Press Complaints, Bush Vows to Cut Down on News Sessions," Los Angeles Times, Feb. 16, 1990, p. A-8*

Paul Houston, also with the *Los Angeles Times,* catches for his readers Bush's emotion over U.S. soldiers killed in Panama.

A visibly anguished President Bush said. . . .

His *voice rose with feeling* as he spoke. . . .   *Paul Houston, "Bush Says Split TV Screen Showed Him as Uncaring," Los Angeles Times, Jan. 6, 1990, p. A-1*

The Associated Press rushes to transmit word of a plane crash, and the writer decides to go with a short, punchy, straightforward lead—a good choice when you're in a hurry. Nevertheless, the writer manages to go an extra step and insert three words that create an image, a mood picture, for readers.

COVE NECK, N.Y.—A Colombian Boeing 707 jetliner with more than 140 people aboard crashed in *fog and rain* Thursday night while on approach to Kennedy International Airport, authorities said. Numerous injuries were reported.   *Pat Milton, AP dispatch for morning papers, Jan. 25, 1990.*

Technique 8: Translating!

Newswriters should *translate,* reducing complexities to simplicities, using every word to draw readers toward understanding. Obviously that means using words readers are likely to know, but avoiding—or explaining—words they aren't likely to know.

An AP writer refers to "viscous goo" in an oil-spill story. Not everybody knows viscous means a fluid with cohesive, sticky consistency.

The *Los Angeles Times* makes it simple: "gooey sludge." Ah, that I understand!

A *New York Times* pro reports a man dies of amyotrophic lateral sclerosis, but quickly adds, "also known as Lou Gehrig's disease. . . ."

Immediately following reference to the gross national product, an AP reporter adds that it "measures the output of all the nation's goods and services."

A *Wall Street Journal* writer refers to "underwriting" and quickly explains it: "A corporation that wants to sell stock or bonds goes to a Wall Street firm, which purchases the securities outright, accepting the financial risk of finding buyers. If the investment bank can sell the securities at a higher price than it paid the issuer, it makes a profit."

You don't need a business degree to understand "underwriting"—and that's how you can tell when a real pro is writing news and translating it. The writing *answers* questions. It doesn't *create* them.

Effective translation often means giving the reader the *meaning* of a term before you use the term itself. An AP pro writes: "The government's *main economic forecasting gauge* rose in December. . . ." Only a full paragraph later does the AP writer use the formidable term, "The Commerce Department's Index of Leading Economic Indicators. . . ."

Quick! How big is a "6-by-6 tunnel" the North Korean army dug into South Korea? A *New York Times* writer translates the answer into meaningful terms: It is "large enough for three soldiers to walk abreast. . . ."

Ever wonder how a jet engine works? A *Seattle Times* writer translates the engineering gobbledegook: "A jet engine sucks air in the front, compresses it with burning kerosene and ejects it at high speed from the back. The discharge moves the plane. . . ."

You've read the Russian words *glasnost* and *perestroika* many times. Could you, without hesitation, define both? Skilled newswriters don't assume you can. Such terms *are* understood by many, however. So, how can you deftly insert definitions without being glaringly obvious or condescending?

Here is how two pros do it:

A *Los Angeles Times* reporter covers Soviet President Gorbachev saying there is need "to broaden and accelerate perestroika, *as his program of political and economic reforms is known.*"

A *Wall Street Journal* reporter on Kremlin affairs: "Despite glasnost, *the policy of greater openness,* the government's inner machinations remain hidden. . . ." (See sidebar below for an expert's view of your newswriter's responsibilities in handling such bureaucratic language.)

Technique 9: Using Numbers to Enlighten, Not Confuse

Numbers put muscle on the frame of a news story. They supply essential specifics—an element of precision—for readers trying to cope in a world of glittering generalities.

A Professional's View: *Be Vigilant!*

Jack Cappon, a long-time AP editor and writing coach, is a foe of bloated language, as he makes clear here.

To say things clearly and concisely takes skill and, above all, vigilance. Bloated language is all around us. Government pumps gaseous bureacratese into the environment. Other institutions, corporate headquarters, the professions and social sciences diligently contribute to the effusion of jargon.

Reporters are professionally exposed to this strangling diction. Their job is to convert it into plain English. Unfortunately, many come down with a bad case of verbiage themselves, and then precision, clarity and grace desert them.[3]

Jack Cappon

However, if you misuse numbers your story can be fatally weakened. Here are some guidelines:

1. A stand-alone number seldom adds much to a story. It's meaningless to tell readers unemployment "increased to 10,000" unless you complete the thought: ". . . increased to 10,000 from 8,698."

2. Raw numbers or figures alone don't mean much to many readers. Figures *plus* percentages often do. Thus, it's much more meaningful to write that unemployment increased "14.9 percent, to 10,000 from 8,698." (You know how to figure percentages, of course: Subtract 8,698 from 10,000 to get 1,302. Divide 1,302 by 8,698, which yields 14.9 percent.)

3. Many numbers entering the news stream are issued for specific periods—days, weeks, months, quarters, years—that are directly comparable to earlier periods. Always relate amounts to the comparable previous period. Thus, it's *essential* to write that "unemployment *in February* increased 14.9 percent, to 10,000 from 8,698 *in February of last year*." Comparing February's figures to January's could be important, but it also could be comparing apples and oranges. Cyclical or seasonal conditions frequently make huge differences, particularly in writing precision economic, business, and financial news (which we'll discuss in a later chapter).

4. Help your readers characterize the size, meaning, impact, and importance of numbers and amounts. The *Los Angeles Times* does this by reporting gang-related killings "skyrocketed." *The Wall Street Journal* uses several devices in this story:

Characterize Size, Meaning, of Numbers

NEW YORK—The ABC television network has agreed to pay a *bracing* 80% increase to keep its coveted contract for "NFL Monday Night Football," *ponying up* a huge $900 million for four seasons. *Dennis Kneale, "ABC to Pay $900 Million in NFL Pact,"* The Wall Street Journal, *Jan. 16, 1990, p. B-1*

The *Los Angeles Times* puts it all together in a story on gang violence in 1989:

Los Angeles police reported that an *unprecedented* 303 people were slain in gang-related killings in the city last year, *a nearly 18% increase* over *the record* 257 slayings logged in 1988. *Darrell Dawsey, "Gang-Related Killings in County, City Set Record in '89,"* Los Angeles Times, *Jan. 12, 1990, p. B-3*

Technique 10: Handling Profanity, Obscenity, and Slang

Language generally regarded as indecent and offensive isn't used in many "family" newspapers or newscasts. Excluded are not only specific words but, often, material or context that create offensive inferences that readers reasonably can draw.

So, in many cases you should "write around" profanity or obscenity and omit them. Sometimes, however, both can be considered essential to reader understanding of an important issue, so discuss the matter with your editor.

Consult Your Editor on Profanity

If both of you decide the material is essential, handling can vary:

"[Expletive deleted]" lets adult readers fill in the blank.

"SOB" for the fuller version often is adequate.

Editors sometimes use the fuller version if it is considered integral to the story—but only deep in the story and, presumably, safe from the eyes of children and other innocents. In a lengthy story about a criminal lawyer defending a killer, a *Washington Post* writer waits until 1,000 words or more go by before inserting an angry statement from a friend of the victim: "[Fred Smith] said his only regret is that 'they don't have a death penalty for that son of a bitch.'" In this case, the *Post* decided using profanity was necessary to illustrate the intense emotion surrounding the event.

Decisions on indecent language often revolve around the same standards used to define news. *Prominence* of people involved, for example, is one yardstick used in deciding how explicit we get. When a well-known football player was arrested on a charge of soliciting sex from an undercover policewoman, AP decided on this handling of details from an arrest report: "When asked what he wanted, [the player] gave a slang response for oral sex and intercourse, [the policewoman] said."

Slang Sometimes Communicates Effectively

With careful writing, you can slide into slang on occasion to reach out and very effectively touch readers. Note how Frederick C. Klein of *The Wall Street Journal* does this in a story on Boston Red Sox baseball players in spring training. Note also how his second paragraph pulls you into the story with him.

Tests of body composition showed that the Bosox *lugged* an average of 16.2% fat, a higher proportion than that reported for other *male jocks.* By comparison, a group of pro football offensive linemen, who tend toward the massive, had *larded out* at 15.6%.

The ballplayers came up average in flexibility tests, and just above that in muscular endurance, measured by how many elbows-to-knees situps they could do in a minute. They averaged 53 there, *in case you'd like to see how you stack up.* Frederick C. Klein, "Never Was No Spring in Their Training," The Wall Street Journal, March 9, 1990, p. A-11

Note the fine, somewhat slangy touch an anonymous editor displays in putting together this story "from wire reports" on the Great Broccoli War of 1990. (See, I told you in Chapter 1 that Big Vegetable stories would enter your newswriter life!):

WASHINGTON—A defiant George Bush pulled rank Thursday on his wife, his mother and the broccoli growers of America.

"I do not like broccoli," Mr. Bush declared. "I haven't liked it since I was a little kid and my mother made me eat it, and I'm president of the United States and I'm not going to eat any more broccoli."

So there. *"Bush Officially Invokes Vegetable Veto,"* Atlanta Journal and Constitution, March 23, 1990, p. A-4

Technique 11: Signaling You're a Pro

You won't be expected in your first newswriting job to turn out a Pulitzer Prize-winning investigative story. You *will* be expected to cover a school conference or sewer commission meeting, or maybe a two-car accident—and report accurately in clean, error-free writing.

Aside from writing challenges we discussed earlier in this chapter, others often arise for beginning writers. They may seem minor, but how you handle them signals to your editor whether you write like an amateur or a professional. Beware of these:

More Hints to Remember

• Subject and verb agreement. He (singular) *is* going. So *is* she. That's obvious. But also watch *collective* nouns: The army (singular) *attacks* tomorrow. The army *is* attacking.

• Agreement of nouns and pronouns. Singular pronouns refer to singular nouns; plural pronouns to plural nouns: The general speaks tonight. *He* won't tomorrow. *But:* The soldiers halted *their* attack. *They* will resume tomorrow.

• Sequences of tenses. A sentence's principal verb determines the tense of subsequent verbs: The army *tries* to fulfill each mission it *is given*. The army *tried* to fulfill each mission it *was given*.

• Split infinitives. *Yes:* The general agreed to attack soon. *No:* The general agreed to soon attack.

• Misplaced modifier. *No:* Despite its casualties, the general ordered the army to attack. *Yes:* The general ordered the army to attack despite its casualties. (This is an error commonly made by young writers.)

• Contractions. *It's* is a contraction of *it is* . . . they're (they are) . . . you're (you are) . . . who's (who is).

• Words that are pronounced the same but have different meanings are *homophones*. Three seem to bother young writers:

> The army halted *there*. (adverb)
> They counted *their* casualties. (pronoun)
> *They're* ready for the general. (contraction)
>
> *Your* sergeant arrived. (pronoun)
> *You're* the new sergeant. (contraction)
>
> *Whose* sergeant is coming? (adjective)
> *Who's* coming? (contraction)

Is continuing vigilance over grammar beneath your dignity as a newswriter? Before you decide, consider whether you would like your byline on the following clanger. It was fronted by a major West Coast daily (we'll omit names to protect the guilty).

> Two people *are* dead and a third person *was* injured in three separate shootings yesterday.

SUMMARY CHECKLIST

☐ To communicate effectively, newswriting must be lean, direct, precise, and colorful. Above all, it must be *accurate*.

☐ Short, understandable words woven into punchy sentences communicate more effectively than long words in convoluted sentences. The most effective sentence often takes this order: subject + verb + direct object.

☐ Using "live" language is essential to good newswriting. Try for language that transmits images of action, color, movement, vibrancy.

☐ Rhythm in writing, as in music, can transport your audience. Strive for melodious (but not lulling) flow.

☐ Especially in your student years, experiment by "reaching" for a different approach to newswriting. Stretch for language, sentence structure, and analogies that draw word pictures. Beware you don't reach so far that you fall flat.

☐ Using the present tense can make news stories come alive—see it now, hear it now, *feel* it now.

☐ It's essential that your newswriting translates for readers. Break down complex subjects into simple language; avoid jargon and scientific terms many readers don't understand.

☐ Strive for *precision* newswriting that weaves statistics and numbers into substantive but palatable offerings for your readers. Learn to handle—and understand yourself—numbers that can aid comprehension.

☐ Issues and challenges in newswriting include preventing colorful writing from creating inaccuracies in your stories, avoiding exaggeration, ensuring you don't attempt to cover lack of factual substance with dramatic writing, keeping your opinions out of newswriting, and writing in good taste.

RECOMMENDED READING

Discerning reading of major newspapers will reveal a treasure of great newswriting. Especially recommended are: *Los Angeles Times, Chicago Tribune, Dallas Morning News, Washington Post, Philadelphia Inquirer, Boston Globe, The New York Times, Miami Herald.* Some of the finest writing of our time appears in *The Wall Street Journal.* Watch how the pros do it.

Very helpful:

William Strunk, Jr., and E. B. White, *The Elements of Style,* 3rd ed. (New York: Macmillan Publishing Co., Inc., 1979).

James J. Kilpatrick, *The Writer's Art* (Kansas City, MO: Andrews, McMeel & Parker, 1984).

Rene J. Cappon, *The Word* (New York: The Associated Press, 1982).

Brier and Heyn, *Writing for Newspapers and News Services* (New York: Funk & Wagnalls, 1969). It's old but effective.

NOTES

1. If you're *really* rusty, I strongly recommend Brian S. Brooks and James L. Pinson, *Working with Words: A Concise Handbook for Media Writers and Editors* (New York: St. Martin's Press, 1989).
2. "Q and A: Ask Keith Moyer," *Gannetteer,* November 1989, p. 25.
3. Jack Cappon, *The Word* (New York: The Associated Press, 1982, p. 13).

Exercise 2–1   Simplifying the Complex

Rewrite each of the following sentences to (1) simplify or improve sentence structure and (2) substitute short, more easily understood words for those that are long or hard to understand.

1. In the accident, three persons received injuries and were rushed to the hospital with abrasions and contusions.

_____

_____

_____

2. Rejecting charges of misanthropy, the senator spoke from the floor during the debate and shouted with passion that he, in fact, loves people.

_____

_____

_____

3. He declared that God is omniscient and, in fact, knows all things—that He has infinite knowledge.

_____

_____

_____

4. The corpsman reached the wounded man after crawling to his side through the jungle and performed a tracheotomy.

_____

_____

_____

5. It was, the professor acknowledged with chagrin, "a lapsus memoriae" that will cause great difficulty.

_____

_____

_____

6. An immediate crisis arose. Because high winds came out of the west. They collapsed the parabolic antenna. The radar thus went dead.

_____

_____

_____

_____

7. Nondurable goods were blamed for the general increases in prices because their costs had risen dramatically.

_____

_____

_____

_____

8. Sentenced to 30 days in jail, he was convicted of driving while intoxicated.

_____

_____

_____

_____

9. He complained bitterly and glanced at his wife. That happened as he was led off by a policeman.

_____

_____

_____

_____

10. A policeman for 10 years, the crowd listened quietly as Sgt. Will Nether spoke about crime in the streets.

_____

_____

_____

_____

Exercise 2–2   Sentence Organization and Spelling

Rewrite the following sentences to improve structure and correct misspellings.

1. Accomodation his goal, they listened quietly as he nevertheless spoke passionately.

_____

2. The sherriff, Fred Smith, proceded toward the Wedesday deadline.

_____

3. Communications sattelites sped through the vaccuum. High above earth.

_____

4. The Carribean a drug runner's haven, the narcotics police put many planes over it.

_____

5. For the dangers they encountered, police certainly didn't recieve high saleries.

_____

6. He said it was alright but the sponser objected but he proceded anyway.

_____

7. All though it was suprizing, he put it off. Because he had to many worrys.

_____

8. The affect of the fire was desparate shortages of food. Water. Fuel. Crowds collected at the office to complain about it.

_____

9. He effected the air of a gentleman despite, which offended servivors, quite obviously having been a scoundral.

_____

10. The sentance was to stiff, he complained, but the judge, he said, ignored him and gave him 10 years for burglery.

_____

Exercise 2–3   Issues and Challenges

1. To write that a speaker "strode cockily" to the podium is colorful. In one paragraph below, describe how it also can be inaccurate.

_____

_____

_____

_____

2. Note this sentence: "A huge crowd menaced police." Why is that sentence vague, and what facts would you insert to give it substance?

_____

_____

_____

_____

3. Explain how the following sentence exaggerates. "Chicago residents feel the city's commuter system is antiquated, according to interviews conducted today by a roving reporter at train stations."

_____

_____

_____

_____

4. Rewrite the following sentence to remove the writer's opinion. "The mayor, called by his foes 'a born loser,' submitted a budget that obviously is out of line and the largest in the city's history."

_____

_____

_____

_____

5. What is exaggerated in the following? "Residents of three cities refused to pay taxes. It was a nationwide people's revolution."

_____

_____

_____

_____

6. Rewrite the following sentence to remove exaggeration. "A huge crowd of 300 swept through Times Square, demonstrating how close New York City is to anarchy."

_____

_____

_____

7. Rewrite the following to move it closer to objectivity. "The running back, a real show-boater, taunted his foes by doing a victory dance in the end zone. Sports writers long have accused him of show boating."

_____

_____

_____

8. Specify three facts you think would strengthen the following. "Despite his small size, the running back piled up enormous yardage in his long career."

_____

_____

_____

9. Rewrite the following to eliminate exaggeration. "All the moaning and groaning around April 15 every year shows most Americans feel grossly overtaxed."

_____

_____

_____

10. Which facts would you search out and insert in this sentence to make it more informative? "The company's profits rose by $6 million, the second-largest increase ever."

_____

_____

_____

_____

Exercise 2–4   Sentence Structure

In the following, put fragments together in complete sentences.

1. He is 59. Name: Fred Smith. Job: Jackson County sheriff. In the news because: was arrested today on charges of dealing drugs. Has been sheriff for 11 years.

_____

_____

_____

2. She is 54. Name: Mrs. Fred Smith. In the news because: her husband was arrested today on charges of dealing drugs. The Smiths have been married 19 years. She fainted when narcotics detectives arrested Smith in their home. Her first name is Myrtle.

_____

_____

_____

3. Cocaine was found in the house. About six ounces. So was a small quantity of heroin. Sergeant Bill Lester said police ripped up floorboards and found the dope.

_____

_____

_____

4. Sheriff Smith's dog, a Labrador, was shot. It attacked detectives, according to Lester. It had been trained as an attack dog, he said.

_____

_____

_____

5. Some officials said Smith's arrest was proof that drugs permeate the community. "When you find drugs under the floor of the sheriff's house you know drugs have spread throughout the community," said District Attorney I. M. Friendly. Officials agreed.

_____

_____

_____

6. The sheriff was visibly angry. Led away by detectives, he shouted angrily. A reporter heard him shout, "This is a setup."

_____

_____

_____

7. Smith was booked on only one charge: selling narcotics. Friendly said other charges would be filed, however.

_____

_____

_____

8. Mrs. Smith said a lawyer was being retained. An expert in criminal law, she said he is Jason Smooth. She said her husband had been framed.

_____

_____

_____

9. Nobody at the county building seemed to know answers to what comes next. Reporters asked who would take over the sheriff's department. County Commissioner Jim Leskee said he didn't know.

_____

_____

_____

10. George Wilson is 36. He has been a sheriff's deputy for 13 years. Other deputies said he might be an interim sheriff candidate. They told a reporter that.

_____

_____

_____

Exercise 2–5   Using Living Language

Write more colorful, vibrant ways of expressing the following thoughts:

1. Fire *moved* through the old house.

_____

_____

2. Victims *asked* for help.

_____

_____

3. Firefighters *drove* to the scene.

_____

_____

4. Flames *burned* the old house.

_____

_____

5. Swinging clubs, guards *moved* the crowd back.

_____

_____

6. Then, like a huge, unstoppable wave, the crowd *moved* forward.

_____

_____

7. The two cars *hit* each other at the intersection.

_____

_____

8. The plane *fell* from the sky.

_____

_____

9. The soldiers *took* the hill.

_____

_____

10. The enemy *left* the hill.

_____

_____

Exercise 2–6   Translating

Rewrite the following sentences using simpler phrases or words for any you feel many readers would find difficult to understand. If you believe technical language must be used, translate it for readers.

1. Smith's attorney said he would seek immediately a writ of habeas corpus.

2. "This bust wasn't handled by the narcs," one detective said. "We took it down."

3. One witness, however, said he saw an officer wearing a jacket with "DEA" on the back.

4. The district attorney said the city should build a Hadrian's Wall against drug dealers.

5. Sometimes, the district attorney said, there "seems to be an inverse relationship between drug traffic and police effort. The harder we try, the more drugs there are." He spoke in despair.

6. A minister said firm action is needed against drug dealing "to keep inviolate the sanctity of the American home."

7. The minister said he saw the finger of "the Prince of Darkness" in the drug trade.

8. "Well," the district attorney replied, "I'm no Merlin and I don't have rabbit tricks."

9. Ken Crawford, president of Eastside Neighborhood Association, said, "I don't mean to be bilious about this but it's time we got somebody to break a few heads on the streets."

10. With that, the district attorney adjourned the meeting *sine die*.

Exercise 2–7   Using Numbers

Write complete sentences either (1) making proper use of numbers or figures or (2) answering questions below.

1. Which additional statistics would you want to write in one sentence about the following? "He said rainfall reached record levels last night."

_____

2. What is missing from the following sentence? "Auto production was up just under one percent in February."

_____

3. "The fast guard scored 39 points, a personal career high." What is lacking from that sentence?

_____

4. Why is the following sentence not entirely valid journalistically? "He said unemployment rose 18 percent in February from January levels."

_____

5. The sentence below reports an increase in unemployment. Rewrite the sentence to characterize for readers the size of the increase. "He said unemployment in the county increased to 20,000 from 10,000 in one month."

_____

6. Insert a sense of dimension in the following sentence that will help readers characterize the size of the difference. "The pitcher's salary is 73 percent higher than it was just three years ago."

_____

7. Put the following fragments together in no more than two complete sentences. "For the past four months, traffic deaths have increased steadily. The figures were 92, 105, 108, 111, respectively. The police chief said he is 'terribly concerned.'"

_____

8. What is lacking, in terms of journalistic validity, in the following? "The anchor's salary rose to $2 million."

_____

9. What questions should you anticipate from your editor if you hand in the following sentence? "The salary range is very attractive."

_____

10. If the mayor's salary increases to $98,000 annually from $83,000, what percentage increase has he received?

_____

Exercise 2–8   Signaling You're a Pro!

Rewrite the following sentences to correct errors in grammar and/or spelling.

1. The Board of Education met Monday night. They will delibarate again Wednesday at noon.

2. The Board authorized the principle of the high school to soon proced.

3. The Board wrestled with all the problems it is given.

4. Despite their objections, the Board suggested the groups leave.

5. It's first edition was filled with troublesome errors.

6. "Its going to be a difficult night," the editor said. "Many ambulences are on the scene and the whole thing looks like a municiple disaster."

7. "Whose coming?", the photographer asked the reporters, emphacizing the need for speed.

8. "Your going," the editor said, pointing at the young reporter. "And your in charge," he said, nodding at the city editor. Nobody paniced but they sure moved hurridely.

9. Two bills were defeated in the Senate yesterday but a third is passed in what certainly was a blow to the Democrats.

10. Despite their defeat, the senator told his fellow Democrats to summerize their political agenda and activitys.

Chapter Three

The Fundamentals of Style: Lean and Clean

Think of the enormous challenge we present our newspaper readers: We rush from revolution to football game to traffic court, sweeping the world for hundreds of thousands of facts. We write hurriedly, dividing time into artificial components to meet our self-imposed deadlines for morning and afternoon papers. We stack hundreds of stories, photos, graphs, statistics in long gray columns, amid the commercial clamor of our advertising.

Then, we throw (literally!) a huge, complex document, sometimes weighing pounds, at our busy, preoccupied readers, and we say, "Now, work your way through this and you will be informed."

Luckily (for *both* buyers and sellers of newspapers), we've devised ways of making that huge package attractive and readable.

In Chapter 1, we looked at how professionals select news their readers *want,* as well as need. That can make newspapers not only attractive but also crucial to readers. In Chapter 2, we explored the colorful, vibrant newswriting so essential to making newspapers effective communicators.

We now turn, in Chapter 3, to other ways pros ensure that newspapers are accessible and manageable sources of information. We'll do this in two sections:

First, we'll concentrate on writing in direct, precise language that is lean and clean—language that, while colorful and vital, doesn't carry excess baggage. Our goal is simplicity in writing that explains the complexities of the world we cover.

Second, we'll look at some hints on preparing news copy and editing it. Preparing it properly is a signal of professionalism.

Most newspapers follow the same style in grammar, punctuation, capitalization and other usages. This adherence to a common style started when newspapers pressured the nation's primary general news services, The Associated Press (AP) and United Press International (UPI), to transmit copy in the same style and form to aid editors using news interchangeably from the rival agencies. Ever since 1960, both AP and UPI have published stylebooks that represent a consensus among newspapers and are alike in style and usage rules. AP's *Stylebook* is most widely used because, among other things, it contains detailed treatment of many aspects of newspaper law important to newswriting. Style and usage rules of most concern to young newswriters have been selected from AP's *Stylebook* and appear on page 461. You will need to consult this material as you read Chapter 3 and complete the exercises.

By chapter's end you will understand many of the writing and editing procedures that professional newswriters follow to ensure newspapers provide readers with a consistency and recognizable day-to-day coherency. That coherency can make a newspaper an effective communicator—and a comfortable, predictable old friend, as well.

THE STRAIGHT AND NARROW PATH TO CLARITY

We all appreciate graceful writing that wanders leisurely here and there, uncovering and highlighting interesting or amusing (if not particularly important) delights for casual readers.

There's room for some of that in newswriting. But not much. We've got to catch our busy readers and move them quickly, *directly* toward understanding information. Your chances of succeeding are improved enormously if your newswriting is lean and clean and keeps to the straight and narrow path—straight through a single sentence, a paragraph, an entire story. Your chances of leading readers to the end improve even more if your writing places no obstacles on that path and creates no sidetracks or diversions.

All that requires adhering to standardized style and ruthlessly eliminating excess wordage, nonessential thoughts, and other baggage that weigh down your readers.

Adhere to Standardized Style

Which paragraph below communicates most effectively?

1. The featured speaker, in the main event of the evening, said Gannett Company Incorporated, with eighty-nine newspapers, claimed daily circulation of six million, 29 thousand, seven hundred and forty-five newspapers sold every day, and 5.6 million on Sundays. The speech lasted about an hour and a half, starting at 7 o'clock in the evening and running until 8:39 p.m. in the evening.

2. The featured speaker said Gannett Co. Inc., with 89 newspapers, claimed circulation of 6.02 million on weekdays, 5.6 million on Sundays. The speech lasted from 7 p.m. to 8:39 p.m.

Obviously, the second example communicates better. Why?

Its *style,* particularly in use of numerals, is consistent. Style is *not* a set of arcane rules established by people with nothing better to do. Style is designed to facilitate effective communication.

Example 2 communicates better because it is *lean,* free of redundancies ("8:39 p.m. in the evening") that in the first example sidetrack and confuse the reader. Moreover, the second example is *clean* and to the point, free of excess wordage. It helps—doesn't hinder—the reader searching for information.

And that's why news organizations have stylebooks and why many editors you'll work with are near fanatics in demanding clean, precise copy: Writing within an established, consistent stylistic framework communicates most effectively because it leads readers quickly toward comprehension of information.

Professional newswriters—and their editors—are especially alert in four problem areas: bloated writing, abstract words and constructions, redundancies and cliches. We'll look at each in turn.

Eliminate Bloat, Abstractions, Redundancies, Cliches

YOU AND THE WAR AGAINST BLOATED WRITING

It's eternal, this war. It must be waged, though, because bloated writing turns off readers. Also, newspapers—and other media—simply don't have room for over-writing.

Yet, sloppy newswriters create bloated copy because, frankly, it is easier and faster to write "long" than "short." It takes little thought to slam together long, stuffy words in hackneyed, ordinary phrases to form bloated, meandering sentences and paragraphs.

But, ah, writing short! That takes effort. It requires writing and rewriting with loving care to find words with punch and precision, then lace them together in clear, direct sentences and paragraphs that pull—entice—your readers forward. (Note the Wordsmith at Work.)

Start by avoiding the temptation (and we all feel it) to exhibit erudition through employment of extraordinarily complicated words of many syllables that may create a state of disorder in the minds of your readers. There, you see? I was tempted to show you, in a long-winded sentence, that I know "erudition."

Here is a rewrite eliminating bloat: Start by avoiding the temptation to display your learning by using big words that may confuse your readers.

Word substitutions that illustrate how you can eliminate bloat are contained in the list below.

accelerate	speed up
accommodations	rooms
apprehend	catch, arrest, seize
commence	start, begin
finalize	complete, end
conflagration	fire
intoxicated	drunk
methodology	method
remuneration	pay
terminate	fire, end

Use Words Familiar to Readers

In sum, use words likely to be familiar to your readers, words with specific, not abstract, meaning. In *The Word,* his tome (or scholarly volume, which *he* would call a "book"), AP's writing coach, Rene Cappon, cautions against using "The Elegant Variation"—stuffy, fancy words some writers use because they consider them elegant ("edifice" for "building," for example).[1]

Of course, you cannot sacrifice precision for short words. If a word of many syllables is necessary, use it. But explain what it means:

> The professor lectured on proto-humans, or early primates with human characteristics.
> The doctor said she suffered from hydrophobia, an abnormal dread of water.

Don't "Write Like You Talk"

Bloat gets really serious if you unthinkingly string together wordy, redundant phrases. You don't communicate effectively by writing in informal language used in shoes-off, chat-across-the-kitchen-table conversation. Like, you know what I mean? "Writing like you talk" may be fine for a chatty column, an occasional feature, or a mood piece. But precision *news*writing requires disciplined, thoughtful effort.

Wordsmith at Work

As violence sweeps Southern California, *Los Angeles Times* editors assign staff writer Paul Dean to a "take-out"—major story—on exactly what happens when someone is shot. Note Dean's use of present tense, his precise detail, and his short, punchy sentences.

Juan Antonio Mendez never felt what hit him. A bullet does that. The small lead plug moving close to the speed of sound shocks and deadens the tissue and organs it crushes.

Fear and confusion heighten the torpor of a gunshot wound. And at this point in his armed robbery of an electronics store in Koreatown, Juan Mendez is in full panic.

The plan has come apart. A young Brinks guard, Ramiro Garcia, isn't showing scared. Mendez's partner was able to grab the canvas cash sack from Garcia's left hand. But the guard isn't flinching, and that could mean he is ready to shoot it out.

Mendez has no time to change moves, to control the next moments of his life, to run, to yelp, to back down or cancel his commitment to violence.

He does have one moment to cock the hammer of his own gun, a museum piece—a rusted, single-action, frontier-style .44 six-gun made by Remington in the 1890s.

But the guard is faster. Garcia's left hand sweeps the barrel of Mendez's handgun aside. His own revolver, a Brink-issue Smith & Wesson with a four-inch barrel and a full load of six .38 Special rounds, clears its black leather holster.

Boom! Garcia's first shot hits Mendez high in the left chest. The range is so close that flakes of unburned gunpowder are forced through Mendez's brown sweater. They tattoo the edges of the chest wound.

Boom! Mendez fires, but it is more of a reflex. The shot goes wild and slaps sideways into a store wall.

Boom! A second bullet hits Mendez's chest, dead center. He stumbles, turning. Boom! A bullet in the right arm, from triceps through biceps and into the left knee. Mendez falls.

Flat on his back, eyes fading, Mendez's dirty sneakers twitch against a display case of home security systems. "Double Entry Security," promises the sign. "Because Your Security and Peace of Mind Are Important."

Mendez flops an arm across his bleeding chest.

It is three days before Christmas.

Juan Mendez has just 58 seconds to live.

Paul Dean, "The Anatomy of a Bullet Wound," *Los Angeles Times,* Jan. 14, 1990, p. E-1

For example, eliminate redundancies and bloat in common sayings or phrases used in everyday language and substitute shorter, punchier versions:

at this point in time	now
with the exception of	except
in consequence of	because
due to the fact that	because
having to do with	about
gave their approval	approved

in the near future	soon
at the present time	now
in order to	to
in the event that	if

Now, note horrors that can emerge if you unthinkingly construct full sentences from "elegant" (but pompous) words and bloated, redundant phrases:

NO	YES
The conflagration roared through the dilapidated structure and, it goes without saying, it was a terrible tragedy.	The fire roared through the shabby building. (If it "goes without saying," why say it? Anyway, "terrible tragedy" is redundant.)

NO	YES
It is interesting to note that the proliferation of adverse weather conditions established an all-time record for low temperatures.	The spread of bad weather created record low temperatures. (Why say "It is interesting to note" when obviously, that is why we're writing about it? And, note the editing of "all-time record." All records are for all time, until the next one is set, a fact that escapes many sports writers.)[2]

Bloat assumes monumental proportions if you let it infect entire paragraphs. Note:

The obviously intoxicated operator of the enormous truck accelerated up to and past the roadblock as police officers attempted to apprehend him, but due to the fact that police were ordered not to open fire on him he eluded them and drove onward down the highway. At this point in time, police say they have identification of the driver and say they hope to make an arrest in the near future.

That two-sentence, 71-word monster is ludicrously bloated. Let's trim it:

The drunken driver of the huge truck sped past the roadblock as police tried to arrest him. They were ordered not to shoot, and he escaped down the highway. Police said they knew the driver's identity and hoped to arrest him soon.

That boils down to a tight 42 words in three punchy sentences. Which communicates better?

YOU AND THE ABSTRACT ISSUE

The issue here is that a confusing situation can be created for readers if newswriters fashion a climate in which they use too many abstract nouns, such as *issue, situation* and *climate.*

The preceding paragraph, for example, can be written much more effectively. I could have written: Readers can be confused if a newswriter uses too many abstract nouns.

Abstract nouns name ideas, qualities, attributes. Misuse of them blunts your newswriting because many are vague and unfocused in meaning. What, for example, is an "issue"? It can be anything people discuss, negative or positive, good or bad.

Abstract Nouns Blunt Writing

Note the difference:

The soldiers discussed the impending problem.	The soldiers discussed the impending attack.

You construct in your readers' minds a completely different picture if you use the concrete noun "attack."

Concrete nouns name something material—a house, bridge, tree. They strengthen your writing. But even concrete nouns must be selected with great care. Note the difference:

Concrete Nouns Add Strength

The soldier picked up his weapon.	The soldier picked up his pistol.

Professional newswriters don't leave their readers wondering whether the weapon was a rifle, grenade, knife, pistol, or other implement of war.

Developing a reporter's eye for details and selecting nouns that describe them precisely will convey your meaning much more effectively.

Develop an Eye for Detail

Much vague, unfocused language slips into print because writers (and their editors) don't take an extra minute or two to try for something more concrete. Note how the following can be fixed so simply:

One debate was on the *question* of education.	. . . on education.
The factory's production *facilities* were modern.	The factory was modern.
Police tried to shut down all drug-dealing *operations*.	. . . all drug dealing.
The *experience* of war horrified him.	War horrified him.
The *problem* of poverty troubled the council.	Poverty troubled the council.
A rise in stock market prices was an encouraging *factor*.	. . . was encouraging.
She was a woman of gentle *character*.	She was a gentle woman (or, even better, She was gentle.)

REDUNDANCIES: BE CONSTANTLY ALERT ALL THE TIME

The message or point to be made and driven home here is obvious and very clear: Don't repeat something again and again when one telling or recounting will do.

Grouped as they are above, redundancies—unnecessary repetitions of ideas—jump off the page and look ridiculous. As you rush to write under deadline, however, they can sneak into your copy and not appear so obvious. How many times have you encountered the following beauties?

acute crisis	general public	personal friend
brutal slaying	grateful thanks	sink down
circle around	grand total	temporary reprieve
close proximity	main essentials	true facts
concrete proposals	more preferable	12 midnight
dead body	old adage	vitally necessary
entirely absent	past history	

Redundancies clog our writing. So many are in print and on air that it's easy to assume they are acceptable. They aren't—and this is another argument against "writing like you talk." You might mention a "completely full glass" in casual conversation over a kitchen table. But professional newswriters don't put that on front pages.

Don't Reach for Redundant Modifiers

Some writers believe they can't make their point without reaching for redundant modifiers to give words an extra—but unnecessary—jolt: *new* record, *pair* of twins, *staunch* supporter.

Let's face it, most redundancies result from just plain sloppy thinking. But occasionally confusion can arise over what is proper. In such instances, think it out: Can a high jumper set an *old* record? Can there be *three* twins?

CLICHES: AVOID THEM LIKE THE PLAGUE

Ever see your friends' smiles fade when they realize you are once more telling the same tired, old joke? Well, imagine readers' faces when they realize a newswriter is using the same tired cliches.

In this sense, language is like a joke: Both wear out if repeated too often; unless selected carefully, both can drive off an audience.

Only Lazy Writers Use Cliches

Cliches, moreover, are evidence of a deeper problem: Writers who use them are lazy, uninterested, or incapable of reaching for new, forceful ways of using the language to make a point with precision and efficiency.

Don't you just want to gnash your teeth or roll your eyes when a writer stampedes ahead and deals out two or three of the following in one fell swoop?

add insult to injury	foul play	supreme sacrifice
almighty dollar	grave crisis	trapped like rats
bloody riot	hail of bullets	uneasy truce
coveted trophy	hungry as a bear	upset the apple cart
do your own thing	left up in the air	watery grave
eyeball to eyeball	long arm of the law	world-class
flat as a board	selling like hot cakes	

Even the pros get lazy on occasion. Thus a *Los Angeles Times* writer has the sheriff's department *rocked* by money-skimming allegations. (We all know, of course, it is the White House, Washington and Congress that are rocked by scandals). An AP writer has adventurers arriving at their destination *weary but jubilant* (as have all adventurers since Marco Polo). And, shots do not *ring* out. Ask someone who has heard them; they, in fact, have a flat, rather nasty sound.

If you reach for a way to express yourself and grab something that feels comfortable because you've read it so many times, drop it. It may be a cliche and injurious to the health of your writing. (The sidebar on page 79 offers a pro's views on developing language skills.)

Now let's turn to preparing copy the professional way.

HINTS ON COPY PREPARATION

The moment you walk into a newsroom for your first job you and your writing start signaling how professional you are. Make sure your copy signals "professional" to those—including your boss—who edit it.[3]

In part, this means you must deliver copy that is accurate, well reported (more on that later in Chapter 8), well written and easy to "work." That is, deliver copy

A Professional's View
You and Your Language Skills

Margaret Holt, business editor of the Fort Lauderdale (Fla.) News/Sun Sentinel, *says sharpening their communications skills is a major challenge young journalists face.*

The single biggest problem for young journalists is inadequate communications skills, including poor language skills. That translates into the lack of old-fashioned accuracy and attention to detail.

Communication problems show up at the front end of the reporting process. New reporters rush out, often without understanding an assignment. Ego gets in the way. They're afraid to appear as inexperienced as they are. They fail to clarify expectations. Big mistake. Ask.

With visions of Page One, they're crushed when their 2-inch masterpiece gets shredded. They want to be writers, after all.

First things first. A fundamental: The best writing flows from accurate, thorough reporting. It is built on facts. Another fundamental: Don't assume anything, not about the information or the assignment itself. Ask.

Do your homework. Double-check facts. Nothing undermines credibility more than stupid mistakes, such as misspelling a name.

Get facts. Really listen to sources. Think. Does what was said make sense? Ask again. You represent the reader.

Be precise. Is that accident victim 41 or 45?

It's OK to ask dumb questions. Our job is to get information. Sometimes, we have to ask about the obvious, which can be embarrassing. Everybody knows. . . . Well, everybody doesn't know. Often, young reporters are afraid they will look dumb, so they fail to question things.

Margaret Holt

Your Copy Must Conform to Style

that conforms to certain mechanical and stylistic specifications your newspaper establishes. Create copy that lightens the burdens on overworked copy editors.

For starters, signaling "professional" means *never* putting on paper or your word processor screen anything you wouldn't want to see in print. No jokes, no obscenities—and no love letters, one of which was transmitted on an AP wire by mistake, killing both a romance and a career.

Some mechanical specifications that follow are basic. You can win copy-desk allies (important to you) by learning them:

1. When typing on paper or printing out from your word processor, use standard 8-½-by-11-inch paper. Double-space everything.

2. Open with a "slugline" to help your editors keep track of your story as they handle it and many others simultaneously. Form may vary but it will be something like this:

• Fred Smith
Jan. 16, 1992
Factory fire

Whether editors use pencils or computer terminals, they hunt down misspellings, errors in grammar and faulty style. Newswriters signal their professionalism by submitting ''clean'' copy without such errors.

(AP photo,
used with permission)

You don't need a 100–word slugline. But it must be specific enough to differentiate your story from others. (There may be five fires on January 16; yours is the *factory* fire.)

Byline, a Badge of Honor

A byline—"By Fred Smith"—is attached by your editor (not you) and at many newspapers is granted only to staffers who go beyond the usual in their reporting and writing. A byline is a badge of honor. Build yours as a signal of quality and credibility. Protect it and what it stands for—your professionalism—by ensuring that it never appears over inaccurate, sloppy writing.

3. Start your story one-third the way down the page, leaving room for a headline or instructions from your editor. Leave margins of at least an inch on both sides and the page bottom.

4. Any story originating outside the city of publication opens with a "dateline." Styles vary, but will be something like this:

- PORTLAND, Ore., Jan. 22—

- WASHINGTON—

Your newspaper's style may require all caps for the city and the state (normally the state is included to avoid confusion, in this case with Portland, Maine). A well-known city, such as the nation's capital or New York, normally doesn't need further identification. (You will have noted, of course, that a "dateline" really is a "place-line." We still call it a dateline even though most newspapers no longer include the date in it.)

5. Never divide a word at the end of a line. That can create confusion in the typesetting process over whether the word should be hyphenated. Never divide a paragraph at the end of a page. A page should be a complete, self-contained "take"—copy that can be edited and sent to typesetting even as you complete another "take."

6. If your story runs longer than one page, write "more" at the end of the first page. The second page should open with a slug something like this:

- smith/factory fire/add one

- smith/factory fire/p. 2

7. When your story is finished, write at bottom of the page: "-30-" or "###" or "-0-." (Incidentally, "-30-" was transmitted by telegraphers in olden days to signal "end of message," thus our use of it today.)

The Mechanics of Editing

Most writing and editing occur on screens, of course, but if you are working on paper, edit your copy with black pencil, correcting errors, eliminating unnecessary wordage, and thus "shaping" or fine-tuning your story. Don't worry about clean typing unless the story is such a shambles that you must redo it to make it readable. Never use "white-out." Edit with symbols recognized universally by copy editors as shown in Figure 3.1 on p. 82.

Style and You

The AP calls its stylebook "The Journalist's Bible." So many editors agree that almost certainly it will be your stylebook as a professional newswriter.

Proper style *must* be learned, for this course and for a successful career as a journalist. Get a copy of *The Associated Press Stylebook and Libel Manual* and start learning it. For quick reference, some important sections of the stylebook are excerpted at the back of this text. Consult this appendix when in doubt on a question of style, punctuation or usage. Your ability to write in proper style will be one important signal of your professionalism on the job.

SUMMARY CHECKLIST

- [ ] Professional newswriters create direct, precise, lean copy in conformity with the newspaper's mechanical and style specifications.

- [ ] News stories communicate best when shorn of redundancies, bloat, abstract words and constructions, cliches.

- [ ] In the war against bloat, avoid multisyllabic words or explain fully their meaning.

- [ ] "Writing like you talk" is not acceptable; everyday language contains too many redundancies ("at this point in time" for "now").

- [ ] Whenever possible, eliminate abstract nouns, which name ideas, qualities, attributes. Substitute concrete nouns, which name material things—house, bridge, tree, lake.

- [ ] Hunt down, search for, find, locate and ruthlessly, without mercy, eliminate redundancies.

☐ Language, like old jokes, can be used too often. The result is cliches, and they "upset the apple cart" (an awful cliche) with discerning readers—and make writers look stupid.

☐ *The Associated Press Stylebook and Libel Manual* is the "journalist's bible." Demonstrating in class or in your first job that you know style is like signalling you are a "genuine professional."

FIGURE 3–1

Editing

The Defense Department said today	indent
it had proposed spending	run in
110 million for a new jet fighter	insert missing $
to be named the "Cobra."	transpose letters
The jet was thought once	transpose words
to be too expensive for the	separate words
Navy but officials said	lower case; no cap
all services, including the navy--	insert dash
would use the plane	insert period (ALSO ⊙)
Over the week end,	join together
one official said,"We have every	insert quotation marks
hope of success.	
He added,"So does the navy."	insert comma
But Senator Fred Smith said	abbreviate
the white house wouldn't comment.	capitalize
For twelve hours, the Defense	use figure 12
Department	
counted 8 separate incidents.	spell out eight
Finally, the sen said he	spell out senator
would ffinally go to the people.	take out f
For him him, that was a tragedy.	take out him
STET	
Sen. John Jones joined	don't make correction
the debate with Wilsen.	spell as written (also use "wilsen (cq)")
Its a certain	insert apostrophe
thing,whether that was	insert semicolon
Anti war groups booed.	insert hyphen

Other symbols:
 Story continues MORE
 story ends — 30 —
 ⌈flush left
 flush right⌉
 ⊃center⊏
 set uppercase
 set lowercase
 set in italics
 BF set boldface

RECOMMENDED READING

The Associated Press *Stylebook* and a thesaurus, a dictionary of synonyms and antonyms, are musts, of course. Also:

Brian S. Brooks & James L. Pinson, *Working with Words* (New York: St. Martin's Press, 1989).

Terri Brooks, *Words' Worth* (New York: St. Martin's Press, 1989).

George Hough, *News Writing,* 4th ed. (Boston: Houghton Mifflin, 1988).

The *Washington Post*'s *Deskbook on Style,* 2d ed., compiled and edited by Thomas W. Lippman, is an example of how major news organizations tailor style to their individual preferences. It also has excellent sections on ethical and legal issues, obituary writing and the role of the *Post*'s ombudsman, or reader advocate.

NOTES

1. Jack Cappon, *The Word* (New York: The Associated Press, 1982), p. 29.
2. The AP *Stylebook* has an excellent section on usage in sports writing.
3. For a look at editing from a copy editor's viewpoint, see Robert E. Garst and Theodore M. Bernstein, *Headlines and Deadlines,* 4th ed. (New York: Columbia University Press, 1982).

Exercise 3–1   Eliminating Bloated Words

Substitute more common words for the following.

1. affirmative _____

2. aforementioned _____

3. apprehend _____

4. cognizant _____

5. commence _____

6. encounter _____

7. enhance _____

8. incarcerated _____

9. interrogate _____

10. laceration _____

11. purchase _____

12. purloin _____

13. remunerate _____

14. residence _____

15. substantial _____

16. sufficient _____

17. terminate _____

18. ultimate _____

19. utilize _____

20. vehicle _____

Exercise 3–2 Trimming Bloated Phrases

Boil the fat out of the following by editing or rewriting.

1. She resigned her position as president.

_____

2. He commented to the effect that her move was unjustified.

_____

3. He then determined the truth of her statement.

_____

4. They agreed to make inquiry about the outcome.

_____

5. They were determined to participate in the decision-making process.

_____

6. He then resigned his office as vice president.

_____

7. That caused her to revise downward her estimates.

_____

8. Many in the audience then threw their support behind her.

_____

9. Two junior officers tendered their resignations.

_____

10. Immediately, Smith voiced his objections.

_____

11. Clearly, he was in possession of the necessary votes.

_____

12. The secretary stressed the point that his objection was improper.

_____

13. That sprung a surprise on the audience.

_____

14. They refused to register a stamp of approval on the measure.

_____

15. The president urged them to take into consideration three measures.

_____

16. He made a speech about the necessity of action.

_____

Exercise 3–3   Tightening

Rewrite or edit the following to tighten and eliminate redundancies and cliches.

1. It goes without saying they admired the coveted trophy.

_____

_____

2. It was a brutal murder and it remains to be seen whether police can solve it.

_____

_____

3. The fact is that seasoned observers felt it was of paramount importance.

_____

_____

4. Circling around the issue, politicians on more than one occasion evaded the truth.

_____

_____

5. Swinging into high gear, they put into effect a poverty program.

_____

_____

6. It was an effort second to none and drew thunderous applause.

_____

_____

7. They threw caution to the wind and plunged into the fight.

_____

_____

8. Stocks were selling like hot cakes and brokers were put through their paces.

_____

_____

9. He lived to a ripe old age, 89.

_____

_____

10. They were trapped like rats and voiced loud objections.

_____

_____

11. He was raised cradled in luxury but still was a diamond in the rough.

_____

12. Given the green light from his boss, he fired three of them.

_____

13. Fred Smith was back in the saddle as chief executive officer of Smith, Inc.

_____

14. His son was determined to follow in the footsteps of his father's example with every fiber of his being.

_____

15. The father's game-plan was to engage in conversation with employees because that would enable him to succeed in accomplishing his goals.

_____

16. She put the finishing touch on her tasks and, as luck would have it, her teacher approved.

_____

17. Plans were made to announce the winners at the gala event.

_____

18. They were united in holy matrimony and afterward there was eloquent silence.

_____

19. It started off with a roar and the building went up in flames.

_____

20. He was in possession of the facts but undertook to study new angles.

_____

_____

Exercise 3–4   Editing Practice—I

Using symbols discussed in this chapter, edit the following to tighten and correct errors. Make sure your final product conforms to AP style.

1. the original source, the *New York Times* reported the bribe was three hundred and twenty-nine dollars.

2. The Alton Telegraph of Illinois however stated the data is incorrect and that the effort was totally destroyed.

3. Governor Fred Smith, Doctor Jane Phillips and General Frank Barnes were in common accored on the egenda.

4. the dabate started at 6:50 p.m. in the evening and lasted until 12 midnight, creating complete chaos.

5. When the messenger arrived at 119 North Fulton Drive the cops and FBI were their.

6. Its clear they had the accused suspect completely surrounded.

7. Everone agreed his skill will effect the outcome because his 20 year old opponant is to weak.

8. The burglar stuck a gun in his face in broad daylight on Main Street, an actual experience few has.

9. Crowds marched on the capitol of Washington in a demanstration brief in duration.

10. A dollar and 6 cents was the fee.

11. the city is comprised of five Districts, each short of basic essentials.

12. The U.S. supreme court ruling was a consensus of opinion cetain to anger loyal Republican supporters of president Bush.

13. they agreed to meet on both Wed. and Fri, a schedule different than normel.

14. The 5 foot 10 inch tackle was no match for his opponant, who was six-two.

15. The total was ten million dollars, about 458 thousand less than expected.

16. everyone thought he was drowned accidentally in the river, which is 2 miles wide.

17. Embarassing as it was, the name was really unique for a person so small in size.

18. he was only a high school gradute, but Driver Fred Smith sure could get maximum posible performance from that truck.

19. The disease still persists despite Doctor Jim Wilsons boasting of results achieved.

20. Less firemen were assigned that necesary, which wasnt good planning ahead.

Exercise 3–5 Editing Practice—II

Edit the following to tighten and correct errors. Conform to AP style.

1. while results were meaningles, staunch foes of the plan insisted one of the last remaining barriers is obtaining qualified experts. Forecasts were that ⅗ of the crowd would be flyers, more preferable to civilians in terms of maximum possible impact.

2. Fewer grain was expected in the harvests, reducing down the chancs of major breakthrus the general public demanded. however no 2 harvests ever was exactly identical any way.

3. With such radical transformation of the general public's expectations, the reason for optimism is because serious crisis can be avoid. that was his message at the noon luncheon.

4. all the girls were university graduates who personally had experienced the results achieved thru mutual coperation. So they frequantly would make inquiries regarding where each group headquartered.

5. Prime minister Margaret Thatcher proved uterly indestructible, in a political sense, She guided her nation as if she were a ship in stormy seas, despite its worst economic crisis ever.

6. When a world leader views his challenges, included among them always is economics. Its refered to as todays most critical problem, irregardless of which countrys are involved.

7. A leaders problems always comprise the homeless, to. the gov. registered his stamp of approval to better funding to face up to the problem.

8. Fred Smith Senior was there, alright. Its clear he and the Lt. Gov. were close bosom budies. Their political enemies refered to them as twins.

9. when the sentence was passed, judge Wilson Frank said he would present a report to the bar association, which had registered a complain with him, which of course he said he would ignore.

10. He called the marshall foreward and told him the media was to be bared. The marshall said he would make inquiry regarding how many newsmen would come.

Exercise 3–6   Editing for Precision—I

In even the shortest story, accuracy and precision are important. Edit the following, using editing symbols studied earlier in this chapter and AP style. Then list five questions you would ask the reporter who telephoned in this version.

Mr. Manny Krenshaw, an auto mechanic, who works at Olson's Garage, at 6723 Seaside Drive, won first prize yesterday morning, it was announced, in a University of Michigan poetry writing contest.

A University spokesman, Prof. Henry Freeman, dean of the university's English department, said Krenshaw's entry, which is titled, "A Mechanic's Muses," was selected by judges who throught its very far suprior to a great many entrys by nationally recognized poets from places like Harvard and Yale and other great universities.

–0–

Questions you need answered to round out this story:

1. _____

2. _____

3. _____

4. _____

5. _____

Exercise 3-7   Editing for Precision—II

1. Edit the following story submitted to your newspaper by a staff correspondent, John Nance, from Washington, D.C. Use editing symbols studied earlier. Conform to AP style. Try for lean, precise language free of errors.

U.S. Senator Franklin Good, Minnesota-Democrat, made a statement today promising he'd do all that's possible to fight AIDS. Good told newsmen and women the media is essential to the fight because it can take the issue to a plurality of voters accros the country.

When asked if he would voice objections to the level of federal speding on AIDS, Good said in the press conference he was in possession of information that spending would be lowered down. He stressed that again and again in his talk with newsmen.

For one thing he said, current spending in the region of about three hundred-and-fifty million dollars was totaly and complete inadequate.

AIDS, he said, is a national problem, not one that can be handled in the capitol city.

2. Your editor asks you to edit the following, boiling it down to no more than 100 words. Retain the essential elements but eliminate nonessentials.

Three persons were killed and 3 injured in a 3-car pileup at about 10:30 a.m. Wednesday morning on Winter Rd., 2 miles south of the city limits.

Police from both the city and county forces sped to the scene in their cars because it wasnt clear at the immediate time where the accident was, in the city or county. The cars were totally demolished.

Ambulances from the county force sped victims, including the three injured, to local hopsitals. Six persons were in the three cars involved. official police said they are having enormous difficulty identifying the dead, as well as the injured, because all of them reside in homes outside the state border.

many people stoped to witnes the cleanup efforts. But traffic continued to flow. It was because the accident occured at a time when commuters werent driving to and from home and office.

3. Your editor wants a "brief" of about 50 words from the following.

Jonathon White, who lives at 118 North Adams street, pled nolo contendere in Superior court wednesday at 10:45 a.m. in the morning to charges that he passed bad checks worth one-hundred-forty-five dollars. The district attorney, Frank Adams, told judge Norman Channels that the Federal Bureau of Investigation wants to talk over some matters with White. Adams said it obviously goes without saying that White should be held until the federals get a chance to do so. He asked Channels to order White held for them. White, cool as a cucumber, simply nodded when told he would be held.

Exercise 3–8   Editing for Leanness

Edit the following in conformity with AP style. Eliminate diversions that might prevent readers from moving smoothly from beginning to end. Edit out nonessentials.

In their meeting last night, the city council agreed to meet again next month as scheduled and also voted four to two to make available between $2 and $3 million for narcotics control efforts in the city.

President Welton Walls of the council said nothing extraordinary likely will heppen in the next couple weeks so it would be okay to just meet as scheduled next month. Members heartily applauded him.

On narcotics control, Walls said the cost of more effective police efforts certainly would be over two million dollars but he hoped it wouldn't hit three million. The money will go for salaries for new undercover agents to be employed and trained for work against drug sellers, he said.

Federal Bureau of Investigation specialists in under cover police surveliance work will train the city's new agents in the beginning, Walls said. He told newsmen at a press conference that the federals could move the citys efforts into an effective realm.

The council agreed to meet Sept. 16 at which time it will open its doors to the general public for a full discussion of spedning the $2 to #3 million. The meeting will be in the Councils' meeting room, in City Hall, at 6:30 p.m. on Tuesday evening.

Exercise 3—9   Editing Practice—III

Edit the following in conformity with AP style.

Temperatures rose over 20 degrees in just one hour yesterday to set an all-time high record of 103 for a July 3rd. The all-time high was hit at precisely 12 noon.

About 50 per cent of the city's schools was closed and local hospitals reported at least 100 persons were seriously ill with heat prostration cases.

Many companys closed there operations down and sent employees home because air conditioning systems were unadequate.

One school principle, Doctor Stephan Wander, of Westside Elem., said it was damned hot on that side of town and three children in his school had to be rushed to local hospitals in ambulances. Ms. Winifred Wilson, principle of Southside H.S., said she had to close her doors to. Wander and Wilson's schools were to reopen tomorrow when weathermen forcast the unprecedented all-time high temperatures will fall down a bit.

Sherrif Barton Downs said his departments' annual Sherrifs' summer Festival, scheduled for July 4th, wouldnt be held. To damned hot, he said.

Teen-aged students flocked in numbers to banks alongside the Red river to find ways they could cool off a bit. Local tv stations telecast the unexpected holiday that got underway as soon as the schools closed there doors down.

Weather records show the whole day was nearly unique.

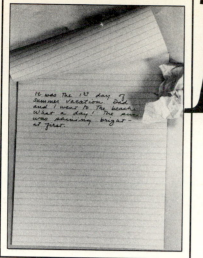

Part 3

Building Your Personal Newswriting Style

You've studied in this book some of the tools essential for professional newswriting—a definition of news, a working knowledge of lean and direct language, an understanding of copy preparation. Now we turn to building your personal newswriting style.

With hard work you can build skills that, at minimum, meet professional standards for clean, understandable writing. If you've got talent—and are willing to work *very* hard—you can go further and build a personal writing style that will draw readers into searching the pages for your byline, a style that will cause your colleagues to say, "*There* is a writer!"

In Part 3 we examine four major steps you can take toward building that kind of newswriting style.

In Chapter 4 we look at how to organize the *structure* of a story. You must "design" the story in your mind, even if roughly, before you start writing. Think as an architect thinks: "What should this structure accomplish? Should it serve as a functional three-bedroom, ranch-style home or a stylish townhouse? And, how will I arrange things, from foundation to roof, to get it built?" In newswriting, as in architecture, plan the structure *before* you put the first brick in place.

Once you've designed the rough structure of your story you can start crafting a lead paragraph.

Pointers on writing *first paragraphs or "leads"* are in Chapter 5. Professionals strive for leads that are strong, unusual, catchy—leads that hook and hold readers. We probably put too much emphasis on lead writing when judging the overall professionalism of a newswriter. But if your lead doesn't entice readers into your story you have accomplished nothing.

In Chapter 6 we study "Helping Your Readers Along," how to *move them past your lead* and deeper into the story. Don't abandon readers after the lead. Pull them along with carefully crafted sentences, paragraphs and transitions.

In Chapter 7 we turn to building a "Bridge of Confidence" with your readers—*developing credibility* in the body of your story, demonstrating to readers that you write accurately, honestly and with authority.

Thus, we begin in Part 3 a crucial next stage in your journey toward professional newswriting. At the end of this stage you should be well along in building your personal—and distinctive—writing style.

Chapter Four

Organizing the Story

Your goal in organizing a news story can be stated simply: Communicate to readers clearly and directly, in minimum wordage, and do so accurately and fairly, with balance and integrity.

Of course, accomplishing that can be complex. Luckily, you have available for the task a wide array of organizational structures and writing approaches.

In Chapter 4 you will study structures and approaches used by professional newswriters. These include the *inverted pyramid, linked boxes,* the *neck of the vase* and the *chronological* structure.

You will learn also that whatever writing structure you use, your news story must have certain information elements: *who, what, where, when, why* and *how.* Recite them as your newswriter's mantra. Professional journalists spend their lives pursuing those elements in the news and communicating them to readers, viewers and listeners.

WHAT INFLUENCES YOUR STORY'S ORGANIZATION

In selecting an organizational structure and writing approach for your news story, consider four factors:

First, the type of material—facts, ideas, concepts, images—you must communicate. For example, writing about the city council's new budget might take a lean approach—a hard-news angle with lots of dollars-and-cents facts. Writing about a hotel fire could take quite another approach, perhaps one that reaches for human drama and images of sirens and lights flashing in the night.

Consider Material to Be Communicated

Second, consider the timing and competitive context in which you are writing. Covering the city council meeting tonight for tomorrow morning's paper will require one organizational structure—probably direct reference to "The City Council voted 9–2 last night. . . ." Writing that story for *tomorrow afternoon's* paper, after radio, TV and perhaps a morning newspaper competitor have reported the 9–2 vote, will take quite another structure—perhaps one that moves the story ahead by reporting *reaction* to the vote among politicians or the public. The vote itself could be subordinated for later explanation. For example:

Consider Timing and Competition

> Councilman Fred Smith said to-
> day the City Council's vote to . . .
> was a travesty.
> The council voted last night. . . .

Consider Audience's Lifestyle and Needs

Third, in organizing a story you must consider your audience, its lifestyles and its news needs. For example, if writing for a morning newspaper audience of hard-charging business executives, you'll need a lean, clean structure that—bang, bang, bang—gives them a quick news "fix" as they rush for their offices. Some newspaper writing wanders pleasantly, amusing readers who willingly plow through hundreds of words to find little tidbits the writer has cleverly secreted. There is a real need for that style—but not at 7 a.m. for executives gulping coffee and searching for news that will dictate whether they should buy or sell in the day ahead, whether fortunes will rise or fall. Conversely, those same executives may constitute a completely different audience, with different news needs, if you catch them in their commuter trains en route home. For commuters, and other audiences you catch during leisurely moments (such as Sunday mornings), you can deal out the facts more slowly.

Consider Your Writing Ability

Fourth, your writing ability will dictate which organizational structure you use. For beginners, a good bet is a simple, straightforward structure that presents the facts clearly and with balance. As your skills improve, strive for new and more imaginative ways of structuring stories. Although journalists have been writing news for hundreds of years, with everything from quill pens to computers, each story you write can be an exciting new venture into creative territory. If you have the skill, you can employ approaches and structures that will take you across new frontiers in communicating through the printed word.

In selecting story structure you also must plan on including crucial news elements—the "Five W's and How."

BASIC INFORMATION ELEMENTS: THE FIVE W'S AND HOW

Fortunately, editors once hung up on narrowly defined (and limiting) rules of writing increasingly are open these days to imaginative new approaches. Many editors now will give you a single rule of writing and story organization: If it works, use it.[1] Nevertheless, every news story *must* communicate certain information elements, whatever unique structure or characteristics you give it. Watch carefully and you'll see the pros pausing over the keyboard after they've written three or four paragraphs and mentally ticking off the following six elements, termed the Five W's and How.

Who

People Are News

People—what they do and what's done to them—make news. Whatever the story, find the people in it and tell your readers about them. Is the federal budget deficit a story about money? No. It's a story about how we Americans spend beyond our means, how much is owed by every man, woman and child among us—and about how other people (government leaders, politicians, special interest groups) are trying to solve the problem. *Money* isn't the story in the city council's new budget. The story is what services city spending will provide the people of your town and how much they must cough up in taxes to provide them. A hotel fire story isn't only a story about a fire. It's a story about *people in a fire*. Make certain your story organization highlights who is involved in the news event or who is affected by it.

What

Highlight What *Really* Happened

Don't skirt it. Don't hide it in clouds of verbiage. Go directly, clearly, simply to it: What—*precisely* what—is your story all about? And, organize your story so the "what" is explained early on (sometimes you will delay this in writing news features; more on that later). *Caution:* You often must peel back layers of facts to reveal for

Getting the "people" angle takes The Associated Press's Donna Cassata into the Streets of Washington, D.C., for comment from a fan as the Redskins football team wins a berth in the Super Bowl.

(AP photo
used with permission)

your readers the *real* "what." For example, a city council vote to increase spending may appear to be the "what"—whereas the *real* "what" is that the new spending will be for fighting drug-related crime. Thus, don't highlight the spending vote and bury, deep in your story, the crime-fighting angle. Both angles must be featured early in your story. Similarly, don't organize an accident story so the first paragraph reports two cars collided, then hold to the ninth paragraph the *real* "what"—that six persons were killed. Your first requirement is to ensure you truly understand what the story is all about. That, in turn, requires you to develop a probing, inquisitive mind. Think of the old joke: Two psychiatrists meet on the street. One says, "Good morning." The other thinks, "What did he *really* mean by that?" When organizing a news story, think: "What is it *really* about?"

Where

If you report from outside the city in which your newspaper is published, the dateline will answer where the story was developed (we don't use datelines on stories occurring in city of publication). But sometimes the "where" element is much more

Explain Where News Broke

than mere geographic location inserted willy-nilly in your story. For example, if two skydivers exchange marital vows while plummeting toward earth the "where" is the story. And if the mayor holds an impromptu news conference while jogging be sure to describe that "where" in some detail. That is, the "where" element can be real news. Conversely, if the mayor holds the news conference in his office, as he has weekly for five years, that "where" probably need not be mentioned. Certainly it need not be mentioned in the lead. At what point in your story—and how fully— you must describe the "where" is a judgment call, obviously. Good rule of thumb: If the "where" is unusual or truly operative to reader understanding, describe it fully. Otherwise, subordinate reference to it—or eliminate it entirely—when organizing your story.

When

The "When" of News Is Critical

Readers need to know the timing and sequence of events you are reporting. Hence, explain the "when" (or time) element and place it with care in your story. For example, readers need to know whether the police chief criticized the city council's anti-drug budget before, during, or after the council's debate over it. If before, perhaps the chief was trying to go around the council and build public support for more spending. If during, perhaps the chief was engaging openly and fairly in the political process to win over council members. If after, perhaps the chief was serving notice he (or she) was unhappy with the council, with the chief's own ability to fight crime—and, dear reader, political trouble may be ahead in Our Town. That is, the *meaning* of an event can be changed by when the event occurred in a sequence of events. Accurately reporting the sequence and, thus, the meaning is crucial in professional newswriting.

Often, a precise time element isn't necessary. It's enough, for example, to write that the council voted Wednesday night. No need to write the vote was at exactly 9:48 p.m. In this example, in fact, the precise time creates a *blind alley* for readers who will wander along it (and away from your story's main thrust), while wondering, "What meaning am I to draw from the fact the vote was at exactly 9:48 p.m.?" However (as in all newswriting), use judgment in handling the time element. If debate lasted all night, and the vote didn't come until 3:36 a.m., you obviously should mention the unusually late hour.

Use judgment also in deciding where in a sentence you place the time element. Good rule: Whenever possible, place it near the verb: "The City Council voted Wednesday night to spend $1 million on fighting drug-related crime." It doesn't work to write, "The City Council voted to spend $1 million on fighting drug-related crime Wednesday night." (What? Spend $1 million on Wednesday night?)

Three other factors to consider as you organize your news story:

1. One time element early in the story establishes the time for the entire story. That is, if the city council voted Wednesday night, say so in your lead—and everything else in the story falls under the Wednesday night time element. Don't keep repeating the council met Wednesday night, discussed taxes Wednesday night, voted Wednesday night.

2. If a second time element enters the story and you must switch your readers from one time element to another, do so with great care. Don't write a lead that mentions the Wednesday night vote, then switch in the second paragraph to what the police chief said on Thursday, then back to Wednesday night, then back to Thursday for more of what the chief said. Limit the number of switchbacks and provide smooth transition.

3. We're in the *news*paper business and timely, topical writing is what we're about. But just because an event didn't occur last night or this morning doesn't mean it isn't news. There is such a thing as *old* but still valuable news. We'll

discuss later how to organize a story to focus on an event and its impact, not on when it happened.

Why and How

These final two elements are essential to an effective news story because busy, preoccupied readers need more than unadorned facts to understand the complex issues we place before them. Consider our front pages and newscasts: war or peace, inflation or recession, money or lives won or lost. Who among us doesn't need to be led gently, with analytical and explanatory writing, through the whys and hows of such stories? Yet, unless you're careful, inserting analysis and explanation can push you over straight news reporting and into another world of personal observation and opinion. Good rule: Quote *authoritative sources* on the whys and hows. Your readers question why the police chief is acting as he is in the controversy over anti-drug spending. They wonder how the political debate is proceeding. And, importantly, they deserve answers from authoritative sources on all sides of the controversy—in tightly attributed quotes. Organizing your story to weave in such authoritative analysis, fairly and with balance, is essential to effective communication with readers.

Let's next examine options you have for story structures that present the six elements just enumerated.

Weave in a Story's Why and How

CHOOSING YOUR STORY STRUCTURE

An Old Standby: The Inverted Pyramid

Envisage a pyramid balanced upside down on its tip. The largest and most important building blocks—those in the foundation—are in the sky and meet your eyes first. Their position signals their importance.

Now, run your eyes down the sides of the pyramid. The blocks get smaller and less important as the sides converge into the tip. Viewed this way, the pyramid tip could be severed and those large, important foundation blocks still would be visible.

We structure the inverted pyramid news story for these purposes:

1. Its first paragraph presents the most important facts of the entire story. Generations of newspaper readers have learned to sweep their eyes across the lead to absorb quickly the most important information and decide whether to read deeper into the story.

2. After the lead, the inverted pyramid structure arranges additional facts in *descending order of importance*. Readers have learned that the position you assign a fact within a news story signals your judgment of its news value.

Arrange Facts to Signal Readers

3. This structure permits editors to cut from the bottom up—without sacrificing crucially important facts—if they must trim a story to make it fit available space. The mechanical reality is that we can print (or broadcast) only the news that fits. That is primarily why, after decades of use, the inverted pyramid structure remains a favorite for newspaper stories written and edited hurriedly under deadline pressure.

4. The inverted pyramid structure also is a concession to another reality: No one, least of all subscribers with busy lives to lead, can read *all* of a bulky newspaper every day. We intentionally create newspapers of hundreds of stories and thousands of words as *menus* from which readers can select items that meet a wide variety of reading desires. The inverted pyramid structure is perfect for rapidly grazing the pages—grabbing a bite here, another there, and halting for some serious munching when the reader locates a particularly tasty morsel.[2]

News service writers covering spot news favor the inverted pyramid structure. They're under competitive pressure and often must dictate stories via telephone from the scene. Newspaper editors using their stories trim them to different lengths. When rushed, you'll find the inverted pyramid lends itself perfectly in dealing out facts in straightforward manner. An example:

OSLO, Norway—A suspicious fire swept through a ferry carrying about 490 people in the North Sea before dawn Saturday, killing at least 75 people and leaving 75 missing and presumed dead, authorities said.

The manager of the Danish company that operated the American-owned ship, which was carrying Danish and Norwegian tourists, said he believed the tragedy was caused by arsonists who set two fires on separate decks.

The dead were found in cabins and on the car deck, where many people were apparently sleeping in their vehicles on the overnight trip from Norway to Denmark aboard the 10,000-ton Scandinavian Star, officials said.

"There was a lot of smoke and flames. It looked rather horrible," helicopter pilot Nils Martinsson, who helped in the rescue, told Swedish radio.

Firemen found 75 bodies on the burning vessel, said Elsebeth Roalso of the Coastal Rescue Center at Sola, Norway.

Seventy-five people were missing and presumed dead . . .

Erik A. Wold, The Associated Press, dispatch for morning newspapers, April 8, 1990.

Note in the example above the skill that the AP writer uses in packing essential facts into his lead paragraph, yet ensuring it is readable. If you wanted to stop reading after the first paragraph you would have the essential facts.

Note below how another AP writer employs the inverted pyramid, this time to catch human drama through use of quotes.[3]

TAMPA, Fla.—A college student accused of stuffing her newborn son in a dormitory toilet was found innocent of murder by reason of insanity Saturday.

[Laura Smith] fell into the arms of her defense attorney and exclaimed, "I knew in my gut I wasn't guilty," after the acquittal was read. Family and friends burst into applause and tears.

"I thank God and everybody who helped me get through this," the tall, slim 18-year-old defendant said. "I love you all."

Hillsborough Circuit Judge Richard Lazzara said he did not believe hospitalization was necessary in light of the insanity finding but said [Smith] should remain under psychiatric care.

The student was charged with first-degree murder in the Oct. 23 drowning of her newborn, 6-pound, 9-ounce boy. If convicted of that charge, she would automatically have been sent to prison for life with the possibility of parole only after 25 years.

Dormitory roommates heard a baby's cries before finding [Smith] in the bathroom covered in blood and rushed her to the hospital. When they returned to the dorm to clean up, they found the baby stuffed head-first in the toilet and covered with bloody towels and sheets.

Defense attorneys argued that [Smith] was temporarily insane, suffering from a dissociative disorder that left her with no memory of being pregnant or even giving birth. *James Martinez, The Associated Press, dispatch for morning newspapers, April 9, 1990*

Obviously the inverted pyramid structure presumes you can isolate the single most important news element for your lead and that all subsequent paragraphs can contain facts of descending importance. But what if that's not possible?

The Linked Boxes Structure

If you have a series of facts to communicate and all have nearly the same news importance, you can wrap each in separate boxes and link them under an all-encompassing or summary lead.

Note how a *Seattle Times* reporter accomplishes that:

> It was a decade that had its share of greed, crime, plague, scandal and war. But remember the '80s for something more noble.
>
> For the decade also was a time of hope and renaissance.
>
> *The walls of communism cracked, then crumbled in Eastern Europe.
>
> *Challenger fell to Earth like Icarus, but tiny Voyager flew on and on, sending home snapshots of neighbor planets, then hurtling toward infinity.
>
> *Terrorists and gangs, shattered dreams and lives, but reasonable people in war-torn countries and drive-by neighborhoods, continued to work for peace.

There were many graphic signs that the '80s held more than a normal decade's share of pain and promise. . .

Sally MacDonald, "For All the Pain on Our Little Planet, Those 10 Years Held Plenty of Promise," *Seattle Times*, Dec. 31, 1989, p. 1.

A *Milwaukee Journal* writer uses the summary lead-plus-boxes structure to handle three equally important questions raised by an aging faculty at the University of Wisconsin:

More than half of the key professors at the University of Wisconsin-Milwaukee and three other UW campuses are at or near retirement age, just as the UW System enters a decade in which the already fierce competition for top faculty is expected to intensify.

Those prospects raise serious questions for students, parents and taxpayers:

*Given the shortage of graduates holding doctorates, will the university system be able to find qualified professors to fill these positions?

*Will the system be able to meet the salary competition from other colleges and universities?

*Will there be benefits to the situation, perhaps an infusion of overdue new blood into the university system? *Richard P. Jones, "UW Facing Gaps as Faculty Ages," Milwaukee Journal, March 11, 1990, p. 1*

In the following example, notice how AP structures a "roundup" story with a summary lead, backs that up with a second paragraph of roundup material—then attaches three "boxes" of specific information that supports the lead paragraph:

Pull Threads Together in "Roundups"

An anti-hazing campaign aimed at countering the image of Greek rows as gin-soaked "Animal Houses" appears to be gaining on campuses from the University of Southern California to Dartmouth.

Worried by their images, as well as the possibility of lawsuits, fraternities around the country are moving to eliminate hazing. Some want to eliminate pledging, the practice of having a period between the recruitment of a member and his formal initiation, when hazing is most likely.

Two of the nation's largest fraternities, Tau Kappa Epsilon and Zeta Beta Tau, have decided that the most effective way to end hazing was to ban pledging altogether in their chapters.

Kappa Delta Rho also approved a long-range plan that includes a move

Wordsmith at Work

The "roundup" structure is perfect for pulling together many related developments in a news story that breaks simultaneously in different places. *But* this structure must be written carefully to enable readers to follow as you move from one fact to another, from one geographic location to another.

Note below how an Associated Press pro opens his second, third, and fourth paragraphs with language carefully selected to help readers easily switch from event to event, location to location.

> DHAHRAN, Saudi Arabia—U.S. warplanes knocked out an Iraqi mobile missile launcher and scored possible hits on three others overnight, the military said today. U.S. Marines fired artillery shells into Kuwait.
>
> Off the coast of Kuwait, a British Royal Navy helicopter blew up an Iraqi patrol boat with a Sea Skua missile, a pool report said. Iraq's naval fleet is all but out of commission, with most of its vessels either sunk or destroyed.
>
> In the skyborne assault, French Jaguar fighter-bombers used laser-guided missiles to hammer an Iraqi artillery position in Kuwait and fortified positions in southern Iraq, the French Defense Ministry said today. Two Marine A-6E Intruder attack planes bombed suspected artillery sites in southern Kuwait overnight, a pool report said.
>
> In the Marine artillery attack, gunners fired more than 100 rounds at a suspected Iraqi artillery battery in Kuwait, a pool dispatch said. Iraqi troops did not return fire and no U.S. casualties were reported, the dispatch said. . .
>
> John King, The Associated Press, dispatch for afternoon newspapers, Feb. 8, 1991

Note above how effectively John King uses roundup story structure to give his readers the full sweep of the Gulf War. Other AP dispatches written on that day focus on individual actions and provide more information and, particularly, human interest details that King has no room for in his roundup.

Also note how King inserts attribution to authoritative sources throughout his story, and does that so carefully that reading flow is not interrupted. A "pool report," incidentally, is from a few reporters chosen by the military to visit combat areas and provide information to those other reporters left behind for security reasons. Pools are a form of "censorship at the source" that reporters resist.

to no pledging by 1995. Phi Sigma Kappa amended its constitution to allow for experimentation with non-pledge programs. Alpha Epsilon Pi introduced new membership education programs.

The National Interfraternity Council, which represents fraternities at 900 college campuses, weighed in with an anti-hazing campaign of its own, stressing that the image of fraternities everywhere was suffering from hazing incidents that harmed pledges physically or psychologically. . . . *The Associated Press, dispatch for morning newspapers, Jan. 1, 1990*

Both the inverted pyramid and the lead-plus-boxes format have great strengths. They deliver to the reader, quickly and in minimum wordage, the story's most crucial facts. Used properly, they can pack emotional wallop into the first three or four paragraphs by letting the unadorned facts tell the story.

However, both the inverted pyramid and the lead-plus-boxes framework have weaknesses. Both are used so often that an awful sameness can settle across newspaper writing. Too many writers use those structures unimaginatively, simply stacking facts atop each other. The result frequently is cold, impersonal writing. And, because both structures present facts in descending order of importance, readers quickly discover stories becoming progressively weaker and less interesting as they probe deeper down through the paragraphs. Many stop reading as a result.

Fortunately, you have available other story structures that present facts in much more colorful and human (and, thus, more readable) terms.

The Neck of the Vase

Think of a flower vase, its slender neck beautifully crafted, more to catch your attention than to serve a utilitarian purpose. The neck descends narrowly but gracefully until it suddenly bulges, and the vase, this thing of beauty, suddenly takes on a very practical purpose—holding water.

You can use that same structure in building news stories. It is enormously powerful for, basically, two reasons:

First, you can search through the broader complexities of a multi-issue occurrence and select a single—and manageable—thought that your readers can focus on as you lead them, oh, so gently, deeper into your story.

Second, this story structure often enables you to extract from coldly impersonal events, which almost defy understanding, the human factor—the people element—and highlight it in terms everyone can understand.

Emphasize the Human Factor

For example, do you understand the complexities of arbitration of disputes in the stock brokerage business? No? Well, *The Wall Street Journal*'s Michael Siconolfi figured that most people don't, so he used a 100-year-old widow as the "neck" of a story to entice us into the subject. Here, in part, is how he did that:

> (Clara Smith) doesn't know much about the stock market. But (Mrs. Smith), a widow who is 100 years old, remembers one lesson from the Crash of 1929: Don't buy stocks on borrowed money.
>
> So imagine her surprise when, in late 1988, she got a margin call for $8,000 to bolster her depleted stock account. Her broker . . . had borrowed tens of thousands of dollars in her $350,000 retirement account, her lawyer says.
>
> (Mrs. Smith), a retired Tempe, Ariz. grade-school principal who is legally blind and partially deaf, had signed a margin agreement that allowed her broker to trade in her account with borrowed money. But on the bottom of it, she scrawled: "I can't read the above fine print. I sign this on your recommendation."
>
> She went to arbitration and, in her complaint, accused her broker of making unsuitable investments and trading excessively to drum up commissions. Last September, a three-member panel of the National Association of Securities Dealers ruled in her favor. It ordered her broker to pay her $250,000 in compensatory damages plus $1 million in punitive damages--the largest punitive award ever granted in an investor arbitration case. — TRANSITION PARAGRAPH
>
> The securities industry has long pressed arbitration on its customers. When opening a brokerage account, many investors sign a standard agreement binding them ahead of time to accept arbitration, rather than resorting to a lawsuit, in the event of a dispute with their broker. But now the tables have turned: As punitive awards to investors balloon, arbitration is rapidly becoming a financial threat on Wall Street.
>
> That's important because investors have been flocking to arbitration. They filed 6,101 arbitration cases against brokers and securities firms in 1988 . . .

Examine key elements in the example above.

First, the *Journal* writer takes a terribly complex (and seemingly dull) but important story into his readers' hearts by picturing a 100-year-old widow whose retirement fund is suddenly shrinking. This becomes not a story about stock trading or arbitration but, rather, a tale of *human victims*—and any reader can understand that.

Second, the writer develops the widow angle enough—but not too much. That is, the widow is used to sketch the human dimension of this story and "set up" reader interest. But the story doesn't become one about a widow. In the fifth or transition paragraph, the "neck" ends, the "vase" broadens and the story becomes an account about arbitration in the securities industry—the writer's intent all along.

Third, in the fifth and sixth paragraphs (and in subsequent paragraphs we have no room to reproduce here) the story leads readers into strongly factual background—number of cases, lawsuits and so forth. That is, in *news*writing, the "neck-of-the-vase" structure must move readers quickly from anecdotal opening to hard, factual reporting.

Quickly Get to Hard News

Note below how an *Atlanta Constitution* writer quickly moves his readers through the neck and, in the third paragraph, into the vase.

[Freddie Smith] was just another drug peddler. He wore flashy clothes, hung out with his fellow dealers in the housing project where he lived, and, before police arrested him and his suppliers in a drug sweep last summer, he was cocky and tough.

[Freddie Smith] is only 12 years old.

He is among a rapidly growing number of pre-teen drug dealers whose cases are clogging metro Atlanta's juvenile courts.

Prosecutions on drug charges against juveniles jumped 150 percent in Fulton County from 1988 to 1989. They more than doubled the year before that—and nearly doubled the year before that, according to Fulton officials. Metrowide statistics show a nearly fivefold increase in juvenile drug cases from 1986 to 1989. . . .   *Douglas A. Blackmon, "More Kids Dealing Drugs Like the 'Big Boys,'"* Atlanta Constitution, *Jan. 26, 1990, p. 1*

Below, two *New York Times* writers stretch out the neck a bit more. But, with an exquisite touch, they weave in gripping detail. Stop reading after the second paragraph—if you can!

It was all over in a few seconds, but what lingers in [Fred Smith's] mind is the sight of his 14-year-old grandson, sinking to his knees on a Brooklyn sidewalk.

The two of them had just left church together, and when they heard shots being fired, [Mr. Smith] crouched quickly, turning to look for the boy.

"He was moving very slowly," said [Mr. Smith], the owner of a men's clothing store in the Crown Heights section. "Very gently."

A bullet had entered the boy's right cheek and exited through the left side of the back of his head.

[Mr. Smith's] grandson, Billy—shot on Jan. 3, 1989, by a man being chased by police—became the first innocent bystander killed in New York City last year. But he was hardly the last.

Before the year was over, at least 30 people in the city had died from stray bullets. . . .   *Suzanne Daley with Michael Freitag, "Wrong Place at the Wrong Time: Stray Bullets Kill More Bystanders,"* The New York Times, *national edition, Jan. 14, 1990, p. 1*

Note below how a *Los Angeles Times* writer laces together three isolated incidents in a neck of dramatic detail.[4]

In January of last year, a black family in Tujunga discovered a noose hanging from a tree on their front lawn. A racial epithet was chalked on the tree trunk.

In February, a young "skinhead" in La Crescenta threatened his Jewish teacher with a gun.

In June, two "gay bashers" attacked a man in Hollywood, beating him with bricks and rocks until his leg and ribs were broken.

Those were just three of 378 hate crimes—those motivated by race, religion or sexual orientation—that were reported in Los Angeles County in 1989, making it the worst year for such activity in the past decade, according to two studies released Thursday. . . . *Sheryl Stolberg, "Decade Ended in Blaze of Hate," Los Angeles Times, Feb. 23, 1990, p. B-3*

With "neck-of-the-vase" stories you can let your creative juices flow as you craft readable, interesting copy out of complex, seemingly dull subjects. However, the form has limitations.

Neck-of-the-vase stories have "soft" leads not suitable for reporting "hard" news stories, such as last night's city council meeting or a tornado that struck town this morning. For such "spot" news stories either the inverted pyramid or the lead-plus-boxes structure is a good bet.

The neck-of-the-vase format doesn't work if you get carried away in describing the person or single anecdote you are using as an intro. Simply, 500 words on the widow would be too much in the *Wall Street Journal* example above. And, the *Los Angeles Times* writer would bore us silly if she laced together 20 isolated incidents of hate crimes, instead of three.

Conversely, cutting the neck of the story too short won't work, either. You must develop enough of the individual or anecdote so readers "see" the picture you're sketching and get hooked into following you deeper into the complex material you're trying to convey.

Vase Structure Requires Writing Discipline

Exiting with a Kicker

The single person or anecdote you use to entice readers into the neck of your story sometimes can be used effectively to give the story a strong ending, or "kicker." This means organizing your story not only with a slender neck for an intro but also with a second slender passageway for an exit at the bottom of the story.

This story structure looks like this:

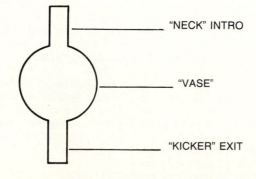

A *Wall Street Journal* writer organized her story that way in writing about the psychological damage suffered by survivors of air crashes:

WADSWORTH, Ohio—Flight attendant [Gail Smith] still thinks about the young blond woman in the window seat.

As United Airlines Flight 232 made its fateful emergency approach to Sioux City, Iowa, last July 19, the young woman cried inconsolably. "She was sobbing and saying, 'I have to get to Chicago. I have a husband and two young children waiting for me,'" [Ms. Smith] recalls with a shudder. "I hugged her for a few minutes and kept telling her to pray."

The young mother was one of the 112 people killed when the DC-10 cartwheeled, broke apart and caught fire. But 26-year-old [Ms. Smith]—dazed and badly bruised—stumbled away from the worst U.S. air accident of 1989. Now, still haunted by what she saw—a body cut in half, a woman without a foot—she is engaged in a struggle of her own to vanquish the ghosts of the tragedy and to resume her career.

At this point, the *Journal* story broadens into discussing how flight attendants are trained to perform in crashes, in addition to details of the Sioux City crash. It quotes psychologists on the depression, guilt and anger that overcome flight attendants after a crash. The story describes how company and union officials reacted to the crash. Then, hundreds of words after enticing readers with an intro based on the flight attendant (the pseudonymous Gail Smith), the writer uses her once more to conclude the story with a kicker:

On a recent hop from Cleveland to Chicago, the morning darkness was lifting. Out the left window, the sun was rising above a velvety floor of purple clouds. [Ms. Smith] looked out and smiled. "This is why I love flying," she said.

She is excited about going back to work, but she knows she won't ever forget Flight 232. She will have a new uniform, but she has saved her old torn blouse, stained with the blood of an injured passenger—a souvenir of a nightmare. *Laura McGinley, "A Flight Attendant, DC-10 Survivor, Struggles to Come Back,"* The Wall Street Journal, *Jan. 18, 1990, p. 1*

A *Christian Science Monitor* writer uses a single individual as both the neck intro and exit kicker:

PRAGUE, Czechoslovakia—Ivan Krempa was born a peasant's son in rural Slovakia. When the Communists took over, he joined them. The party guaranteed him a spacious apartment. It set aside a comfortable country retreat for weekends and vacations. In return, Krempa repaid his benefactors with unwavering support.

After the Soviet invasion of Czechoslovakia in 1968, the most prominent Prague Spring participants lost their jobs and hopes for the future. University professors were turned into window washers, engineers into stokers, lawyers into bus drivers.

Krempa was brought before a party committee and asked his opinion of the invasion: Did the Prague Spring represent a counterrevolution? He nodded. This loyalty soon was rewarded with an appointment as director of the Institute of Marxism and Leninism.

Today throughout Eastern Europe, millions of Communist Krempas are fighting to keep their jobs. They make up the so-called *nomenklatura*, filling the police and Army, along with important posts in almost every walk of life. . . .

Here, the story broadens into a discussion of what other East European non-Communist governments are doing with similarly privileged Communist *nomenklatura*. The story reports on developments in Poland and Hungary, as well as Czechoslovakia, and describes promises being made to the former Communist officials to keep them from becoming restive. The story then narrows once more and "exits" with our Czech friend who served as the neck intro:

None of these promises reassure Communists like Krempa. He has not been feeling well. He spent a few weeks at a spa, recovering from nervous tension, he says. Upon his return, he plunged into rewriting an account of the events of 1968.

Following Soviet leader Mikhail Gorbachev's declaration that the invasion was a mistake, the Czechoslovak party is rushing to create its own updated history. *William Echikson,* Christian Science Monitor, *dispatch for morning newspapers on Jan. 18, 1990*

The neck-plus-kicker structure is strong because the person used in the intro can provide thematic continuity for your readers. They have a real person to identify with as you pull them forward through technical, financial or other complex material. And, if you've whetted your readers' appetites properly in the neck of the story, they'll read through the entire story to find out what happens in the end to the person.

People Give Stories Thematic Continuity

Weaknesses of this structure are twofold: First, it has to be handled deftly. Overwriting either the neck or the kicker can destroy the thrust of your story. These devices are *not* what your story is all about; that "bulge" in the middle, with its wider view and explanatory detail, provides the guts of your story. Second, the neck-plus-kicker structure requires skillful editors. They can't simply trim your story from the bottom if it's too long. Rather, they must hunt in the interior of the story for wordage that can be sacrificed, and that takes time and patience—both in short supply as deadlines approach.

Structuring Your Story Chronologically

Some news stories are so complex they defy conventional writing structure. Picking a single dominant fact for an inverted pyramid structure is impossible. Neck-of-the-vase organization won't work either.

What to do? Well, one solution may be simply to unfold the facts *as they occurred*—and let the story tell itself. That's what one *New York Times* master craftsman did:

When the siren screams, police chases, milling throngs and traffic jams had subsided around the Empire State building yesterday at lunchtime, a passer-by asked a security guard what had happened. The guard sighed. "What's the use?" he said. "If I told you, you wouldn't believe me."

What happened, in roughly chronological order was this:

(1) Two men seeking to promote their adult-education school announced they would throw $10,000 in dollar bills from the 86th floor of the skyscraper. (2) Two other men chose the same time to hold up the Bankers Trust branch in the building, and after firing a shot found themselves pursued up 34th Street by plainclothesmen, a store detective and the welter of reporters and cameramen awaiting the promoters.

(3) The suspects were tackled and disarmed in one of the most heavily photographed arrests of recent times.

(4) The promoters, unaware of the commotion, got out of a taxi on 34th Street with five clear plastic bags full of money. (5) After some understandable confusion about the loot from the bank and the bags of money, the promoters were denied admittance to the tower on the grounds of public security but were pursued around the marble lobby by people snatching at the bags for samples. (6) The would-be philanthropists were taken away in a patrol car for their own safety.

(7) The shaken promoters announced they were studying other means of sharing their profits. (8) The suspects were charged with armed robbery.

The spectacle of two men trying to throw away money without success while two others a few feet away tried to steal some, also without success, proved diverting to strollers out for the first coatless day of 1982. . . . *Paul L. Montgomery, "A Failed Giveaway Meets a Foiled Getaway," The New York Times, March 13, 1982, p. 1*

A *Los Angeles Times* writer uses the chronological structure in telling the dramatic and moving story of a hero at an accident scene. The chronological structure works here because it "walks" the reader through the event, step by step:

Professional editors judge young writers on their ability to write clearly, accurately in conformity with rules of correct grammar and usage and with the reader in mind. Here, *Seattle Times* editor John Saul (seated) and The Associated Press's Mark Berns, visiting the *Times*' newsroom, check a news story.

(AP photo used with permission)

Ray Abboud is a one-man army when he takes to the streets of Los Angeles.

That's what he was Wednesday night when he saw a head-on collision near the downtown Civic Center.

Abboud, 31, said he maneuvered his own car into position to shield the accident victims from being hit by other motorists traveling in the 600 block of 1st Street.

Then he dispatched members of a growing crowd of onlookers to call authorities.

Then he aided two badly injured women trapped in the front seat of one of the wrecked cars.

Then he discovered that a 9-year-old girl on the floor of the back seat was not breathing and performed mouth-to-mouth resuscitation until he revived her.

Then he noted the motorist that hit the women was sneaking off. Abboud chased down and captured the suspected drunk driver and dragged him back to the scene.

Then he helped clear a path through stalled traffic along 1st Street so that professional rescuers could reach the scene.

"I just got mad," said Abboud, owner of an East Los Angeles clothing store and a part-time singer. "Everybody was just standing there doing nothing. I kept thinking it could be my own little girl lying there."

Los Angeles police confirmed Abboud's account of the incident. . . . *Bob Pool, with contribution from Nieson Himmel, "He Gives the Performance of His Life at Accident Scene,"* Los Angeles Times, *Feb. 16, 1990, p. B-3*

In the example above, the lead is simple, just 16 words. It avoids all nonessential detail—including the time element, which is subordinated to the second paragraph. Don't junk up your leads. Focus on the essential. Precisely when the incident occurred is secondary in this example.

The writer begins five paragraphs—the fourth through eighth—with the same word, "then." This surely violates somebody's rules of good writing. But it certainly dramatizes the fact that this "one-man army" was rushing from crisis to crisis, handling life and death by himself. Again: Forget the writing "rules"; if it works, use it.

In the tenth paragraph, the writer neatly inserts independent confirmation—from police—that it all happened as the "one-man army" said it happened. *Always* insert confirmation from authoritative sources but do so as unobtrusively as possible.

Incidentally, look again at the ninth paragraph in the example above. Note how the writer deftly inserts the fact that the rescuer is a "part-time singer." For a kicker, the writer concludes with this:

Abboud said he was trying to avoid heavy traffic on the Hollywood Freeway about 6:15 p.m. Wednesday when he turned onto 1st Street. He said he was headed to Hollywood to pick up equipment for a charity singing engagement Saturday.

"I'm going to write a song and dedicate it to that little girl," he said. "It's going to be a song about drunk drivers."

Chronological stories can have great strengths: They are excellent story-telling devices wtih a tempo close to informal speech patterns you probably use in chatting with friends. The pace nicely varies the staccato, bang-bang rush of hard news stories that dominate newspaper pages.

But that relatively slow tempo is a major weakness of the chronological structure. It's not appropriate for writing hard news, when your mission is to sort out and present clearly the crucial elements sought by fast-paced readers. When you write chronologically, readers must plow through the entire story, hunting for primary news elements and assessing their relative importance. Those are tasks *you* undertake for readers when you write with the inverted pyramid or the linked-boxes structure—stacking the most important news elements at the top and, by that positioning, signaling their relative importance.

Other Structures

A story structure variously termed "time delay" or "suspended interest" is useful for sparking reader interest. It opens like a chronological structure but gets more quickly to hard news. A *Seattle Times* writer uses this variant in reporting, with heightening suspense, how two Laotian refugees awaited arrival in Seattle of their policeman father from Laos:

Craning his neck and peering through a wall of glass, 20-year-old Sourasith Boupharath intently scanned the faces coming toward him in the busy terminal of Seattle-Tacoma International Airport.

He waited and watched, as the minutes and passengers passed, for one face in particular, but admitted he was not entirely sure he would recognize it.

"When I think of him," he said, "I see him dressed as a police officer."

Minutes later, it was no police officer who emerged slowly through the glass door of Sea-Tac's international-arrival gate. It was a slight, quiet man of 54 in a blue-gray suit and striped shirt.

Yet Sourasith, along with his 22-year-old brother, Sourasack, had no trouble recognizing the face and the smile as that of their father, whom they had not seen in 15 years.

"He still has the curly hair," Sourasith beamed.

The hugs and smiles and kisses of their reunion capped a story that began in 1975 in troubled Laos, as the Communist regime strengthened its grip over the country and its institutions. . . . *Jack Broom, "Reunion Caps a 15-Year Drama," Seattle Times, April 10, 1990, p. B-1*

A *Boston Globe* writer uses the "delay" effect, leading a news story with a bit of *history:*

WASHINGTON—Winter came hard to Western Europe in 1947. The Allied victory at war had turned sour in peace. Food was short, fuel was short, economies were stalled and unrest was rolling across the continent.

The U.S. response: the Marshall Plan, an aid program that today would cost $100 billion or more. It sparked the growth that has turned Western Europe into a stable powerhouse and a mammoth market for American goods.

Another hard winter is now on its way, this one in Eastern Europe. So, too, many predict, are shortages, stagnation and the danger of unrest.

But this time the U.S. has responded differently, offering $1 billion thus far and calling others, especially Germany and Japan to carry most of the burden. . . . *Peter G. Gosselin, Boston Globe dispatch for afternoon papers of Dec. 28, 1989*

Like the chronological structure, the "delay" organization of a news story can grab reader interest. A Laotian refugee anxiously scanning faces in a crowd, a bit (a *small* bit) of fascinating history—both work well in the examples above. Caution, however: The "delay" device is a "soft," not hard news, intro. Use it too often or with stories inappropriate for that structure and your readers will be ex-readers, jumping ahead through the pages in search of more hard news with a faster pace.

"Listen" to Your Story's Rhythm   Sometimes, you can "listen" to the facts of your story and sense a rhythm that, if you can capture it, gives you perfect story structure.

For example, a *New York Times* writer reporting on random shootings "hears" a capricious rhythm—one victim sits on a park bench, gets shot and lives; another walks a city street, gets shot and dies. On one hand you live, on the other, you die:

A young doctor was sitting on a bench with her brother in Central Park last week when a stray bullet, apparently fired from long range, struck her in the chest. She lived.

A young dental assistant was walking home with her roommate from a pizza parlor in the Bushwick section of Brooklyn a few hours later when a stray bullet, apparently from the gun of a man shooting at another man on a crowded street, struck her in the chest. She died.

If there was ever any comfort in the knowledge that most murder victims know their attackers, even that has fallen prey to the random violence inflicted on New Yorkers and other city dwellers. Death by bad luck, typically at the hands of drug dealers with powerful weapons, has a powerful effect. . . . *Richard L. Madden, "Increasingly, Stray Shots Find a Mark," The* New York Times, *national edition, March 18, 1990, p. E-20*

A Knight-Ridder writer walks with President and Mrs. Bush among U.S. servicemen wounded in the invasion of Panama. The writer "listens" to the story develop, decides wonderfully strong quotes are its core—then structures the story around them. The writer *steps back and lets the quotes tell the story:*

Search for Strong Quotes

SAN ANTONIO, Texas—A little girl in a ruffly blue dress stood by her father's bed in a dingy hospital ward and told President Bush about her favorite Christmas present: "My daddy."

That was the heart-stopper on this last day of 1989 as Bush and the first lady visited the bedsides of dozens of U.S. fighting men wounded in the Panama invasion and recuperating in military hospitals here.

Among the hurt was the daddy of 8-year-old Noella Almeida in blue ruffles.

"We tried to tell them how grateful we are," said the President, his eyes filling with tears, as he left the last of the injured—and their loved ones—in the Army hospital at Fort Sam Houston.

"You identify with these families. This little girl there . . . ," the President said, obviously haunted by Noella, whose father, Sgt. 1st Class James Almeida, is recovering from fragmentation wounds he received during the Panama invasion five days before Christmas.

Next, the writer broadens the story to give background to the Panama invasion and to describe the hospital. But the structure throughout rests on a series of punchy quotes:

Meeting the commander in chief is "a pretty neat experience. Kind of a rough way to do it, though," Marine Sgt. Gregory Johnson said through clenched teeth.

His jaw was broken by a bullet in the chin, with the bullet now lodged—safely, he said—in his back.

"There are a little post-mortems here and there but it was a wonderful thing and we're all very, very proud of you," Bush said to Johnson, 24, and three other wounded men in one

spare room at the medical center at Lackland Air Force Base.

"We're proud to be able to do it," Johnson fired back from his cranked-up bed.

"It just makes tears come to our eyes for what they've done," said Alan Reeves, eyes indeed brimming. He is the proud father of Army Sgt. David Reeves, who was shot in both shoulders and shook left-handed with the president.

Then, still "hearing" the rhythm of those gripping quotes, the writer exits the story with a kicker built on what the Bushes said to reporters after leaving the hospital.

"Tell them about the boy with the flag," prompted Mrs. Bush.

"You tell them," answered the president. So she did.

A young serviceman paralyzed by the fighting handed the president "a little American flag," she said. "And he said, 'This is from all the men in Panama. And I want you to have this from them and we thank you for sending us.'"

"He meant it," she said. "You can't fake that." *Ellen Warren, Knight-Ridder News Service dispatch for afternoon newspapers on Jan. 1, 1990[5]*

Issues and Challenges:
Lessons to Structure By

The stories in this chapter provide important lessons for you in structuring news stories.

First, note that *the structures are simple,* formed primarily of lean sentences woven together in uncomplicated fashion. Their magic is that the writers (professionals all) avoided forced, convoluted writing. Strive for an easy flow, a rhythm in your story organization and writing.

Second, *the writers had general audiences in mind* when they structured those stories. Note there are no unexplained technical terms or words newspaper readers cannot easily understand. *But* those stories are not grand orations flung before audiences of thousands; they are written as if directed at a single individual—stories told almost in one-to-one fashion. When writing, many pros "tell" their story to a friend, their mother, a colleague, and ensure the organization and language are suitable for them. News service editors once instructed young writers, "Tell it to the Kansas City milkman." When you are writing, "tell" your story to the milkman or someone you know.

Third, the example stories are structured in *a form appropriate for both the material being communicated and the reader audience.* The AP writer covering the North Sea ferry disaster used the inverted pyramid. Telling that story chronologically or in a "time delay" structure would be completely inappropriate for readers anxious to learn details of the "hard" news event. Similarly, *The New York Times* story about the 14-year-old boy shot outside church in Brooklyn would have been ruined if structured as an inverted pyramid.

Fourth, each example *structure is focused clearly and directly on the main point* of the story. The writers create no blind alleys for readers to follow, no clouds of verbiage to hide the core of the story. And, note how often people—recognizable, *real* people—are used to lead readers to the point of the story in dramatic, compelling ways. Ruthlessly eliminate clutter from your story.

Fifth, the newspaper stories are structured to *relay great amounts of detail,* something no competing medium—not TV, not radio, not magazines—has the time or space to do. *But,* our example stories are structured to deal out information in manageable "bites." Readers are not overwhelmed with great spoonsful of facts, numbers, technical terms in any single paragraph. In writing highly detailed stories, *pace yourself* as you ever so gently increase the amount of information you place before your readers.

You have seen in this chapter examples of how to structure news stories. What's next? It's how to get readers into the story by fashioning a compelling, attractive lead paragraph. To that challenge we turn in Chapter 5.

SUMMARY CHECKLIST

☐ The organizational structure you choose for a story depends on type of material you must communicate, the timing and competitive context in which you are writing, your audience and its information needs and your writing abilities.

☐ Whichever structure you use, your story must contain six information elements: *who* is involved, *what* is happening, *where, when, why* and *how?*

☐ For fast-breaking, hard news, a story structure hard to beat is the *inverted pyramid,* which presents the most important news elements first, then arranges others in descending order of importance.

☐ The *linked-boxes structure* permits you to write a summary or all-encompassing lead, then arrange additional facts of equal importance in a series of "boxes" or paragraphs linked below.

☐ A *neck-of-the-vase* structure often is perfect for "soft" news stories because you can use an individual or single anecdote as a vehicle for pulling readers into details deeper in your story.

☐ Most news stories must be written so they can be edited quickly from the bottom up by editors trying to fit them into available newshole (space in the paper). However, when conditions permit, try for a carefully crafted "kicker" that permits readers to exit your story with an unusual anecdote or dramatic quote.

☐ Complex stories that don't fit the inverted pyramid or "neck" structures often can be organized successfully in chronological order that simply lays out facts in the sequence they occurred.

☐ The "time delay" or "suspended interest" structure uses the human interest approach of chronological organization but more quickly takes readers into the hard news you want to communicate.

☐ The stories in this chapter demonstrate that successful story structures are simple and often aim at general audiences but really are "told" to an acquaintance of the writer. And, successful structures focus clearly on the story's main point, dealing out details not all at once but in manageable "bites."

RECOMMENDED READING

Students of story structure will be rewarded by reading the *Boston Globe, The New York Times, Washington Post, Philadelphia Inquirer, Dallas Morning News, Los Angeles Times, Seattle Times, Chicago Tribune* and *Milwaukee Journal.* Some of the best writing (and editing) in print today is in *The Wall Street Journal.* Note particularly the *Journal's* superb front-page use (often in column one and column six) of the "neck-of-the-vase" structure. For a faster, human interest approach to structure, see three tabloids: *New York Daily News, New York Post, Philadelphia Daily News.*

For magazine *news* writing, note the story structures in *Time, Newsweek* and *U.S. News & World Report.* Note particularly how *U.S. News* is taking a hard news approach with its "news you can use" format.

Professional guidance on story structure and editing is available from the American Society of Newspaper Editors, which publishes writing hints in its *Bulletin* and periodic special studies from P.O. Box 17004, Washington, DC 20041, and from The Associated Press Managing Editors Association, 50 Rockefeller Plaza, New York, NY 10020. Don Fry publishes frequently and brilliantly on writing from the Poynter Institute for Media Studies, 801 Third St., South, St. Petersburg, FL 33701–9981. Note also the feature "Editorially Speaking" published by Gannett Co. monthly in *Gannetteer.*

NOTES

1. Changing attitudes in newsrooms were examined in detail by The Associated Press Managing Editors and summarized in six case studies published as "APME Writing & Editing," Boston, MA, October 1988. It's available from APME, 50 Rockefeller Plaza, New York, NY 10020.
2. Packing the "Five W's and How" into the inverted pyramid structure is discussed particularly well by Mike Foley, managing editor, *St. Petersburg Times,* in "Formulas Can Lead to Good Writing," published in "Writing, A Special Report from APME's Writing and Editing Committee," Issue No. 156, September 1985, p. 5.
3. Hints on why so much strong writing gets on The Associated Press wires can be gleaned from Rene J. Cappon, *The Word* (New York: The Associated Press, 1982).
4. For years, *Los Angeles Times* was derided by many journalists as over-written and poorly edited; today it is a treasury of fine writing worthy of study by all aspiring journalists.
5. Like most major groups, Knight-Ridder sells news from its newspapers to other newspapers.

Exercise 4–1   Organizing the Story

The type of material you must communicate will often dictate your story structure and writing approach. Examine two "hard" news and two "soft" stories from The Wall Street Journal *and* The New York Times *(or other newspapers your instructor designates). In about 200 words, discuss how the facts, ideas, concepts and images in those stories led the writers to take different approaches to structural organization and writing. For example, did a "spot" news development dictate use of the inverted pyramid? Did a less timely event lead to use of "neck-of-the-vase" approach? Be certain to write in clean AP style.*

Exercise 4–2   Structure and Timing

The timing of a news event has great impact on story structure and writing approach. Examine five news stories published by The New York Times *(or another morning newspaper designated by your instructor) covering news events that broke the day before. In about 200 words, (1) describe the stories' structures (inverted pyramid, "neck," etc.) and (2) comment on why those structures are (or are not) appropriate for the stories covered.*

Exercise 4–3   Structure and Audience

The type of audience you serve must be considered in your selection of a story structure and writing approach. Examine coverage in The Wall Street Journal *and* The New York Times *(or other newspapers your instructor designates) of the* same news event. Comment in about 250 words on how the two stories resemble each other, how *they differ and how you think the writers factored their different audiences into their writing approaches.*

Exercise 4–4   The Five W's and How

Examine the lead story on the front page of today's New York Times *(or other newspaper designated by your instructor) and describe below, in about 250 words, its Five W's and How. Precisely what are they? Where are they placed in the story? Is their placement correct? If not, how would you have placed them? Be sure to identify the "real" what.*

Exercise 4–5   Writing an Inverted Pyramid—I

These are the facts of an inverted pyramid story published in the San Francisco Chronicle. *Use these facts to write, in the space below, an inverted pyramid story.*

Officers announced yesterday arrest figures for the Christmas holiday weekend. Arrests were made by the California Highway Patrol (CHP). Arrested were 2,114 suspected drunken drivers. That's far more than the 1,491 arrested last year. The Patrol is making a concerted effort to keep drunken drivers off the highways. That was responsible for the 41 percent increase in statewide drunken-driving arrests. That statement is by Susan Cowan-Scott, the patrol's commander of public affairs. She said CHP officers demonstrated "a real, aggressive attitude" toward drunken drivers. CHP officers made 274 drunk driving arrests during the holiday period in the Golden Gate Division, which includes San Francisco and the nine Bay Area counties. The holiday period was from 6 p.m. Friday to midnight Christmas Day. The 274 arrests were 72 more than last year.

Exercise 4–6   Writing an Inverted Pyramid—II

Following are facts of a story published in the Augusta (Ga.) Herald. *Write an inverted pyramid story from them.*

Monday, Jesse Carroll was elected chairman for 1990 of the Richmond County Board of Commissioners. He won a unanimous vote. It came on the first ballot. Nominations split along party lines. Republican Herb Beckham was nominated by Commissioner Lee Neel. After it was apparent Carroll had the four votes he needed to win, Neel moved to make the vote unanimous. Carroll is a Democrat. He voted for himself and three other Democratic commissioners voted for him, too. Carroll is from the 86th District. He said, "I would like to say that I'm especially pleased that this is unanimous. I'm looking forward to a good year. I know with your help, we'll do that."

Exercise 4–7 Writing an Inverted Pyramid—III

Write an inverted pyramid story from these facts, which were published in the San Francisco Chronicle *on Feb. 22, 1990. Position in your second paragraph the "why" element.*

Yesterday, the Labor Department issued a statement. It said inflation took a sharp turn for the worse last month. Consumer prices jumped 1.1 percent. That was the biggest monthly increase since June 1982. The chief economist at Carroll McEntee & McGinley Inc., a New York investment firm, Lacy Hunt, issued a statement. "Virtually everything rose. It's clear that inflation is creeping upwards," Hunt said. Most of January's increase in the Consumer Price Index came from record price increases for fuel oil and fresh produce. Both resulted from December's cold weather.

Exercise 4–8 Writing an Inverted Pyramid—IV

Write an inverted pyramid from the following facts, which were published in the Washington Post.

Yesterday, John M. Poindexter, former national security adviser, was convicted by a federal jury. On all felony charges against him. They were conspiracy, lying to Congress, obstructing Congress. Those charges were lodged against him in his Iran-Contra trial.

He is a retired Navy rear admiral, aged 53. He was the highest-ranking Reagan administration official brought to trial in the Iran-Contra affair. When the jury foreman pronounced him guilty, in U.S. District Court, he showed no emotion. Poindexter was said by the prosecution to have participated in an illegal coverup. To protect former President Ronald Reagan from the political fallout of the biggest scandal in his presidency. For Independent Counsel Lawrence E. Walsh, the verdict was his most sweeping victory. For more than three years, he has been involved in the criminal investigation. The verdict ratified a central tenet of his inquiry, that at the highest levels of the Reagan administration conspiracy to coverup the scandal existed.

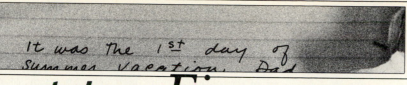

Chapter Five

Leads That Hook Readers

Now begins your serious romancing of readers.

All we've studied thus far is preparation for this moment. Defining news, considering style, experimenting with story construction—all are *technical* preparation for mastering the *art* of enticing readers into reading what you write.

Your primary lure is a *lead*—or *introduction*—of one, two, three or even more paragraphs that promise readers reward for reading further. You create that promise by capturing a news event's essence and summarizing its most important elements. In that process, you define the story's newsworthiness and establish its priority and relevance in the day's news flow.

Or, putting it simply (not a bad idea in lead writing), your lead beckons, "Hey, reader! I've got something here you should read. Briefly, it's this . . . and here's why it's important. . . ."

In this chapter we will look at lead-writing options that professional newswriters use to shout that message. These include *hard and straight* leads, *double-element* leads, and others I label as *what and real what* and *who* leads, plus leads that emphasize the *when, why* and *how* of a story. We will also study *look-ahead* and *special-peg* leads. Study how the pros do it—but don't be limited by their writing devices. You can be different in exciting new ways and develop many successful approaches to lead writing *if* what you create truly engages readers, pulls them into your story and jump-starts their minds into action.

When you finish this chapter you should possess new writing strengths that will help you start that process.

LEADS HARD AND STRAIGHT

The first mission of your news lead, obviously, is to *communicate important news,* or strongly, unmistakably and alluringly signal readers that it lies waiting in subsequent paragraphs. Properly crafted, "hard and straight" leads accomplish that quickly in minimum wordage and with maximum impact.

Such leads seldom are beautiful, poetic musings. They're workhorses in the newswriter's stable—strong and able to pull readers straight ahead into quick understanding. Note how the *Los Angeles Times* writer in the following example uses just 39 words in a *single-element lead* paragraph (one with only one central thrust) and effectively communicates *what* happened, *when, who* did it and *why.*

> The Los Angeles Coliseum Commission voted 8 to 0 Wednesday to support the concept of demolishing and reconstructing the Coliseum as a means of either keeping the Raiders playing in the city or attracting a new professional football team.
>
> The only commission member opposed to the idea, Los Angeles County Supervisor Pete Schabarum, left the meeting before the vote for another engagement. The decision cleared the way for the stadium's private managers, Spectacor Management Group and MCA Inc., to proceed with negotiations with Raiders owner Al Davis in hopes of reaching a firm agreement to keep his team in Los Angeles. . . . *Kenneth Reich, "Commission Approves Overhaul of Coliseum,"* Los Angeles Times, *Jan. 11, 1990, p. B-1*

Limit Leads to Essential Detail

Note above how lean and clean the first paragraph is. Essential details are summarized nicely for rapid comprehension by readers. Names and elaborating details that might junk up the lead are held to subsequent paragraphs. That frees the first paragraph to lead readers straight to the primary element of hard news—the 8–0 vote. Note particularly how a less-important angle (that one commissioner opposed the idea) is left to the second paragraph.

Note below how a *Wall Street Journal* writer strikes with single-mindedness directly to the core of one of the most dramatic stories of our time.

> WASHINGTON—The U.S. went to war in the Persian Gulf last night. *Gerald F. Seib, "Waves of U.S. Planes Attack Iraq As War Breaks Out in Persian Gulf,"* The Wall Street Journal, *Jan. 7, 1991, p. 1*

Keep your leads free of stray or secondary thoughts that might lure readers away from your story's main thrust. Think this way: If directing someone rushing to a hospital you would outline the simplest, straightest route. You wouldn't describe all the tourist delights that could be sampled by wandering down side streets. When writing leads, keep your readers moving down a straight path, too.

Below is a "hard and straight" lead that, while far from beautiful, communicates clearly and directly news important to readers in Appling, Ga.—that landfill fees are being increased. Note, however, this lead introduces a *second main thrust* in the story (mayor objects) without diverting readers. The writer accomplishes this by opening her lead with a clause that introduces the second thrust *and* emphasizes its importance by positioning it first in the paragraph. Just 26 words are used to lure readers in with a lead that contains two principal thoughts.

> APPLING, Ga.—Despite protests from Grovetown Mayor Dennis Trudeau, the Columbia County Commission on Tuesday approved a new rate schedule for landfill fees for cities in the county.
>
> Under the new schedule—effective Jan. 1—Grovetown will pay $1.20 per cubic yard for garbage it dumps in the county landfill. Before Jan. 1, the city paid 75 cents per cubic yard.
>
> The commissioners voted 3–2 to charge cities that have a landfill 60 percent of the commercial rate—which is $2 per cubic yard. Cities without a landfill would pay 80 percent.
>
> Grovetown has a landfill for such things as limbs and leaves, but not garbage. Harlem—the county's only other incorporated area—contracts with a commercial hauler to collect its garbage so the new rate schedule will not affect that city.
>
> "My patience is growing thin for being charged, being charged and being charged," Trudeau told commissioners. . . . *Amy Swann, "Grovetown Gets New Landfill Fee; Mayor Irked,"* Augusta (Ga.) Chronicle, *Feb. 7, 1990, p. 2-C*

Note above how the writer parcels out elaborating details in the second through fifth paragraphs. Her approach meets five goals you should strive for in writing "hard and straight" leads:

1. Limit your lead paragraph to minimum wordage and one, perhaps two, main news thrusts (in the above example, rate approval and mayor's protest).

2. Quickly and smoothly take your readers to additional essential details (the new $1.20 rate Grovetown will pay starting Jan. 1). Note the writer's smooth transition ("Under the new schedule . . .") that leads readers from the first paragraph and into the second.

3. Add details in manageable "bites." The writer above holds off until the third paragraph the precise vote and other secondarily important facts. Don't jam too much into a lead (or any other single) paragraph. Readers won't laboriously hack their way through an impenetrable jungle of facts. Let them see a little light ahead as you lure them forward.

Add Details in Manageable Bites

4. *Quickly back up the main thrust of your lead.* In the example, the new rate schedule is explained in the second and third paragraphs. The lead's second idea (mayor's objection) is explained by the quotation in the fifth paragraph ("My patience is growing thin . . ."). *Remember:* Your lead is *your promise to readers* that your story contains news they need. Get them to it quickly in subsequent paragraphs.

Quickly Back Up Your Lead

5. Plan a paragraph—call it the "housekeeping" paragraph—that backgrounds the story and puts it in perspective. In the example above, the housekeeping paragraph is the fourth. It explains why Grovetown needs the landfill.

Insert Explanatory "Housekeeping" Paragraph

In writing hard and straight leads, a temptation is to pack too many separate thoughts into the first paragraph but think you are communicating effectively if you keep wordage to a minimum. For example, read once (and *only* once) the following lead. Read at your normal pace, then jot down the primary idea it is designed to communicate.

EAST BERLIN (AP)—The German states united their economies and erased their borders Sunday while 10,000 East Germans waited in line for Western currency on the huge square where they toppled Communism. *The Associated Press dispatch for Sunday newspapers, July 1, 1990*

See? There are just 29 words in that first paragraph above—but it is virtually incomprehensible in one reading because it contains *four* separate ideas: (1) economies united, (2) borders erased, (3) 10,000 people wait, (4) communism toppled. And, in the full version (which we cannot reproduce here), one of the four (the square) isn't explained until the seventh paragraph—far too deep in the story to back up a principal element in the lead. *Remember:* If a news angle is important enough for first-paragraph mention, it's important enough for you to explain in paragraphs that immediately back up your lead paragraph.[1]

THE DOUBLE-ELEMENT LEAD

With practice, you'll be able to write *double-element leads*—single paragraphs containing two core thoughts—that readers can comprehend easily. Note below how a *Washington Post* writer lets his first paragraph run long (40 words) and inserts two core ideas (name change, Honecker's note) but still gives readers a smoothly flowing lead.

EAST BERLIN—East Germany's Communist Party, continuing its struggle to remake itself in an emergency party congress, changed its name today and released a month-old note from deposed party chief Erich Honecker saying he accepted "full responsibility" for the country's crisis.

New party leader Gregor Gysi, chosen just last week, announced to a standing ovation that the Socialist United Party of Germany would now be called the Socialist Unity Party of Germany–Party of Democratic Socialism. Gysi said the leadership decided "to have a double name, to supplement the existing name" to accommodate both those members who want to make a complete break with the past, and those who don't.

Continuing a landmark meeting begun last weekend, the party's new leadership released a report describing Honecker's 19-year rule of the country as corrupt and misguided in its last years and maintaining that his ouster Oct. 18 forestalled "a civil war-like bloody conflict" with the masses of East Germans who had taken to the street to demand reforms.

The 77-year-old Honecker, who is reported to be gravely ill, conceded in the note made public today that he had "deceived" himself about the economic situation and popular feelings.

"I take full responsibility for the situation that has arisen," Honecker wrote in the letter. . . .   *Jackson Diehl, "E. Germany Changes Party Name,"* Washington Post, *Dec. 17, 1989, p. A-1*

Deal Out Additional Facts Smoothly

In the example above, the *Post* writer achieves smooth flow by dealing out facts in manageable "bites" and carefully structuring his second through fourth paragraphs to back up the first. Note the two promises to readers in the first paragraph. One (name change) is explained in the second paragraph, the other (Honecker's note) in the third. *That* is how to back up a lead paragraph.

Note also above how the *Post* writer quickly backs up the Honecker note angle with Honecker's own words—a partial quote ("deceived") in the fourth paragraph and a full quote in the fifth. Meaningful direct quotes add enormous strength to backing up a lead.

In the example below, the *double-element* or *combination* lead (or, as the pros say, the "combo lead") works well in the first paragraph. Its two core elements (currency and Soviet tolerance) are understood easily. But there is a problem in the backup. Can you spot it?

EAST BERLIN—The West German finance chief Friday suggested circulating his country's currency in East Germany, and the Soviet Union showed its greatest tolerance yet for unifying the states.

The idea of the prosperous West merging with the impoverished East continued to shape the debate over how to rescue East Germany from economic collapse and political paralysis.

East Germans have brought their economy to a standstill with strikes, protests and spiraling absenteeism as the country careens toward its first free elections March 18.

Dresden Mayor Wolfgang Berghofer, an influential and popular reformer, said complete collapse is imminent unless workers are given a convertible currency this year and the steady flood of people leaving the country is stopped.

"My fear is that in the next few days and weeks an exodus of hundreds of thousands will develop, and if this situation is not quickly counteracted, it will lead to political and economic collapse," Mayor Berghofer said.

Premier Hans Modrow also acknowledged this week the nation is nearing collapse.

Untold thousands are working illegally in East Berlin, earning West German marks that have at least 10 times the buying power of the meager ostmarks they earn in their jobs in the East.

West German officials previously have proposed plans for eventual convertibility of the ostmark, but Finance Minister Theo Waigel suggested Friday that a more immediate and effective measure might be wholesale introduction of the deutschmark.

Meanwhile in Moscow, Soviet Foreign Minister Edward A. She- vardnadze proposed that Europeans, Americans and Canadians vote on unification because they suffered so much in World War II. . . . *The Associated Press, dispatch for morning newspapers, Feb. 3, 1990.*

The backup problem above is that the lead paragraph's second main thrust (Soviet tolerance) isn't explained until the *ninth* paragraph. Don't make your readers wait that long before you fulfill your lead's promises.

"WHAT" AND "REAL WHAT" LEADS

You have a wide variety of writing options when structuring leads to emphasize the "what," or what happened in an event, and the "real what"—what it means. One approach:

DETROIT (AP)—The Standard & Poor's Corporation down-graded its credit rankings today for the Ford Motor Company and the Chrysler Corporation, signaling sagging faith in the auto industry's finances.

The other big Wall Street credit rating company, Moody's Investors Service Inc., said it would decide by the end of the month whether it would change Chrysler's rating.

The ratings reflect how Wall Street views the credit worthiness of companies and their subsidiaries. Lower ratings generally mean companies must pay higher interest to borrow in the credit markets.

S & P dropped Ford one notch in its ratings, to double-A-minus, considered a high level of investment-grade securities, from double-A. Chrysler fell to the agency's lowest investment-grade level of triple-B-minus, from triple-B. *The Associated Press dispatch for morning newspapers, June 15, 1990*

Note above the "hard and straight" treatment in the first paragraph of *what* happened: Standard & Poor downgraded its credit rating for Ford and Chrysler. An amateur writer might stop there. But the AP pro quickly (and wisely) adds the "real what"—that the downgrade of the ratings signals "sagging faith in the auto industry's finances." Note the sequence of (1) *what* happened, followed by (2) what it means, the "real what."

Explain Real Meaning of "What"

Also note above the AP writer's skill in writing the first paragraph in language easily understood by non-expert readers, then gently escalating (but always quickly explaining) the story's technical details. The third paragraph, for example, is superb "housekeeping." It explains clearly what credit ratings are all about and nicely backs up the "sagging faith" angle in the first paragraph. Note fourth paragraph mentions of bonds are closely tied to explanations of what investment grades mean. *Translate* technical terms for your readers.

Always Translate Technical Terms

Sometimes your lead paragraph should assign first priority to the "real what" over the "what." This often is required when your readers likely are unfamiliar with material you are covering. An example:

PANMUNJOM, Korea (AP)— North Korea and South Korea took a major step toward reconciliation Tuesday by agreeing to an unprec- edented meeting between their top government leaders.

The talks could be held as early as August, officials said.

Delegates from the countries met at the border truce village of Panmunjom and agreed to sign an accord July 26 that would outline a proposed agenda and procedures for the first meeting of prime ministers.

It would be the first such meeting since the division of the peninsula in 1945 into the communist North and capitalist South. The North invaded the South and touched off the Korean War 40 years ago last week. . . .

The Associated Press dispatch for morning newspapers, July 4, 1990

In the example above, the "what" is that North and South Korean officials agreed to meet. Unless readers follow Korean developments closely, they likely won't recognize the significance of that. Thus the AP writer gives first-paragraph priority to the "real what," or meaning, of that agreement: that a major step toward reconciliation has been taken. (Incidentally, note the AP writer's fourth paragraph of "housekeeping" details. It puts the story in an historical context that explains why the agreement is so significant.)

Obviously, even though you are covering an event and clearly see the "what," you won't always be able to discern the "real what" or meaning of an event. That need not deter you from writing an interesting and informative lead. Note the example below:

TOKYO—As diplomatic tea-leaf readings go, this one was a doozy.

On the 40th anniversary of North Korea's founding last month, aging dictator Kim Il Sung was delivering his usual windy speech to the assembled masses of Pyongyang, blasting "U.S. imperialists" and the "fascist rule" of America's South Korean "stooges." Then, suddenly, Mr. Kim held out an olive branch:

"We should develop good-neighborly, friendly relations with those capitalist countries that respect the sovereignty of our country," Mr. Kim said. "We will also develop economic and technical cooperation and cultural exchange with capitalist countries that don't have diplomatic relations with us, on the principles of equality and mutual respect, and promote friendly relations with the peoples in these countries."

Almost alone among communist societies, North Korea has remained aloof and hostile to much of the non-communist world, while its main allies, the Soviet Union and China, have decided to overhaul their socialist systems by improving political and economic ties with Japan and the West. No one knows for sure what to make of Mr. Kim's latest comment, and North Korea, one of the world's most secretive societies, isn't elaborating. Officials in Tokyo and Seoul are intrigued but don't know if it represents a change in policy. . . . *Urban C. Lehner, "Rumors of Peace Stir on Korean Peninsula," The Wall Street Journal, Oct. 7, 1988, p. A-20*

In the example above, the obvious "what" is that North Korea's dictator seems to be holding out an olive branch. But what does that mean? The *Journal* writer neatly catches the essence of mystery in a "tea-leaf reading" first paragraph and then, with engaging honesty, points out in the fourth paragraph that "No one knows for sure what to make of Mr. Kim's latest comment. . . ."[2]

Lesson: If you don't understand the "real what," don't pretend you do. With imaginative writing you can craft a lead that not only is honest but also catchy and readable. After all, a mystery, a question without answers, a problem without solutions—all can be *news*. Ensure your writing captures the mystery.

Write to Capture Mystery

Incidentally, note the timeless lead paragraph in the example above. Reporters aren't always quick to pick up news from North Korea (and, sometimes, other sources). But when you read the example, did you note how the *Journal* writer neatly inserted the fact that the speech took place the *previous month?* (It's in the second paragraph.) Old news is still news when handled with such skill. (On the subject of writing skills, see the sidebar on p. 131.)

Wordsmiths at Work

A touch of humor can make winners out of otherwise mundane stories. Examples:

American Isuzu Motors is giving Joe Isuzu, that pathological liar, the boot. Honest.

The car maker said it will drop the humorous but sometimes controversial pitchman this August, when it begins introducing its 1991 model year cars. . . . "Joe Isuzu to Get Boot," *The Wall Street Journal*, June 5, 1990, p. B-6

The Joe Isuzu "liar" advertising campaign that made the little-known Isuzu automobile a household name and elevated David Leisure—the actor who played Joe Isuzu—to the stature of a cult figure, has been so successful it may run for the next century.

(That's a lie.)

Actually, after four years, Isuzu is giving liar Joe Isuzu the boot . . . Jeffry Scott, "Isuzu Is Giving Liar Joe Isuzu the Boot—And That's the Truth," *Atlanta Constitution,* June 5, 1990, p. B-1

Get ready for a four-letter word.
Snow.
An estimated 4 inches of it could be on the ground in Seattle and elsewhere in Western Washington by tomorrow morning. . . .   Dee Norton, "A Chill in the Air, and Snow, Too," *Seattle Times*, Feb. 14, 1990, p. A-1

MIAMI—Two teen-agers, apparently bent on a kidnap-for-ransom scheme, abducted an 18-year-old woman, exchanged shots with her father, sped off in a car and then called the whole thing off—because they had to be home by 10 p.m., police said.   Knight-Ridder Newspapers dispatch for Jan. 12, 1990

NEW YORK—Donald J. Trump, the billionaire real-estate developer, has long attached his name to objects of his desire: Trump Tower, the Trump Shuttle and Trump, the board game. Now, add one not as pleasant: Trump v. Trump, the divorce.

The maneuverings of Mr. Trump and his wife, Ivana, began in earnest today, with all the trappings of power, money, publicity and shrewdness that helped create the empire of hotels, casinos and office towers that bear the Trump name.

Though the couple's separation after 12 years was announced on Sunday, its full potential as the first great celebrity divorce trial of the 1990's began to develop today. . . .   Nick Ravo, "Trump, the Divorce Case: Clash Starts Over a Pre-nuptial Pact," *The New York Times,* national edition, Feb. 13, 1990, p. A-14

LEADING WITH THE "WHO" ELEMENT

Handling the "who" element in leads can be tricky because (1) you must identify the most important "who" angle, but (2) you must judge carefully how specific and detailed to be in describing the "who."

Pursuing the "real what" in a news story, this American correspondent interviews Prime Minister Yitzak Shamir of Israel. Witnessing history in the making is a dividend for reporters.

(AP photo
used with permission)

In the example below, the writer judges that two presidents—Bush and Noriega—are the obvious "who" and must be identified by name and title in the first paragraph. "President Bush" is a name that will grab reader attention. At the time, Manuel Antonio Noriega was in the news every day, so his full name is required in this lead:

WASHINGTON (AP)—President Bush said Friday he is "not seeking a deal" on a reduced charge for Manuel Antonio Noriega and vowed to "bend over backwards" to avoid saying anything that would interfere with the deposed Panamanian ruler's trial. *The Associated Press dispatch for afternoon newspapers on Jan. 6, 1990*

In the example above, the AP writer doesn't assume readers know "Noriega," thus the reference to "deposed Panamanian ruler's trial." Consider how silly the lead would sound if it opened with "The President of the United States said Friday . . ." or referred only to the "deposed Panamanian ruler" and didn't mention Noriega by name.

Sometimes a person's association with a name in the news requires focused treatment in your lead. Why was Neil Bush an important "who" element in the news in the early 1990s? Because (1) he was President Bush's son and (2) he was discussed in the savings and loan bailout crisis—in that order. Hence, in the following example, a *USA Today* writer handles the "who" element to emphasize the connection with the President:

> Savings and loan regulators Thursday released conflict-of-interest accusations against President Bush's son, Neil, and ordered him to answer them at a public hearing in September. *"Neil Bush Is Ordered to Explain Loans," USA Today, July 6, 1990, p. 5-A*

If the precise name of the "who" element is relatively unimportant, your lead can omit the name and, rather, describe what makes the person significant. An example:

> ROCHESTER, N.Y.—A paroled killer charged in the slayings of eight women was ordered held without bail Friday and authorities say they have linked the man to a total of 11 killings over the last two years. *The Associated Press dispatch for afternoon newspapers, Jan. 6, 1990*

In the example above, the important "who" is "a paroled killer." His actual name, not widely known, is best left to later mention (AP held it to the third paragraph). That frees valuable first-paragraph space for punchy language that catches readers' eyes—"paroled killer . . . slayings . . . killings."

Good rule: In handling "who," mention name and title if both likely will be recognized by readers as important. Otherwise, define what makes the "who" important ("paroled killer") and hold the actual name to later mention.

Often, the "who" of a news story is the receiver or object of action and so dominates an event that the "what" angle must be subordinated. An example:

> NEW YORK—Hundreds of thousands of residents of Manhattan's fashionable upper East Side and the Bronx were left without power Friday when a massive gas explosion and five-alarm fire ripped through a Consolidated Edison Co. plant, killing one person, injuring 29 others and sending a huge plume of flame and column of black smoke over the electrical facility.
>
> Scores of people were trapped in stalled elevators in darkened high-rise apartment buildings . . . *John J. Goldman and Lisa Romaine, "Gas Explosion, Fire Cut N.Y. Power," Los Angeles Times, Dec. 30, 1989, p. A-24*

In the *Los Angeles Times* example above, the "what" element (explosion and fire) affects hundreds of thousands of residents. Thus, the "who" element is most important. Often an otherwise unimportant event becomes news if it involves or even is merely witnessed by many people. A small plane crashing in a forest may be a minor event; one crashing before thousands of viewers at an air show becomes a significant event. A power outage in Two Fork, Ga., isn't big news; one that darkens the nation's largest city is—particularly to residents in the nation's second-largest city, Los Angeles, who would be similarly stricken in such a disaster.

HINTS ON HANDLING THE "WHEN" ELEMENT

The "when" element is an integral part of any news story, and how deftly you work it into your leads is an important test of your professionalism.

Handling "when" is simple in a "hard and straight" lead. Mostly, you plunk it into the first paragraph, near the verb: "The City Council voted Wednesday night to . . . ," or, "President Bush declared today that. . . ."

It's sometimes difficult, however, to handle the "when" if circumstances require subordinating the time element to a more newsworthy element in your first paragraph. Note how a *Seattle Times* writer handles "when" in the following. The scenario: On *Thursday* night, there is a shootout. The *Seattle Times* is an afternoon paper, so the event breaks after Thursday's edition. Early *Friday*, TV and radio cover the story. So does the competing morning *Seattle Post-Intelligencer*. For *Friday afternoon's* edition, the *Seattle Times* handles the story this way:

EVERETT—Two Everett police officers and a bystander were injured in an exchange of gunfire at a housing project here before the suspect apparently killed himself.

Everett police last night responded to a report of an armed man holding people hostage in an apartment when the man broke a window and began firing at officers.

One officer, 75 yards from the unit, was grazed in the back and a second was injured by a bullet fragment, Everett police said.

A 19-year-old Everett man was hit in the abdomen by a stray bullet as he looked out a window of an apartment almost a block away, police said.

Everett Police Sgt. Harold Shoemaker said today that police believe the bullet was fired by the man in the housing project. *Michael Arrieta-Walden, "3 Wounded in Shootout," Seattle Times, Feb. 16, 1990, p. E-1*

Avoid Emphasizing Old Time Elements

In the example above, the writer omits "when" from his first paragraph because inserting "Thursday night" in a lead paragraph being read late Friday afternoon or Friday evening would say, in effect, "Hey, reader! Here's news . . . but it's about 24 hours late. . . ." Holding the "when" to the second paragraph avoids that, and doesn't detract from the news value of the story. In fact, that arrangement emphasizes the "what" (shootout) and that, not *when* it occurred, is the real news.

Caution: Learning to manipulate time elements, as in the example above, doesn't relieve you of responsibility for *updating* your story with the freshest possible news for your readers. Note the fifth paragraph above does that with a "today" (Friday) time element.

"Second-Day" Leads Carry Story Ahead

Sometimes you must create a "second-day" or "follow" lead when updating a "running" (or continuing) story. This can carry the story forward into a new dimension for readers already familiar with some details of it. In the next example, a *Milwaukee Journal* writer puts a second-day lead on a story already 24 hours old:

Two violent deaths at the lakefront in less than a week should not alarm the public about security in the area with the city's festival season in full swing, police and Summerfest officials said Thursday.

Their assurances followed a fatal shooting Wednesday night on N. Lincoln Memorial Dr. after a fight between people in two cars. . . .
Mark Lisheron, "Summerfest Fans Reassured About Safety," Milwaukee Journal, July 6, 1990, p. A-1

In the example above, we see how the sequence of timings can require a second-day lead: The shooting (second paragraph) occurs Wednesday night, after that day's *Milwaukee Journal* goes to press. The story is covered Thursday morning by the *Milwaukee Sentinel.* For its readers Friday afternoon and evening, the *Journal* advances the story with first-paragraph treatment of official assurances that the public should not be alarmed. This sometimes is called a "reaction lead"—a second-day reaction to the event itself.

The strength of the second-day or reaction lead is that it carries readers into new information not already learned from a competing newspaper or radio or TV. A weakness is that too many writers hang second-day leads on unimportant developments. For example, the *Milwaukee Journal* lead above would be weak if it reported merely that, "Police continued to hunt today for the attackers who. . . ." In leading with official reaction, the *Journal*'s writer pegged his story to a question certain to be asked by many Milwaukee residents: Is the lakefront area safe? Don't try to advance a story with a second-day lead pegged to anything but truly important news.

The "when" time element, then, can be the *focal point* of your story, or it can be *almost irrelevant.* First, an example of handling with precision a time element crucial to a story's focal point:

BUCHAREST, Romania—The birth of the new Romanian nation took place at 2:30 p.m. Friday, Dec. 22, in Studio No. 4 of the National Television building here.

That was when the rebel leaders went on the air to announce that the dictator Nicolae Ceausescu, under siege in the Communist Party headquarters in central Bucharest, had fled for his life. . . .   *Rone Tempest, "Romania Had Its Rebirth in a Television Studio,"* Los Angeles Times, *Dec. 30, 1989, p. A-18*

In the *Los Angeles Times* example above, the "when" is part of important history. Thus the precise time is necessary in that lead.

Below is an example of a time element that's nearly irrelevant. In fact, the "what" so clearly is the most important dimension of this story that the "when" time element seems inserted only out of some sense of journalistic obligation to complete the Five W's:

Sometimes "When" Is Nearly Irrelevant

As the flag that draped Sonny Lamb's coffin was folded, precisely and reverently, hundreds of police officers saluted.

They wore uniforms of different colors with patches and badges of different shapes. They take orders from different chiefs and patrol different cities.

But Thursday they stood together.

A squad of riflemen fired a muf-fled salute and, from the Alabama hillside, a lone bugler blew taps. And still the honor guard folded the flag, carefully, in slow motion.

Finally, it was handed to Columbus Police Chief Jim Wetherington who stooped to present it to Evelyn Lamb, widow of the slain officer . . .   *Richard Hyatt, "Hundreds Salute Fallen Brother,"* Columbus (Ga.) Ledger-Enquirer, *Dec. 15, 1989, p. A-1*

The above example, published on Friday, is a superb example of how a day-old (Thursday) time element can be subordinated in a *timeless lead.* And, note that inserting the precise time element in the third paragraph ("but Thursday at 2:36 p.m. they stood together") would ruin the story's flow by creating a blind alley that readers would follow, wondering, "Why is precisely 2:36 p.m. important?"

In the *Wall Street Journal* example below, two writers deftly handle a *yesterday* time element with a second-day lead that focuses on a new dimension of an event.

The scenario: President Bush abandons his "no new taxes" pledge. This is very big news. All day and into the evening, TV and radio carry it. Business and financial news services flash it around the world. The next morning, the *Journal* obviously cannot simply announce old news—that Bush is abandoning his pledge. Instead, the *Journal* uses this approach:

WASHINGTON—In a deliberately unassuming four-sentence statement released yesterday morning President Bush abandoned his longtime pledge of "no new taxes," immediately changing the national debate from whether taxes will be raised to whose taxes will be raised.

The carefully worded statement listed "tax revenue increases" as one of the elements necessary for budget deficit reduction. White House officials refused to elaborate. But clearly, the president now is ready to negotiate a budget deal with Congress that could include new or higher taxes. . . . *Allan Murray and Jeffrey H. Birnbaum, "Now It's Official: Bush Embraces Tax Increases to Narrow Budget Gap,"* The Wall Street Journal, *June 27, 1990, p. A-1*

Did you notice the *Wall Street Journal* writers in the above example left a yesterday time element in their second-day lead? Many readers would not notice because the writers expertly pitched the story ahead to focus not on taxes being raised but *whose* taxes will be raised.

PITCHING LEADS AHEAD WITH "WHY" AND "HOW"

No writing device is more useful than the "why" and "how" elements in pitching a lead ahead. This involves using "why" and "how" in second-day leads to explain *today* something that happened *yesterday*.

Note below how an AP pro explains on *Tuesday* the "why" and "how" of a tragedy that occurred on *Monday*—and, in the process, neatly takes readers ahead into new understanding of a story covered earlier by radio and TV:

MECCA, Saudi Arabia (AP)—A ventilation-system failure was blamed Tuesday for a stampede in a packed pedestrian tunnel linking this holy city with a tent city. Diplomats said about 1,400 pilgrims suffocated or were trampled to death.

Sources said a power failure caused the air conditioning in the 1,500-foot-long, 60-foot-wide tunnel to switch off in 112-degree heat Monday, setting off the stampede. . . . *The Associated Press dispatch for afternoon newspapers of July 3, 1990*

Below, a *Syracuse* (N.Y.) *Post-Standard* writer uses "why" and "how" to pitch ahead a story on two armored car guards robbed of $10.8 million:

A hankering Tuesday for a morning snack may have caused the undoing of a Monroe County security team, who became sitting ducks for the second-largest armored car heist in U.S. history during an unauthorized stop at a convenience store.

Thomas Ryan, spokesman for the Monroe County Sheriff's Department, said a shipment of $10.8 million bound for the Federal Reserve Bank in Buffalo was seized at 7:20 a.m. Tuesday by armed robbers, according to accounts from the driver and guard hired to protect the Armored Motor Service of America vehicle. . . . *Sean Kirst, "2nd AMSA Heist Nets $10.8M,"* Syracuse (N.Y.) Post-Standard, *June 27, 1990, p. A-1*

In the example above, clever writing not only pitches the story ahead but also points up the irony of guards getting robbed of $10.8 million while stopping for a snack that probably cost a dollar or two.

The "Look-Ahead" Lead

This writing device is extremely useful for several purposes:

• You can use it to summarize developments to date in a news story and simultaneously pitch the story ahead.

• You can alert readers to an upcoming event but avoid a "program lead," a deadly dull, unimaginative creature that simply states an event is planned. ("The City Council will meet Wednesday night." "Fall semester classes start Friday.")

Avoid "Program" Leads

Program leads are to be shot on sight. Instead, use "look-ahead" leads as *USA Today* does in a Friday weekend edition to tell readers an economic summit is planned:

LONDON—President Bush and Western leaders are trying to settle their differences over aid to the Soviet Union as they head to the economic summit in Houston next week.

Heating the Western debate: a startling appeal for help Thursday from Soviet President Mikhail Gorbachev. *Jessica Lee and Mark Memmott, "NATO Leaders Debate Aid to Soviets," USA Today, July 6–8, 1990, p. A-1*

In the example above, *USA Today* creates an active, informative, multidimensional lead for what could have been a routine "meeting-will-be-held" story. Note handling of time elements: Next week is the "when" element in the first paragraph (written in present tense, "are trying"). The writers then move smoothly, in the second paragraph, to the Thursday (yesterday) time element.

Other "look-ahead" examples:

George Bush and Mikhail Gorbachev meet tomorrow to discuss nothing less than unwinding the global order spawned by World War II.

Gerald F. Seib, Walter S. Mossberg, Peter Gumbel, "Bush, Gorbachev Meet With Limited Agenda, Historic Opportunities," The Wall Street Journal, Dec. 1, 1989, p. A-1

KENT—The boys are good buddies. They are teen-agers. And they are hard-core basketball fans.

A King County Superior Court judge will decide if they are also cold-blooded killers.

Tomorrow, 14-year-old Ray and 15-year-old Steve (not their real names), both from the Timberlane area of Kent, are scheduled to go on trial as juveniles in the slaying of Brett Tolstedt. . . . *Christy Scattarella, "2 Kent Teen-agers: 'Cold-blooded Killers'?," Seattle Times, Jan. 23, 1990, p. A-1*

King County Executive Tim Hill will propose tomorrow that county voters move to establish a regional government to grapple with growth.

In a speech to the County Council, Hill is expected to call for a petition campaign to elect citizen "free-holders" to draft a new "city-county" charter. That charter could shift power significantly among the 150-plus local governments within the county.

A draft of Hill's speech was obtained by The Times. In it, Hill says a new charter should establish a "two-tier" county government. . . . *Eric Pryne, "Major Changes in Government?," Seattle Times, Jan. 28, 1990, p. A-1*

Dangers in writing look-ahead (or "is expected") leads:

First, you can predict an event (a meeting, the outcome of talks, a trial beginning) and be wrong. Plans change, talks don't proceed as expected—so be cautious. Note in the example immediately above that the reporter pegged his look-ahead lead on a copy of a speech he had obtained. Still, if the speaker changed his mind and delivered a different speech, the newspaper would have to explain to readers why a proposal, which the lead paragraph predicted without reservation, wasn't made.

Second, you can get tangled in cumbersome writing unless you handle look-ahead leads with skill. Note the following example. The scenario: South African black leader Nelson Mandela visits Florida before flying to Michigan. The *Flint* (Mich.) *Journal,* an afternoon paper, must go to press *before* Mandela leaves Miami. An additional complication: Mandela is scheduled to arrive in Michigan at 2:10 p.m.— *before* the Flint paper reaches subscriber homes (most afternoon papers aim for delivery about 4 p.m.). The approach:

DETROIT—Nelson Mandela was to fly away from controversy in Florida today and land to a hero's welcome in Michigan.

Gov. James J. Blanchard and Detroit Mayor Coleman A. Young head a delegation that was to greet the black South African leader at his scheduled 2:10 p.m. arrival in Detroit. *"Detroit Hero's Welcome Awaits Rebuffed Mandela,"* Flint *(Mich.)* Journal, *June 28, 1990, p. A-1*

In the above example, "was to fly away" and the 2:10 p.m. time element create problems. First, the lead is cumbersome and hardly enlightens readers who can see the arrival televised before the *Journal* even is delivered—or, at the least, can watch it in living color on the evening news. Second, by giving it first-paragraph priority, this lead assigns improper importance to Mandela's plane trip. After all, plane trips aren't news these days.

Lesson: In writing look-ahead leads don't get tied up trying to be so timely that you stumble over time elements. The mechanical facts of newspaper production can trip you, and TV will beat you. Here, an AP writer fashions a look-ahead lead based on Mandela's departure from Washington *but* avoids problems by omitting precise time of departure:[3]

Remember: TV Is Faster

WASHINGTON (AP)—Nelson Mandela leaves the capital today assured of some political support and buoyed by a tumultuous rally where he was serenaded, praised and nearly worshipped by more than 19,000 Washingtonians. *The Associated Press dispatch for afternoon newspapers of June 27, 1990*

PRECISION VS. GENERAL LEADS

A crucial judgment you must make when handling statistical data is how much detail you can insert gracefully in your first paragraph and not choke readers. *Always,* your goal is *readability,* so read your lead aloud. If *you* choke for air midway through, so will your readers. If *you* require three readings to understand it because too many facts are jammed into your lead paragraph, so will your readers.

Below is an example of how you can omit precise figures from a lead paragraph and, instead, *characterize the meaning* of those figures. The result is a readable *general lead:*

NEW YORK (AP)—New York City has surpassed Detroit to become the robbery capital of the nation, according to figures compiled by the city's police department.

New York's rate of robberies in 1989 was 1,271 reported for every 100,000 in population, police said. Detroit's figure was 1,095 and the District of Columbia came in third with 1,055. . . .   *The Associated Press dispatch for Sunday newspapers, April 22, 1990*

Look again at the AP lead. Would you be attracted to the story if its second paragraph, with its jumble of figures, were the lead? The writer anticipated that a *precision lead* paragraph, jammed with figures, would drive off readers.

Sometimes, of course, the facts of a news event scream for a *precision* lead paragraph. An example:

ATLANTA (AP)—A year after a white supremacists rally in downtown Atlanta turned violent, 50 Ku Klux Klan members and supporters gathered at the state Capitol Saturday, as 2,400 law enforcement officers kept about 100 counterdemonstrators safely away. *The Associated Press dispatch for Sunday newspapers of Jan. 7, 1990*

Consider why the story above demands a precision lead: The story—the "real what"—is the irony of *50* Klansmen being met by *100* counterdemonstrators—all watched by *2,400* law officers. A general lead that didn't use precise numbers to point up that ironic contradiction would fail.

Lesson: In considering whether to write a precision or general lead, judge two factors.

First, what are the primary news elements in the story? Are they highly technical details, facts and figures that require precision treatment in the first paragraph? Or, can the news elements be summarized or characterized for better readability in a general lead?

Second, have you decided from the *readers' viewpoint*? Consider not simply whether you can jam the facts in; consider, rather, whether readers can absorb and comprehend them.

Write From Readers' Viewpoint

REFINING EMPHASIS IN LEADS

Lead paragraphs are designed, of course, to extract one or several news elements from your entire story and signal their importance by giving them priority treatment. Sometimes, however, you may want to emphasize a single element *within* the lead paragraph itself.

Dashes can be used to set off facts and give them special emphasis, as *Los Angeles Times* writers show here:

On the eve of trial, Los Angeles County supervisors on Tuesday passed up a chance—possibly their last—to settle a lawsuit designed to help a Latino win a seat on the county board, and a federal judge was asked to delay the June supervisorial election. *Richard Simon and Frederick M. Muir, "District Suit Heads for Court," Los Angeles Times, Jan. 3, 1990, p. B-1*

> RICHMOND, Va.—Lawrence Douglas Wilder, the grandson of slaves, stood here Saturday in the one-time capital of the Confederacy and took the oath of office as governor of Virginia—the first elected black governor in U.S. history. *Art Pine, "First Elected Black Governor Takes His Oath," Los Angeles Times, Jan. 14, 1990, p. A-1*

The *colon lead,* infrequently used in days bygone, now appears in some of the nation's finest newspapers. Like the dash, the colon can give special emphasis to news elements within your lead. Examples:

> Sen. Alfonse M. D'Amato says he made a promise to the people of New York when he ran for the Senate in 1980: "Elect me, I'll fight for you." *Jim McGee, "D'Amato's Pothole Politics and Paper Trails," Washington Post, April 22, 1990, p. A-1*

> The Issaquah Alps Trails Club, which lobbied successfully to protect thousands of acres on the Eastside from development in the 1980s, has a big, bold idea for the '90s:
> A publicly owned greenbelt, several miles wide, stretching along the south side of Interstate 90 from Bellevue to Snoqualmie Pass. *Eric Pryne, "Time is 'Ripe' for an I-90 Greenbelt," Seattle Times, Jan. 4, 1990, p. B-1*

Opening a lead paragraph with a phrase can emphasize a point:

> After almost a year of study, the Army has rejected a Pentagon advisory group's recommendation that women be allowed in some combat jobs on an experimental basis. *Molly Moore, "Army Rejects Combat Roles for Women," Washington Post, April 22, 1990, p. A-15*

> WASHINGTON—In his first State of the Union address, President Bush tonight proposed sharp new reductions in the number of Soviet and United States troops in Europe. He said the cuts had been made feasible by the rapid collapse of the Soviet empire. *R. W. Apple Jr., "Bush Calls on Soviets to Join in Deep Troop Cuts for Europe as Germans See Path to Unity," The New York Times, Feb. 1, 1990, p. A-1*

> In its largest transaction ever, Koll Co. agreed Tuesday to pay $532 million to buy property in 19 states from Union Pacific Corp., the nation's second-largest railroad company. *Michael Flagg, "Koll Spending $532 Million on Property," Los Angeles Times, Jan. 3, 1990, p. D-14*

Below, a superb writer uses two words—"even" and "reputedly"—to emphasize the tragic fact that foods long available throughout much of the world (oranges and bananas) only now are available in backward Bucharest:

> BUCHAREST, Rumania—Sacks of coffee beans and other long-unseen goods, beef, pork, chocolate bars, even oranges and, reputedly, bananas, appeared in the stores here today, belated Christmas presents from the brief, violent revolution that overthrew Nicolae Ceausescu. *John Knifner, "Rumanians Finding a Bounty of Food They Long Missed," The New York Times, Dec. 29, 1989, p. A-1*

Lesson: any newswriter can slap together facts in a lead. Pros handle the language with loving care and gracefully weave in subtleties and nuances that take readers into a story with special feelings and impact. Use the available tools—punctuation devices, carefully selected words, sensitive arrangement of news priorities.

THE SPECIAL PEG LEAD

Lead writing, in major part, is your search for words, themes, facts—call them "news pegs"—familiar or important to your readers and, thus, likely to attract them into your story. Professional newswriters grab for special pegs on which to hang stories.

Below, a *Los Angeles Times* writer uses the marital problems of financier Donald Trump, widely discussed in 1990, as the peg for a roundup story on prenuptial agreements:

For better, for worse. For richer, for poorer . . . 'til the prenuptial pact do us part.

That may well be the official marriage vow of the 1990s. Just ask Donald and Ivana Trump, who last week announced their plans to divorce—and to duke it out over an amended prenuptial agreement that has him gloating and her steaming.

The Trumps are not alone. Other notables who were at loggerheads over such agreements last year included:

• Convicted hotelier Leona Helmsley, who at one point was accused of violating the terms of her prenuptial agreement by trying to gain control of her husband's estate.
• Actor William Hurt, whose former live-in lover unsuccessfully alleged that they had entered into a prenuptial agreement.
• And Washington Redskins owner Jack Kent Cooke. . . . *Darlene Sordillo, "When Couples Write a Pact for Parting," Los Angeles Times, Feb. 21, 1990, p. E-1*

(Incidentally, note above the second-paragraph use of slang: ". . . duke it out. . . ." This effectively signals readers, "Hey, this isn't exactly an earth-shattering story . . . but you might enjoy reading it . . .").

Note below how a *Chicago Tribune* writer uses a one-year anniversary as a peg for a fresh approach to a story. The general "one-year-ago" approach of the first, second and third paragraphs gives way, in the fourth and fifth paragraphs, to precision reporting that updates readers on what occurred in the past year.

Anniversary Pegs Sometimes Effective

After one year of living dangerously, another began yesterday for author Salman Rushdie and those connected with his strange case.

A year ago, the Ayatollah Ruhollah Khomeini broadcast this "fatwa," or religious decree, over Tehran radio: "I inform the proud Moslem people of the world that the author of 'The Satanic Verses' book, which is against Islam, the Prophet and the Koran, and all involved in its publication, are sentenced to death."

Last Friday, the late Khomeini's successor, Ayatollah Ali Khamenei, reportedly said in a sermon that Khomeini's fatwa, "is still valid and must be implemented."

For Penguin's Viking branch, which won a bidding war for the right to publish "The Satanic Verses," the year has brought 30,000 abusive letters to its U.S. headquarters, 5,000 to its London offices. The firm's London warehouse has been evacuated six times because of bomb scares.

There have been 11 other bomb alerts, only six of them false alarms. . . . *R.C. Longworth, Chicago Tribune dispatch for Feb. 15, 1990*

Note below the special peg is a *visual image* probably familiar to virtually every American—the red-and-white soup can of Campbell Soup Co. This lead would be less effective if pegged only to "Campbell Soup Co."

The family that has controlled the Campbell Soup Co. for more than a century and made its red-and-white soup cans a common sight in the nation's cupboards has split over ownership of the giant food maker. *"Dispute Among Campbell Heirs Boils Over; Three Say They'll Sell," Los Angeles Times, Dec. 29, 1989, p. D-1*

Sometimes you need not actually describe the special peg. Readers cannot miss the point of the following lead—published the day before St. Valentine's Day:

NEW YORK—Romantics, take heart! There's an epidemic of marital fidelity in America today.

Nine out of 10 people said they've never been unfaithful to their spouses and 80 percent said they would marry the same person again—at least that's what they claimed in a Gallup Poll released Monday. . . . *Kiley Armstrong, The Associated Press, dispatch for afternoon newspapers of Feb. 13, 1990*

Make Readers Shout, "Hey, Maude!"

Think of special peg leads as you search for the "Hey, Maude! factor"—a symbol or memory that causes readers to sit up and exclaim to their spouses, "Hey, Maude! Listen to this . . ." (or, of course, "Hey, Charlie . . ."). For example, write about President John F. Kennedy's assassination, and Americans who were 15 or older that day will recall instantly where they were and what they were doing when they heard the tragic news. Mention spaceship Challenger blowing up, and younger Americans will have memories, too. If writing for Americans of college age, perhaps the following will spark emotions and serve as special pegs: Michael Jackson's white glove, McDonald's golden arches, an old building on campus, the football team's mascot. If worked into leads, such special pegs have good chances of catching reader attention.

You'll find one of the greatest dangers you face as a newswriter is slipping into *monotony,* letting a dull predictability settle over your writing. Don't let it happen. Strive for variety in your leads. We turn now to other useful devices.

QUESTION LEADS

News writing is designed, of course, to *answer* questions, not ask them. Occasionally, however, leads that ask questions can entice readers into stories.

Below, *The Wall Street Journal* leads a story on financier Donald Trump by asking a question on many minds at the time:

Why would bankers shell out $20 million more in loans to a man who already owes $3.3 billion and appears to have little prospect of meeting all of his debt payments on his own? Fear of bankruptcy court appears to be the best answer. *Milo Geyelin and Neil Barsky, "One 10-Letter Word Put Pressure on All to Agree on Trump Bailout: Bankruptcy," The Wall Street Journal, June 27, 1990, p. A-1*

Does the following question lead catch *your* eye?

POYNETTE, Wis. (AP)—Was Lori Bringe murdered or did she take her own life? Nearly two years after she died, family members and investigators continue to search for answers. *The Associated Press dispatch for afternoon newspapers of July 5, 1990*

And, does the question lead in the following *compel* further reading?

Calculate the winter rain and the harvest rain (in millimeters). Add summer heat in the vineyard (in degrees centigrade). Subtract 12.145. And what do you have? A very, very passionate argument over wine.

Prof. Orley Ashenfelter, a Princeton economist, has devised a mathematical formula for predicting the quality of red wine vintages in France. And the guardians of tradition are fuming. . . . *Peter Passell, "Wine Equation Puts Some Noses Out of Joint," The New York Times, March 4, 1990, p. A-1*

QUOTE LEADS

Test your own reading habits. Do you often glance down a column, stopping when you see quotation marks? Many readers do. They are interested in what other people say—particularly in the precise words used to express anger, sorrow, love, hate.

Unfortunately for the newswriter, many people in the news don't deliver their emotions in nicely rounded quotes that lend themselves to neat leads. But when they do, use those quotes. Here is an example:

"I intend to be at the execution," the gentle, gray-haired woman said quietly. "I want to see him die."

The tall, handsome, often charming man Clara Smith was talking about is Bill Jones, 34, adopted son of a police chief, doting father of twins and skilled television cameraman who did commended work on a documentary about the heritage of Eskimos.

He is also the man accused of strangling five California women—one of them Clara Smith's daughter—after raping at least two of them and two other women, all in the space of 18 days. . . . *Eric Malnic, "Man Awaits Death Sentence for Murders of 3," Los Angeles Times, Jan. 29, 1990, p. A-3*

Note above how the writer packs enormous punch in his first paragraph by contrasting that hard, bloodthirsty quote with its source: a "gentle, gray-haired woman" speaking "quietly." You can build lasting word pictures from such contrasts.

Another quote lead:

MOSCOW—"My Son Was Not Born to Die in Azerbaijan!"

The hand-lettered sign, held up by a Russian mother at a weekend rally in Moscow, demanded the withdrawal of the troops sent to Azerbaijan and Armenia to prevent a potential civil war between the two southern Soviet republics. . . . *Michael Parks, "Troop Call-up Leaves Ethnic Russians Bitter," Los Angeles Times, Jan. 29, 1990, p. A-1*

Issues and Challenges

One of the challenges in stretching for imaginative leads is to ensure you don't stretch too far—and miss. Below is a discussion of how to sense when you're stretching too far.

For *beginning* writers, the "hard and straight" lead that covers the Five W's and How is most important. It's the workhorse of our craft and, in its own way, is a thing of beauty when shaped to communicate clearly and precisely. Master it first.

When you do begin stretching for other, more imaginative types of leads, make sure your creative drives aren't overheating and getting you into trouble.

You'll know you're in trouble when you start reading the minds of chimpanzees:

> The 18-year-old chimpanzee had one thought on her mind from the moment in April when she first saw the Detroit Zoo's new $7.5 million Chimps of Harambee exhibit: getting out of it.

You'll know you're in trouble when you portray nonessential details so vividly that your readers can think only of chopsticks, speared chicken, and an open mouth, not the news:

> Seattle City Councilwoman Dolores Sibonga spears a piece of chicken with her chopsticks, holding it poised near her mouth as she considers a question about the proposed deal to build an arena and keep the SuperSonics basketball team in town.
>
> She has been here before, been asked to give tax breaks to professional sports franchises. She went along with a deal to keep the Mariners from moving to another city and regretted it.
>
> "I helped put the Mariner deal together, and it was a mistake," Sibonga says, shoving the chicken into her mouth with a vengeance. . . .

You'll know you're in trouble when you get carried away and write that pride (or anything else) is breaking out, like measles, all over a city:

> Unabashed pride broke out Thursday in the city of Detroit, so accustomed to insult from within and without. The spark was a serene man named Mandela, who touched down in America's heartland for just a few hours to remind his people of their common struggle for respect.

You'll know you're in trouble when readers need a cast of characters and scorecard to understand your writing because you've swept the courtroom floor and dumped everything into your lead:[4]

> Superior Court Judge George Bryant on Friday heard a plea of not guilty from a woman accused of murdering a Royston man, accepted a plea of insanity from a Hart County man who shot two people, and sentenced an 18-year-old Madison county man to serve jail time for allegedly setting fire to a Comer teenager in January, during arraignments at the Madison County Courthouse.

There are dangers in using quote leads. First, not often will you find quotes, as above, that fit so nicely into leads. Don't lead with a quote that fails the test:

- Does the quote express recognizable emotion clearly and precisely?
- Does it characterize the story?
- Will it *pull readers in?*

Second, when stumped for an idea on how to lead a story you may be tempted (we all feel it) simply to reach into your notes for a quote—any quote—for your opening paragraph, whether or not it is appropriate. A quote lead, that is, can be the lazy newswriter's way out of a dilemma. Don't be a lazy writer.

SHOCK LEADS

You'll handle plenty of shocking news in your newswriter career, and often your challenge will be to find ways of writing it without making your readers ill over their breakfast. Sometimes, however, isolating the shocking nature of an event can create compelling leads:

Castration.
  The word sends shivers up many spines. So when the call for castration of violent sex offenders began gathering surprisingly strong support from an array of lawmakers last week, critics were both startled and unnerved . . . *Jim Simon, "Castration: Would It Stop Offenders? Experts Split,"* Seattle Times, *Jan. 15, 1990, p. A-1*

LOS ANGELES—Whenever Jim Lee opens his refrigerator, his two carefully hoarded bottles of Seconal are there, reminding him that he is soon to die, and that like large numbers of people with AIDS, he is preparing when the time is right to take his own life.
  "I don't need these pills to remind me that I'm dying; whenever I look in the mirror and see my Kaposi's I'm reminded," he said, referring to the cancerous blotches that are a common mark of AIDS. "Whenever I have a fever I'm reminded."
  Doctors and social workers and AIDS patients say there are many people like Mr. Lee, facing the near certainty of an agonizing death, surrounded by friends and lovers dying in the same ugly way, who have made long-term preparations for suicide. *Seth Mydans, "AIDS Patients' Silent Companion Is Often Suicide, Experts Discover,"* The New York Times, *Feb. 25, 1990, p. A-1*

THE "YOU" LEAD

Writing for a newspaper's mass audience, it's difficult to address in your leads any single individual. Sometimes, however, the "you" lead can be effective:

If Judge John Rochester throws the book at you, you had better read it.
  And be prepared to discuss it.
  Rochester, an 18th Circuit judge who serves Coosa, Clay and Shelby counties, uses a novel approach to justice with some offenders.
  He assigns them books to read.
. . . *Nancy Wilstach, "Criminals and Literary Punishment,"* Birmingham (Ala.) News and Post-Herald, *Feb. 24, 1990, p. A-1*

> If someone offered you an effortless way to boost your immune system, make more money, free yourself from addictions, lose weight or attract new friends—for less than $20—would you go for it?
>
> Many people do, buying sublimi-nal audiotapes that purport to send to your subconscious mind powerful messages that can improve your outlook and your life. . . . *Robin Lichenstein, Newhouse News Service dispatch for afternoon newspapers of Dec. 28, 1989*

"You" Leads Have Weaknesses

You'll note two weaknesses in "you" leads. First, most cannot be taken literally. Chances are slim that you or any other "you" in the reading audience will ever stand before Judge Rochester or seek effortless ways to boost your immune systems. Second, "you" leads can drive away readers who quickly discern they aren't the typical "you" being addressed. That is, you writers—all of you—risk limiting your reading audience with "you" leads.

CONTRAST LEADS

Contrast (or counterpoint) leads carry enormous punch if fashioned to lead readers in one direction, then suddenly jerk them the other way. Think of telling a joke in reverse: Instead of craftily pulling listeners along in joke-telling, then surprising them with a contrasting punch line at the end, you *open* this kind of lead with contrast. Examples:

> SAN JOSE, Calif.—They call it the drug that does nothing: It doesn't lead to addiction. It doesn't make the user high. It doesn't cause nausea. But it can help addicts overcome the heroin habit. . . . *Bill Ramano, Knight-Ridder Newspapers dispatch for Dec. 28, 1989*

> FLAT ROCK, Mich.—Here in the very shadow of America's Motor City, the Japanese are doing something that the Big Three auto makers still find difficult: They are building world-class quality cars with American workers. *James Risen, "Carbon Copies," Los Angeles Times, Jan. 22, 1990, p. D-1*

> Manuel Noriega, recently Panama's supreme ruler and now federal prisoner No. 41586, huddled with his lawyers yesterday to plot strategy for his unprecedented legal battle. *"Noriega Plots His Defense," San Francisco Chronicle, Jan. 6, 1990, p. A-1*

SUMMARY CHECKLIST

☐ Whichever style lead you write, it must communicate important news or signal readers that news lies waiting in subsequent paragraphs.

☐ "Hard and straight" leads are strong when they cover the Five W's and How in minimum wordage and are held to one or two core ideas.

☐ A lead is your promise to readers of news to come, so back up that promise by explaining the lead's core ideas in immediately following paragraphs.

☐ Deal out elaborating details in manageable "bites" that readers can absorb without choking.

☐ Include, quickly after your first paragraph, a "housekeeping" paragraph that backgrounds your story and puts it in perspective.

☐ News feature leads can be extremely effective on hard news stories that are best told with feature-style writing.

☐ When writing leads that emphasize the "what" of an event, be certain to explain the "real what"—the meaning behind what happened.

☐ Leading with the "who" element can be tricky because you must judge whether the person involved should be named or described ("John Smith" or "a paroled killer").

☐ The "when" element requires deft handling because it can be the focal point of your story or nearly irrelevant.

☐ The follow, or reaction, lead can move a news story ahead into new territory for your readers.

☐ Using "why" and "how" elements can pitch a story ahead by explaining *today* an event that occurred *yesterday.*

☐ Program leads ("Classes start tomorrow") must be avoided; instead, use look-ahead leads that explain or describe an upcoming event. ("Classes start tomorrow with University enrollments at an all-time high.")

☐ Always strive for readability when deciding whether to write a precision lead heavy with statistical data or a general lead that characterizes the meaning of those data.

☐ You can achieve variety by writing leads that open with questions, quotes, shocking facts, or that address readers as "you."

☐ Whichever writing device you consider, the "hard and straight" lead is the workhorse of our craft and must be mastered first.

☐ Special peg leads search for words, events or memories, such as anniversaries or well-known symbols, that are likely to spark reader interest.

RECOMMENDED READING

After reading *about* lead writing in this chapter you should head for your school library's newspaper collection. You'll find there a wide variety of leads. Decide for yourself, based on what you've seen in this chapter, which leads are good, which are bad. If you have access to them, the following newspapers offer consistent examples of leads that are strong (and sometimes brilliant): *The Wall Street Journal, The New York Times, Chicago Tribune, Seattle Times, Boston Globe, Miami Herald, Dallas Morning News, Los Angeles Times.*

For varying views on lead writing, see Rene J. Cappon, *The Word* (New York: The Associated Press, 1982); Bruce D. Itule and Douglas A. Anderson, *News Writing and Reporting for Today's Media* (New York: Random House, 1987); George A. Hough III, *News Writing,* 4th ed. (Boston: Houghton Mifflin, 1988); The Missouri Group, *News Reporting and Writing,* 3rd ed. (New York: St. Martin's Press, 1988).

NOTES

1. Few newspapers ration wordage in their leads or emphasize single-element "hard and straight" leads as does *USA Today*. Editors are deeply divided over the effectiveness of *USA Today's* short, punchy style, but the paper offers students many examples of leads that "tell it fast and straight."
2. For outstanding examples of news stories that define the "real what," see *The Wall Street Journal*. This newspaper is masterful at explaining highly complex matters in lay language.
3. Associated Press writers feed news wires that never stop, serving media with differing deadlines around the world and thus become expert at handling time elements, pitching stories ahead and using follow-up or reaction leads. These are skills you would need particularly if working for a major metropolitan newspaper publishing several editions daily.
4. For additional examples of writers who went wrong, see Rene J. Cappon, *The Word* (New York: The Associated Press, 1982). Cappon uses delightful wit in describing writing pitfalls.

Exercise 5–1   Leads Hard and Straight—I

From the following facts, write a "hard and straight" *lead paragraph that answers who, what, where and when.*

It was the worst ferryboat disaster in Scandinavian history. Authorities said that. A ferry, Danish-operated, caught fire. It happened in the North Sea. Early this morning. Tonight, 46 people were still missing. At least 100 died. Use a London dateline.

Exercise 5–2 Leads Hard and Straight—II

In about three paragraphs, write for Friday morning a "hard and straight" lead from the following facts. Make certain you assign first priority in your lead paragraph to the most important element (or elements).

Mayor Tom Bradley's 1990–91 budget package went before the Los Angeles City Council's Budget and Finance Committee. That was on Thursday. A net cut of $7 million from the package was recommended by the committee. The cut recommendation included an additional 2% spending reduction across the board for most departments. Bradley's plan called for hiring 400 police officers and 115 more Fire Department emergency medical service employees. Those plans were left intact. Bradley's revenue-producing measures were unchanged also. They included a 10% business tax increase, a doubling of fees for sanitation trucks and a new parking tax aimed at people who drive to work.

_____

_____

_____

_____

_____

_____

_____

_____

_____

_____

_____

_____

_____

_____

_____

_____

_____

_____

_____

_____

Exercise 5–3 Short, Punchy Leads

In about 20 words, write from the following facts a short, punchy lead paragraph that catches the jury's decision and the horror of what the man was convicted of doing.

This happened yesterday. Jurors on a King County jury convicted James Smith. He earlier had been imprisoned for one assault on his son. This time he was convicted of first-degree manslaughter. The jury decided this time that he recklessly beat his 3–year-old son to death. Smith lives in Auburn.

_____

_____

_____

_____

_____

_____

_____

_____

_____

_____

_____

_____

_____

_____

_____

_____

_____

_____

_____

_____

Exercise 5–4   Dealing Out Statistical "Bites"

From the following information, write for Monday morning a first-paragraph lead that characterizes or summarizes the single most important meaning of the facts. Then, deal out the figures in two additional paragraphs to back up your first paragraph. It is to be written for an Atlanta newspaper audience.

The FBI released crime statistics Sunday night. They show: Miami was second in serious crimes per 1,000 residents. Its rate was 189 per thousand. Dallas was third with 168. These are figures for cities with populations of more than 300,000 in 1989. Indianapolis's rate was the lowest of reported crime, at 43 per thousand. Atlanta was the most crime-ridden city by far. Its rate was 210 per 1,000. That happened before. For several years, Atlanta has been at or near the top of various crime rankings. So, once again, Atlanta had the highest crime rate of any large city in the country.

Exercise 5–5   Precision Lead Writing

Write for Sunday from the following information a precision lead paragraph that points up the irony of the situation, then add a backup paragraph. Use an Atlanta dateline and write for a paper in Georgia.

Two opposing groups demonstrated Saturday in Atlanta and Forsyth County. The two groups were overwhelmingly outnumbered and separated by officers in rows. There were about 35 white supremacists on one side, 75 followers of civil rights activist Hosea Williams on the other. The two groups remained apart and the rallies were uneventful. The total cost to Georgia law enforcement for making sure the groups remained apart was at least $650,000.

Exercise 5–6 Emphasizing Elements Within a Lead

Write a lead paragraph emphasizing that Nelson Mandela spent 27 and a half years in prison before finally winning his freedom today. Then, back up your lead paragraph with second and third paragraphs of quotes. Use a Cape Town dateline.

After winning his freedom, Mandela promptly urged his supporters to increase their pressure against the Government. It's a white minority Government. That Government had just released him. He urged that on his supporters at home and abroad. Mandela spoke to cheering crowds. He spoke from a balcony of Cape Town's old City Hall. He said, "We have waited too long for our freedom. We can wait no longer. Now is the time to intensify the struggle on all fronts. To relax our efforts now would be a mistake which generations to come will not be able to forgive."

Exercise 5–7 Writing A Look-Ahead Lead

Write a two-paragraph look-ahead lead from the following facts. Be sure to avoid a simple "program lead."

Councilor Edna Kindreck proposes a "noise control" ordinance. There are exceptions for ball games, parades and other activities. It's aimed at forcing people to keep the sound from boom boxes, radios and television sets within their own property lines. And inside their own dwellings. The Columbus Council will vote next week on the ordinance. Kindreck's ordinance also would regulate the output of car radios to within 25 feet of their source.

_____

_____

_____

_____

_____

_____

_____

_____

_____

_____

_____

_____

_____

_____

_____

_____

_____

_____

_____

_____

_____

Exercise 5–8   Writing "What" and "Real What" Leads

From the following information, write a lead paragraph that states both the "what" and "real what," or meaning, of this event. Then, back up your lead with two or three paragraphs of detail.

A Fenton Township man, Jerry Elrich, a former volunteer firefighter, was awarded $27,500 by a jury. He convinced the Central District Court jury Friday that Fenton Township violated his civil rights by not reinstating him after a debilitating back injury in 1981. The verdict could mean greater employment rights for volunteer firefighters throughout the state. Elrich is 44. The jury, in reaching its verdict, found that Elrich was an employee of the township and has the protection of state employment laws. The ruling will be appealed. If it survives appeal it could mean that local governments throughout the state might be forced to pay "on-call" firefighters and other types of volunteers an hourly wage. That is the fear of some municipal officials.

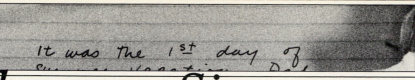

Chapter Six

Helping Your Readers Along

So, you've selected a structure for your news story, crafted a bright, attractive lead, and now everything else in your story will fall in place easily?

Don't believe it.

Laboring over a lead, but then casually knocking out random paragraphs on everything else that follows won't work. Readers need your painstaking help *throughout your story* as they navigate toward understanding the news. If your writing becomes haphazard you in effect abandon your readers—if they haven't already abandoned you.

It's easy to forget readers need your help all the way through your story, and that in pulling them ahead you are *competing* for their time and attention. In newspaper work, you spend your career in news, thinking it, talking it, socializing with newspaper colleagues who follow the news closely. You spend hours, even days or weeks, putting together a single news story, searching its every dimension to master it with complete understanding. But, what then becomes perfectly clear in your professional journalist's mind doesn't automatically flow through your writing and become clear to your readers. They, after all, devote their days to things other than news, and in competing for their time, you *compete with everything else that crowds into their busy lives.* On average, they turn to their newspaper once daily—and then for only 25 minutes or so. And within that time span you and your story *compete against everything else in the paper,* from front-page headlines to comics to stock market prices.

To succeed in newswriting, then, you must do more than catch readers' attention with your lead. You also must *sustain it* throughout your story. In this chapter we turn to techniques that you can use to pull your readers deeply into your story, to *help them along.*

We'll study how to tie elements of your story to promises you made in your lead—the *tie-back factor.* We'll look at building a *train of human interest* to carry readers forward. Then, we'll look at clear writing that keeps straight your story's *cast of characters,* in addition to its other elements—*what, why, where, when.* We'll examine writing devices you can use: *identifiers, comparison, characterizations* and *transition words.*

THE TIE-BACK FACTOR

Readers who go beyond your lead are demonstrating willingness to search for details because you sparked their interest. Make the search difficult and they'll go elsewhere. Encourage them along the way and they'll stick with you.

One quick way to assist their search is to construct carefully your *backup paragraphs*—those immediately following the lead—to "tie back" clearly to the lead's primary news elements.

Note how simply, but effectively, that is achieved in the example below. The writer opens by promising details of a Federal Aviation Administration report, then flags them by opening the second and third paragraphs with "FAA" references that tie back directly to the lead:

WASHINGTON—The Federal Aviation Administration said it opposes requiring use of child-safety seats in planes because the end result would be an increase in highway deaths.

The FAA, at a congressional hearing on child-restraints, cited a number of new. . . .

The FAA analysis goes like this: Requiring the seats for small childen would. . . .   *Laurie McGinley, "FAA Cites Deaths in Cars in Opposing Kids' Seats in Planes,"* The Wall Street Journal, *July 13, 1990, p. A-10*

Below, a *New York Daily News* writer superbly crafts a second and subsequent paragraphs that tightly tie back to the lead:

Joe Smith Sr. had a heart-to-heart with his son yesterday. It was unlike any of the talks they had years ago as they fished in the Long Island Sound off Glen Island.

This father-son chat took place in the deathhouse of Virginia State Penitentiary, Richmond. Joe Sr. has less than a week to persuade his namesake to fight for life.

On Friday, the boy he used to take fishing will be strapped into an electric chair and executed at age 31 for murdering a man who was his benefactor and lover.

"The chair . . . it's a couple of steps from me," said Joe Jr., now confined to a basement cell around a

corner from the room where he will die. "I can't see it but I hear them testing it. You feel the ground vibrate, and it seems like you can almost smell it, man."

The execution comes in somewhat record time, even for Virginia, which subscribes to the strict justice of the pro-death penalty South.

Condemned a year ago, Smith, a drug addict who spent most of the last decade in New York prisons, has refused to file appeals to his sentence, an option that could extend his life for up to 10 years. . . .   *Don Gentile, "Time to Die & to Grieve,"* New York Daily News, *June 25, 1990, p. 2-C*

In the example above, writer Don Gentile uses three tie-back devices:

1. He opens his second paragraph with "This," a *specific reference* to his first paragraph's "heart-to-heart." Similar specific references can be built around "the," "that," "those."

2. Gentile's second paragraph "father-son chat" also is a specific tie-back, to his first paragraph's "heart-to-heart."

3. The writer's third-paragraph reference to "the boy he used to take fishing" ties back to the second sentence of the lead paragraph, ". . . as they fished in the Long Island Sound off Glen Island."

But what *really* carries readers ahead into this story? It's writer Gentile's skill in creating a *human interest train of thought* in just three paragraphs (father-son, fishing, deathhouse), then loading readers on board and steaming ahead. Thus hooked, *they'll not leap off until Gentile wants them to.*

Create Human Interest Train of Thought

After all, what is a tale about death row in Virginia State Penitentiary? A *news story* like all those other news stories that shout at us every day from front pages and the tube.

What is it when a story describes a father talking to his condemned son? *A tragedy.*

See the difference?[1]

Incidentally, in our discussion above, did you sort of "get into" the father-son tragedy? Did that make our discussion of tie-back factors interesting? Would you like to learn more about the writer who so skillfully pulled you into that tragedy? If so, remember in writing your own news stories that *nothing* pulls along readers as effectively as involving them in first-paragraph human interest and then tying the rest of your story to that. Note also how I identify Don Gentile of the *New York Daily News* and refer to "*his* first paragraph" and "*Gentile*'s second paragraph." I tried to acquaint you with a live human being and carry you forward with a discussion of his writing rather than construct a dry, impersonal discussion of tie-back factors. As you help your readers along, personalize—let them identify with *real people*. Things, ideas, concepts, corporations, nations—they don't have the pull of real people.

Introduce Your Readers to Real People

Note below this briefer "human interest train of thought":

[James Smith] lived and died on the streets. Tuesday, he was given a home.

The unmarked plot in Crest Lawn Memorial Park in northwest Atlanta was beyond his means, but Fulton County paid to bury him there, as it does for more than 150 down-and-out people each year. About a quarter of them, like [Smith], are homeless.

"For some of them, death is a release and a relief," said the Rev. Howard Creecy Jr., one of the county chaplains. "It gives them a permanent home, something they haven't had in a long time. It's one of the most decent things that the county does." *David Corvette, "Dignity in Death," Atlanta Constitution, Feb. 7, 1990, p. B-1*

Want to know more about [James Smith]? Writer David Corvette hurries to tell you:

[Mr. Smith's] daughter, [Alice], said her father worked construction jobs until he was injured several years ago. He began drinking heavily, she said, and eventually took up residence on the streets, living out of his shopping cart. He refused offers to stay with her, she said.

The story above really is about how many paupers Fulton County, Georgia, must bury each year. But only deeply dedicated readers would follow writer Corvette into his story if it opened with something like this: "Fulton County buries about 150 down-and-out people each year at a cost of approximately $1,735 per funeral. . . ."

Editorial cartoons can use humor as an effective means of communication. Here, *Atlanta Constitution* cartoonist Mike Luckovich gives readers an amusing, yet insightful look at the news by tying together two elements: Soviet leader Mikhail Gorbachev's domestic problems and the then-current film *Driving Miss Daisy*. Both meet the ''timeliness'' definition in news.

(Used with permission of Michael Lukovich)

Answer Questions That Your Writing Raises

Were you attracted to the first-paragraph mention in the story above of down-and-outer Smith being "given a home"? Note how writer Corvette ties back to that in his third-paragraph quote. Don't raise questions in your leads unless you tie back and answer them quickly. (For examples of how other writers succeed by tying the human elements into their stories, see the sidebar.)

By the way, did you notice above how we identified the *Atlanta Constitution* reporter as "writer David Corvette" and "writer Corvette"? Don't expect readers to memorize names in a story's cast of characters. Help them along with such devices as "*writer* Corvette."

KEEPING THE CAST OF CHARACTERS STRAIGHT

If you focus on the "who" element in your lead and establish reader recognition with one or several persons you must help your readers along by keeping the cast of characters straight in subsequent paragraphs.

Wordsmiths at Work

The true professional newswriter develops the knack of helping readers understand large, complex and impersonal issues by reducing them to *human terms*. Here is how to make "economy" and "recession" come alive:

> The economy is teetering on the brink of a recession. Will the U.S. tumble into one soon, or will the economy slowly struggle back to solid growth?
>
> Among economists, the consensus is it will stage another miracle recovery, much as it did after slowing alarmingly in 1986. . . .
>
> But for [Charles Smith], the economic landing has already been plenty hard. He was dismissed in November from his job as a housekeeping executive at an Atlanta motel—told, he says, that "hotels are cutting the fat. What I know is that I'm only a couple of weeks away from the poverty level of saying I'm homeless."
>
> Nor is economic weakness any stranger to [Betty Jones], laid off recently at Cummins Engine Co., a victim of a poor trucking market that is hurting sales of the Indiana company's diesel engines. Worse, she says, the fact that she was laid off and hired three times last year makes other companies wary. "Employers think I'll go right back if Cummins has jobs again," she says.
>
> Stories like theirs filter down. . . .   Lindley H. Clark Jr. and Alfred L. Malabre Jr., "Does Recession Loom? Most Experts Demur, But People Are Wary," *The Wall Street Journal*, Jan. 26, 1990, p. A-1

The author of the following example shows how to make an obituary glitter, in this case with memories of the late Arthur A. Houghton Jr., who was renowned for his management style while president of Steuben Glass:

> It is part of company folklore that about a month after assuming control of the new subsidiary, Mr. Houghton, dissatisfied with its products, spent a Sunday smashing every piece of glass in a company warehouse in Corning, N.Y.
>
> Armed with short lead pipes and clad in overalls, gloves and goggles, he and John M. Gates, an architect and company vice-president, flailed away at 20,000 items valued at $1 million. With an interest in art that he wanted to combine with business, Mr. Houghton had decided to start from scratch by destroying the old products that were not selling and trying to create a quality glass business that would incorporate imaginative design in technically superb crystal. He said he wanted to "produce crystal in the highest standards of design, quality and workmanship, glass which would rank in history among man's greatest achievements."   George James, "Arthur Houghton Jr., 83, Dies; Led Steuben Glass," *The New York Times*, April 4, 1990, national edition, p. B-13

(Destroying $1 *million* worth of Steuben glass? Now, *there's* a "Hey, Maude!" factor.)

How to move what otherwise would be a routine traffic story into the big leagues of *stories that matter* is conveyed in this example:

> Classmates at Cherry Creek High School knew Summer Saville-Ball as a caring teenager who liked to spend time with her friends.
>
> That's what she was doing Friday when she and two other Englewood teen-

age girls, out for a walk in south Denver, tried to cross a busy street just a block from Saville-Ball's home.

Two of them didn't make it.

A car slammed into Saville-Ball, 14, and Carolyn Tebbens, 15. Saville-Ball was killed. Tebbens suffered a broken leg and was in stable condition last night at Denver General Hospital.

Denver police still were investigating. . . .

"She [Saville-Ball] was really nice," said classmate Celena Dieker, 14. "She gave a lot of encouragement to us all."

Added 14-year-old classmate Ann Henry: "She was an easy person to talk to because she was a good listener."   "Denver Girl, 14, Remembered as 'Real Nice,'" *Denver Post,* Jan. 28, 1990, p. B-1

Note how the author of the next article uses the human element to pull readers into a discussion of Iraq's occupation of Kuwait during the Gulf War:

KUWAIT CITY—In the Arab culture, Kalid Shalawi observed, it is sign of weakness for a man to cry. But he unashamedly wept today as he described seven months of bloody occupation by the Iraqi army.

"Sometimes I sit alone and start crying over what has happened in Kuwait. It is worse even than people thought," Shalawi said.

As acting chief of the medical section of Mubarak Hospital, Kuwait's largest, Shalawi said he saw the worst of the occupation—victims of torture, bullet riddled bodies that came into the surgical wing with hands tied behind the backs, young men who had been chopped wtih axes.   William Claiborne, "Kuwait Doctors Charge Torture, Killings by Occupiers," *Washington Post,* March 1, 1991, p. 1

In the previous section, two writers did that: The *Daily News'* Gentile, with father and imprisoned son; the *Atlanta Constitution*'s Corvette, with homeless man buried. (Note, incidentally, in the preceding sentence, how I've helped *you* along by reminding you which papers Gentile and Corvette write for. Give *your* readers such reminders.)

Below, a writer pegs his lead on *two* individuals who have strong reader recognition, then structures subsequent paragraphs around them—around recognizable real people, not ideologies or institutions.

VATICAN CITY—Soviet President Mikhail S. Gorbachev promised Pope John Paul II yesterday that his country would grant religious freedom to its citizens and invited the pontiff to visit the Soviet Union.

And John Paul, who was born in Poland and has crusaded against Soviet domination most of his life, invoked the "blessings of Almighty God" on Gorbachev and wished him success with his program of perestroika.

The historic meeting of communist leader and Catholic Pope. . . .

The two men emerged beaming from a 75-minute meeting. . . .
Steve Goldsmith, "Soviet Vows Religious Freedom," Philadelphia Inquirer, Dec. 2, 1989, p. A-1

Below, a *Philadelphia Inquirer* writer on the same front page helps readers along by tying back to first-paragraph mention of President Bush:

VALLETTA, Malta—President Bush arrived on this Mediterranean island yesterday to prepare for the most important meeting of his political career, but was forced to divert attention from his weekend summit with Mikhail S. Gorbachev to handle a crisis in the Philippines.

The President, who begins two days of shipboard talks with the Soviet leader today. . . .

Bush, who looked tired. . . .
White House Chief of staff John H. Sununu said the President. . . .
Bush began his day. . . .
The President toured the carrier. . . .
At one point, a jet flew past him. . . . *Owen Ullmann, "A Distracted Bush Arrives for Summit,"* Philadelphia Inquirer, *Dec. 2, 1989, p. A-1*

Sometimes your cast of characters is formed of individuals not recognizable by name. Your challenge then becomes a bit more difficult:

Ever wonder whether that electronic scanner is correctly reading the prices of your groceries as they go zipping by at the checkout counter?

A bill passed yesterday by City Council would give shoppers a chance to double-check.

The measure mandates a return to the days of individually priced items.

It was hailed by senior citizens, dozens of whom were gathered in Council chambers, and panned by supermarket operators.

Seniors say. . . .
Supermarket operators say. . . .
Anthony S. Twyman, "Council Bans Calls for Grocers to Price Items," Philadelphia Daily News, *March 1, 1990, p. 4*

Above, the writer neatly separates his cast of characters into two groups—seniors and supermarket operators. Throughout the rest of the story, it's simple for readers to understand who is being quoted.

Here are two other ways of quickly tying back on the "who" element:

A 48-year-old Austin woman testified in state District Court on Tuesday that she had no idea that a woman charged with plotting her murder had taken out an insurance policy on her life.

[Patricia Smith] told a jury. . . .
Anne Belli, "Target of Alleged Murder Plot Gives Testimony in Trial," Dallas Morning News, *March 21, 1990, p. A-25*

WASHINGTON (AP)—Dimintrios I, the first Greek Orthodox patriarch to visit the United States, says civilization is threatened by a turn away from morality and spirituality.

The spiritual leader of 250 million Orthodox faithful will spend. . . .
The Associated Press dispatch for afternoon newspapers, July 3, 1990

In the tie-back below, the "who" element is "they." Do you think it works?

Mount Airy residents won a major victory yesterday in the continuing urban war between neighbors and nuisance bars.

They shut down two of them.

And they did it by using the legal system to pressure the bar owners into leaving quietly and selling their bars to people from the neighborhood. . . . *Beth Billin, "Residents Win Fight: Nuisance Bars Are Closed,"* Philadelphia Inquirer, *Dec. 2, 1989, p. B-1*

George Esper, Associated Press special correspondent who covered the Vietnam War from Saigon, interviews an official from the "other side"—Trinh-xuan Lang, who became Vietnam ambassador to the United Nations after the war. Reporting complicated international developments requires clarity on who is representing what position.

(AP photo used with permission)

The danger in the above tie-back is that "they" could be mistaken for "nuisance bars"—except that the lead paragraph so clearly is pegged on "Mount Airy residents."

In general, when you see "they," "them," "their," "its" in your copy, stop and consider carefully whether the tie-backs or antecedents—prior references—will be obvious to your readers. They may not be clear. (There, you see? When you read, "They may not be clear," you couldn't be sure whether "they" referred to *readers* in the previous sentence, *prior references,* or *tie-backs.* Better: "Prior references may not be clear to your readers.")

Be careful particularly when leading your readers out of a paragraph that mentions several persons. For example:

Recheck Clarity of Antecedents

> Smith, Jones and Allen were candidates for the office.
> *No: He* said he was best qualified because of his experience and education.
> *Yes: Jones* said he was best qualified because of his experience and education.

Another good rule: Once you've identified the "who" for your readers, stick with the identifiers you've fixed already in their minds. For example, if you lead with "Sheriff John Smith," stick with "Smith" or "the sheriff" throughout. Don't repeatedly lead readers astray with new (and vague) references to "the lawman" . . . "the officer" . . . "the black-haired officer" . . . "the 6-foot officer". . . "the official".

Issues and Challenges

A major challenge in structuring news stories is how to convince readers to continue reading—how to entice them deeper into your story with images and quotes. Here, a newswriter in the Chicago bureau of The Associated Press, Sharon Cohen, describes how she goes about structuring an enticing story.

A long time ago one of my colleagues gave me some common sense advice: "Write your story as if you're telling it to someone."

It's a good tip to remember, especially when trying to explain issues that seem so big and complicated, such as billion dollar farm programs or school-funding formulas.

When writing one of those stories, I map out in my mind how I'd explain it to someone, then go from there, using people to illustrate the point, whether it's a farmer living on food stamps or an inner-city kid whose school doesn't have enough money to buy books. It makes the subject more manageable and readable.

In longer pieces, I don't write a formal outline first, but usually jot down a quick list of major points that need to be covered and then start thinking about how they're going to fit together.

Everyone develops his or her own methods of writing. These are some guidelines I try to follow:

After conducting interviews, I try to go over my notes as soon as possible so details are fresh in my mind, whether it's the tone of a grieving mother's voice, how a shriveled corn stalk looks or what special mementos are in someone's office.

Before writing, I read my notes over and look for the strongest quotes. Often it's a process of sifting through similar comments and trying to find the one that best captures the point I want to convey. I also look for obvious holes to see what I haven't asked, what other calls I have to make or other research I have to do.

After a few paragraphs, I stop and read what I've written to see how it sounds and to eliminate wordiness. I do that again a few times after I've finished the story.

I also spend lots of time reading the work of my AP colleagues to see how leads are written and stories organized. It's one of the best ways to learn.

Sharon Cohen, AP Chicago, Associated Press Managing Editors' 1990 Writing Committee Report, p. 11

KEEPING THE "WHAT" STRAIGHT

If you peg your lead on the "what" element or *issue* in a news story you'll seldom have the luxury of structuring subsequent paragraphs around a recognizable person that readers can identify with easily. You'll need extra writing skill to help your readers keep the *issue* straight.

In the example below, a writer uses tie-backs in every paragraph to keep readers tightly focused on the issue:[2]

WASHINGTON—The Supreme Court ruled 6–3 yesterday that police can set up roadblocks to stop and question all motorists in an effort to catch drivers impaired by alcohol or drugs.

The decision is expected to encourage law enforcement officials. . . .

Overturning lower-courts in Michigan, the court ruled. . . .

Saying public safety should prevail in such instances, Chief Justice William H. Rehnquist, writing for the majority, said that . . . .

But Justice John Paul Stevens, in a sharply worded dissent, charged that. . . . *Aaron Epstein, "Sobriety Checks Upheld," Philadelphia Inquirer, June 15, 1990, p. A-1*

Don't Lose Your Writing Momentum

Some issues are so complicated you must devote many words, high in your story, to help readers keep them straight. The danger, of course, is that your writing can lose momentum and that the *news* angle can disappear as your story dissolves into background matter. In the following example, the writer devotes the first two paragraphs to news, then two paragraphs to essential background, and (in the fifth paragraph) picks up momentum again on the breaking news:

WASHINGTON—Sen. Alan Cranston (D-Calif.), who in 1986 solicited a controversial "soft-money" contribution of $85,000 for the California Democratic Party from Lincoln Savings & Loan owner Charles H. Keating Jr., will support a ban on all such fund-raising activities by state parties that escape federal regulation, an aide disclosed Sunday.

Cranston's administrative assistant, Roy Greenaway, said the senator will back a Democratic plan to prohibit the practice in the future, even though he fears it is not tough enough to entirely eliminate the soft-money phenomenon.

"Soft money" is the term used to describe the millions of dollars currently being spent by the state parties

in presidential and congressional elections. In 1988, it is estimated, each of the presidential campaigns raised at least $20 million in soft money, which was spent by the state parties.

Soft money now escapes federal regulation because the state parties claim it is being spent only on behalf of state and local candidates. But national party officials admit that they collect and distribute soft money primarily to affect the outcome of congressional and presidential races.

To compensate for the proposed ban on soft money, Greenaway said, Cranston will propose to raise. . . . *Sara Fritz, "Cranston Will Support Bill to Ban 'Soft Money,'" Los Angeles Times, Feb. 19, 1990, p. A-24*

As the example above illustrates, you need to parcel out background carefully and in small "bites" to avoid killing the momentum of your story. Sometimes you can explain an issue with minimum wordage. For example, readers of the following lead may wonder why the White House is being so careful. Just 15 words (italicized in the third paragraph) explain why:

WASHINGTON—The Bush administration is trying to enlist coca-eating insects in the war against drugs, but the White House sought to assure Andean leaders yesterday that "neither troops nor caterpillars" would go into their countries without an invitation.

Scientists at the U.S. Department of Agriculture's research center in Beltsville, Md., are experimenting with the notion of deploying legions of malumbia moths in the illicit coca fields of Peru and Bolivia with the hope that, in their caterpillar stage, they would feast on the drug-producing coca leaves and thus ruin the harvest.

The research is at such an early stage, however, that it has not been discussed with the South American leaders, *some of whom have already demonstrated a wariness of U.S. intervention in their internal affairs* [emphasis added]. Baltimore Sun *dispatch for afternoon newspapers of Feb. 21, 1990*

Of course, in the example above the issue is much more complicated than those 15 italicized words indicate. Deeper exploration would have to include history of U.S. policy in Latin America. But the brief explanation in the third paragraph above serves to "hold" readers until more detailed background can be inserted later in the story.

At times, helping readers along on issues requires considerable detail, but detail can be interesting if handled properly. Don't you find the detail in the third paragraph of the following a fascinating addition to the story's treatment of the issue?

GAITHERSBURG, Md.—Richard Davis holds the weight of America in his hands. It's a just weight, he believes. But he isn't too sure about the one in France.

Mr. Davis is the Keeper of the Kilo—the one man in America charged with making sure that this country's official kilogram weighs exactly that. He stores the kilogram—a 1½-inch cylinder of platinum and iridium—in his laboratory safe here and studies it as if it were an Old Master.

This is the weight from which all other weights in the U.S. are measured. If America's kilo is off, so is every bathroom and butcher scale in the nation, not to mention laboratory balance. (In 1959, the U.S. set the weight on one pound at precisely 0.45359237 kilograms; one kilogram equals about 2.2 pounds.)

But the King of Kilos is the international kilogram, which is locked away in France, and something weird is happening: It is losing weight, threatening to mess up measurement world-wide. . . . Bob Davis, "Move Over, Oprah: Now Even Weights Are Losing Weight," The Wall Street Journal, July 12, 1990, p. A-1

KEEPING THE NUMBERS STRAIGHT

You will drive readers away quickly with a lead pegged to numbers that never are explained in subsequent paragraphs.

Note how the writer in the following example helps readers along by breaking down the lead's $93.8 million in unmistakably clear fashion:

A $93.8 million package of Denver Public Library improvements cleared its first hurdle yesterday when a city council committee approved it.

If the proposal makes it through the council and is signed by Mayor Federico Pena, Denver voters could face their second major bond election in nine months.

The package includes a $61.1 million replacement for the 34-year-old Central Library at 14th Avenue and Broadway. Another $21.4 million would be spent renovating, expanding and building branch libraries.

The rest of the money, $11.3 million, would be spent on. . . . *Kevin Flynn, "Council Panel OKs Upgrading of Library," Rocky Mountain News (Denver), Jan. 18, 1990, p. 6*

When handling numbers, or amounts, as in the example above, two rules apply:

First, don't make readers hunt through your story to find the elements that total the number or amount given in your lead. Lay out the component numbers or amounts clearly.

Always Add Numbers Again

Second, when you use numbers, *always stop and add them once again* to ensure they are correct. Discerning readers will.[3]

Sometimes, keeping the numbers straight doesn't involve dollars or complex figures. Nevertheless, if your first paragraph mentions a number, or an amount, you must lead readers directly and quickly to its components. Note:

Charlotte-Mecklenburg school officials say three planned new elementary schools can be integrated without crosstown busings.

Two—planned for southwest and northeast Mecklenburg—could draw enough black students from surrounding areas, they say.

The third school, in northwest Charlotte between Beatties Ford Road and Lakeview Drive, would. . . . *John Minter, "Plans For Schools Offered," Charlotte (N.C.) Observer, June 14, 1990, p. 3–C*

The following first paragraph mentions two children. Note how quickly the authors provide details for each, devoting the second paragraph to one, the third to the other. This story would not be effective if one child were covered in, say, the first five or six paragraphs, with the second shoved more deeply in the story.

One brain-dead child was disconnected from life-support systems while another child clung to life at Children's Hospital yesterday, as authorities investigate both cases as possible child abuse.

Two-year-old [Billy Smith] of [106 Tree Lane] in Conifer died at about 7:30 a.m. at the hospital, where he'd been comatose since being admitted Monday with brain inju-

ries. Jefferson County sheriff's detectives continued an investigation.

Meanwhile, a 16–month-old boy was in critical condition with a head injury at Children's Hospital. Denver police arrested the mother's live-in boyfriend in connection with an investigation of child abuse. . . . *Tony Pugh and John Ensslin, "Abuse Probed in Tots' Injuries," Rocky Mountain News (Denver) Jan. 18, 1990, p. 7*

KEEPING THE "WHERE" STRAIGHT

Don't make readers arm themselves with atlas and compass in order to understand the geography of your story. Here are some hints on helping readers along on their reading trek.

If you write under a dateline, *everything* in your story is assumed to have happened there. If you need to shift locale, do so clearly. For example, the following article carries a Sacramento dateline because it was written by a staffer in the Sacramento bureau of the *San Francisco Chronicle*. Note how the first two paragraphs deal with the *statewide* drought:

SACRAMENTO—California is face to face with one of its worst droughts of the 20th century.

Water supplies throughout a state graced with only slightly more than half its normal rain and snow-fall are dangerously low. Already, water shortages have produced pockets of pain in a few communities scattered across the state.

In subsequent paragraphs, the writer needs to focus on the *San Francisco Bay Area,* where the *Chronicle* primarily circulates. Note how readers are moved from Sacramento to the Bay Area:

But for the most part, a rare combination of good fortune and good planning have made it likely the vast majority of Bay Area residents, and most of the state, will survive the long, dry summer of 1990 with only minor inconveniences. . . .

Although the Bay Area appears prepared to meet the continuing water crises, other areas are not so fortunate.

In the last paragraph above, the writer is signaling readers to be ready for another shift, this time away from the Bay Area and to "other areas." Those include Ventura, so the writer begins the next segment of the story this way:

In the town of Ventura, 30 miles south of Santa Barbara, four-person households must live on 294 gallons of water per day, roughly 40 percent of their normal consumption.

Ventura's water-supply outlook. . . . *Tupper Hull, "Bay Area Is Well Prepared for Another Drought Summer,"* San Francisco Chronicle, *April 22, 1990, p. A-1*

Below, note how the writer opens with a Dallas-Fort Worth "where" element, then shifts to two paragraphs on the wider U.S. picture and, in the fourth paragraph, moves readers back to focus on Dallas-Fort Worth:

Inflation has risen faster than economists had predicted, and in Dallas-Fort Worth the increase in consumer prices easily is outpacing the national average, the U.S. Bureau of Labor Statistics reported Tuesday.

Despite the greatest retreat in 55 years last month for fuel prices, the cost of living in America rose 0.5 percent last month, the bureau reported.

The culprit was clothing. Apparel prices shot up with the introduction of new spring lines and kept inflation high enough to deter any lowering of interest rates, economists said.

In Dallas-Fort Worth, government data showed, higher apparel prices were heavily responsible for. . . . *Kevin B. Blackistone, "D-FW Inflation Outpaces U.S. Rise,"* Dallas Morning News, *March 21, 1990, p. A-1*

Your Dateline Is a Promise to Readers

Writing under a dateline is your promise to readers that you physically are in that city. It's a *mortal journalistic sin* to fake a dateline. If you're not there, don't say you are. Foreign correspondents often write from a capital city and must mention other cities in their territory. Below, two correspondents switch from dateline city to another city where the action is.

First, in a story datelined Moscow, a *Washington Post* correspondent needs to refer to a meeting in the city Vilnius:

MOSCOW—Hundreds of Lithuanian men who deserted the Soviet army ignored Moscow's deadline today to turn themselves in to authorities, and the republic's leadership protested the movement of a convoy of tanks through its capital as a "predatory" show of military power in the continuing secession crisis. . . .

At a meeting in Vilnius, leaders of Latvia and Estonia—neighboring Baltic republics pursuing their own independence drives—expressed full support for Lithuania. . . .

In Vilnius, the republic's president, Vytautas Landsbergis, charged that. . . . *David Remnick, "Lithuania Protests Convoy of Tanks,"* Washington Post, *March 29, 1990, p. A-1*

It doesn't take much: "At a meeting in Vilnius . . . ," "In Vilnius . . . ," and you have shifted readers neatly onto new geography.

Note below how smoothly a *Los Angeles Times* pro switches you to Vilnius after a Moscow-dateline lead and four subsequent paragraphs:

MOSCOW—Lithuanian leaders meeting in a special session Monday drew up emergency plans for the survival of their economically dependent republic if the Kremlin carries out a threat that could effectively seal Lithuania's borders to critically needed raw materials. . . .

Lines formed, meanwhile, at gasoline stations in the capital city of Vilnius. . . . *Masha Hamilton, "Lithuanians Draft Survival Strategy,"* Los Angeles Times, *April 17, 1990, p. A-1*

It's not only overseas correspondents writing about exotic foreign cities who must be careful to shift readers as action in the story shifts. Suppose, for example, a speaker attacks the mayor of your town at a Chamber of Commerce luncheon and you get reaction from the mayor's office:

John Smith, Republican candidate for mayor, charged Friday that Mayor Charlene Drew is incompetent and should be turned out of office.

"She's no leader, and our city deserves better," Smith told the weekly Chamber of Commerce luncheon at Downtown Hotel.

Drew slashed back, charging her opponent with "blatant partisan politics" and "gutter tactics."

In a statement released from her office, the mayor said. . . .

It's the last paragraph above that shifts readers from the luncheon to the mayor's office. It's important to be explicit *how* and *where* the mayor responded. If she had been at the luncheon and jumped to her feet, shouting at Smith, *that* obviously would need to be in the story. Reporting that she replied by releasing a statement from her office adds new understanding for readers.

Two good rules to observe:

Handle Geographic Switches Carefully

First, keep to a minimum the number of geographic switches in a story. Readers go crazy jumping back and forth between different locales while trying to understand a story's news flow.

Second, if you must switch geography, bunch your references. That is, try to give your readers four or five paragraphs from Moscow, then four or five from Vilnius—not one from Moscow, one from Vilnius, another from Moscow, then another from Vilnius. . . . And, when you do switch, alert readers *early in the switching paragraph:* "In Vilnius, meanwhile. . . ."

KEEPING THE "WHEN" STRAIGHT

The dimension of time, like geography, can be terribly confusing for readers unless you write with great care. A couple of good rules to follow:

Label Time Switches Clearly

First, limit the number of time switches you pull in a story. Taking readers from the present to the past, then to the future, and back again can be bewildering.

Second, when you do pull time switches, label your moves clearly.

The problem of time switches arises, of course, because we often must explain *today*'s news against a background of *yesterday*'s developments—and project all that against what might happen *tomorrow*. Note how a *Los Angeles Times* writer does that in a story that opens with a *today* time element, then shifts backward in time:

Local economists who have analyzed Mayor Tom Bradley's proposed $3.6 billion budget warned Monday that the city is spending more money than it is raising and is headed for serious financial trouble.

The grim reports are the latest in a series of bad financial news for Los Angeles that has emerged in recent weeks.

Last month, Bradley announced a hiring freeze for nearly all city departments and last week he proposed a new city parking tax and a 10% increase in the city's business tax.

Despite the drastic measures, Lynn Reaser, senior economist for First Interstate Bancorp, said Monday. . . .
Jane Fritsch, "City Budget Spells Trouble, Analysts Say," Los Angeles Times, April 24, 1990, p. A-1

In the example above, there are *five* time elements in four paragraphs—"Monday" (in the lead), "recent weeks" (second paragraph), "last month" and "last week" (third), and back to "Monday" (fourth). But writer Fritsch switches so smoothly you hardly notice.

Warning: When you open with a *today* element but need, in subsequent paragraphs, to move backward in time to pick up background explanation, quickly resume the *today* thrust. Moving backward in time is like interrupting your story to insert housekeeping details on an issue: If you delay too long in resuming with fresh "today" news, your story loses momentum. Note in the example above that the writer devotes just 53 words to "old" time elements in her second and third paragraphs before resuming, in her fourth paragraph, the forward thrust of her story with the today ("Monday") time element.

Below, a Knight-Ridder reporter opens with a "yesterday" time element, goes backward in time in his second paragraph—then uses a single word, "Now," to pull readers back to the present in the third paragraph:

CAPE CANAVERAL, Fla.—Plagued by weather delays before yesterday's blastoff of the shuttle Atlantis, the space agency said it might ease some of the strict launch rules concerning weather conditions that it established after the Challenger disaster.

Weather standards have delayed six of nine shuttle missions since Challenger exploded in January 1986, killing the seven astronauts aboard. That accident was blamed, in part, on cold temperatures.

Now, officials of the National Aeronautics and Space Administration say they have enough new data to. . . . *Martin Merzer, Knight-Ridder Newspapers dispatch for afternoon newspapers of March 1, 1990*

Here, a writer pulls readers smoothly from "a year ago" to "yesterday":

A year ago they were high school dropouts. Depressed. Isolated.

Yesterday, though, they sat in caps and gowns. Smiling. Proud. They were part of the graduating class of. . . . *Henry Goldman, "Ex-Dropouts in Work-Study Program Get Diplomas and A New Outlook," Philadelphia Inquirer, June 15, 1990, p. B-1*

Timeless Summary Leads

Note below how a *Washington Post* writer, in a story published on a Sunday, opens with a *timeless summary lead* ("After years of bickering . . .") and, in his third paragraph, *thrusts the story ahead* to expected developments ("This week. . . .").

After years of bickering with Japan over specific trade disputes, the Bush administration decided last July to try a new approach—a frontal assault on "Japan Inc.," the tightly knit Japanese business practices and economic policies that U.S. trade officials believe give Tokyo much of its competitive edge in the world.

This approach, the first time two sovereign nations have tried through negotiations to pull apart each oth-er's economic systems and demand changes in them, has raised the tense trade relationship between the United States and Japan to a new pitch following President Bush's personal intervention in talks with Prime Minister Toshiki Kaifu in February.

This week, the negotiations reach a crucial point. . . . *Stuart Auerback, "Japanese Trade Talks Reaching Crucial Point," Washington Post, April 1, 1990, p. A-1*

Note the time sequence below: (1) *timeless lead* paragraph, (2) *tomorrow specific* in second paragraph, (3) *last month* in third paragraph. Why do you think the writer is so time specific in her second paragraph?

Anheuser-Busch and Rainier Brewery have taken conflicting positions over a state liquor control board proposal to label beers that contain more than 4 percent alcohol by content.

The board is conducting a series of hearings on the proposal, with the second scheduled at 9:30 a.m. tomorrow at the board's offices in Olympia.

In the first hearing last month, Anheuser-Busch, producer of Budweiser, told the board. . . . *Dee Norton, "Debate Brews on Beer Labels," Seattle Times, April 3, 1990, p. D-1*

In the second paragraph above, a specific time element is required because the writer must signal time (and place) of a public hearing readers might want to attend. A major responsibility of any newspaper is to give readers such operative information—call it "news to live by."

Provide "News to Live By"

If you doubt my emphasis on orderly handling of time elements really is necessary, try to sort out the time sequences in the following story on New York City police searching for a crazed "Zodiac" killer. The story was published on a Monday afternoon:

The hastily assembled Zodiac Task Force hit the scarred streets on the Brooklyn-Queens border just after midnight Thursday, searching for the killer.

Hours earlier, Chief of Detectives

Joseph Borrelli noted the shooter's desperate need for attention. "Perhaps all the publicity may have satisfied his need," he said.

Later, a handpicked team of detectives left the Richmond Hill station house and saturated the area—hoping to get lucky.

"It's going to be a long night," said one cop as the task force, headed by Lt. Daniel Kelly, left the three-story stone building at 1:30 a.m.

Cops were the only people out in East New York and Woodhaven that morning. . . .

Now, look again at the story above. Can you sort out *which morning* is referred to in the fifth paragraph? (Sorry, but I don't know for sure, either. The reference apparently ties back to the lead's "after midnight Thursday" but would that mean the morning of Thursday *or* Friday?)

In Chapter 4 we studied the strengths of chronological narratives in stories. These lay out time sequences in orderly, understandable fashion and present attractive "you-are-there" detail. However, weaknesses are that they carry "soft" leads, often gather momentum slowly, and most of the time aren't appropriate for hard, breaking news stories. Be of good cheer: It's sometimes possible to open a story with a hard "today" news lead, then shift into chronology that readers find so attractive. The tricky part comes in shifting from a hard-news, inverted-pyramid lead to chronological treatment. Note this handling:

Shifting From Hard News to Soft Chronology

A Los Angeles County sheriff's deputy testified Wednesday that he screamed to his partner to kill a member of the Nation of Islam as he and the Muslim wrestled on the ground for control of his service revolver.

"Kill him, kill him. He's got my gun," Deputy William Tackaberry said he exhorted David Dolson, a trainee deputy under his charge, just before Dolson fired a shot into the head of 27-year-old Oliver Beasley, killing him. . . .

Here, the writer expands into six additional paragraphs on trial testimony. It is straight "he said . . . they said . . ." writing about the trial on that particular Wednesday. However, the story is so dramatic that the writer wants to move into a chronological description of what happened in the shooting. She does this by shifting time elements backward from testimony with this "switchback" paragraph:

The incident occurred Jan. 23 outside an apartment complex on West 106th Street in the Athens District of Los Angeles County. . . .
Andrea Ford, "'Kill Him, Kill Him; He's Got My Gun,'" Los Angeles Times, April 19, 1990, p. B-1

With the transition paragraph above, the writer now picks up chronological treatment of the fight and killing.

Below, a reporter switches from timeless lead to a chronology on how writer Hunter S. Thompson became involved in legal difficulties (of which he eventually was cleared).

WOODY CREEK, Colo.—It is, as the Doctor might say, a nasty little tale. It's a story of naked lust or maybe vicious treachery. Either way, it's tawdry to the bone.

The Doctor, a.k.a. Hunter S. Thompson, is the eccentric bestselling author who has been a cultural icon to political junkies and college students for 20 years with his commentaries and tales of wild living and drug abuse.

But at age 52, the man whose life is the inspiration for the maniacal character, Duke, in the Doonesbury comic strip, finds himself enmeshed in a most uncomical situation. It's one Thompson himself might have conjured up, but. . . .

It began one night, back in February, when he consented to meet a woman. . . . *Dan Morain, "Gonzo Time," Los Angeles Times, April 23, 1990, p. E-1*

IDENTIFY, COMPARE, CHARACTERIZE

As readers move through your story they search for a frame of reference—perhaps an example or comparison—that will help readers understand what you're describing for them. It doesn't take much to help them along.

You can *identify* a person or corporation with a couple of words, just enough to trigger readers' recollections. I've italicized examples in the following:

In a last-minute deal with bankers yesterday, Donald J. Trump narrowly avoided missing a payment deadline that could have led to personal bankruptcy.

But for the *once-invincible* developer, the deal comes at a humbling cost. . . . *Richard D. Hylton, "Banks Approve Loans for Trump, But Take Control of His Finances," The New York Times, June 27, 1990, p. A-1*

Avon Products, Inc. announced that its cosmetics would soon be made and sold in China. *The beauty products* company said it had begun a joint venture with a Chinese partner. . . . *The Associated Press dispatch for morning newspapers of Feb. 1, 1990*

Comparisons as Illustrative Devices

Comparisons are among a writer's most potent illustrative devices. For example, can you look out a window and estimate for a friend a distance of 100 yards? Difficult, isn't it? Now tell your friend to *visualize the length of a football field*. Well, that's exactly 100 yards. Easier, right?

Note the comparison used so superbly below to illustrate a difficult concept in computer technology:

While some problems can be solved now by supercomputers using one or a handful of processors, massively parallel systems can greatly speed up computations with thousands of processors running simultaneously, *much as if thousands of gates were added to a congested highway toll station.* *David E. Sanger, "Japan Sets Sights on Winning Lead in New Computers," The New York Times, April 30, 1990, p. A-1*

How fast did Californians buy lotto tickets? An AP pro explains:

> Californians dreaming of a possible record jackpot of $62 million or more grabbed lotto tickets *at the stunning rate Tuesday of up to 525 each second—15 times normal—*state officials said. *The Associated Press dispatch for Feb. 21, 1990*

How do conservatives grade President Bush and his staff? Another AP pro puts it in terms we all understand:

> Conservatives give President Bush grades ranging from "B" to "D" but rate Vice President Dan Quayle an "A" or "A-minus" in a critique of the first year of the Bush administration.
> John Sununu also gets top grades.
> . . . *W. Dale Nelson, The Associated Press dispatch for January 7, 1990*

In a story on student suspensions in Portland, Ore., the *Sunday Oregonian* makes a comparison with national rates to put the local story in an understandable framework:

> There were 2,228 students suspended during the 1988–89 school year, for a suspension rate of 4.4 percent of the district's 51,182 students. . . .
> Nationwide, the total suspension rate for public schools was 5.7 percent in 1985–86, the most current year with available figures. . . . *Holly Danks, "Schools See More Violence,"* Sunday Oregonian, *Nov. 26, 1989, p. B-1*

A *Seattle Times* reporter reveals the State of Washington could be collecting another $295 million each year in taxes—but isn't. To help readers understand the magnitude of that number the writer makes a comparison:

> As an example of what $295 million in tax receipts might buy, it's just short of the $300 million sought by the state's teachers for higher salaries. Instead, teachers will get only about one-tenth of that in the budget passed by the Legislature. . . . *Carlton Smith, "$295 Million in Taxes Uncollected,"* Seattle Times, *April 3, 1990, p. A-1*

Here's an historical comparison that succeeds because the writer doesn't assume all readers recall what "Munich" means in diplomacy:

> "This is another Munich," said Lithuanian President Vytautas Landsbergis, *recalling the appeasement of Adolf Hitler that doomed Czechoslavakian independence in 1938 and helped bring on World War II.*
> *David Lauter, "President Decides Against Sanctions in Lithuania Crisis,"* The Los Angeles Times, *April 25, 1990, p. A-1*

Here is a comparison that fails because the writer assumes all readers recall an Austrian statesman (Prince Klemens von Metternich, 1773–1859):

> Both sides appear to understand this as they ponder the consequences of a moribund Warsaw Pact, a North Atlantic Treaty Organization that has lost its main mission, a united Germany and a disintegrating Soviet bloc. *Making sense, and stability, of it all is a challenge worthy of Metternich.* R.W. Apple, Jr., "A Summit Without Maps," The New York Times, May 28, 1990, p. A-1

Characterize the Meaning of Events

Characterizing the meaning of a news event can move readers toward understanding.

Examples:

Bankers restrict a financier's credit and call in some of his loans. It's complicated financial maneuvering that's difficult for non-expert readers to understand, but a writer superbly characterizes it:

> . . . his bankers, who in the past had eagerly backed his grand visions, *now have him on a short leash.* Richard D. Hylton, "Banks Approve Loans for Trump, but Take Control of His Finances," The New York Times, June 27, 1990, p. A-1

Demonstrators in Seattle demand a law to prohibit discrimination on the basis of someone's sexual orientation. What does that mean?

> What that means, in practical terms, is that it would be illegal in Washington to deny housing to a woman just because she is a lesbian. It would be illegal to fire a man from his job because he is gay. Mark Matassa, "Homosexuals Renew Efforts in Olympia," The Seattle Times, Jan. 25, 1990, p. A-1

In Washington, D.C., the House Judiciary subcommittee pushes along to its full committee, with "an adverse recommendation," a proposed ban on flag burning. Heavy stuff! Hard to understand—then, a smart writer makes it clear by characterizing the real meaning:

> Such a recommendation is a parliamentary maneuver that means most members of the panel opposed the amendment but sent it on to the parent committee anyway. David Hess, "Flag Burning," The Charlotte Observer, June 14, 1990, p. A-1

West Germany's chancellor outlines a plan for creating a German federation. Can't you just hear readers muttering, "So much has been happening in Germany I can't keep it all straight. . . ." "Frankly, I don't know how far-reaching the plan is. . . ." So, the writer characterizes the plan:

> It represents a major leap beyond
> the policy of taking "small steps"
> toward improving relations with East
> Germany that virtually all West Ger-
> man governments have pursued.
> *Ferdinand Protzman, "Kohl Offers An Outline*
> *to Create Confederation of the 2 Germanys,"*
> *The New York Times, Nov. 29, 1989, p. A-1*

Note the last three examples above are *full paragraphs* of characterization inserted in news stories to help readers understand and, thus, encourage them to read further. Believe it: If your readers are confused by the first, say, five or six paragraphs of your story, you'll not lure them further. A paragraph of characterization, strategically placed, can give them a "second wind" of interest. However, note the examples *are short and extremely clear.* When you interrupt the hard-news momentum of your story to insert a paragraph of characterization or background you risk losing readers. You give them a *natural stopping point,* where they can think, "Ah, now I understand," and move on to the comics or stock prices. Hold such interruptions to minimum wordage and quickly resume your story's flow.

Don't Give Readers Natural Stopping Points

In the following examples, writers use just a *few words,* early in their stories, to characterize an event or person. Such insertions give readers a beginning point for understanding the dynamics of a story (as does, "In unusually strong language . . ." in the first example). But they are so short and incomplete that they *must* be explained in more detail deeper in the story. Nevertheless, note how just a few words can set the tone of a story for readers:

> *In unusually strong language,*
> Milwaukee Congressman Jim Moody
> attacked. . . .   *Craig Gilbert, "Moody*
> *Attacks Kasten on Taxes," The Milwaukee*
> *Journal, July 6, 1990, p. B-1*

> [An editor] *has a reputation as an*
> *outspoken maverick.*   *Alex S. Jones, "At*
> *U.S. Newspaper Editors' Talks, Criticism and*
> *1960's Headliners," The New York Times,*
> *April 6, 1990, p. A-12*

> Mr. Fitzwater, *in his most upbeat*
> *comments of the week on this issue,*
> said . . . :   *Bill Keller, "Bush and Gorba-*
> *chev Work on Trust at Camp David," The New*
> *York Times, June 3, 1990, p. A-1*

> The state's *controversial* learnfare
> program is being damaged. . . .
> *Amy Rinard, "State Audit Targets MPS Attend-*
> *ance," The Milwaukee Sentinel, July 3, 1990,*
> *p. A-1*

Using Linkage Words

Have you noticed many paragraphs in this chapter open with, "In the example above . . ." or, "Note below . . ."?

Those are *linkage words* I use to help you sort out various elements being discussed. Think of them as road signs: "Now, please turn your attention here . . ." or, "Proceed in this direction. . . ."

Below, the italicized linkage words help readers move smoothly through a news story:

Federal environmental officials on Tuesday released a $106-million, short-term solution to the groundwater pollution problems in the San Gabriel Valley, a decade after the widespread contamination was first discovered.

Under the plan, a dozen of the most tainted water wells will be cleaned up first and officials will undertake other efforts to contain the spread of contamination.

At the same time, U.S. environmental Protection Agency officials acknowledged that no government agency can supervise and finance the cleanup of what has become one of the worst pollution problems in the West. *Berkley Hudson, "Short-Term Plan for Cleaning Up Water Released," Los Angeles Times, April 18, 1990, p. B-1*

Note that in the above example the second paragraph's "Under the plan . . ." links readers to the first paragraph's "short-term solution." In the third paragraph, the writer uses "At the same time . . ." to carry readers to a new thought ("officials acknowledged").

Below, just two words (italicized) link two paragraphs:

Soviet President Mikhail Gorbachev warned Friday that he would cut off the flow of vital goods to the breakaway republic unless its leaders rescinded within two days laws designed to bolster Lithuania's March 11 declaration of independence.

In response, Lithuania's leaders yesterday drafted a curt and defiant letter to Gorbechev. . . . *"U.S. 'Deeply Disturbed' Over Threat to Lithuania," Seattle Times and Seattle Post-Intelligencer, April 15, 1990, p. A-1*

In the example below, a writer discusses orders designed to halt sexual harassment at the United States Naval Academy. Then, the writer shifts readers to an anecdotal ending that illustrates that one woman cadet remains undaunted. I've italicized linkage words that make the transition:

The order regarding physical contact with plebes reinforces an existing regulation, but increases the punishment to include expulsion.

Despite the problems that prompted the new orders, the outgoing class sounded optimistic. "I love this school and have no regrets," said Ens. Tara Traynor, 23, of Philadelphia, who will report soon to Naval Flight School in Pensacola, Fla. "I'd do it again in a heartbeat." *Eric Schmitt, "990 Are Graduated at Naval Academy," The New York Times, May 31, 1990, national edition, p. A-11*

Linkage Words Help Readers Shift Gears

Linkage words are valuable when you want to signal readers to shift reading gears and be prepared for a new thought. Below, the writer leads with one thought (trading after normal hours) and shifts to another (trading electronically) in the second paragraph. The linkage words that help readers shift gears open the second paragraph: "In another sharp break with tradition. . . ." Then, in opening his third paragraph ("The plans . . ."), the writer signals he now is going to discuss *both* thoughts from the first and second paragraphs.

For the first time in its nearly 200-year history, the New York Stock Exchange will begin trading after its normal hours later this year and hopes to start trading during the night in 1991, exchange officials told brokerage firms yesterday.

In another sharp break with tradition, the new trading will be conducted electronically, away from the trading floor. *In addition,* some of it may bypass the exchange's specialists, the floor traders through whom all transactions are now routed.

The plans, which were disclosed by people who have been briefed by exchange officials, are an attempt to. . . . *Floyd Norris, "Big Board Plans Trading at Night; Electronic Transaction to Begin," The New York Times, June 14, 1990, p. A-1*

Note below that once a *Detroit Free Press* writer gets his lead hooked into you, he uses linkage words so well you have difficulty shaking loose from the narrative:

Carol Robinson has been through the grief and anger that came from losing her husband, Wayne, to a brain tumor last year at age 45.

And she has felt the guilt, *too,* because she had survived.

"I tried to stop myself from crying because I thought, how could I feel sorry for myself when I was the one that was still here," she said.

Though the hurt is still there, Robinson, 47, has been drawing inspiration lately from the small black and white magnetic sign that used to hang in her husband's office.

It says "Make It Happen" and now, from *its place* above the stove in her West Bloomfield home, *it* serves as a reminder to Robinson and her three children, who range in age from 15 to 23, that you can achieve what you want through hard work.

The *hard work* these days is. . . . *Robert Musial, "Widow Fights Grief with Activism," Detroit Free Press, June 29, 1990, p. H-1*

Read again the second paragraph of the example above. Do "and" and "too" make you think that the second paragraph is a *continuation* of the first? Do you think that to understand the first paragraph you must read the second? If so, writer Musial succeeds—and I think he does. Note, incidentally, in the fifth paragraph above how "it" and "its" complete the transition from "the small black and white magnetic sign" in the fourth paragraph. That's smooth use of linkage words.

Here are other linkage words you can use to open a paragraph and tie back to the preceding paragraph:

or	moreover	for example
but	nevertheless	meanwhile
in addition to	this	meantime
also	that	at the same time
still	for instance	simultaneously
however		

Use transition words with precision. For example, don't use "meanwhile" to shift readers to another geographic locale, to another person, or to another time dimension. "Meanwhile" means "at the same time." Use it only for that meaning.

REMEMBER: CLARITY

I've discussed in this chapter many writing devices you can use to help your readers move along in your story. Handled carefully, they can strengthen your writing greatly.

However (a linkage word), never forget your greatest tool is, simply, *clarity* in writing. However manipulative you become in throwing around transitions, linkage words or other writing tricks, you'll lose readers *if readers cannot understand the point you're trying to make.*

Sometimes (another linkage word), achieving that understanding (linkage again!) will require you to forget trying to craft well-rounded, beautiful sentences, and merely use a typographical device (the asterisk) to isolate and identify main points in your story. An example of how that is done to move readers briskly through a garbage story:

Jack Aldridge, assistant to the Columbus public service director, said city officials are likely to suggest a multi-faceted approach that would include:

*Separating out some types of waste at the landfill.

*Development of a disposal site for lawn clippings and tree limbs.

*A system to separate bulky items, like refrigerators, from garbage.

*A voluntary recycling program, under which the city would provide drop-off points for cans, bottles and newspapers. . . .   *Ben Wright and Ken Edelstein, "City Manager to Propose Landfill Extension Plans,"* Columbus (Ga.) Ledger-Enquirer, *Feb. 13, 1990, p. A-3*

Incidentally, did you notice the example above is this book's second use of a story about garbage as an illustration? I did that to make a point: In a news career, it's not all Big Story, Washington, Moscow, the fast track. You'll handle (figuratively, of course) a ton of garbage stories. Handle them as jewels. Help your readers through them and—as we'll discuss in the next chapter—write them with such strength and authority you'll be able to build, whatever your subject, a *bridge of confidence* to your readers.

SUMMARY CHECKLIST

☐ Your newswriter's responsibility goes beyond fashioning a catchy lead and into writing the entire story in a manner that helps readers along.

☐ It's extremely important that your backup paragraphs "tie back" clearly to your lead's primary news elements.

☐ Nothing pulls readers through a story like creating *human interest* in your lead, then unfolding details in subsequent paragraphs.

☐ If your lead focuses on the "who" element you must keep the "cast of characters" straight in readers' minds through subsequent paragraphs.

☐ If you lead with the "what" element you'll need keen judgment in inserting explanatory background at strategic points in your story.

☐ In leading with emphasis on numbers and amounts, make sure you subsequently spell out clearly the components of those numbers and amounts— and add them again to ensure you are correct.

☐ Limit the number of switches in locale you force on readers in a single story, and when you do switch, label your moves clearly.

☐ You'll lose readers quickly if you constantly switch time elements from present, to past, to future. Switch infrequently and only with clear labeling.

☐ Using a "switch back" paragraph, you can move away from a hard news lead with a "today" time element and take readers backward to chronological treatment of details.

☐ *Identifying* a person or corporation ("Avon . . . the beauty products company . . .") helps readers understand your story.

☐ Reader understanding is enhanced if you *compare* an event to something they understand (conservatives give President Bush "grades ranging from 'B' to 'D'").

☐ *Characterizing* the meaning of an event aids reader understanding (bankers have a financier "on a short leash").

☐ You can pull readers from one paragraph to the next by using *linkage words: however, in addition, meanwhile, in response, also.*

☐ Many writing devices are available to help you pull readers along but your strongest tool in writing is *clarity.*

RECOMMENDED READING

By now you should be a regular reader of newspapers. Read your local and nearby metropolitan newspaper, of course. But also sample other papers, including those cited in this chapter. Your best "case book" is published every day—in New York City, Philadelphia, Washington and other cities known for outstanding print journalism.

Other helpful sources: Theodore M. Bernstein, *The Careful Writer* (New York: Atheneum, 1965); Philip Meyer, *Precision Journalism* (Bloomington: Indiana University Press, 1973); Roy Peter Clark, *Best Newspaper Writing* (winners of American Society of Newspaper Editors competition, published annually by Poynter Institute, St. Petersburg, Fla.); Louis L. Snyder and Richard B. Morris, *A Treasury of Great Reporting* (New York: Simon & Schuster, 1949).

NOTES

1. Strong human interest writing in the *New York Daily News* and *New York Post* is featured with all the splash and color those tabloids can muster. But equally strong, if not so flamboyant, human interest writing can be found in less sensational dailies. Note particularly the style of *The New York Times, The Wall Street Journal, Philadelphia Inquirer* and *Los Angeles Times.*
2. Few issue stories are more challenging for writers on a continuing basis than the U.S. Supreme Court. With only minimal advance indicators on what justices will say, reporters must handle extraordinarily complicated stories under deadline pressure. Few do better than those writing for the *Baltimore Sun, Washington Post, The New York Times* and the *Philadelphia Inquirer.*
3. At least a basic accounting course and, depending on your ability with numbers, perhaps an advanced course, would be excellent preparation for a newswriting career. If you shudder at the thought, count the number of economic, business and financial news stories on tonight's evening news or tomorrow morning's front page.

Exercise 6–1   The Tie-Back Factor

Study front-page writing in today's New York Times *(or another newspaper your instructor designates) and describe, in about 150 words, a particularly strong—or weak—example of the tie-back factor. Discuss how the writer handled tie-back in backup paragraphs. Rewrite a poor example to illustrate how tie-back should be handled. Be certain to write in clean AP style.*

Exercise 6–2   The Transition

Two separate news elements are in the facts below. (1) Hollywood has increased the number of protected buildings, and (2) there has been agreement to rehabilitate El Capitan. Write a lead based on element No. 1, and back that up with a second paragraph. Then, fashion a transition and discuss the El Capitan element in your third paragraph.

The Community Redevelopment Agency on Thursday doubled the number of local structures protected. They are protected under the agency's preservation policy. Winning increased protection Thursday from demolition and change were Hollywood High School and 93 other Hollywood buildings. Los Angeles city officials and private preservation activists alike hailed the massive expansion of the agency's preservation policy. The expansion comes at a time when Hollywood is set to undergo a billion-dollar redevelopment effort. Facts on the second news element: El Capitan (now the Paramount) theater is on Hollywood Boulevard. The original splendor of its East Indian-style auditorium will be restored. Walt Disney Co. and Pacific Theatres Corp. have agreed to rehabilitate the landmark completely.

Exercise 6–3   Switching Locales

Below are the facts of an AP weather story. Many locales are mentioned. Write a story leading with evacuations from Elba, Ala., then piece together the rest of the story. Be certain to fashion smooth transitions so your readers can keep the geography straight. Write for the Sunday Oregonian *in Portland.*

Rescuers in boats had to go to the aid of people in Elba, Ala. They plucked people from trees and rooftops. At least 1,000 people were evacuated from the town. The town is in southern Alabama. The flood occurred when a levee broke Saturday. Six people drowned when their car ran off a back road into a rain-swollen creek. A bridge had washed out. The six drowned elsewhere in Alabama, not Elba. Across southern Alabama, since Thursday, when thunderstorms moved in, more than a foot of rain has fallen. Much of the South had bad weather. Schools and roads were closed in northwestern Georgia and, on Saturday, flood warnings were issued. About 35 homes were flooded. That was in Jackson County, Mississippi. Several roads there were washed out. Officials said in two days 14 inches of rain fell. The region is going to get more rain. That's the forecast. There were no immediate reports of injuries in Elba. The levee that broke is on the Pea River. It ruptured about 6:30 a.m. WKMX radio reported witnesses said only the roof of a middle school was visible and that water filled the first floor of the county courthouse.

Exercise 6–4   Multiple Locales and Issues

Below are facts from a Los Angeles Times *drought story. Write a story leading with the Southern California situation. Then describe the situation in Los Angeles. In about your fourth paragraph, insert "housekeeping" details that explain the overall drought situation. Finally, add a paragraph on the drought in other cities.*

Today is the official end of a disappointing rain and snow season in the distant mountains that supply most of the water for Southern California. It is the fourth straight disappointing rain and snow season. So, today begins Southern California's most severe water crisis since 1977. This summer, most cities and water agencies are faced with possible shortages. So, they now are really scrambling. They are passing water conservation laws, dusting off old measures left on the books from the 1977 drought. That one was statewide. The scramble was revealed in a *Los Angeles Times* survey of Southern California locales. Los Angeles is the region's biggest water user. If residents don't cut water use 10% in the next month the city has threatened rationing this summer. Spring runoff into the giant reservoirs run by the state and the U.S. Bureau of Reclamation is expected to fall to a level as much as 67% below normal. That's the problem. The reservoirs already are lowered by three years of drought. Los Angeles' water supply is less than half of normal. It's in the eastern Sierra Nevada. An even more crippling situation is faced by areas such as Santa Barbara, which depend on local water supplies. Officials in Santa Barbara already have banned lawn watering and garden watering. But you can water from hand-held buckets. In San Clemente, yards may be sprinkled only every other night this summer. No new landscaping may be planted.

Exercise 6–5   Developing a Human Interest Train of Thought

From the following facts, write a story that focuses on the victim and establishes reader interest in her. Carry your readers along for at least four paragraphs with details and quotes focused on her and the tragedy.

This is a tragedy that occurred about 1 p.m., on Cedarest Road. A girl in Dunn Loring was killed. A trash truck backed over her yesterday. She was two years old. The accident was ironic. It occurred barely a month after her family moved to a secluded suburban cul-de-sac specifically to protect their small children. They wanted the children protected from the dangers of busier streets.

Her mother said, "It was like we were finally getting what we wanted for our kids." The mother is Nancy Liberatore. She spoke in an interview last night. She was choking back tears as she spoke. Here is what happened: Whitney Michaela Liberatore, the girl, was bundled up in her snowsuit. She was outside playing with her brother. He is four. They were playing with two other children on Cedarest Road. Then, the garbage truck rumbled down the street in reverse. An 8-year-old boy, Brian West, lives across the street. He tried to snatch Whitney out of the path of the truck. But she darted away from him, apparently thinking it was part of a game. Whitney's father rushed out his front door. He had heard the truck. He rushed out just before his daughter was struck and killed instantly.

Exercise 6–6   Keeping "When" Straight

The following facts are from an Atlanta Constitution *story published on Thursday. Write a story beginning with a lead that looks ahead to the meaning of the proposed smoking ban. In your second paragraph, work in the "tonight" angle. Later in your story, insert background pegged to what happened on Tuesday.*

The Fulton County school board is considering an anti-smoking policy. It is a new, sweeping policy that is under consideration. Under it, prep football fans would have to leave their cigarettes at home. So would school visitors and employees. Scheduled for tonight at 8 p.m. is an initial vote. The vote is on the new, revised policy that would ban all smoking. All smoking on school grounds. Employees—under existing rules—are prohibited from smoking. While in the presence of students, that is. Rather, in the presence of students on school property or while attending or supervising student activities. They may smoke in designated areas, however. The current policy does not address smoking by visitors, although Fulton County students are banned from smoking. At all times. Four of the seven school board members, at Tuesday's work session, cited recent studies. Studies on the health hazards of secondary smoke. The four said they favor a policy that is tougher.

Exercise 6–7   Focusing on Locale

The Chicago Tribune *circulates in the suburban communities of Skokie and River Forest. From the following, write a story, using a lead that focuses, first, on Skokie and, second, on River Forest. Schaumburg should get No. 3 priority in your story. Conclude with a general paragraph on what Thompson and McClure announced.*

This all came in an announcement on Monday. Steven D. McClure and James Thompson made it. McClure is director of the Department of Commerce and Community Affairs. Thompson is governor. They announced grants for eight new civic centers. They also announced additions to four existing civic centers around the state. The grants total forty-four million, 100 thousand dollars. The department rejected a request for a convention center in Schaumburg. That was for $20 million. The department said backers of the Schaumburg center must apply again. They must apply by July 31 for funding. That is, if they want the funding in the new fiscal year. That year started Sunday. The River Forest award was for $1.9 million for a new community center. Skokie got $10.2 million. For a new performing arts center. The awards were made by state economic development officials on Monday. They were announced Monday by Thompson and McClure.

_____

_____

_____

_____

_____

_____

_____

_____

_____

_____

_____

_____

_____

_____

_____

_____

_____

Exercise 6–8　Keeping "Who" and "Where" Straight

Your challenge in this exercise is to write a story that smoothly leads readers through the "who" and "where." Write from the following facts for the Milwaukee Sentinel.

The original news story appeared on Tuesday. In the *Milwaukee Sentinel.* The dateline is Oshkosh, Wisc. Lt. Douglas Jahsman said the following. He is with the Town of Menasha police. He said a 23-year-old member of the New Greeks rock band was arrested Monday. In connection with the alleged rape, the gang rape, in May, at a local motel, of a 15-year-old girl. She is from Milwaukee. The band member is from Windermere, Fla. He is Fred Smith. He turned himself in, under a prearranged agreement, according to Lt. Douglas Jahsman. He turned himself in to the district attorney's office. In Winnebago County, that is. The charges he—Smith, that is—faces are twofold: first, charges of physical abuse of a child. Second, being a party to the crime of assault—sexual assault—on a child. Warrants are out for others, issued by authorities. That's according to the lieutenant. He said warrants are out for the arrest of three other band members. In connection with the incident. There is no charge against a fifth band member, Jahsman said. He isn't a suspect.

_____

_____

_____

_____

_____

_____

_____

_____

_____

_____

_____

_____

_____

_____

_____

_____

_____

_____

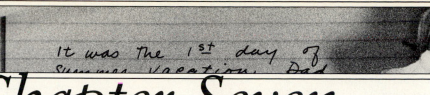

Chapter Seven

Constructing the Bridge of Confidence

We turn now to how you build and maintain your single most important asset as a newswriter: your credibility. No matter how strong your reporting or how beautiful your writing, you will not succeed as a journalist unless editors and readers alike regard you as credible.

Building credibility is a crucial process that starts *now,* in this course, every time you touch a keyboard. (After all, your instructor could well be asked one day by a hiring editor whether you are a responsible, professional person.) You must develop a passion for accuracy, detail and precision, and sharpen writing techniques that *demonstrate that passion* to editors and readers through items that appear under your byline.

Maintaining credibility is a career-long effort. The goal: recognition of your byline as a symbol of accuracy, reliability, professionalism.

Think of building a *bridge of confidence* to your readers by designing a believable story structure and then riveting to it the facts, one by one, that create credibility. *Give your readers reason to believe.*

We'll discuss in this chapter techniques you can use: quoting authoritative sources, which shows readers you are providing the best available expert information; inserting graphic details into your story, which demonstrates the thoroughness of your reporting; and—always—double-checking your facts.

PUBLIC DOUBTS ABOUT JOURNALISTS' CREDIBILITY

In striving for credibility, you, like every newswriter, begin with two major disadvantages.

First, the public has considerable doubt that we journalists *can* or *want* to get the news right. For example, a 1989 survey by the Times Mirror Co. asked thousands of people this question: "In general, do you think news organizations get the facts straight, or do you think that their stories and reports are often inaccurate?"

Responses:

	General Public	Govt. Leaders	Academic Elites	Business Leaders
Get Facts Straight	54%	54%	51%	23%
Inaccurate	44%	43%	45%	77%
Don't Know	2%	3%	4%	0%

These findings[1] (which are consistent with many others in recent years) are even more shocking when considered against a backdrop of general feeling among the public that we *don't want* to be accurate. The Times Mirror survey found that a majority of the public believe the press tends to "favor one side" in writing on issues. Many see "political bias" in what we print.[2]

In developing your personal credibility, in proving you *do* want to get it right, you inevitably will carry some of the negative baggage the Times Mirror poll found in the public's general attitudes toward the press. You'll find, for example, friends and strangers alike addressing complaints to you about, "Oh, *you* people *in the media* never get it right"—as if "you" includes you and all those who write for newspapers, magazines, TV, radio and other forms of communication. People with a beef over something said by a TV talk-show host or a magazine columnist often will include you in their critical net.

You Begin *Without* Credibility

Your second major disadvantage in building credibility is that you arrive on the job *without any*. What, after all, can you display to editors and readers on your first day that *proves* you are a credible journalist? You can't show them journalism's equivalent to bar exam results or a license to practice medicine, both of which are at least some indication of proficiency. No, your challenge is to demonstrate every day, *with every word* you keystroke, that you are accurate and reliable. And you must keep it up, day after day, story after story—always guarding against the mistake, the momentary lapse, that can draw down your carefully hoarded reservoir of credibility. Draw down that reservoir, give cause to doubt your reliability, and you will have enormous difficulty building it up again.

As you attempt to fashion credibility links with your readers, you'll find a major barrier is their general lack of understanding about the press as an institution and how you, the newswriter, go about your work. The Times Mirror survey, for example, found even the most celebrated journalists "often go unrecognized by more than half of the national news audience" (although TV news *personalities* are more visible). The survey also found the public often unaware of the "most fundamental facts, about the news business. . . ." (Only 4 out of 10 respondents, for example, could accurately define an editorial).[3]

Lesson: Your readers don't know you personally, don't understand your motives, and certainly don't understand the mechanics of covering the news and publishing newspapers. So, you must devise ways of, in effect, saying *in your writing,* "Folks, I've done a thorough reporting job for you. I'm quoting authoritative sources, and giving the news to you as straight as I can." You must write, that is, not only to attract readers with a snappy lead and then pull them into the body of your story but also to demonstrate you are putting before them a credible, accurate story.

Write to Demonstrate Your Credibility

Let's look at ways you can make that obvious in your writing.

QUOTING AUTHORITATIVE SOURCES

People expect many things from the American media: entertainment and diversion from TV sitcoms, background melodies from radio, adventure from travel magazines, titillation from supermarket tabloids.

From you, the newswriter, they expect *news and information,* accurately reported and written to reveal its meaning and impact on their lives.

Authoritative Attribution Needed

Demonstrating in the internal structure of your story that you have obtained that news—that you have the goods—from authoritative sources is the single most important step you can take toward making your writing crackle with believability. Note, for example, how a *New York Times* writer demonstrates explicitly the source of his story:

WASHINGTON—Calling the drug problem "the toughest domestic challenge we've faced in decades," President Bush tonight proposed a national drug control strategy that focuses heavily on increased law enforcement against drug sellers and users.

In an address prepared for delivery from the Oval Office, Mr. Bush adopted a tone of urgency in warning that drugs were a grave threat "sapping our strength as a nation."

"There is no match for a united America, a determined America, an angry America," Mr. Bush said. "Our outrage against drugs unites us, brings us together behind this one plan of action, an assault on every front." *Bernard Weinraub, "President Offers Strategy for U.S. on Drug Control,"* The New York Times, *Sept. 6, 1989, p. A-1*

The story above illustrates the most basic technique you have for demonstrating your story's authoritativeness: Attribute to the source by name (President Bush, in

Attribute Sources by Name

Quoting ordinary citizens caught in a war lends credibility to a news story, as does quoting official sources. Here, Sam Dillon, a *Miami Herald* expert on Latin America, talks with women and children in Managua during Nicaragua's civil war.

(Knight-Ridder photo used with permission)

the example above), use partial quotes (lead and second paragraph in the *Times* article), then a full quote (third paragraph of the *Times* story). Readers cannot doubt where this story comes from.

Incidentally, why do you think writer Weinraub opened his second paragraph with, "In an address prepared . . ."? (The story was written *after* the president's speech was prepared but *before* it was delivered. Weinraub's language was a *hedge* in case the president changed his speech during delivery and revised quotes that were the main thrust of the story. In later editions, after the speech was delivered, the *Times* eliminated hedging language.)[4]

Stress Source's Credentials

Sometimes the *names* of your sources won't add to the authoritativeness of your lead, but the *roles* they play in the news will. Write to emphasize the role:

CLEMSON, S.C. (AP)—The chief negotiator in a 6½-hour restaurant hostage drama said Monday he was "scared to death" during the ordeal and relieved when the gunman gave up without shooting anyone.

"People were counting on us to get them out of there alive," said Bruce Cannon, one of three Greenville County Sheriff's deputy trained in hostage negotiation strategies. *The Associated Press dispatch for afternoon newspapers of Feb. 6, 1990*

Demonstrate Source's Credentials

Note above how The Associated Press writer leads with a "blind" (unnamed) source *but* then quickly, in the second paragraph, lays out the source's name and credentials. If you lay before your readers what a source tells you, you owe your readers details on the source's credentials so readers can judge for themselves the credibility of what you have written. Look again at the second paragraph in the above example. How could you demonstrate for readers additional facts that would strengthen their understanding of the source's credentials? How about mentioning the officer's age? If he is 62, readers will know he's not a rookie. How about mentioning his number of years as a negotiator? If he's been a negotiator for 20 years, he's experienced. How about mentioning he was trained by FBI experts in hostage negotiations? In those ways you can signal readers on how strong your source's credentials are.

Beware Sources Who Request Anonymity

At times, news sources speak with reporters only on condition they not be named. You must be careful because some sources, particularly in government and politics, float "trial balloons." That involves making anonymous statements so the source can judge public reaction without taking responsibility. Or, sources issue anonymous statements to boost their own careers or departmental positions in the never-ending tug and pull of politics. Nevertheless, much important news surfaces only because reporters agree (carefully and in consultation with editors) to grant anonymity. In such cases, you must do all you can to *characterize* the authority and rank and thus, reliability of your sources. For example, consider this *New York Times* story:

WASHINGTON—President Bush appealed to President Mikhail S. Gorbachev today to avoid military force in Lithuania as the Administration sought to balance its formal support for Lithuanian independence with its concern for stability in Eastern Europe.

While the Administration has taken a muted approach in its public statements to avoid increasing tension between Moscow and Lithuania, officials said it has privately warned the Soviet Union that the use of military force would be a serious setback for relations between Moscow and the West. . . .

A senior United States official said "the aspirations of the Lithuanians must remain our primary objective. . . ."

In his second paragraph above, the *Times* writer attributes background interpretation to "officials." That doesn't give readers much reason to lend full confidence to the story. So, in a subsequent paragraph, attribution is pegged to "A *senior* United States official," which gives readers at least some help as they judge for themselves the authoritativeness of this account. Deeper in the story, the writer signals readers on *why* the Bush administration is treading so delicately and why the *Times* is forced to quote anonymous officials:

At a time when American interests have become increasingly entangled with Mr. Gorbachev's political fortunes, Administration officials are privately expressing surprise, and apparently some frustration, that Mr. Gorbachev has not gained more control over the pace of Lithuania's quest for independence.

The United States has carefully avoided offering any solution to either side. Mr. Bush said this approach was intended to avoid inflaming tension. . . . *Andrew Rosenthal, "Bush Urges Gorbachev to Avoid a Military Assault in Lithuania,"* The New York Times, *March 23, 1990, p. A-1*

In the example above, how could the source identification ("senior United States official") be strengthened? Well, it would help readers to judge the story's credibility if they knew whether the source is a "senior *White House* aide" or "senior U.S. *State Department* official," and so forth. Give your readers as much source identification as possible.

Incidentally, note in the above example that although the *Times* writer inserts attribution to an authoritative source ("senior United States official"), the story's even flow is not interrupted. Your eyes probably move across that attribution without halting. But for readers who want to know the source of what they're being asked to believe, attribution is there. Also note how the writer strengthens his credibility by displaying for readers the behind-the-scenes maneuvering in the Bush administration. Many readers aren't aware of how reporters work or that they are privy to "inside" information. By weaving such details into your writing you enhance *reader understanding* and *your credibility*.

"Inside" Details Strengthen Your Credibility

In the example that follows, a writer takes another approach by explicitly stating why an anonymous source is being quoted. Note that the language (in italics) serves to strengthen the story's credibility:

ORLANDO, Fla.—When Betsy decided 16 months ago to do something about her drinking problem, she went to the only recovery program she thought would work—Alcoholics Anonymous.

But she knew she was going to have a philosophical dilemma when the others in the room bowed their heads at that first meeting and recited the Lord's Prayer. Then she read the

second step of the 12–step AA program—the one about believing in a higher power. Betsy didn't believe.

"In the very beginning, I did not have a God," said Betsy, 50, who *asked that her real name not be used because anonymity is a cornerstone of AA*. . . . *Susan M. Barbieri,* Orlando Sentinel *dispatch for afternoon newspapers of Feb. 13, 1990*

Issues and Challenges:
The Newswriter and Objectivity

Rewarding, socially useful careers abound in *advocacy journalism*. By wearing an advocate's label you can take a position, express a viewpoint, and use writing skills with great impact to save whales, strive for or against abortion, or crusade for any of the thousands of causes active in today's society.

But you won't have credibility as a *news*writer if you do.

If you make any statement—any *commitment*—when you choose to become a newspaper reporter it is that you have joined the ranks of those who see great merit in striving for facts, for keeping their personal views out of their writing and presenting all sides of issues as objectively and dispassionately as possible.

This concept is controversial. Some journalists say true objectivity cannot be achieved, that each of us is the sum total of personal experiences, and, no matter how hard we try, we inevitably will view the world differently, with highly personal if not prejudiced attitudes. Others argue that journalists *should not* even try for objectivity, that news is far too complex for straightforward reporting of facts and requires interpretation if readers are to understand its complexities. Too often, this presumes reporters are somehow able to locate and understand "truth," then lead readers to it.

Whatever the merits of those objections, most American newspapers make objectivity a goal and will insist that you, as a beginning newswriter, strive for it. (Later, when you're more experienced, you may write *editorials* advocating the newspaper's position on issues, *commentary* or *analytical pieces* interpreting the news, or *personal columns* offering your opinion on any subject, within limits of libel law and good taste!)

As for objectivity, beware of traps in five areas: They are *story selection, source selection, story structure, language selection* and *timing and context*.

Story selection

Unless given a specific assignment, a newswriter typically can opt each day to pursue any of scores, if not hundreds, of story ideas. Even when covering a "beat"— a specific news area or subject—the possibilities are endless for "trending" the news simply through story selection.

Let's say, for example, you're on the police beat. Today you have time to do an "enterprise" piece—a story going beyond "he said, they said" and looking behind the scenes, wrapping up developments in a single, easily comprehensible package for readers. You could (1) do a story on how many crooks the city police department catches, or (2) do one on how many crooks it *doesn't* catch. One story reflects well on the police chief; the other doesn't. The danger is in letting your personal feelings about the chief creep into your decision on which story to do. If you're sore at the chief, step back from the story selection process and ask yourself which story truly is more important and which best serves your readers' interests.

In a wider sense, the danger is that you can opt, even subconsciously, to do only those stories that agree with your thinking. Let's say you are strongly anti-abortion, for example. Do anti-abortion stories simply seem more newsworthy than pro-abortion stories? Examine your own secret passions, commitments, prejudices (we all have them) and eliminate them from the story selection process.

Source selection

The next decision that can destroy objectivity and put special "spin" or direction on a story is your selection of sources to interview. Are you unthinkingly gravitating toward sources who are anti-abortion? Are they, well, more congenial than pro-abortion sources? Do people whose thinking agrees with yours seem smarter than others? We'll discuss this later with reporting techniques, but a test of your objectivity in source selection is:

Whether your sources are *authoritative,* truly in a position to know and deliver the information you need, and

Whether you have selected sources from *all sides* of the issue at hand.

A Republican janitor in City Hall cannot provide authoritative, balancing comment on the city budget submitted by the Democrat mayor.

Story structure

However objective you are in selecting story idea and sources, you can throw a story awry by improper presentation of facts. Open with 10 paragraphs of the anti-abortion viewpoint and hold until the 11th paragraph the other side's position and you have destroyed the objectivity of your story. *Balance* in story structure, essential to objectivity, does *not* mean establishing some silly measurement such as providing three column inches of type for one viewpoint and precisely three inches for another. Balance does *not* mean giving space or treatment to patently stupid "balancing comment." The Ku Klux Klan may be a serious news story; its racial theories aren't. Balance *does* mean exposing readers to various authoritative, reasoned viewpoints of a controversy as you lead readers through a story.

Language selection

A subtle way of unthinkingly letting objectivity slip from your writing—or maliciously putting spin on it—is selecting language that creates unbalanced impressions in readers' minds. Note the difference if you write that a politician "stiffly acknowledged the crowd's applause" or "smilingly waved back at the applauding crowd." What a difference it makes if you write that a murder defendant "answered with remorse" or "responded cockily" to the prosecutor's questions. Was a *Wall Street Journal* reporter dispassionate in writing that a source "began lamely" to speak? What picture did a *New York Times* reporter create by writing of a U.S. Senate aide "strutting into a committee room . . . whispering into the ear of his mentor . . ."? What's the difference between "smile," "grin," and "grimace"? A great deal, if you use them interchangeably to describe, say, how the president of the United States responds to a reporter's question.

Complete neutrality in language arguably cannot be achieved—and probably shouldn't be. Catching the nuances of life for your readers is part of your job, and precision use of properly descriptive language is one of your tools. But striving for objectivity requires fair, evenhanded use of language.

Timing and context

There is a great difference between doing a series on crime in the streets when the mayor is not running for reelection—or just weeks before she is. Readers can draw entirely different perceptions from precisely the same story, depending on when it is published and other news developing around it. It's not enough to strive for objectivity in selecting, sourcing, structuring and writing a news story. Its impact must be considered, too. That, like most issues in ethics, is controversial among journalists. Some say reporters and editors who hesitate on stories because they might have adverse impact are judging news not on its merits but, rather, on possible public reaction. That "ethical-reactive" approach, some say, can lead journalists to avoid controversial stories. Others say a story's impact must be judged before publication in this era of nuclear weapons, near panic over public health threats, economic unrest and other emotional issues.

Often you'll need to protect your source from official retribution for speaking out. Always let your readers know why. In a story on the inability of New York City police to stop drug traffic, a *New York Times* writer enlists reader understanding:

"It's never really going to change," said an embittered Bronx narcotics detective. "The whole system collapsed years ago, and nobody's willing to own up to it.

"There's so much money in drugs," said the detective, who asked not be named to avoid trouble with his superiors. "Power is money and money is power. That's the vicious cycle. When I make retirement in 12 years, the drugs will still be here."

John Kifner, "Bush's Drug War: Scorn on Besieged Streets," The New York Times, Sept. 8, 1989, p. A-1

Caution: Were New York police inclined toward retribution, could they run down a "Bronx narcotics detective" who will retire in "12 years"? If you agree to protect a source, ensure that you do.

QUOTING SURVEYS AND DOCUMENTS

When quoting documents or survey results, always inform your readers who issued them—and why.

Readers draw one conclusion if you quote from a "Master Plan for City Beautification" and let it go at that. They draw quite another if you go a step further and explain the plan is camouflage for a chamber of commerce scheme to establish a nuclear waste dump on the city's outskirts—and "beautify" it by planting trees around it.

Plans, documents, survey results—all can be issued with ulterior motives, just as those unidentified officials can drop their anonymous quotes on you for special reasons.[5]

Note how explicit the *Sunday* (Portland) *Oregonian* is in telling readers who sponsored a poll on public attitudes toward Mayor Bud Clark, who conducted it *and* what survey methodology was used:

More Portlanders are critical of Bud Clark's job performance than at any time since he became mayor in 1985, according to a poll conducted for The Oregonian.

Almost three-fourths of Portland voters rate the mayor's job performance as either fair or poor. Only 25 percent said that they thought the mayor was doing a good job, and a mere 2 percent said that Clark's performance was excellent.

The figures from a poll, conducted Feb. 2–4 by Griggs-Anderson Research, represent a dramatic decline in the mayor's standing with the public since 1988. In another poll, taken 10 months ago, almost half said that Clark was doing a good or excellent job. . . .

Always Explain Polling Methodology

In a chart depicting poll results, the *Sunday Oregonian* adds this:

About the poll: Griggs-Anderson Research conducted telephone interviews with 400 randomly sampled registered voters in Portland between Feb. 2 and 4. The sampling error is plus or minus 4.9 percent, meaning that in 19 out of 20 cases the true result would be within 4.9 percent of the poll results. *Gordon Oliver, "Poll Shows Mayor at Lowest Ebb," Sunday Oregonian, Feb. 11, 1990, p. B-5*

In the example above, writer Oliver is not only completely open about who sponsored the survey, but also adds another dimension that builds reader confidence in how he handled the story:

> Clark refused to talk about the poll results. "He said, 'I'm not going to comment on a poll,'" said Tim Gallagher, an executive assistant to the mayor.

Always seek—and insert in your story—balancing comment. Readers don't trust one-sided stories (any more than *you* trust classmates who say their grades are plummeting because professors "don't like me"; surely, you wonder, there's another side to that story). And, if the other side won't comment, tell readers that too. Covering a flap over Jane Pauley's departure from NBC's "Today" show and Deborah Norville's ascent, a *Wall Street Journal* writer demonstrates to readers he sought balancing comment:

Carefully Insert Balancing Comment

> Mr. (Mike) Gartner, the NBC News president, declines to comment on any aspect of this story. NBC News Senior Vice President Dick Ebersol, who orchestrated Ms. Norville's ascent, didn't return phone calls. *Kevin Goldman, "Was Today Mess Just a Plot to Make Jane Pauley a Star?," The Wall Street Journal, March 12, 1990, p. A-1*

QUOTING OTHER MEDIA

It's considered bad form among newspaper folks to quote other media too often. That's believed to indicate you and your newspaper lack initiative. And, of course, if you're quoting another newspaper all the time why shouldn't readers drop you and read it? But sometimes you must quote other media, and when you do, explain why *and* establish their credentials.

Note how the *Washington Post* provides background to readers when quoting an Indian newspaper in a story on possible war between India and Pakistan:

> The Times of India, an influential English-language daily with close ties to the government, reported today that India's home minister, Mufti Mohammed Sayeed, now believes that war with Pakistan "would be fully justified if the objective of freeing Kashmir from the stranglehold of the secessionists was achieved."
>
> The newspaper quoted Sayeed as saying privately. . . .
>
> The reported remarks, coupled with a statement by Prime Minister V.P. Singh this week that Indians should prepare themselves psychologically for war with Pakistan, mark the first time that Indian leaders have suggested that alleged interference by Pakistan in Kashmir could justify an offensive war. *Steve Coll, "Assault on Pakistan Gains Favor in India," Washington Post, April 15, 1990, p. A-25*

Below, a writer attributes a story to "news reports," then provides details that help readers decide for themselves how reliable the reports are:

NEW DELHI—At least 29 people were killed and about 25 wounded today in Srinagar, capital of the state of Jammu and Kashmir, when Indian troops fired on pro-independence crowds, news reports said.

The United News of India, quoting the Kashmir radio, said 15 people were killed and 20 wounded when troops fired at crowds. . . .

The government-run All India Radio reported that seven people were killed. . . . *Sanjoy Hazarika, "Indian Troops Kill 29 Protestors in Secessionist Rally in Kashmir," The New York Times, March 2, 1990, p. A-1*

QUOTING RUMORS AND TALES FROM TRAVELERS

Our business is reporting facts we've checked and double-checked. Sometimes, however, a rumor or unconfirmed report can be so extraordinarily important that you must report it. When you do, take pity on your readers and explain precisely what you have (and have not) pinned down.

Note how an *Atlanta Constitution* pro handled a rumor:

WASHINGTON—As unconfirmed reports surfaced Tuesday that Kremlin leader Mikhail S. Gorbachev plans to resign as head of the Soviet Communist Party, the Bush administration scrambled to assess them and their possible effect on relations between the two superpowers.

In a report Tuesday from Moscow, Cable News Network said Mr. Gorbachev is considering resigning his post as head of the Communist Party but would retain his position as Soviet president. . . .

CNN said it had been told by a "well-informed and usually reliable Communist Party source" that Mr. Gorbachev. . . . *Andrew Alexander, "Gorbachev to Quit Party Leadership?," Atlanta Constitution, Jan. 31, 1990, p. A-1*

The *Atlanta Constitution* aided readers in another way that day: Phil Kloer, TV critic, published a detailed analysis of how CNN (Cable News Network) broke the story, who the correspondent was (Steve Hurst, "a 12–year Moscow veteran with NBC and The Associated Press . . ."), and how the networks characterized the rumor (CBS mentioned "rumors"; ABC, "a swirl of rumor and speculation"; NBC said there was "lots of speculation but no confirmation").

Unfortunately, rumors can have all the devastating effect of confirmed news. On Wall Street, the Dow Jones industrial average, a closely watched indicator of investor sentiment, fell 10.14 points on the Gorbachev rumor.

And, of course, rumors can be wrong. The day of the Gorbachev story, the *Constitution* also fronted this story:

TORONTO—Contrary to rumors around Atlanta earlier this week, Toronto is not pulling out of the race for the 1996 Olympics. Furthermore, some Toronto leaders do not consider Atlanta as their city's chief competition for the bid. *Barry Brown, "Toronto Sticks With Campaign for Olympics," Atlanta Constitution, Jan. 31, 1990, p. A-1*

You Seldom Win in Reporting Rumors

Remember this unfortunate *fact* about *rumors:* If you report them and they later prove wrong, you'll likely be remembered by your readers as having dished out erroneous reports—even if you originally labeled them "rumors." Newswriters seldom win by reporting rumors.

Much of the information you handle as a newswriter comes to you second (or third) hand. Note below how a *New York Times* veteran correspondent handles traveler reports from isolated Albania:

BONN—Western diplomats and people who have traveled recently in Albania are discounting reports of anti-Communist demonstrations in the northern part of the county. But they see signs that the Albania government has grown concerned that the Democratic tide rolling through Eastern Europe may yet threaten Europe's last Stalinist citadel.

The reports of unrest in the isolated country of 2.3 million people came mostly from neighboring Yugoslavia. . . .

One report by Tanjug, the official Yugoslav press agency, said. . . .

A Western diplomat who spent most of Jan. 11 in Shkoder said. . . .

In recent months, Albanians who live along the country's borders. . . .

While dismissing the reports of demonstrations, Westerners in Tirana, the Albanian capital, and other cities noted. . . . *David Binder, "Westerners Discount Reports of Unrest in North Albania," The New York Times, national edition, Jan. 31, 1990, p. A-8*

Note above how writer Binder illustrates the *character* of the information he is reporting by opening each paragraph with explicit details on his sources. Binder *levels with his readers*—and, consequently, readers who have followed his byline for years read him with confidence. For many young newswriters, inserting attribution without interrupting narrative flow is a large problem. It need not be.

Readers don't find attribution as interruptive as you might think. They read quickly over "he said . . . she said . . . they said . . ."—and that, incidentally, is the best way of inserting attribution in your writing. And, if you insert attribution with care, you lessen even more the possibility it'll destroy your writing rhythm. For example:

No:

She said the plane was reported overdue.

He said the plane crashed last night.

They said an investigation is under way.

Yes:

The plane was reported overdue, she said. It crashed last night, he said.

An investigation is under way (as always following a plane crash, so no attribution is necessary).

When inserting attribution it's not necessary to tie each fact directly to its source, as in the illustration above. It's only necessary to arrange facts and attribution logically so readers can determine, with reasonable ease, where you got your facts. For example, a writer reports the arrest of a member of a rock band on charges the band member raped a 15-year-old girl. In the lead and each subsequent paragraph, the writer tightly ties facts of the story to "police said." But repeating "police said" gets monotonous. So, to vary things a bit, the writer groups two paragraphs of facts under a single sentence of attribution (italics added):

Ways to Avoid Repetitious Attribution

According to the warrants:

The girl drove with friends May 11 from Milwaukee to attend the rock concert at a Town of Menasha bar.

Later, the girl accompanied a 17-year-old friend to the band's hotel

room. When the 15-year-old arrived at the motel, one of the band members ran out of his room, grabbed her and carried her into a room where he and other band members forced her to have sexual intercourse.

You also can group paragraphs of facts under single sentences of attribution such as these:

Police gave these details:

Witnesses gave this account:

Testimony revealed this picture:

Her account:

His advice:

Their proposal:

REPORTING GRAPHIC DETAILS

Inserting graphic details in your writing is one of your best devices for demonstrating to readers that you've fulfilled your journalistic responsibility for reporting accurately and fully. Graphic details can demonstrate you were there, that you have the facts.

For example, can you doubt the *Los Angeles Times* reporters who wrote the following story were really on the job?

A 12-year-old Hesperia boy who wandered away from a church group during an outing in the San Gabriel Mountains in the Angeles Forest died Sunday, just hours after rescuers found him partially frozen under a blanket of snow on a narrow ridge where he had spent the night.

After an all-night search in dense fog, snow and strong winds, a Los Angeles County Sheriff's Department rescue team found Ruben Allred at 10:25 a.m. after spotting a tuft of his blond hair sticking out of a "little mound of snow" about a mile from where he was last seen, Sheriff's Sgt. Gordon Carn said.

The boy was face down, arms pulled tightly to his sides, hands clutching his light cotton jacket close to his chest. He was clad only in the jacket, jeans and tennis shoes, the sergeant said.

"Judging from the snow built up around the boy," Carn said, "he probably tried to tuck himself in at about 12 [midnight] to 2 o'clock."
Sheryl Stolberg and John H. Lee, "Lost Boy Dies After Night in Angeles Forest," Los Angeles Times, Jan. 15, 1990, p. A-1

Read again the second and third paragraphs above. Can those writers get you any closer to the "narrow ridge" where the body was found without actually taking you there?

Note below how two *Los Angeles Times* writers assure readers they were on the job when an infamous criminal was released from prison:

Charles David Rothenberg was released from prison Wednesday under the tightest parole measures in California history—nearly seven years after he burned his son beyond recognition in a twisted plot to hurt the wife who divorced him.

At 12:40 a.m., Rothenberg was driven from an undisclosed California prison *under guard by six parole agents,* who delivered him to an unnamed parole destination sometime before 9 a.m., officials said.

Dressed in blue jeans and a chambray shirt and toting two boxes of personal belongings. . . . Nancy Wride and Tony Marcano, "Rothenberg Paroled Under Strict Controls," Los Angeles Times, Jan. 25, 1990, p. A-1

Note above how graphic detail (italicized) is woven into the story. Don't you feel *confidence* in these writers?

Sometimes, graphic detail is most effective if it isn't woven in so subtly but, rather, inserted—bang—in several strong paragraphs in a news story. Below are three paragraphs Andrew J. Glass of Cox Newspapers inserted in a lengthy story about the Gulf War. Employing you-are-there details, Glass takes his readers to the front:

In late January, as a full moon rises in a near-cloudless sky, the Saudi Arabian sand dunes turn fearsomely cold. It is not a good place to get lost. A week of unusually heavy rains have left large patches of deep mud in the desert, which trap unwary vehicles.

Recently, however, the days have turned bright and sunny. The mud is drying up, which makes the troops happy.

Every few minutes or so, Cobra helicopters pass overhead as they patrol the desert roads at what would be called tree-top level if there were any trees. *Andrew J. Glass, Cox Newspapers, dispatch for morning papers of Jan. 31, 1991*

Often, direct quotes inject graphic detail and lend unmistakable authenticity to a story. A *San Francisco Chronicle* writer used direct quotes to describe seven people drowning:

Direct Quotes Give Stories Authenticity

"Throw me a rope!" one of the victims screamed before disappearing.

"It was really horrifying, realizing the rescuers weren't going to bring all those people back," said Pierre LaBossiere, who was on the shore watching the dramatic rescue.

"It was sickening watching them one by one falling through the ice. It was very scary and there was nothing we could do." *Michael Taylor, "1 of 7 Bodies Retrieved From Ice,"* San Francisco Chronicle, *Feb. 21, 1990, p. A-1*

Note above how the writer builds *three* paragraphs of quotes around a single attribution ("said Pierre LaBossiere") in the second paragraph *and* neatly explains how the source came to witness the tragedy ("who was on the shore watching . . .").

Using a quote just as you got it—bad grammar and all—can lend enormous credibility to your writing. An AP pro recognizes that:

Skidmore, Mo. (AP)—It has been a year since Kenneth Rex McElroy, described as the town bully, was shot to death on the main street of this farming community. Despite two grand jury investigations, no one has been charged in the killing. Few residents seem to care.

"It ain't easy to feel bad for somebody that never did no good for your town," says the postmaster, Jim Hartman. "I can't think that anyone feels any different than you would about the people who invented penicillin. Nobody tried to hang them for finding a way to kill a germ."

Mr. McElroy was widely regarded as an armed tough who stole livestock and anything else he could. Last summer he was killed in a barrage of gunfire after climbing into his air-conditioned Silverado pickup truck, with his wife Trena and a six-pack of beer at his side. The truck engine burned up in the half-hour he was left slumped in the cab, his foot lodged on the accelerator.

"It's really a shame about the Silverado," said Dave Dunbar, a former marshal who said Mr. McElroy once threatened him with a high-powered rifle. "That was a really nice truck." *The Associated Press dispatch for morning newspapers of July 11, 1982*

Some lessons to be learned in the above:

1. Most of the time you should avoid unnecessarily embarrassing people with direct quotation of their grammatical errors. That's done by *removing quote*

Never Change Language Inside Quote Marks

marks and paraphrasing the quotation, *never* by changing the language inside the quote marks. If you put quotes around it you signal readers that is *exactly* what was said.

2. If a quote catches the mood of your story, *use it,* bad grammar and all. The King's English wasn't spoken that day in Skidmore when they surrounded the bully's pickup truck.

3. Tune your eye (and keyboard) to quotes that support your lead.

Note in the fourth paragraph above how the former marshal evidences more regret about the ruined pickup truck than the slain man—which, of course, is irony that supports the lead and central thrust of the story.

Using extended direct quotations from a transcript can reveal for readers the complexities of the news and simultaneously build credibility by illustrating how reporters strive to get it straight. A writer describes the Bush administration's ambiguous diplomatic language in talking about possible deals to free hostages held in the Middle East. The story describes how the White House spokesman, Marlin Fitzwater, bobs and weaves at a news conference, and adds:

Then the following exchange took place between Mr. Fitzwater and reporters:

Reporter: "Are the 400 Shiites being held by Israel and its allies in south Lebanon hostages or prisoners of war?"

Mr. Fitzwater: "We believe all hostages should be released."

Reporter: "Well, what about these 400? Are they hostages in your view?"

Mr. Fitzwater: "I'm not going to get involved in giving definition to those hostages."

Reporter: "Well you certainly are implying that you think they're hostages, since you responded to a question about them that way."

Mr. Fitzwater: "Sorry. We're not going to give a definition to it."

Reporter: "Marlin, why should we not read this as a double standard?"

Mr. Fitzwater: "Because our policy is very clear for one and for all. We don't believe in hostage taking, period." *Thomas L. Friedman, "Hostage Sleight of Hand," The New York Times national edition, May 2, 1990, p. A-1*

The strength of extended quotation from a transcript is the often dramatic detail thus incorporated in your story. The weakness, of course, is that it forces readers to sort through sprawling verbiage in search of meaning—a task you normally must fulfill because most of your readers lack the time, inclination, or journalism training to be reporters themselves.[6]

Tell Readers How You Know

Inserting graphic detail sometimes creates in readers' minds this question: "How could the writer possibly know that?" You are obliged to anticipate and answer that implied question.

For example, don't you wonder how a *Wall Street Journal* writer, in the lead paragraph below, *knew* "alarm bells began ringing . . ."?

Five hundred feet deep in the Norwegian Sea, 250 miles north of Norway, alarm bells began ringing in the Soviet submarine Komsomolets as it spied on the U.S. submarine fleet.

Fire had broken out in the stern, in the seventh compartment. And the killer sub, whose torpedoes were armed with nuclear warheads, was in grave danger.

In his second paragraph, the writer rushes to explain that those details came from a Soviet sailor who was there:

"I jumped out of my cot, pulled on my pants and ran to the central control room," recalls Capt. First Rank Boris Kolyada. There, an officer was feverishly calling on the intercom:

"Seventh, seventh," the officer shouted. But there was no answer from the seaman on duty.

Though the high-tech "Mike" class vessel managed to surface, flames spread rapidly forward to other compartments. For hours, crewmen fought the blaze, smoke and poisonous gases while waiting for someone to answer their SOS. But when the sub went down for the last time, its commander and others remained trapped on board.

But, readers wonder, isn't it highly unusual for American journalists to learn such details of previously secret Soviet disasters? Yes, and the *Journal* writer explains that, too, in the next two paragraphs:

The sinking of a sub is a relatively rare event. The U.S. has lost but two submarines in 25 years, the Soviets five. Because subs are stealthy military vessels, their operations obviously are secret, and detailed accounts of sinkings are scarce.

But thanks to glasnost, this case is different. Admirals have been giving interviews on Soviet TV. Soviet military journals—Naval Digest and Red Star—have printed analyses of the accident, which occurred April 7, 1989. The Soviet press, including Pravda and Izvestia, has printed excerpts from the ship's log and interviews with survivors who have vivid stories to tell. It is all quite astonishing to U.S. intelligence officials. . . . *William M. Carley, "How Secret Soviet Sub and Its Nuclear Arms Sank North of Norway,"* The Wall Street Journal, *March 14, 1990, p. A-1*

Sometimes the best way to answer the "how-do-you-know-that?" question is by writing that you were there. A writer describes excitement in Moscow over the city's first McDonald's restaurant:

"Do you need an invitation to get in?" a teenage girl asked reporters leaving the restaurant after a media preview Tuesday.

"Not tomorrow. Anyone can go then," one reporter replied.

"Really?" the girl shrieked, clapping her hands in delight as she scurried off to tell her friends standing timidly behind her. *T. Elaine Carey, "Moscow Enters Burger Age,"* Atlanta Constitution, *Jan. 31, 1990, p. A-3*

Describing the same event, a *Wall Street Journal* writer doesn't mention "a reporter" was there, but with exquisite use of graphic detail and a strong quote, he makes that plain in the following example.

MOSCOW—When Elizaveta Pavlenko, a sprightly 74-year-old pensioner, heard that McDonald's was opening its first Soviet restaurant in Moscow yesterday, she put on her best fur coat and emerald earrings and went to see for herself. Not one to take any chances, she ate a hearty breakfast at home first.

Sitting in the brightly lit restaurant, the biggest McDonald's in the world with indoor eating for 700, she quickly regained her appetite—and her belief that life can be good even in these troubled times. "It's like a holiday," she enthused, toying with her strawberry sundae. The food and the cleanliness are "wonderful," but what struck her most was the service. "Somebody even showed me to my seat and carried my tray," she marveled. "Now, that has never happened to me before." *Peter Gumbel, "Muscovites Queue up at American Icon,"* The Wall Street Journal, *Feb. 1, 1990, p. A-6*

You recognize, of course, that as vivid as are the two examples above, they still are impersonal—stilted, even—when compared to our most common (and, probably, most effective) form of communication, one-to-one conversation between people. If you were at the McDonald's opening in Moscow, describing it in a telephone call home, you would put it something like this:

> So, *I* go into this new McDonald's and *I* see this darling little old lady . . . and *I* say to her . . . and she says to *me.* . . .

Immediately, your listener would have a personalized mental image of *you* talking a mile a minute to some little old Russian lady, and your effort to communicate effectively would be well under way. Unfortunately, it's contrary to newspaper convention to inject "I" and "me" into your writing except under most unusual circumstances. Many writers even shrink from mentioning "a reporter" was there and, instead, say a *newspaper* was there. An example:

> CONVICT LAKE, Calif.—Rescuer Cris Baitx, using first his fists, then his head, had twice punched his way out of the ice on Convict Lake and was going under for a third time.
>
> Panicked, he was drifting in and out of consciousness in the frigid waters where three teenage boys had already disappeared and four other men struggled to stay afloat.
>
> "I was sure I was gone," Baitx told *The Times* on Tuesday. "I was thinking of my wife and kids and are they going to be OK, because I'm history."
> *Tracy Wilkinson and Joel Sappell, "Rescuers Worked Frantically as Victims Slipped Under Ice," Los Angeles Times, Feb. 21, 1990, p. A-1*

Although reporters aren't supposed to inject themselves into the news, newspapers increasingly are with investigative reporting that *creates news*. When that happens, your writing must make the circumstances clear. For example, this is the lead on a *Los Angeles Times* story:

> Newly obtained information about a devastating blast at Mobil's Torrance refinery reveals that human error caused an explosion that has triggered two years of legal, political and regulatory battles for the nation's fifth-largest industrial corporation.

The reader must wonder, "'Newly obtained information . . . '? Obtained by whom? From whom?" The paper answers:

> The Times obtained Mobil memos and the federal safety report, as well as other documents, months after filing requests with the U.S. Occupational Safety and Health Administration and the city of Torrance under the federal Freedom of Information Act. The documents were gathered as part of the city and OSHA's investigation into the explosion. *George Stein, "Mobil Refinery Explosion Laid to Human Error," Los Angeles Times, Feb. 11, 1990, p. B-1*

Note below how the *Atlanta Journal-Constitution* brings readers fully into the picture on its investigation of whether a candidate for governor paid sales taxes generated by two hotel lodges he owned with his brother.

After inquiries from The Atlanta Journal-Constitution, the candidate's brother, Ray Barnes, inspected the lodges' records. The newspaper's questions were prompted by a tip from a source inside the political community. *Jeanne Cummings, "Barnes Admits Not Paying $9,030 in Sales Taxes,"* Atlanta Journal-Constitution, *June 8, 1990, p. A-1*

So, quoting authoritative sources and using graphic detail are two ways to build a bridge of confidence to your readers. But what's really the most important step you can take?

ALWAYS DOUBLE-CHECK FACTS

Fact-checking can be simple.

A reporter asks, "Who are you?," and *hears* this response: "William C. Brown."

Amateur reporter: "Thanks."

Professional reporter: "That's 'C' as in 'Charles'? And, do you spell it, 'B-r-o-w-n'?"

Response: "No, 'Z' for 'Zeke'. And, it's spelled 'B-r-o-w-n-*e*.' First name is 'Wilhelm,' by the way."

Or, fact-checking can be complex, difficult, time-consuming. It can involve massive search of computerized reference works or your newspaper's dusty clip file in the "morgue" (library); it can involve rousting people out of bed in the middle of the night for telephoned questions.

Whether simple or difficult, fact-checking must take you as close as you can get to the perfect, error-free story. For whatever your efforts to achieve credibility, you'll fail if even minor inaccuracies creep into your writing. Mr. Brown*e*, for example, never will quite believe you again if you misspell his name in print. Neither will his spouse, children, relatives, neighbors, business associates . . . the circle of public disaffection with your writing—*your byline*—can widen infinitely from such errors. And, after all, *why should* readers trust your ability to handle a news story's main thrust if you can't spell the principal's name correctly? (See the sidebar on p. 208 for an example of painstaking fact-checking by some AP pros.)

In writing your story, double-check these facts:

1. *Names and titles,* both personal and corporate. Few facts are more crucial to your story's credibility—or easier to check. For certain, the principals in your story won't mind if you ask *them.* And note: Precision is required in such things as whether it's Smith & Son, Smith & Son Co., Smith & Son Corp., or Smith & Son Ltd. . . . (In that connection, recall we noted earlier in this chapter that 77 percent of business leaders believe news organizations are inaccurate. *They* know the difference between a family grocery and a corporation. If *you* don't, check page 52 of *The Associated Press Stylebook and Libel Manual,* 1987 edition.)

Recheck Names, Titles Ages, Locations, Dates

2. *Ages and personal background.* Many people are sensitive about their age. *No* reporter should be afraid to ask. (*Remember:* There are no dumb questions in our business; only dumb reporters who fail to ask.) And get personal background straight. If you think Mr. Brown*e* gets upset when you misspell his name, you should hear him when a newspaper makes errors in his religious, corporate, family or social background!

Reporters Can't Be Afraid to Ask

A Professional's View:
Painstaking Care Builds Credibility

The Associated Press has a reputation for accuracy, and the following account illustrates why. It was written by Richard Rosenblatt, an AP New York sports writer, and published in AP Log, a weekly report for editors and reporters on how news stories were handled. Note the double-checking by AP staffers—and AP members—after CBS fired its well-known sports announcer, Brent Musberger.

Brent Musberger fired?

Yeah, right.

I was ready for something like this. April Fool's Day wasn't going to make a fool of The Associated Press, at least not if I could help it.

As the national sports supervisor on April 1, I walked into the office on alert. For years, media have fallen prey to professional hoaxers, all of whom view April 1 as the high, holy day.

With that knowledge, I began compiling the sports digest. Within hours, the alarm sounded.

Ron Blum, the "Sports on TV" writer who this day was the rewrite man, took a call from Susan Kerr, CBS Sports spokeswoman. Ron has dealt with Ms. Kerr and believed it was she.

Ms. Kerr was calling from Denver, where the media had massed for the next day's NCAA basketball championship game between UNLV and Duke—on CBS.

She read a short statement that said Musberger's contract was not being renewed and his last assignment would be calling the title game.

Blum began writing an "urgent" (an AP story assigned high priority for transmission) while I called (AP) Denver to alert our sports crew to what might be happening.

Then the nagging questions: Brent fired? The day before a big event? With no warning? And why would Ms. Kerr call us in New York when hundreds of reporters were in the same hotel in Denver?

"Let's get back to her, get her to FAX the release," I said. "I want more confirmation. Get Brent on the phone. Get (CBS Sports president Neal) Pilson."

We got Ms. Kerr and again she confirmed the story. So did Robin Brendle, another CBS spokeswoman. "I swear, it's not an April Fool's joke. It's true," another CBS PR person said.

"FAX me the release," I said.

She did, and a bio, too.

At this point, Rick Warner, one of our reporters in Denver, was at CBS' hotel headquarters, trying to get Pilson.

Blum got through to Musberger's room and got someone who identified himself as "Tubbs." He said he'd take a message.

Tubbs called back, identifying himself as Jimmy Tubbs, Musburger's personal assistant. He read a statement that said Brent was surprised at the news.

Blum called Brendle, who confirmed that Tubbs was Musburger's assistant.

Ms. Kerr called back: "I've got Pilson for you."

While Blum was talking to him, he signaled the story was "for real" and moved the urgent.

It was 2:15 p.m., EDT—75 minutes after the first report of Musberger's dismissal.

This was no prank.

It was to almost everyone else.

First, radio stations called. From Los Angeles, St. Louis and Kansas City.

"This Brent story you guys have, it's true? It's April Fool's Day, you know," was the usual query.

"I know. It's true," I said.

Then WFAN, the all-sports radio station in New York, called:

"This isn't true about Brent, is it? You're being fooled."

"No, we're not. Its' true," I said.

Then Bill Taaffe, TV writer for Sports Illustrated, called:

"That Brent story you have can't be true. I've known Brent for 20 years and I never heard of Tubbs," he said.

"Bill," I said, "we've got Pilson on the phone. He's confirmed it."

Then came the clincher.

CBS Sports in New York called:

"That's not true," said the CBS research assistant, who had gone to high school with Blum. "It's a joke. Why did you put that out? It's not real."

"Yes, it is," I said.

By 2:50 p.m., a writethru (a completely new, updated and rewritten story) was on the wire, Warner was tracking down CBS executive producer Ted Shaker, Tubbs and other CBS executives.

The phone calls started slowing down.

Richard Rosenblatt, "Musberger Fired? On April Fool's Day? Nah!" *AP Log,* April 9, 1990, p. 1

3. *Location.* Put City Hall at the corner of Smith and Elm streets, when everybody in town knows it's at Smith and Oak, and you're dead. (And be *certain* you don't have Oak Street traffic running one-way east; everybody but you knows it runs west.) *Precise* location in your story lends credibility. It demonstrates you are a newswriter who cares about the basic building blocks of a story, and the reader confidence you gain with that will aid you in getting across as believable other primary news elements of the story. (Newspaper styles vary on how precise to be. Some editors want a drug raid written as occurring at "Apartment 2-B, on the second floor of a red brick multiple-family dwelling at 1109 E. Maple St." Others, to protect the privacy of uninvolved neighbors, want "a second-floor apartment in the 1100 block of East Maple St.")

4. *Dates.* Write that the school board's public hearing will be Wednesday night—when, oops, you meant Thursday night—and you can draw subscription cancellations, not only complaints, from angry readers who bundled up and set forth on the wrong night. That also won't do much for your credibility with your editors. Get the time right too—and double-check both.

Now, after confirming those basic "building-block" facts, take a wider view of your story:

1. Is your central narrative on what happened correct? Does it, as written, truly describe the news event as you understand it? Our earlier discussions showed how slippery the language can be when you're trying to depict an event accurately. Does your language firmly and accurately grasp it?

2. Does your story accurately *answer all obvious questions* arising from the event and why and how it happened? And, does your writing anticipate and *answer implied questions,* those likely to arise in your readers' minds? For example, if you write that 150 new cases of AIDS occurred in your city, you answer only one very obvious question if you report that hospital facilities are available for victims. Implied questions are many: Is this disease reaching true epidemic proportions here? Is it threatening our general populace? Is our blood supply safe? What can *we,* your readers, do to protect ourselves?

Rethink Accuracy of Your Central Narrative

Yes, we have just completed yet another rundown of the newswriter's basic checklist: the Five W's and How. Again and again, you must return to questioning whether your story fulfills your basic newswriter's mission of explaining—accurately—who, where, what, when, why and how.

But there's more to double-checking the internal dynamics of your story:

A Final Checklist for Accuracy

1. Be certain any *comparisons* are accurate. Are you correct in comparing those 150 new AIDS cases to the "Black Death plague"? Remember, the plague killed *millions* when it swept Asia and Europe in the Middle Ages.

2. Particularly rethink any *characterizations* in your story of a person's beliefs, thinking, feelings and, especially, intent. Remember, even the best reporter can determine only what a person says, not what he or she *thinks* or *feels*.

3. Look again, too, at any technical language or jargon. Is your *translation* correct? It may be colorful and catchy to describe, say, a new giant computer as "an electronic way of counting on your fingers more quickly." But does that really translate the computer's capabilities?

4. How about any *identifiers* you've used? If you identify a corporate raider as a "bear in a corporate china shop" you've (1) used a cliche, and (2) you've butchered it—the trite phrase you're searching for is, "*bull* in a china shop." And (3) you've not *really* described the person accurately.

5. Reread that "housekeeping" paragraph. Does it correctly isolate, define and provide background for the *central issue* in your story? Beware that you didn't over-simplify in your effort to keep background to a minimum so as to avoid interrupting the momentum of your story.

6. And, certainly, *add the numbers again.* Do the components within the story equal the total number mentioned in your lead?

Being inaccurate—flat out, 100 percent wrong—will destroy your newswriter's credibility faster than anything else. But exaggertion—even in its milder forms—comes in a close second.

For example, most of us go through entire careers in journalism without being present to write about a world record being set—in anything. Thus when you're double-checking facts before turning your story over to an editor, pause and think again if you see these words in your writing: biggest, smallest, richest, poorest, hottest, coldest, oldest, youngest, brightest, dumbest, fastest, slowest. . . .

Use those words and you may hear, "Oh, you people in the media never get it right. . . ."

SOURCES FOR DOUBLE-CHECKING

You can check facts by using resources in three broad categories.

Interviews

Interviews Are Best for Double-Checking

We'll explore interviewing more deeply in the discussion of reporting techniques (Chapter 8), but this resource, obviously, is enormous. It involves not only the principals in your story but also others in a position to know: their friends (and enemies), families, neighbors, attorneys, accountants, bankers, employers . . . the list is endless. *Remember: Many* people know a great deal about other people—even the most publicity-shy recluse. Of course, many people in the news are served by others whose job it is to provide you information. They include agents and public relations consultants (who, of course, tend to give you *one side* of the story—the best; so beware). However, many objective, dispassionate sources, for the cost of a telephone call, will talk with expertise on every conceivable subject: Bankers love to talk about banking, attorneys about the law, scientists about science. When you have facts to double-check, put your reporter's legs in action, tune your nose for news, locate authoritative sources—and ask. If the sources you contact say they don't know, ask them who does. Ask, ask, ask.

Your Newspaper's Resources

For readily available information on news of yesterday, today and tomorrow, your newspaper probably is the best resource in town. Back copies of newspapers, often available on microfilm, are day-by-day chronicles of much that's happened in years past. Many newspapers computerize morgue files of clips, providing fast access to background material. Get to know your newspaper's librarians—well. They are gold mines of information and often maintain files that are particularly strong in three areas: local personalities, corporations, and major news events of the past. But a word of caution: Errors *do* slip into newspaper reporting and, thus, into newspaper files. Don't take too much for granted when pawing through old clips.

If your newspaper uses AP service, it is a *member* (not client) of AP, and that gives you an enormous resource. If you are doing a story on, say, local crime rates, a call to The Associated Press can get similar rates for other cities of like size, your state, the nation—and add a valuable, wider perspective to your story. As a membership organization, AP puts high priority on serving its newspapers and can give you, even on the smallest daily, international resources from which to draw.

Many newspapers also have computerized information services, such as Nexis, that provide access to other newspapers' morgues or data banks. Soon after you arrive for your new job, thoroughly check out your newspaper's resources.

By the way, newspaper lore *is* correct: The city editor and veteran reporters indeed are walking repositories of local history and information. Seek their advice and counsel. But don't make a practice of leaning on them too heavily. (For example, by shouting across the busy newsroom, "How do you spell Cincinnati?" Nothing annoys veterans more than young reporters who don't know how to use a dictionary, atlas, stylebook or other desktop reference works.)

Standard Reference Works

On a local level, city directories list address-by-address information on adult names, occupations, telephone numbers, and other facts. And they also list names and numbers of *neighbors* who might be able to help you track down information on a person. Telephone books provide quick double-check on names and addresses. Chambers of commerce and city governments often issue helpful fact books on population, economy, tax receipts, business activity, and so forth.

Most state governments issue lists of agencies, officials and telephone numbers handy for fact-checking. A wealth of information is available for the asking in most states: marriage and divorce rates, tax receipts, auto registrations, and so forth.

On the federal level, massive information resources are available. Two publications list much of it. The *Monthly Catalog of United States Government Publications* indexes government documents by author and subject. The *United States Government Manual* shows you where publications originate. The *Congressional Directory* lists government employees and agencies.

Don't overlook old standbys: *The World Almanac* is invaluable. *Who's Who* publications carry biographical data from the world, America, sections of America and occupational specialties (finance and industry, religion and so forth). *Facts on File* provides background information, heavy with figures, for many subjects in the news. And, perhaps atop a file cabinet, covered with dust, you'll find somewhere in your newspaper various encyclopedia that are crammed with facts and figures. Dust 'em off.

Professional organizations can respond quickly with factual material (along with their own propaganda, if you're not careful). They exist on national, state and local levels for doctors, accountants, lawyers, electricians, plumbers, teachers—you name the occupation, an organization exists that can help you.

Of course, one of your first stops when you arrive on your new job should be at your local library. Establish personal contact with reference librarians. They generally are helpful types who can put a finger on just about any fact you might need.

And, it is facts, facts, facts that build that bridge of confidence we're all after.

Summary Checklist

- [ ] Credibility, a newswriter's greatest asset, is built over a career through dedication to accuracy, detail and precision.

- [ ] A barrier to credibility is widespread public feeling that journalists can't and don't want to get the news right.

- [ ] To build credibility you must not only write snappy leads and pull readers into your stories but also demonstrate you are putting before them a credible, accurate story.

- [ ] Quoting authoritative sources is the single most important step toward making your writing crackle with believability.

- [ ] Provide details on your sources' credentials so readers can judge the credibility of what you are asking them to believe.

- [ ] Whenever possible, let your story show readers how the news was obtained and from whom.

- [ ] In quoting survey results and documents always report precisely who issued them and why; let readers judge your sources' motives.

- [ ] When you must quote other media, explain to readers why and establish the credentials or authoritativeness of the source you're quoting.

- [ ] When forced to write unconfirmed reports or rumors, give readers precise details on what you have (and have not) pinned down.

- [ ] Newswriters shouldn't worry that inserting attribution destroys the narrative flow of their stories; readers mostly pass easily over "He said . . . she said. . . ."

- [ ] Inserting graphic detail in your writing helps demonstrate to readers you've reported accurately and fully.

- [ ] Direct quotes can add drama and believability to writing.

- [ ] Professional newswriters anticipate questions that will arise in readers' minds (such as, "How can the writer possibly know that"?) and answer them in the story.

- [ ] Before turning your story over to an editor, double-check your facts.

- [ ] Double-check names, titles, ages, personal background of principals in your story. Also check location and dates—completing yet another review of the Five W's and How.

- [ ] Also check whether your central narrative truly describes the news event. Review the appropriateness of any comparisons, characterizations, translations of jargon, and use of identifiers.

- [ ] Double-check facts through interviews, in addition to your newspaper's resources (its morgue, AP, computerized information sources) and standard reference works.

RECOMMENDED READING

For an excellent start toward understanding the media's credibility problem, see Times Mirror's continuing series, "The People & The Press," Times Mirror Center for The People & The Press, 1875 I Street, NW, Suite 1110, Washington, D.C., 20006. Also extremely helpful: "Relating to Readers in the '80s," a survey commissioned by the American Society of Newspaper Editors and conducted by Clark, Martire & Bartolomeo, Inc., May 1984; "Changing Needs of Changing Readers," sponsored by ASNE in 1978; "Credibility," a 1984 survey by Associated Press Managing Editors Association; "Newspaper Credibility: Building Reader Trust," ASNE Research Report, 1985, P.O. Box 17004, Washington, D.C., 20041.

For examples of outstanding writers handling graphic detail, see Meyer Berger, *The Eight Million* (New York: Simon & Schuster, 1942); Roy Peter Clark, ed., *Best Newspaper Writing* (St. Petersburg, Fla.: Poynter Institute, published annually); Gerald Gross, ed., *The Best of the Post* (New York: Popular Library, 1979); Louis L. Snyder and Richard B. Morris, *A Treasury of Great Reporting* (New York: Simon and Schuster, 1949); Louis L. Snyder, ed., *Masterpieces of War Reporting* (New York: Julian Messner, Inc., 1962).

NOTES

1. "The People & Press, Part 5," Times Mirror, November 1989, p. 26. The survey, conducted by the Gallup Organization, interviewed 1,507 members of the general public, 96 government leaders, 100 "academic elites," and 79 business leaders.
2. "The People & Press," Times Mirror, January 1986, p. 10.
3. Ibid, p. 9.
4. Many news releases are issued routinely in advance of delivery, and they are published or broadcast with similar hedging language. Some government reports are issued days in advance with an "embargo" note stating when they can be published.
5. Growth of politically acute special-interest groups gives rise to a multitude of reports and surveys issued for partisan purposes but not always so labeled.
6. For insights into interplay between reporters and politicians see presidential press conference transcripts regularly published in *The New York Times*. Following the pattern of questioning revealed in the transcripts is excellent training for young newswriters.

Exercise 7–1   The Credibility Factor

Interview separately two friends on their opinions of the credibility of your college newspaper or local daily. Question them on attitudes toward the general believability of the newspaper and *any specifics they mention. Below, in about 200 words, write a general summary lead, followed by a story heavy with direct quotes. Be precise in describing names, ages, background and credentials of your interviewees.*

Exercise 7–2   Credibility and Unanswered Questions

Search the front page of today's Wall Street Journal *for examples of questions left unanswered in news stories. Scrutinize stories for jargon that's not translated. Question whether stories are written for a lay audience or experts. Note any unanswered "implied" questions. In about 150 words, discuss your findings in precise detail.*

Exercise 7–3   Catching Quotes

In this exercise your instructor will read a statement to the class (or speak extemporaneously, with a tape recorder handy). In 200 words, write below a general lead that summarizes the instructor's statement. Then, write a story of mainly direct quotes. This exercise is designed to test your ability to reproduce exact quotes faithfully and to paraphrase correctly those you don't catch with precision.

Exercise 7–4   Finding Authoritative Sources

In this exercise, draw up a list of authoritative sources you would approach if given a story assignment. List below their names, ages, addresses, telephone numbers, and, importantly, their credentials that make you regard them as "authoritative." You will need sources on all sides of any controversies. At your instructor's discretion, draw up lists of local sources you would approach on one or several of these issues:

Abortion   Controversy over rock music lyrics
Child abuse   Graduation rates for athletes
Drinking laws in your town   Enrollment levels and projections at your school
Student loan availability   Importance/efficiency of student government

_____

_____

_____

_____

_____

_____

_____

_____

_____

_____

_____

_____

_____

_____

_____

_____

_____

_____

_____

_____

Exercise 7–5   Spotting Holes

Study the lead story in today's New York Times *(or another newspaper your instructor designates) and, in about 200 words, address these questions: Does the writer establish credibility by including sufficient attribution and quotations from authoritative sources? Does the writer use anonymous sources and, if so, are readers told why? Are any anonymous sources described fully enough so their credentials are established for readers? Is graphic detail used? Do you see any implied questions raised in the story but unanswered by the writer? In general, do you have confidence this writer "has the goods"? Is this an account you trust?*

Exercise 7–6   Precision Handling of Facts

The following two cases were handled today in Harris County Superior Court by Judge Jackson Smith. Write a general combo lead, then handle each case in the detail you think it merits. This is a test of your ability to handle detail carefully and accurately.

John Jones, 26, P.O. Box 86, Elk Grove, pleaded guilty to possessing a controlled substance (cocaine) and was sentenced to three years supervised probation and a $1,000 fine and $50 fees, at $75 a week beginning Friday. A misdemeanor marijuana possession charge is being dismissed.

Ray C. Green, Route 1, Box 263, East Point, pleaded guilty to possessing cocaine April 25 and June 15, 1989; sentenced to three years in prison and four years supervised probation on each count, to be served concurrently. Two charges of selling a controlled substance, possessing drug-related object and possession of a firearm by a convicted felon were dismissed.

Exercise 7–7   Using Quotes

The following exchange took place between President Bush and reporters at a news conference. Write a summary lead, then use both question and answer in partial or full quotes as you complete your story. Use "today" as your time element.

Q.   Mr. President, the conflict in Israel between the Israelis and the Palestinians seems to become increasingly violent.

A.   Yes.

Q.   Do you think the Israelis at this point are acting appropriately and responsibly?

A.   Well, I have called on both sides for restraint. I've called on the Israel forces to show constraint. I'm worried about it. I am troubled about the loss of human life in this area.

     . . . And the answer is to get these talks going. And I will do everything I can to—to get the talks for peace going.

Q.   Well, Mr. President, is there anything that the United States can do with its enormous clout with Israel, to push the Israelis to be more open to these peace talks?

A.   Well, the problem we face right now is this, almost an interregnum. I mean, there's no firm decision-making government in place. So we're in a bit of a hiatus because of that.

Exercise 7–8   Publishing Graphic Details

Examine a news story that your instructor will designate (in today's New York Times, *or another newspaper) for use of graphic detail. What graphic detail does the writer include? Does it add to the credibility of the story? Is detail insufficient? If so, in what ways? If you were the reporter/writer, which additional detail would you seek to better tell the story to readers? Respond in about 200 words.*

Part 4

The Art of Reporting, Legal Traps and Ethical Questions

We turn now to three subjects that must be studied by any aspiring newswriter: *reporting skills*, the basics of *press law*, and how to start building a *personal code of journalistic ethics*.

Reporting is important because it is the foundation of all we do in journalism. Only by reporting news accurately, fairly and as fully as possible can we discharge our responsibilities as journalists. And only by developing your reporting skills simultaneously with your newswriting skills will you qualify eventually as a professional. We'll look at how to develop reporting strengths in Chapter 8.

Understanding press law is important because there are dangerous legal traps awaiting you out there in the media world. Libel law is a particularly dangerous club being used against journalists, and you must understand that you—as well as your newspaper or magazine or broadcast station—are personally liable for what you write. This is covered in Chapter 9.

Ethics are much discussed these days by journalists and the public alike. You'll probably find on your first job that your employer has a *corporate* code of ethics of conduct, but that in developing a *personal* code you are on your own. We'll discuss in Chapter 10 some ideas for you to consider as you begin sorting out your own position on important ethical issues.

Chapter Eight

The Art of Reporting

Most careers in American journalism are built primarily on *reporting skills,* not great writing. Oh, it's terrific to be a brilliant writer. It gives you an enormous edge over most other journalists and eases your communication with readers. So, you should certainly strive to become a great writer. But if you don't make it you still can be successful *if* you learn to "smell" news and develop a bulldog determination to get it—and *if* you then lay atop all that the clean, direct, understandable writing we're discussing in this book.

Unquestionably, understanding reporting techniques is essential to you in mastering basics of newswriting. Hence, we turn now to three aspects of newsgathering: First, the newspaper structure in which you will work. Second, developing sources. A reporter without sources is a cowboy without a horse, a soldier without a rifle. Third, how to get what you want from an interview. Finding sources is one thing; getting news out of them is another.

By the end of this chapter you should move forward with greater confidence in your development as a newswriter because you will understand the larger context of where news is found and how to get it.

ORGANIZING TO FIND AND BRING IN NEWS

Harrison Salisbury, a *New York Times* Pulitzer Prize winner, recalls being transferred home after nearly six years in Moscow and receiving his first local reporting assignment: garbage.

Salisbury, then virtually the dean of foreign correspondents covering the communist world, was ordered to cover New York City's problems with its mountains of garbage. Garbage!

Salisbury didn't see the assignment as demeaning. He says he agreed to do garbage, thinking, "I would do it in style. No *Times* reporter had ever ridden a garbage truck. I would."

The result was *the* definitive coverage of garbage in a lengthy series of stories the *Times* kicked off with prominent front-page display. Salisbury then labored long on a series about teenage gang violence in Brooklyn (a foreign correspondent in Brooklyn!), which was done so well the *Times* distributed 10,000 reprints. Soon, Salisbury was riding his stories about garbage and other seemingly secondary subjects to new heights as a renowned reporter.[1]

Ultimately, your success as a reporter will depend on such spirit, imagination, and hard work. Finding news value in the seemingly insignificant, accepting any assignment, then doing it better than anyone else—all these are traits of great report-

Executive Editor Bob Haring of the *Tulsa* (Okla.) *World* discusses local news coverage with Metropolitan Editor Debbie Jackson.

(Used with permission of *Tulsa World*)

ers. They compulsively ask, probe, experience, get involved in the world around them. Great reporters live to track down news, often on solo hunts, and drag it home! (See the sidebar for one editor's views of what makes good reporters.)

Reporters must also work as part of a newsroom team in a disciplined corporate structure that's necessary to get newspapers on the streets. If you and others in the newsroom don't pull together, the newspaper will fail financially and, thus, journalistically. So, yes, your first day on the job you'll be expected to arrive filled with enthusiasm, then generate your own story ideas, develop your own sources, bring in your own stories. But you'll also be expected to fit smoothly into the larger structure your newspaper has built to gather news and win in the hotly competitive media marketplace.

You Must Fit Into Newsroom Structure

NEWSROOM STRUCTURE

Newspapers once were particularly important in our society primarily because they alone chronicled arrivals in this world (with birth announcements), then marked movements through life—school graduation, marriage, children, promotion at work (or, perhaps arrests!). Finally, newspapers reported exits from this world (in obituaries).

Today, newspapers, particularly at the community level, still cover such important life stages. But they also have added whole new dimensions of sophisticated coverage of news—and that's where you, the aspiring reporter, come in. Business, finance, economics, science, sports, the arts and entertainment—name your hobby

A Professional's View:
The Attributes of Good Reporters

Bob Haring began as a reporter and rose in the executive ranks of The Associated Press before becoming executive editor of the Tulsa (Okla.) World. Here he outlines what makes good reporters.

The most important attribute for good reporters is curiosity.

They must be nosy, to want to know what's going on and why. And the best reporters have the broadest range of curiosity—they're interested in everything.

The second-most important attribute is a willingness to ask questions. Good reporters ask questions whether they're being paid to gather information or are just satisfying curiosity.

Third is a genuine interest in and fondness for people. That goes along with asking questions. Good reporters are interested in the people they talk to.

Fourth is a keen sense of observation. Good reporters are aware of what's going on around them and notice changes. Good reporters will see a new sign that announces a new business, notice a new car in the driveway that heralds a promotion, etc.

Good reporters are not afraid to admit they don't know something. Reporters who ask dumb questions don't make dumb mistakes.

Good reporters also have a strong element of common sense. This is just an ability to know when something's brewing, when something just doesn't make sense, when there just has to be some explanation for a seemingly unexplainable incident.

Part of this is training. Reporters who learn to add up the figures in a press release, to question the spelling of a name, etc., over time develop this ability to "smell" a story.

What kind of training helps build good reporters?

The broadest kind of education. Reporters need education in history, government, economics—plus, of course, strong basic reading and writing skills. I'd recommend a course in accounting, perhaps also one in statistics. Some background in science is essential.

In today's environment, it helps to understand something of business—how corporations are organized, how they work, how to read annual reports and financial statements.

Reporters also need to learn how records are kept, where are the sources of information, how to use a library and various computer databases.

Reporters also must be writers—and editors. The purpose of reporting is to communicate, to impart information clearly and correctly, through writing. Remember that it's impossible to write too simply to be understood. Realize that if you can't define a word, your readers probably won't understand it.

Above all, realize that reporting and writing are skills that constantly evolve and improve with practice. Skilled writers learn all the time—and learn from others.

Bob Haring

or interest and some publication somewhere employs reporters to cover it. To qualify, you must prepare in both "horizontal" and "vertical" dimensions.

Reporters need horizontal—or broad—education in liberal arts courses and many "life experiences." Possessing broad background is important because often the first task given beginners, particularly on small newspapers, is *general assignment reporting*. This involves covering a wide variety of stories—a fire today, a murder tomorrow, the board of education the next day—rather than being assigned to a "beat" focused on cops, courts or other narrow news areas.

However, newspapers (and other media) are rapidly redefining news and how it must be reported. As we saw in Chapter 1, the trend is toward specialized coverage for markets of readers with narrow news interests. Those reader groups then are "sold" to advertisers who pay to reach them. For the newsroom, this strategy requires a tightly organized journalistic thrust that will gain competitive advantage by delivering special-interest news with expertise, depth and detail that other media cannot match.

Prepare for Specialized Reporting

Newspapers, therefore, need reporters who are broadly educated but who also have vertical—or in-depth—preparation for specialized reporting. For example, many reporters are writing for expert readers, not general audiences. Covering medicine, science or the arts for readers who are physicians, scientists or opera singers requires expertise that many general-assignment reporters years back simply could not muster. Therefore, in subsequent chapters of this book we will begin edging our discussion of newswriting toward basic skills needed to begin in specialized reporting.

The specialization is clear, even among small papers. The *Quincy* (Mass.) *Patriot Ledger,* an afternoon six-day paper of about 87,000 circulation, assigns staff to each of these specialities:

- books
- fashion
- films/theater/lifestyle
- food
- radio/TV
- religion
- sports

A nearby competitor, the *Boston Globe,* a morning paper of 516,000 circulation daily and 787,000 on Sundays, is typical of metropolitan papers with many full-fledged specialty departments:

auto	food	religion
books	garden	restaurants
business	medical	science
drama	music	sports
education	radio/TV	travel
fashion	real estate	

Specialized News Now Fronted by Dailies

Newspapers, naturally, assign reporters to other, broader news categories. At the *Globe,* they include city, regional, national, and foreign news, in addition to special weekly coverage of New Hampshire (a state in the *Globe's* circulation area) and a Sunday magazine. Importantly, specialized news once relegated to pages deep inside newspapers now is displayed prominently on page one. Daily, both the *Globe* and

Patriot Ledger, like all papers, run front-page stories about business, science, education, or other specialty interests.

Now, envisage yourself interviewing for a job at the *Globe* or *Patriot Ledger* and being asked how you see yourself eventually fitting into the newsroom at either paper. "I can cover a fire" won't cut it. Neither will, "I'm great at covering speeches. . . ." You'll need to answer that you can do both *and* bring in-depth, expert background and skill to covering at least one news specialty.

Many newspapers even are redefining traditional news categories such as "fashion," "finance" and "auto." This, too, signals that you will need in-depth reporting expertise.

The *Seattle Times*, for example, doesn't have an "auto" specialist. It has a reporter who writes "Getting There," regular coverage of *commuting* throughout the metropolitan area.

The *Santa Ana* (Calif.) *Orange County Register* assigns "topic" reporters to "Southern California culture," "Relationships," "Making Money," "Learning." The *Register's* "auto" specialty now is "Getting Around," and covers travel by plane, train, bus and car, as well as governmental issues pertaining to it.

Major newspapers often subdivide topics even more narrowly. Among its nine

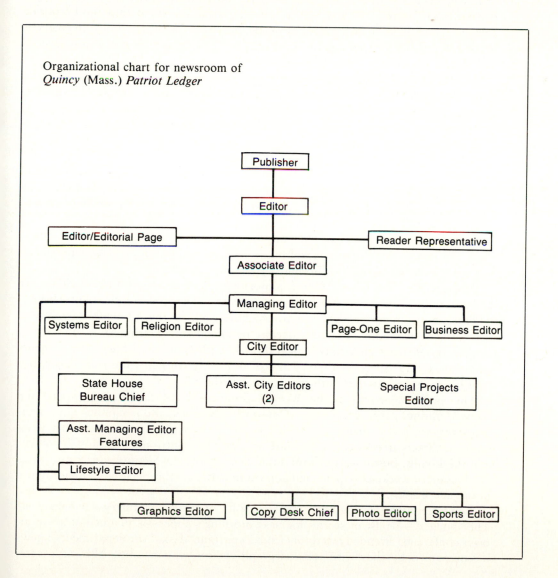

Organizational chart for newsroom of
Quincy (Mass.) *Patriot Ledger*

music critics, *The New York Times* employs specialists in classical music and rock. The *Los Angeles Times*, like many newspapers, has special "urban affairs" writers. And, naturally, newspapers still cover garbage—only now with "environmental" writers.[2]

Table of Organization Shows Structure

The formal structure of a newsroom is traced in a "table of organization" showing flow of authority and responsibility. See our example of an organizational chart, adapted from the *Patriot Ledger*. Note that the "reader representative," or ombudsman, reports directly to the editor on what the public is saying about the newspaper. The reader representative also critiques the newspaper from the public's standpoint, as an aid to the editor in improving journalistic performance. Other assignments in the table of organization are self-explanatory except, perhaps, the "systems editor." This person is in charge of newsroom computers, data banks, and, often, computerized research done to assist reporters in gathering and analyzing data for their stories.

THE NEWSROOM PROCESS

It will be some time before you get your own box in the newsroom table of organization, or receive those other trademarks of success within the corporate *structure*—a title on your door and rug on the floor. But from the start you'll be involved in the newsroom *process* of identifying news, getting it and writing it, and you should understand how the process works.

Editors responsible for arranging coverage, editing copy and publishing the newspaper use reporters as "assets" (along with time, money and newshole, the space in the paper dedicated to news, not advertising). But the underlying dynamic in the newsroom process goes far beyond assembly-line creation of a "product." Newspapering attracts people who want to shine light in dark corners, change things, *do good* and simultaneously beat somebody—another newspaper, a magazine, or TV competitor or maybe just the odds against getting a particular story. The best and most competitive of such people frequently rise to the top, so you'll find generally that your editors, though perhaps jocular or seemingly cynical, are very serious about their craft.

How Newsroom Policy Is Set

Titles vary in newsrooms. The chief news executive normally is the *executive editor,* or *editor.* This person establishes overall newsroom policy and supervises a *managing editor* and others who put out the paper each day.

At the *Tulsa* (Oklahoma) *World,* a morning paper of 123,000 circulation daily and 240,000 on Sundays, the chief news executive is Executive Editor Bob Haring, who began as a reporter, then rose to executive ranks in the AP before taking over the *World*'s newsroom. "I directly oversee news content," Haring says, "and generally decide on front-page play. I deal directly with sports and photo departments and oversee three special writers. I also deal directly with city and state desks, but coordinate those activities with the managing editor."

The managing editor is the *World*'s production coordinator, overseeing the "copy" (editing) desk, computer systems and operations, and personnel. An *associate managing editor* selects features from the AP, Knight-Ridder, and other news services; directs free-lancers (non-staff writers who contribute occasional stories), and the Living, Business, and Entertainment sections. A *Sunday editor* supervises production of weekend papers (and at most newspapers this person is a major figure in the newsroom).

News planning, Haring says, involves "a lot of regular and irregular meetings." The "budget"—or list of stories for next morning's paper—is planned at a 4 p.m. news conference attended by editors from important "desks" (or departments): news (accompanied by the "wire" or "telegraph" editor who handles AP), city, state,

At the *Tulsa* (Oklahoma) *World,* Executive Editor Bob Haring leads daily news conferences where editors discuss story ideas, assign reporters, and map out next day's content.

(Used with permission of *Tulsa World*)

sports, business, graphics, and photos. The associate managing editor represents Lifestyle and Entertainment. The general character of the Sunday paper is planned on Wednesdays, with late-breaking news being inserted up to deadline time Saturday.

Each department, in turn, has internal meetings of editors and reporters to plan coverage. Haring meets daily with writers handling editorials, plus op-ed page coverage (news and opinion displayed on the page opposite the editorial page).[3]

As a beginner, you won't attend news-planning sessions. But your supervising editor might offer one of your story ideas as worthy of pursuit, or suggest you handle a story idea generated in the planning session. Under best conditions, an assignment will be discussed with you by a senior editor who will suggest news angles or approaches to take, sources to contact, and give you writing guidance. But don't be surprised if, on your first assignment, you are given no guidance whatsoever. It's traditional in many newsrooms to test beginners on whether they have the initiative to take a bare idea and develop it by themselves into a publishable story.

You'll Be Tested on Initiative

In many newsrooms, work schedules are set in writing at least two weeks in advance so you'll know whether you're on days, nights, general assignment (GA) or a beat. Individual story assignments are made in a written daily schedule ("sked"). Your editor will often order approximate wordage for a story and give you a deadline when it is due. Some papers not too concerned about journalistic quality keep track of reporters' performance with a "story count"—a record of quantity of stories produced. Papers more concerned with quality will give reporters the time and wordage necessary to produce the best-possible story and not press you for a large number of stories.

After you keyboard your story into the newsroom computer it is pulled out by an editor assigned to copy reading and headline writing. In your beginner days, your copy might be looked at first by a supervising editor assigned to your "break-in." With luck, you'll get constructive, professional guidance. But you're heading into a demanding, fast-paced business, so be prepared for some rough handling. That, too, is traditional in some newsrooms. The first story I wrote for The Associated Press was balled up (we typed on paper in those days) and thrown at me—not *back* to me; *at me*. For those times, the editor's guidance was routinely constructive and professional: "You obviously don't know how to write a [expletive deleted] lead!" he explained.

On the copy desk, your story competes for room in the paper against all other news breaking that day. If your story is of relatively minor importance, the desk's supervising editor will quickly order a copy editor to trim it to specified length and put a one-column headline on it. You may have to search back among classified ads for your story. Or, if you've brought in important news, your story might be considered at the news planning conference for front-page display (or "play"). If you're really lucky, it could be played "above the fold," or on the top half of the page or, even, under a multicolumn headline as the "lead" or primary story of the day. Most newspapers place the lead story in the upper-right corner of the front page. Many readers look there first, and it's a matter of pride among reporters to "lead the paper."

Don't be too disappointed if, in your early days, your stories are "killed" and don't get into the paper. The number of pages that a newspaper publishes is determined by how much advertising is sold, not by how many columns of newshole the editor thinks are required ideally for news. As a beginner, you may handle relatively unimportant stories that are first to be killed on a "big news day" when many more important stories compete for space. (Of course, if your stories continue to be killed *after* your first few months, you better find out whether your performance is deemed substandard.)

It's important to note that the newsroom process is designed to generate news guidelines and story ideas that flow downward to reporters, but also to encourage upward flow of ideas from reporters on the front line. Energetically pushing your story ideas with editors and competing against colleagues for space in the paper is part of *making* your own success. Some editors even create "dynamic tension" in the newsroom by pitting reporters against each other in the belief such competition fuels the news-gathering process, which depends completely, of course, on reporters striving to bring in the news—and the good ones do strive to do so. (See sidebar on p. 234.)

Reporters, in turn, depend on their sources to reveal the news.

Make Your Own Success

THE CARE AND FEEDING OF SOURCES

You cannot have too many sources. Thus the more people you meet and the more hands you shake—the better. It's most important to have sources who are *authoritative* and *strategically positioned* to know what's actually happening, to whom, where, when, why and, of course, how it's happening.

In building your sources, first stake out the geography (the beat) or subject (topic) you'll be covering. You cannot actively cultivate sources everywhere. Narrow your target area. (But *never* pass up developing a source elsewhere who might pay off in the future.)

Develop Strategically Placed Sources

The object of the newsroom process: a
front page with strong local reporting
and a balanced view of state, national,
and international news stories.

(Used with permission
of *Tulsa World*)

Next, look for sources at the headwaters of the "rivers of news" we discussed in
Chapter 1: people, money, power, among others. Much of the news we handle flows
from them.

Among your best sources, of course, are people who originate news, people with
money and power (governmental, political, business, economic, religious, and so
forth) *or* those who make decisions affecting them. Think of having sources positioned along the banks of news rivers at narrow spots—"choke points"—and who
are able to see the entire flow, even if they cannot alter its course.

For example, if you're assigned to cover the county sheriff's department you can

A Professional's View:
Reporting from Hell

Peter Arnett of Cable News Network was strongly criticized by some Americans for going to Baghdad to report from the Iraqi side during the Persian Gulf War. Some critics even labeled Arnett unpatriotic. His response:

The reason I stayed in Baghdad is quite simple: Reporting is what I do for a living. I made the full commitment to journalism years ago. If you ask, are some stories worth the risk of dying for, my answer is yes—and many of my journalist friends have died believing that. I revere their memories, and I would betray them if I did anything less than continue a full commitment to coverage. . . .

I'd go anywhere for a story if there was enough viewer interest and CNN wanted coverage. I'd go to Hell itself for a story if someone important down there wanted to be interviewed. But, then, the labelers would probably declare I was down there because I was an atheist.

Peter Arnett, "The Story From Baghdad," *Washington Post*, March 17, 1991, p. D-1

just bet the sheriff is as much politician as peace officer and more interested in putting a "spin" on the news—that is, releasing it in a manner favorable to him rather than ensuring its free flow. But the sheriff's deputies, who have their own agendas, can be cultivated as sources. So can radio dispatchers. They sit at crucial "choke points," listen to all radio messages and at times alone possess a timely over-overall picture of what's going on. Even the jailhouse janitor can signal you, "Something's up!"

Think of who can signal you on what's news these days on your campus.

For example, are graduation rates for athletes news? How about athletic scholarships and other financial support for football and basketball players? Three people on campus know all about those subjects—the university president, the vice president for academic affairs and the athletic director. But they may be reluctant to volunteer the facts. However, somewhere in the university bureaucracy are junior officials and clerks who handle the paper or computer records on which those facts are recorded. Important details also are filed by someone on campus with your state's board of regents and the National Collegiate Athletic Association, among others. Who stands at "choke points" on campus, watching all that flow by?

How about student loans? Somewhere in the office of the vice president for finance, and elsewhere on campus, are people who know what student readers want to know: how much money is available, how much is projected to be available next year, at what interest levels, and under what conditions? People with access to those facts are there, waiting for you to contact them.

In just that manner, professional reporters "dope out" where news is and who has it.

Cultivate Sources With Visits   Then starts the cultivating of sources. It takes personal visits (telephoning doesn't work), plenty of *relaxed* chatting (don't push too hard, too fast), and lots of coffee (often more than you should drink). Hand over your business card (with *home* as well as office telephone number) and suggest it be slipped into the desk across which pass all those facts you intend eventually to get. Then, make the same rounds next week and the week after that and the week after that. . . . The pros call it "leg-work" for a reason.

Here's an approach used by generations of your predecessor reporters: "Hi. I'm Smith of the *Tribune*. I'm new in town and just trying to get the lay of the land. Who are you? What do you do? How long have you been here? You don't say! That long, eh? Say . . . how do things work around here?" Does the source have Frederick Remington prints on the office wall? Western art is *interesting!* The source catches butterflies for a hobby? Say, that's fascinating. . . .

Every source has a mother, father, son, daughter, spouse, dog, cat, pet goldfish—something near and dear. Ask about it next time you drop in. *Chat 'em up.*

And record those details, along with names, addresses and telephone numbers (office *and* home) in a "source notebook." They'll help you break important news one day, and the notebook could become your most valuable possession as a reporter. Keep it updated. Remember, sheriff's deputies can become sheriffs one day. So can radio dispatchers. And as you move up the professional ladder, your techniques remain the same. Every successful foreign correspondent has source notebooks listing once-anonymous, low-ranking embassy officials who eventually became ambassadors—and ambassadors who became deputy secretaries of state! Stay in touch with sources even after they or you move on.

Keep a Source Notebook

It's nice to be nice to people. But we're talking here about *working* to develop *professional relationships* with sources that one day you can *use* (don't shy from the word) to get news. That raises the question of how close to get personally to sources (or their pet goldfish). Get too friendly and when the Big Story breaks you may be tempted to pull your punches to avoid embarrassing your friend-source in print. During your cultivation of sources it's best to be straightforward; your job is to get news and print it, along with people's names and addresses, and that's what the chats over coffee are all about.

Officials often are "news-wise." They have likely dealt with many reporters. They know the "game"—in fact, they may be playing their own. And that's good reason to be alert. Ask yourself: Why does the president of a bank (or of a corporation, a university or of the United States) agree to talk to you, a reporter? You probably don't travel in the same social circles. Your personality, while undoubtedly outstanding, isn't *that* great. As a reporter you are primarily a *taker* of information and a *giver* of nothing . . . unless. . . . Ah! Could some sources be trying to *use you*, to get something in the newspaper, just as you are trying to *use them*? Yes, and isn't newspapering wonderful fun?

Beware of Sources Using You

Some people give you news merely because you ask (which is why you always should ask, one way or another, "What's new?"). But many have other motives—empire building, revenge, promotion of a "just cause." (You'll note, for example, that just before federal budget time, "informed sources" begin leaking "news" all over Washington about the just cause of a strong U.S. Navy—or Air Force, or Army, or Marine Corps—and that it alone can defend the nation against newly discovered threats in the Middle East—or Africa, or Asia, or . . .).

Why Sources Reveal News

There's nothing wrong in obtaining news from self-centered, impassioned advocates of a "just cause." Many sources who spilled Watergate details to the *Washington Post* and other newspapers wanted to "get" then-President Richard Nixon. Countless other important stories are broken by prejudiced sources. Just be certain you try to understand your sources' motives and that you double-check what they say and obtain balancing comment.

SUCCEEDING IN AN INTERVIEW

Learning to interview news sources, like learning to ride a bike, is largely a matter of trying repeatedly and, inevitably, falling on your face a couple of times before you get the hang of it.

Interviews Are Your Most Important Tool

But here are some pointers that might ease the learning pain: First, the interview is your most important reporting tool. Documents, computer records, warehouses of bureaucratic files—all leave a paper trail that can be of enormous value to you. But *people,* not paper, break news stories. People provide story ideas, and tip you on where news is found. Consider this: Somewhere in the (literally) *tons* of documents kept by your university or city is a news story. Maybe a great story. But where do you start searching for it? *Some people know.* And, properly stroked as sources, then interviewed carefully, they will reveal the story to you.

Prepare Carefully Before Interview

Second, success *in* an interview is arranged mostly *before* the interview. Reporters who go into interviews prepared are those who come out with news. Learn in advance as much as you can about your interviewee and topic. *Go in with the advantage of knowing more than the interviewee thinks you know.* Check *Who's Who* on the interviewee. Thoroughly background yourself on the topic. Don't open with a banker by asking, "What is a prime rate?" Don't ask a world-famous pianist, "What's a concerto, and who is Tchaikovsky?" On the other hand, don't be afraid to ask if you don't understand a point raised in the interview.

Use Your Own "People Skills"

Third, build your interview technique around your own personality and unique "people skills," not somebody else's model. Some reporters can charm interviewees with humorous conversational openers; many of us tell jokes badly and must fall back on businesslike (but *never* brusque!) talk about weightier matters. Use whatever approach is most natural for you—and the situation. And, although T-shirts and jeans may be the "real you," they simply won't convince either the banker or pianist that you're to be taken seriously. Dress appropriately.

Fourth, build into your technique a routine openness and honesty. You are a reporter who operates on the record and puts facts in the newspaper. Establish that when you request the interview. That doesn't mean you can't "muscle" your way in occasionally: "I'm doing a story for the *Tribune* and have the views of several other persons on you [or your company or your policy] and I know you would like to tell your side." If you weren't born with a streak of toughness, develop one. You might have to ask tough questions. Robert W. Chandler, long-time chairman and editor of the *Bend* (Ore.) *Bulletin,* complains that too many young reporters "do not want to offend anyone. They are unwilling to ask tough questions." Chandler says many would rather write noncontroversial "two-headed calf features."[4]

As a reporter, you have enormous leverage. But your power must be used judiciously and always with integrity. See the sidebar for one news executive's views on your obligations when interviewing.

Let's "walk" through an interview.

Open low key. Don't whip out your notebook and pen, like Billy the Kid in a bank. That says, "This is a stickup . . . give me your facts" and turns off interviewees. Pick something (Remington prints on the wall? A butterfly collection?) to chat about for a moment.

These opening moments set the tone for the coming contest—and that's what a news interview is. The source has news; you're there to extract it. Don't grovel in profuse thanks because the high and mighty one has granted you a few precious moments. You (or, at least, your newspaper) are important too, and the interview will be a richly rewarding experience for *both* of you!

Some news sources are impatient, or on a tight time schedule. If you detect that mood, swing the conversation quickly around to Topic A.

Issues and Challenges:
Your Obligations When Interviewing

Do reporters have obligations to the people they are interviewing? John Ginn, a veteran reporter, editor and publisher, says yes.

A responsible reporter has a massive obligation to understand what each news source is trying to communicate. Similarly, the reporter is obligated to quote and/or paraphrase each source in ways that reflect the meaning intended by the source.

Too often, young beginning reporters fail to meet one or both of these obligations. Their failures erode their personal integrity with both readers and sources (not to mention their bosses), as well as their newspaper's credibility. Such flawed reporting also contributes greatly to the general distrust many in our society feel toward journalists.

There appear to be several causes for these failures by young beginning reporters.

One contributor likely is a combination of low self-esteem magnified by inexperience with the interview task. A young reporter lacking confidence and experience can slip into the trap of trying to impress the source by avoiding lulls in the conversation, of being embarrassed to ask clarifying questions, and shunning comments such as, "Would you repeat that? I want to be sure my notes reflect what you're saying exactly." So the reporter gets preoccupied with thinking about the next question to be asked rather than listening carefully to the source's answer to the current one and being sure he or she understands that answer.

Another contributor to this problem comes when a reporter suspects a source is lying to, misleading, or striving to manipulate the reporter. This happens, of course. A responsible reaction is to quote accurately the abusive source and then to present other information that helps readers conclude the source is lying, misleading, or manipulating. But irresponsibility by a source does not justify irresponsibility by the reporter. So "repaying" such a source by distorting his quote, changing the context, or omitting important elements is not acceptable reporter behavior.

Beginning young reporters who listen carefully and write stories that accurately reflect what sources are striving to say tend to shed the label "young beginning reporter" rather quickly.

An exercise that can help reporters appreciate the need for these skills and possibly help them acquire them is role play. Such role play needs to give each beginning young reporter some opportunities to function as a source for a story while colleagues ask questions and write stories based on responses to those questions. Young reporters who have opportunities to read such stories and to note how certain other reporters failed to capture what they were really trying to say can grow significantly from such experiences.

John C. Ginn, president and publisher, *Anderson (S.C.) Independent-Mail*

Now, you must get your notebook and pencil out without freezing your source. Wait until a fact, figure, or quote is delivered, then say, "Let me take that down to be sure I quote you correctly in my story."

There! Notebook and pencil are out. You have advised the interviewee this talk is on the record. (That means the source's name and quotes may be published.) Now you're in business.

Establish Ground Rules for Interview

Issues and Challenges:
Asking the Proper Questions

Beginning reporters must learn how to extract important information from press conferences. A major challenge is framing questions with precision, then persisting in getting answers.

Let's study how reporters obtained important news from Gen. H. Norman Schwarzkopf, American commander in the Persian Gulf War, at a press conference Feb. 27, 1991, in Riyadh, Saudi Arabia. Gen. Schwarzkopf, using photos and charts, told reporters that more than 50,000 of Iraqi soldiers had been taken prisoner.

The first question asked was broad and *open-ended,* designed to let Schwarzkopf range widely in his reponse:

> Q: I wonder if, in an overview, despite these enormously illustrative pictures, you could say what's left of the Iraqi army in terms of how long could it be before he [Saddam Hussein] could ever be a regional threat, or a threat to the region again.

The general replied at length that the Iraqi army had been seriously damaged. That drew the second question of the press conference—a *close-ended* question, one tightly focused and designed to draw a specific response:

> Q: You said [Iraq has] all these divisions along the border, which were seriously attrited. It figures to be about 200,000 troops maybe that were there. You've got 50,000 prisoners. Where are the rest of them?

By getting specific and persisting with the question above, reporters drew from Schwarzkopf the statement that, "There were a very, very large number of dead in these [Iraqi] units, a very, very large number of dead." That was one of the major stories to come from the press conference.

Later in the press conference, a reporter demonstrated a useful technique—ask a two-part question (you might not get the floor a second time) and frame your question to inject personalities into the story and draw a human response. This was the question:

> Q: Did you think that this [the war] would turn out—I realize a great deal of strategy and planning went into it—but when it took place, did you think this would turn out to be such an easy cakewalk, as it seems? And, second, what are your impressions of Saddam Hussein as a military strategist?

The first part of the double-barreled question above drew a detailed (and coldly analytical) response. The second part, about Saddam Hussein, the general's foe in the war, drew a very human, almost passionate response that became one of Schwarzkopf's best-known statements of the entire war:

> A: As far as Saddam Hussein being a great military strategist, he is neither a stategist nor is he schooled in the operational art nor is he a tactician nor is he a general nor is he a soldier. Other than that, he's a great military man—I want you to know that.

It's important to note that press conferences are designed to let reporters push for details—and if an answer isn't precise, the ground rules permit pressing for the details you need. Note below how the quick exchange of questions and answers clarified an important issue:

> Q: Is there a military or a political explanation as to why the Iraqis did not use chemical weapons?
> A: We've got a lot of questions about why the Iraqis didn't use chemical weapons and I don't know the answer. I just thank God that they didn't.
> Q: Is it possible that they didn't use them because they didn't have time to react?
> A: You want me to speculate, I'll be delighted to speculate . . . [Schwarzkopf then gave a lengthy, detailed answer].

Using a tape recorder frees you to converse more intently without taking notes and, obviously, gives you a precise record of what is said—important in interviews on controversial subjects or with individuals known later to deny statements that create waves. Many officials will use a recorder to keep their own record of the interview. But some sources, less sophisticated in the ways of reporters, are terrified of tape recorders. It's best to ask, "Mind if I use a tape recorder to ensure I quote you accurately?" Then judge the reaction. (*Never* record an interview secretly. You're a reporter, not an undercover agent.)

You've come into the interview with a goal—a specific story or perhaps comment on an earlier story—and in these opening moments you must search for conversational rhythm that will get you there. Don't always go straight in with tough, direct questions. Move cautiously around the edges, look for openings, search for resistance.

If rhythm is established and your interviewee opens up, let the conversation flow, unless talk wanders hopelessly astray. Often if you permit the interviewee to "run" a bit, you'll stumble across a story even better than the one you came for. Make a mental note to return, through questions, to any point that's left unclear.

Think about what is said. Too many young reporters don't. Instead, they lower their heads (breaking eye contact) and furiously, unthinkingly take notes on everything said. Control of the interview is lost and the reporter turns into a stenographer trying to record a speech. You must take *selective* notes, breaking eye contact (and your control of the interview) only to write down particularly important facts or quotes. You can learn to do this only through practice.

As you talk, you're juggling in your mind the relative news importance of what is being said. You're *searching for the lead*. And when conversation reveals it, you circle it with questions, fleshing it out, probing for details. Of course, something said a few moments later could be even more important, and you must juggle news priorities in your mind once more.

Search for the Lead While Talking

If the tempo slows, ask a question that jump-starts conversation once more. An open-ended question ("Tell me about your policy") might encourage new directions. It also might open a rambling monologue with no news value. A closed question ("On which date did you implement the policy?") gets control back in your hands.

Your persistence can be crucial. Russ White of the *Orlando* (Fla.) *Sentinel* recounts being refused an interview by Dr. Norman Vincent Peale, author of *The Power of Positive Thinking*. Too tired, said the 89-year-old Peale. White persisted: "Come on, Dr. Peale, think positively." He got the interview.

If the interviewee evades a question, ask it three or four different ways. Sometimes that unlocks answers. However, the line is narrow between persistence and being overly adversarial—an aggressive, posturing "attack" attitude that treats every news source as a foe. If you get too tough, the interview process breaks down into a tug-of-war, and content suffers. Remember, you're after news, not theater.

If your questions get into areas that the interviewee regards as dangerous, a variety of tactics might be used against you:

- The question-answers-a-question tactic. "Well," the interviewee responds, "what do *you* think the policy should be?" ("Oh," the reporter replies, "I work for the *Tribune,* not the State Department. What do *you* think?")

- The hypothetical tactic. "Well," the interviewee says, "hypothetically [or "ideally" or "under some circumstances"] troops could be sent in." (That's evasive, so you press for a precise response: "Under *current* circumstances, *will* troops be sent in?")

- The intimidation tactic. "That," says the source, "is a dumb question." ("Let me put it this way . . . ," you say, completely *un*intimidated and declining the invitation to back away from the point.)

If your interview turns really sour, the source might say, "Oh, by the way, my answer to that question is off the record [not for publication attributed to the source by name]." Or, midway through the session, the source might say, "We're off the record, aren't we?" If this happens, you must make a tough decision: If you stand by your guns ("No, this is *on* the record, and I'm going to quote you"), you've got a story—and probably lost a source. If you regard your source as supremely important, you might have to negotiate. All news professionals have been trapped that way and most will acknowledge that on occasion they've swallowed their pride and gone off the record to save a source for future use. But you shouldn't let the same source do that to you twice.

It's curious, but some sources, even powerful officials familiar with reporters, sometimes are reluctant to volunteer information outright. Instead, they'll signal you—perhaps with tone of voice or body language—to ask a direct question about it. Listen and watch for such nuances.

Before concluding the interview, *always* ask, "Is there anything else you'd like to tell me?" That can unlock something important.

If the interviewee says no, you have a last chance to fire off the really tough (or "dumb") question. It's OK to be tough (or "dumb") but not too early in the interview. Save that question for when the interview is ending and you have nothing to lose.

Whenever possible, though, leave the interview on good terms. You may need another chat.

SPOTTING NEWS AND FOLLOWING THE PAPER TRAIL

Millions of Americans had jobs and commuted to them normally this morning without incident, just like yesterday morning. Broadly, that's news.

Reporters, however, look for fresh, developing news, and, in a narrow sense, *deviations from the norm* can be your first signal that important news is breaking: Suddenly, some Americans *don't* have jobs; accidents unexpectedly *disrupt* commuting; today is *unlike* yesterday.

If you spot deviations early enough, writing about them will focus public attention on impending problems, goad officialdom to act, *make a difference.* But how can you catch early signals of change? One way is to learn the pattern of things, then watch for disruptions in that pattern.

Imagine yourself looking at a distant horizon. Flat plains stretch evenly, monotonously across your view—then, suddenly, abruptly, the plains are broken by towering peaks and deep valleys. In a news sense, it's in those peaks and valleys that reporters first see disruption of patterns, and it's there they turn initially to ask, "Why? . . . what's going on?"

Watch for Disruptions of Patterns

Now, imagine yourself interviewing the mayor. She drones on and on, as she did last week and the week before, about the Good Life in Our Town. It's so monotonous you could nod off. Then, off-handedly, she throws up a mountain peak: "Could get better, too, if Acme Widgets locates here." Whoa! What was that, Mrs. Mayor? Acme Widgets? Well, she explains, Acme has submitted a feasibility plan for a new production facility in the northwest suburbs. . . .

Maybe the mayor's conversational pattern is broken by a valley: ". . . I'm worried, though, about the unemployment figures. . . ." Whoa, again! Unemployment figures?

For the alert reporter, the monotonous view is interrupted, the pattern broken. From a distance, it appears *news* is developing. What you need now are facts: What does Acme produce? How many workers will it employ? When? Or, if you see the unemployment valley as news: Precisely what are the unemployment figures? How do they compare with last month's, last year's at this time?

In either scenario, you must get up close for a better look. How can you do that? You find—and follow—the paper trail.

Somewhere, someplace, that feasibility plan and those unemployment figures are on file. If you've developed news sources, perhaps one can direct you straight to the documentation. If not, you'll have to "dope out" for yourself where to find the written record. To do that, obviously, you must first learn how things work, how government is structured, how corporations and other institutions are organized.

Too often, young reporters don't know such things. Ted Natt, editor and publisher of the *Longview* (Wash.) *Daily News,* a 25,000-circulation afternoon paper, complains: "Many young persons don't know how communities are structured. They don't know about local government units, state laws, specialized units of government and how revenue-taxing systems work. We often have to teach them which courts have what jurisdiction over various areas of the law."[5]

Learn the Inner Workings

For starters in covering local news (where you probably will begin), you should learn how things work—how the paper moves—in five broad areas:

1. *City (or village) government.* Exact form varies, but important offices include those of the mayor, city manager (paid employee), city clerk, finance department, planning commission, zoning board (which regulates the types of construction permitted in the city and *always* has controversial matters at hand). The city manager, clerk or information office can provide a table of organization depicting the full governmental structure. In city hall, on file either with the clerk or finance department, you'll find the city budget, records of licenses and contracts the city has negotiated, and committee reports of all sorts. Voter registrations, births, deaths, marriages, divorces—all are on file. Check city ordinances or codes—the local "law"— to see how *government* should run; then watch for deviations from the norm. An elected city council enacts ordinances and establishes codes. Its meetings and the entire written record on public matters should be open to you, except for some personnel records on city employees. Check whether your state has an open records law ("sunshine" law) and whether it is being implemented.

Study Government Organization

2. *County government.* The elected county commission is the single most important source of news. It meets regularly and, in sessions open to the public, discusses

Look for City-County Tension

and votes on issues of compelling importance to your readers. The commission raises money (through taxes) and spends it. On file in the county building are the same types of records found at the city level. Even if you're assigned to city news, keep your eye on county government. Relationships between city and surrounding counties are extremely important—and often strained.

Education Is An Important Story

3. *Boards of education.* In many cities and counties, this is where a great deal of the action is, where much of the taxpayers' money is spent, and where many local social issues are fought out. Most boards are elected, but some are appointed. Whichever, they attract the movers and shakers in many communities and, also, controversy. Aside from spending a huge portion of local property-tax revenue, a board of education acts on such things as drug and sex education in schools, busing and other racial matters, type and quality of classroom instruction and size and composition of school faculties—hot topics, all. A board, through its elected president or chair, passes policy to a full-time, paid school superintendent who, in turn, directs local school principals. Records kept by the board secretary and superintendent's office should be open for inspection (except, again, some personnel records). You'll note, of course, that the paper trail extends downward from board to principals to classrooms through *scores* of officials, each a potential news source.

4. *Police.* Learning the structure of police departments is crucial for a local reporter. Three levels are most important: city or village; county; state. Depending on local law (or custom), city and village police respond to direction from the city council or mayor. County sheriffs take orders from the county commission. State police, of course, respond to their headquarters in your state's capital and, in turn, to the governor and legislature. It's important to learn precisely which police documents are, by state or local law, open to you and to *ensure they are kept open.* Watch, particularly, arrest records and booking sheets (or "dockets") kept at local precinct (or office) level. They show who has been arrested and jailed—and why, when, and where.

People Sources Mandatory in Covering Police

Documents aside, police news is one area of coverage where you *must* have strong people sources who can signal you that an arrest has been made but not registered, and so forth. Also operating at the local level are many federal agencies, such as the FBI and Drug Enforcement Agency. It's often difficult to develop news sources in such agencies, but most respond alertly to valid requests for information, and all operate under the federal Freedom of Information Act, which requires that many records be opened to reporters. You should advise your editor immediately if any public documents are denied you.

Learn How Courts Operate

5. *Courts.* This specialized beat often is assigned to only veteran reporters, but you'll encounter court-related matters in virtually every aspect of news. So start learning now the structure of courts and how the paper trail winds through them. *Civil courts* handle legal fights among individuals, corporations, and governments who sue each other over such things as accident cases or contracts. *Criminal courts* are where government seeks enforcement of criminal statutes by trying individuals for crimes. In criminal cases, the government's prosecuting attorney obtains an *indictment,* or accusation, against an individual suspected of an offense. A court issues a *warrant* for the person's arrest. The *charge* is read to the individual in a courtroom *arraignment* and the government presents evidence to a judge in a *preliminary hearing* or to a *grand jury.* If the grand jury finds probable cause that a crime has been committed, the individual is indicted, and asked, in court, to make a plea. If it's guilty, the judge passes sentence. If innocent, trial begins. The prosecutor presents evidence to the jury. A defense attorney hired by the defendant (or provided at taxpayer's expense if the defendant is indigent) attempts to refute the prosecutor and win the client's acquittal. Court clerks and other courtroom personnel often are helpful in pointing you toward the paper trail and helping you understand it. Remember, the prosecuting and defense attorneys are advocates, so *their* interpretation of events must be taken as one-sided.

Read the Fine Print

We've discussed developing official sources and regularly dropping in to ask, "What's new?"

That's important, all right, but don't think it automatically uncovers news.

Officials in Washington, N.C., knew for nine years the town's water was contaminated with cancer-causing chemicals and didn't tell reporters from the *Washington Daily News* (or voters). The paper won a Pulitzer Prize in 1990 for breaking the story only because its 67-year-old editor, William Coughlin, makes a career of looking for peaks and valleys on the horizon. This time he sighted a single sentence on the back of his monthly water bill stating town water had been tested. Why? He wondered. From that slender lead, reporters Betty Gray and Mike Voss broke the story that created a statewide environmental scandal.[6]

Question: Did *you* ever read the fine print on the back of your water bill?

Russell Baker, today a great *New York Times* columnist, recounts getting scooped by competitors his first night as a *Baltimore Sun* reporter covering the police. Baker relied on officials to tell him what was new (and failed to comprehend fine print in a police report on what turned out to be a gruesome murder): "Out of the agony of this episode I learned one of the most important lessons every journalist needs to know about the craft of newspaper reporting; to wit, that only a fool expects the authorities to tell him what the news is."[7]

SUMMARY CHECKLIST

- [ ] Success as a reporter requires spirit, imagination, hard work, and a compulsive desire to ask, probe, experience, and track down news.

- [ ] You are expected to self-start as a reporter and conduct solo hunts for news, but you also must fit smoothly into a newsroom structure designed to gather news and win in a hotly competitive media marketplace.

- [ ] Training to be a reporter requires broad or horizontal education in liberal arts subjects but also in-depth or vertical preparation for writing specialized news for expert readers.

- [ ] Even small papers today require reporters with special talent for covering news such as fashion, food, sports and religion aimed at capturing groups of readers attractive to advertisers.

- [ ] Traditional news categories such as "fashion," "finance," "autos," are being redefined by some newspapers into "topics" such as "Culture," "Making Money," "Getting Around."

- [ ] In the newsroom, the chief news executive normally is the executive editor, or editor. The managing editor often supervises day-to-day production of the newspaper.

- [ ] In many newsrooms, the news-gathering process is driven by intense desire to change things and do good, not merely create a news "product." Expect to work for editors serious about their craft.

- [ ] News sources are crucial to a reporter, and the best sources are authoritative and strategically positioned to originate news.

- [ ] A reporter must be cautious about getting too close personally to sources. The relationship should be professional.

- [ ] Learning to interview successfully is like learning to bike ride: You try and try, occasionally falling on your face, but eventually succeed.

☐   Deviations from the norm often are a reporter's first signal that news is developing. Look for peaks and valleys interrupting the even, monotonous "news horizon."

☐   Once you've stumbled onto the existence of news, follow the paper trail—records, documents, and so forth. This requires learning the structures of local government, boards of education, police and courts and how paper moves in them.

RECOMMENDED READING

For samplings of what drives great reporters and newsrooms, see David Halberstam, *The Powers That Be* (New York: Knopf, 1979); Harrison E. Salisbury, *Without Fear or Favor* (New York: Time Books, 1980). For a look at creation of a news philosophy, see Peter Pritchard, *The Making of McPaper: The Inside Story of USA Today* (New York: Andrews, McMell & Parker, 1987).

The art of interviewing is covered well by George M. Killenberg and Rob Anderson, *Before the Story* (New York: St. Martin's Press, 1989).

Must reading for any beginning reporter is John Ullmann and Steve Honeyman, eds., *The Reporter's Handbook* (New York: St. Martin's Press, 1983). Also see Lauren Kessler and Duncan McDonald, *Uncovering the News* (Belmont, Calif.: Wadsworth, 1987), and *How to Use the Federal FOI Act,* FOI Service Center, 800 18th Street, N.W., Suite 300, Washington, D.C., 20006.

For those beginning to compile a source notebook, start with the listing of news sources published in each July/August issue of *Washington Journalism Review.*

NOTES

1. These and other fascinating stories are recounted in Harrison E. Salisbury, *A Reporter's Tale of Our Time* (New York: Harper & Row, 1988).
2. For further insights into such news categories, see *Editor & Publisher International Yearbook,* an annual that contains staffing breakdowns for every daily newspaper in the United States.
3. Bob Haring letter to author, March 27, 1990.
4. Robert W. Chandler letter to author, April 5, 1990.
5. Ted Natt letter to author, April 17, 1990.
6. Details of the *Washington Daily News* story are in David E. Pitt, "City Gets Clean Water (and Pulitzer)," *The New York Times*, national edition, April 16, 1990, p. A-7.
7. Russell Baker, *The Good Times* (New York: William Morrow, 1989).

Exercise 8–1   Interviewing an Editor

Interview an editor of a local paper designated by your instructor and, in about 300 words, describe (1) the news-room structure and (2) how a story written by a reporter moves through the editing process. Pick an appropriate story structure (inverted pyramid, neck-of-the-vase, for example) and write carefully in AP style throughout. Background yourself by studying the listing for the editor's newspaper in Editor & Publisher International Yearbook.

Exercise 8–2   Specialized Coverage

Examine three consecutive front pages of The New York Times *(or another newspaper your instructor designates) and write, in about 250 words, your analysis of general assignment and specialized reporting displayed there. Which stories obviously are written by specialists? How can you tell? Which categories of specialized writing—finance, economics, science, and so forth—are represented on the front pages? Write in AP style.*

Exercise 8–3 Reporting Assignments

Obtain a table of organization for the administrative structure of your university or college. Then, from the view-point of student readers, list news beats you would assign to reporters as editor of a campus newspaper. Also list news topics or subjects (such as "Campus Living" or "Music") you would arrange to cover. Like all editors, you have finite "resources" for this task: 12 reporters. Use them judiciously to cover important beats and topics. Don't forget general-assignment tasks, either. Write in AP style in about 300 words.

_____

_____

_____

_____

_____

_____

_____

_____

_____

_____

_____

_____

_____

_____

_____

_____

_____

_____

_____

_____

_____

_____

_____

Exercise 8–4 Where to Find News

For each of the 10 news topics listed below, write the name, title, and telephone number of the official or department where you would seek information about it. Bypass the information office or publicity department.

1. Drunk driving arrests last month (town *and* campus).

_____
_____

2. Dollar amount of student loans made *through university* last year.

_____
_____

3. Dollar amount of football scholarships granted last year.

_____
_____

4. Academic calendar (class and vacation schedules) for next year.

_____
_____

5. Total contributions last year to alumni fund/foundation.

_____
_____

6. Projected freshman enrollment for next year.

_____
_____

7. City regulations on opening/closing times for bars.

_____
_____

8. Campus incidence of venereal disease.

_____
_____

9. University president's travel schedule for next week.

_____
_____

10. Biographical data on university vice president for academic affairs.

_____

Exercise 8–5   Accuracy in Interviewing

In this exercise, your instructor will conduct a "news conference" about his or her background. You are expected to obtain full and accurate biographical data and a good grasp of what motivates him or her professionally in teaching. Use a neck-of-the-vase story structure, opening with perhaps a personal anecdote or intro built around a particularly good quote. Make sure you catch quotes accurately and write in AP style. Do this in about 300 words.

Exercise 8–6   Library Resources

Using resources available through the reference desk of your library, answer the following questions:

1. What was total student enrollment of your university or college last year?

_____

2. What was total employment (faculty and staff) last year?

_____

3. Who is chairman of IBM? Where and when was he born?

_____

4. How much was the governor of your state paid (salary only) in 1988?

_____

5. Who won the Pulitzer Prize for international reporting in 1989?

_____

6. How many square miles are there in the state where your school is located?

_____

7. What was the lowest temperature ever recorded in Albany, N.Y.?

_____

8. Was President Bush ever director of the CIA?

_____

9. What is the headquarters address of Knight-Ridder, Inc.?

_____

10. How many stanzas are there in the national anthem?

_____

Exercise 8–7   Precision in Interviewing

In class, interview a classmate for 15 minutes on biographical data, including age, birthplace, current permanent and temporary addresses, number of brothers or sisters, whether mother and father are alive/dead, married/divorced. Also determine courses currently being taken, major or intent to major, and career aspirations. Then reverse roles and submit to being interviewed on the same questions for 15 minutes. Write a 200-word biographical sketch on your classmate and, under your instructor's supervision, submit it for an accuracy check by the person you interviewed. You should verify the sketch written about you. Both sketches should be edited closely, using editing symbols learned earlier in the course, and then submitted to your instructor for grading on accuracy and style.

Exercise 8–8　Questions to Jump-Start Interviews

All reporters occasionally are thrown unexpectedly into interviews without time to prepare adequately on the inter-viewee's background or the topic to be discussed. However, if reporters stay current on the news—and if they learn to "gear up" quickly—they can conduct a satisfactory interview. In this exercise your instructor will name a person currently prominent in the news and give you a specified time to write 10 questions you would ask that person. Your questions must be specific and directed at obtaining views and facts about the news development that makes the person prominent.

Chapter Nine

Press Law and You

We've moved rapidly in this book toward professionalism in the exciting business of newswriting. We've discussed the sometimes heady chase after news and how to stretch for imaginative, colorful ways of writing it.

We now must slow our pace to consider briefly—but very carefully and cooly—a danger confronting anyone who works in today's sometimes frenetic world of news: Legal traps await the unwary newswriter out there. Libel law is being used by some people as a club against the media for real or imagined wrongs. People are increasingly willing to launch civil actions—to sue—out of motives ranging from a desire to restore wrongly impugned reputations to desire for monetary damages from the media or, simply, desire for revenge over something published.

Before writing your first news story you must understand that libel suits often are filed not only against newspapers but also against reporters personally. Suits can be enormously expensive to fight and, if lost, can cripple a newspaper financially and destroy careers.

Therefore, on your first job, editors will require you to understand fundamentals of press law and be extremely careful in handling any story remotely sensitive legally—and many are, even the most innocent-appearing ones.

In this chapter we'll look first at crucial principles of law, particularly libel. Then we'll look at your professionalism as a newswriter as your first line of defense in *preventing* legal difficulty. Your best defense is ensuring that your writing is accurate, balanced, fair, and without malice—so professional that it gives no one grounds to sue successfully.

Caution: The author of this book is not a lawyer. This chapter is far from a definitive discussion of press law. So, while in school, study press law. Before starting your first job, consult local authority, such as your state press association, on laws in your state. (Most press associations make an attorney available for telephone consultation.) And on the job, consult your editor immediately if you have any doubt about how to handle a story that might be dangerous legally.

WHY PRESS LAW?

Must we really look at press law in our study of newswriting techniques? Yes, and for starters, here are three reasons:

• A former chief assistant district attorney sues on charges he was libeled in a newspaper's coverage of his conduct in office. A jury orders the newspaper to pay him *$34 million in damages.*

• A physician says a magazine article leaves the impression he sexually abused his daughter. He sues for $40 million to cover damages he claims he suffered and $200 million to punish the magazine *and* writer.

• An entertainer says a network TV show created the impression he got financial assistance from organized crime figures. A jury awards him $19.2 million in damages.[1]

Still wonder if it's necessary for you to study press law?

The three cases above are samplings of legal problems confronting the media today. Each case involves years of litigation. Each reflects a tendency among juries to take broad swipes at the media by handing down millions of dollars in judgments against them.

Between 1980 and 1986, newspapers lost three out of four libel cases that went to trial. During 1986–1987, damage awards *averaged* more than $1 million. In three out of five libel awards, juries tacked on punitive damages designed not to compensate for actual loss suffered but, rather, to punish the media.[2]

More recently, the media success rate has improved in defending against libel suits.[3] And, most judgments against the media in lower courts are overturned or dramatically reduced by appeals courts, where judges, perhaps unlike juries, rule strictly on law and not on emotion over the media and their role in our society, as jurors might. But legal costs alone in libel suits can be enormous. CBS spent more than $15 million defending against a suit by Gen. William C. Westmoreland. (He and his supporters spent $3 million.) So—win or lose—the damage to media treasure chests and journalists' careers can be huge.

Jurors Reflect Societal Suspicion of Media

Clearly, in ruling so frequently—and harshly—against the media, jurors reflect a wider societal suspicion of media motives and conduct. As a reporter, you will be part of the media institution that, surveys reveal, the public—and, thus, jurors—often regard as arrogant, distant, insensitive and altogether deserving a financial sock on the jaw.

Research shows many Americans regard reporters as self-centered, out to get a good story and "sell newspapers," even if that means harming others or invading privacy. Newspapers and other media often are regarded as "big guys" who don't mind trampling on "little guys" to get what they want.

Many Suits Based on "Unfair" Writing

Why people go the next step and sue newspapers comes through also in research: Many sue out of deep frustration, often over stories a journalist would consider minor, even inconsequential. Those who sue—"plaintiffs"—often feel something written about them is unfair, unbalanced—that they are wronged by images left in readers' minds. Of course, many who sue quarrel with the facts or accuracy of a story, but some also are angered by *impressions* left by it, by what they perceive to be its basic unfairness.

People offended by press coverage often contact the reporter or newspaper to tell their side of the story or simply blow off steam. They have no legal right of access to the media, no right to insist their reply or a corrective story be published. But they want to talk to someone. Too often, they get brushed off by curt reporters or harried editors. Next stop: a lawyer's office.

Obviously, then, discharging your journalistic responsibility by covering the news, while staying free of legal liability, can be complicated. We, therefore, need to take a close look at certain legal principles.

PRESS LAW: THE FOUNDATION

American press law is complex, but its beginnings were simply stated in just a few words, and even today the legal foundation of our media rests on them:

> Congress shall make no law respecting an establishment of religion, or prohibiting the free exercise thereof; *or abridging the freedom of speech, or the press;* or the right of the people peaceably to assemble, and to petition the Government for a redress of grievances.   *First Amendment to the U.S. Constitution*

From that simple but majestic language flowed many U.S. Supreme Court interpretations down through the years that define the legal relationship between government and the media.

First Amendment Is Our Legal Foundation

The First Amendment gives the newswriter strong protection in writing about public officials or, as well, individuals in the public eye. You need only look at this morning's front pages or the evening news to see tough coverage of officials or, say, sports or entertainment figures. Those few words in the First Amendment are the legal basis for the freest, hardest-hitting media in the world.

However, the First Amendment does *not* offer you complete freedom. For example, the U.S. Supreme Court has limited press freedom through wartime censorship, to protect an individual's right to a fair trial, and to prevent publication of obscenity.

First Amendment Doesn't Provide Complete Freedom

And, very importantly, the First Amendment does not hold the newswriter free from liability in *civil actions* initiated by individuals who sue on grounds of defamation. Defamation is the sector of law that must receive our primary attention in this book, for there lie the potentially most damaging legal traps you will face early in your newswriter career.

Defamation is false communication that tends to harm people's reputation and thus lower them in the estimation of their community or deter others from associating with them. *Defamation is injury to reputation* by exposing a person *or business* to dislike, hatred, ridicule, disgrace.

Defamation Is Injury to Reputation

Broadly, defamation comes in two forms: *Libel* is writing, pictures, cartoons or another tangible medium that injures reputation. *Slander* rises from injury to reputation through the spoken word. We'll concentrate on libel.

Libel Is Tangible, Slander Spoken

Many libel cases arise from news writing that alleges criminal behavior, incompetency, inefficiency, immoral, fraudulent or other dishonorable conduct. Particularly dangerous are stories that harm professional reputation and cause financial loss to a person or business.

There are other factors to consider:

A libel must be *published*. But that doesn't mean only on a front page. Even a memo to your editor, say, or a letter to a friend can be judged to constitute publication. If circumstances suggest someone other than the writer and target saw the offending material, it has been published.

Libel Must Be Published

Persons who claim libel must prove they were *identified* in the offending material. However, that doesn't mean you are safe if you omit names, ages, addresses. If a person's identity can be inferred from a story, identification may have been made. So, don't write, "An elderly, white-haired grocer who lives near the school was accused of child molestation" and think you're safe because you didn't name him. Everybody in the neighborhood knows the kindly old gent—only one grocer fits that description—and you've identified him. Conversely, when you *do* intend to identify someone, do so fully enough to ensure no mistaken identification can be inferred. For example, fully identify the accused child molester as "John G. Jones Jr., 54, a grocer who lives at 156 N. Oak St., near Green School." Identify him only as "John Jones, a grocer who lives near a school" and you could have a problem if another John Jones, also a grocer, lives near Little Red School over on Elm Street.

Be Extremely Careful with Personal Identifications

It's not only literal language of a published statement that can make it defamatory. The context of the statement and the overall impression it reasonably creates can also defame. Don't write, for example, about a woman and leave the impression—which a jury could draw—that she is a person of bad moral character or a

***Impressions* You Leave Can Defame, Too**

person of ill repute. *Always* step back from your keyboard for a moment and think: Would a reasonable person reading this reach an unfair, defamatory conclusion about the subject?

DEFENSE AGAINST LIBEL

Be Able to Prove Truth

Truth is the only absolute defense against a libel action. But—and there's always a "but" in law (which is why we have lawyers)—*you must be able to prove* the truth of what you write.

Some experts argue that recent court rulings shifted to the plaintiff (the person who brings suit) the burden of proving that a *false* assertion was made. Nevertheless, if a libel suit against you goes to court you likely will find yourself required to prove—to your editor if not to a jury—that you wrote the truth.

An important distinction: It's not enough to prove you correctly quoted someone; you must prove the allegations, yours *and your source's,* are substantially correct. So, watch those sources who demand anonymity as they feed you potentially damaging material about someone. We'll discuss this in detail later, but you could be required to prove allegations made by a source you are pledged not to identify.

Another important defense against libel charges is *privilege.* It comes in two forms:

Absolute Privilege as a Defense

1. *Absolute privilege* flows from the long-standing principle in American law that public business must be conducted with free and open debate, so partici-

Reporters interviewing Nicaraguan Contra leader Adolfo Calero demonstrate two techniques for catching quotes accurately: notebook and pen, or tape recorder. Note the reporter on the left is recording his own question.

(AP photo used with permission)

pants should be protected from successful libel actions. That protection extends to public and official proceedings and most public records. For example, absolute privilege covers participants for what they say on the floor of the U.S. Senate or a state legislature, or in a court proceeding.

2. *Qualified privilege* sometimes extends protection to the media if they report *accurately, fairly and without malice* from public and official proceedings and public records. *Note:* Absolute privilege does *not* extend to what you report and write, and even qualified privilege can be lost if it's proven you wrote with malice or didn't fairly and accurately summarize the material.

Qualified Privilege as a Defense

Qualified privilege can protect you in reporting what public officials say on many matters that arise outside, say, a court or legislature. You have qualified privilege to report, for example, that the police chief said the grocer was arrested on a charge of child molestation. However, you must report fairly, accurately, and without malice.

Caution: State laws differ on who is a public official and what is an official proceeding or official record. Check local authority to ensure you have qualified privilege before you do anything else. Although the city police chief may be a public official, the city dog catcher may not be, at least within the framework of libel law.

In some instances, defense against libel charges can be built around "neutral reportage." Some—but not all—state courts recognize privilege sometimes exists for fair and balanced "neutral" reporting of charges and countercharges made about public officials or figures by responsible individuals and organizations. This type of reporting occurs, naturally, in political campaigns or controversies over important public issues. Sometimes, that charges are made publicly is news in itself. Must newswriters independently verify the truth of each charge and countercharge? Some state courts say no, that privilege exists *if* reporting is neutral, if the newswriter does not advocate the validity of the charges, if the subject of a charge is given chance to respond, or if the reporting is balanced. "Neutral reportage" isn't a universally accepted defense. But being neutral, fair, balanced and accurate can give your attorney ammunition for constructing a defense.

"Neutral Reportage" Sometimes a Defense

Let's look at important cases bearing on public officials, public figures, private individuals, and how you cover them.

Landmark Cases

In 1964, the U.S. Supreme Court ruled in *New York Times Co.* vs. *Sullivan* that public *officials* must prove "actual malice" to recover damages for defamatory falsehoods in coverage of their official conduct. The court ruled that to prove malice officials must prove those responsible for the story knew it was false when they published it *or* published with "reckless disregard" of whether it was true or false.[4]

This was a major breakthrough for the media although it did not confer absolute privilege on them. The ruling meant the media could cover public officials and—even if some published information was incorrect—should be protected from having to pay damages in a lawsuit.

Note "reckless disregard." This ties back to your *journalistic responsibility* as a newswriter. It's imperative that you check, double-check, and in your reporting and writing make every effort to do a principled, balanced, fair job. And, you should be able to prove in court that you did so.

"Reckless Disregard" and Your Journalistic Responsibility

In 1967, in *Associated Press* vs. *Walker,* the U.S. Supreme Court extended its *Times Co.* vs. *Sullivan* ruling to public *figures.* The AP case involved a former Army general, Edwin A. Walker, who had become active politically. He was present during riots at the University of Mississippi in 1962 and sued The Associated Press for a story about the riots.

The Court ruled that Walker "was a public man in whose public conduct society and the press had a legitimate and substantial interest." Thus did the Supreme Court extend its *Times Co.* vs. *Sullivan* ruling to public *figures,* requiring them to prove actual malice.

Warning: The law is shifting and changing, and since 1967, court rulings have narrowed the definition of public figures. For example, a prominent attorney was found in *Gertz* vs. *Robert Welch Inc.* to be a private, not public, figure. So was a wealthy divorcee well-known in social circles in *Time* vs. *Firestone.* In *Wolston* vs. *Reader's Digest,* the Court ruled that even people involved in a national criminal investigation don't automatically become public figures.

So, even though you're writing about well-known people you may not have protection from *Associated Press* vs. *Walker.* Court rulings indicate a public figure does *not* include someone unwillingly thrust into the limelight. It *does* seem to cover a private person who willingly seeks the limelight and enters public debate.

To establish knowing falsehood or reckless disregard, libel plaintiffs may probe a reporter's state of mind at the time a contested story is written. This means a plaintiff may question news judgments, and newsroom procedures, and may obtain documents or a reporter's notes that might shed some light on state of mind.

Should You Keep Your Notes?

Some libel experts recommend newspapers keep memorandums or other documentation compiled at time of writing as evidence at any later trial that care was taken in doing the story and that reporters and editors were convinced it was true and fair. *However,* other experts argue that reporters should *not* keep notes because the plaintiff's attorneys might be able to use them for their own purposes. Check with your editor on your newspaper's procedures.

Something else to watch: In its *Associated Press* vs. *Walker* ruling, the Supreme Court also dealt with a lawsuit by a football coach, Wallace Butts of the University of Georgia, against owners of the *Saturday Evening Post.* The Court said Butts was a public figure, but that in its reporting and writing about him the magazine ignored "elementary precautions" and engaged in "slipshod and sketchy investigatory techniques." The Court said that the AP's story about Walker was "hot news" but that the Butts story was not, and that although *Saturday Evening Post* editors recognized need for thorough investigation before they published charges against Butts, they published in "reckless disregard for the truth."

Again, we see a need for every journalist to report and write with great care, thoroughly checking facts in a highly professional manner—and to be able to prove that was done.

Note also the Supreme Court's implication that reporters doing so-called investigative stories that are not "hot news" carry an extra burden of confirming the facts. Many young reporters enter the investigative realm early in their careers and are assigned to stories that are extremely important and sensitive, although not "hot news." If you draw such an assignment, proceed carefully.

WATCH THESE TRAPS, TOO

Criminal libel. This involves charges that libel resulted in breach of peace, possibly a *criminal* offense punishable by imprisonment. Newspapers and press associations are fighting attempts in some states to threaten the media with criminal libel. The principles of law and defensive measures detailed in our earlier discussion of civil libel pertain in criminal libel, too.

Test of Privacy is Current Newsworthiness

Privacy. It's a principle well established in U.S. life and law: A person has a right to privacy, to be left alone. Nevertheless, the courts have ruled reporters can write safely about persons involved, even unwillingly, in matters of legitimate public interest. For example, a survivor of a hotel fire has been involved in a news event of public interest, even if unwillingly, and can be shown running naked to safety. When in doubt, ask yourself if there is *current newsworthiness* in the event. If so, chances are the right to privacy has been forfeited. But chances are it has *not* been forfeited, for example, in this scenario: You are assigned to do that feature so beloved in smalltown journalism, the look back at "Our Town 25 Years Ago." Flipping through newspapers of a quarter century ago you come upon a juicy item. Sam Bigtime, the town's leading banker and a pillar of the local church, was arrested 25 years ago today on a charge of drunken driving. Drop it. If he's lived a blameless life since then, there may be no current newsworthiness to that old charge and he may have legal right to privacy in what happened that long ago. (There *may* be current newsworthiness in that item, however, if it concerns a local politician running on a political platform promising harsh treatment for drunken drivers. But this entire area can be tricky legally, so consult your editor.)

False Light. This arises from publication that portrays an individual in "false light" that would be offensive to a person of ordinary sensibility. Such publication *need not be defamatory.* Lawsuits based on false light often charge that a suggestion or implication, rather than outright explicit statement, holds an individual in false light. Sometimes omission of important facts is cited as false light. The defense is truth: If what is stated is true, it cannot hold the individual in "false light."

"False Light" and Truth

Fair comment. It's possible, particularly in smalltown journalism, where every writer must cover many types of stories, that early in your career you will review local theater or musical performances. Perhaps you'll write commentary on, say, art exhibitions, or review books. Publication of such writing can be as libelous as any "hard" news story. However, there is a defense: "fair comment and criticism." It can provide protection if these legal principles are met: You publish opinion and comment on matters of *public interest or importance*. Your facts are true. You report and write fairly and with honest purpose and, certainly, without malice. The "fair comment" principle is why painters, composers, actors (and writers of textbooks) must grit their teeth and suffer under the harshest criticism. They have no legal recourse if the critics are accurate in their use of facts, and are fair, honest and without malice.

The Defense of "Fair Comment"

Now, we've looked at major danger spots in press law. How can you avoid them in your newswriting?

PRACTICAL LESSONS IN LIBEL LAW

Let's examine how you must try to avoid legal difficulties by *being fair* in your writing, by ensuring there is *sound journalistic reason* for what you write, by *treat-*

A Professional's View
Libel: The Grim Reaper

Libel, a published false statement that harms someone's reputation, is the grim reaper of loose journalism. Libel can be devastating to the subject, and an ensuing suit can be debilitating for the reporter. . . . Generally, the best way to avoid libel problems is through sound journalism and a sense of fairness. . . .

Boisfeuillet Jones Jr., general counsel, *Washington Post*[5]

ing every story you write as important, and being particularly careful with stories charging *criminal misconduct.*

Write with Balance, Accuracy, Fairness

As a newswriter, your first defense against libel suits is doing the journalistic job the way it should be done—accurately and with balance. Report and write as dispassionately and objectively as possible. Give all parties in a dispute chance to comment, particularly anyone whose reputation could be harmed by your story. Write in nonjudgmental language, avoiding words or phraseology (see the sidebar below) that could be interpreted as implying guilt or wrongdoing. *Be fair.*

Hurt people in print, wound their ego, embarrass them in their homes, churches, jobs, communities—and they may come after you, trailing a lawyer and seeking revenge as well as monetary award. Stop and think: Does your writing accuse someone of violating society's standards of living and behavior? Does it cause them loss in their profession, business or social circle? If so, you may need expert legal counsel on how to proceed. Obviously, much of what you will write as a journalist may embarrass people or cause them emotional distress. After all, how can you write that Mr. X was arrested as a drug pusher or that Mrs. XYZ was fired as chief executive officer of her company without embarrassing them? But there can be sound journalistic reason for those stories, true news value in revealing to the public what happened. Make sure you don't harm or embarrass simply through sloppiness

Write with Sound Journalistic Reason

A Professional's View:
Word Alert

Stop and think if you find yourself using the following words in newswriting. They are among words libel expert Bruce Sanford says have inspired libel suits when used to describe individuals.

adulterer	scandalmonger
bankrupt	scoundrel
blackmailer	seducer
booze-hound	shyster
coward	skunk
crook	sneak
deadbeat	sold his influence
drug addict	stool pigeon
drunkard	stuffed the ballot box
ex-convict	suicide
fool	suspect
gay	swindler
groveling office seeker	thief
illegitimate	unethical
informer	unmarried mother
kept woman	unprofessional
Nazi	unsound mind
peeping Tom	unworthy of credit
rascal	villain

Bruce Sanford, counsel for Society of Professional Journalists

or carelessness. And *never* harm or cause emotional distress through premeditated intent to wound.

Many times, it's "little" stories that cause legal problems. On big stories—investigative takeouts or stories obviously sensitive—reporters and editors are alert for the slightest nuance that might draw a lawsuit. Frequently, the newspaper's lawyers look over a story before publication. But too often reporters aren't alert when writing two-paragraph police blotter items or accident stories. They get bored and sloppy—facts get mixed up, wrong names and addresses creep into writing. And, if you write the drug raid was at 191 Broad St., and it really was at 291 Broad, you can have a serious problem with the folks who live at 191.

Treat every story you write, even a small one, as the most important in the world. And at that moment it is—*because it is the one you are writing*. Check, double-check every fact. Practice precision journalism.

Practice Precision Journalism

Be extremely careful, for example, in covering the criminal justice system (and many young reporters start on "cops"). Individuals are *arrested* and *booked,* or entered in police records, on specific charges. Be exact in your reporting:

Wrong: Narcotics agents swept through a "shooting gallery" at 291 Broad St. last night and picked up six drug pushers.

Correct: Narcotics agents last night raided what they said was a "shooting gallery" at 291 Broad St. and arrested six people on charges of selling drugs.

And notice the difference here:

Wrong: A car driven by Fred Smith of 291 Broad St. crashed into one driven by an Oklahoma tourist on I-85 last night, killing three persons. Sources said Smith was drunk.

Correct: Cars driven by Fred Smith of 291 Broad St. and an Oklahoma tourist *collided* on I-85 last night, killing three persons. *Police charged* Smith with driving while intoxicated.

Some categories of news obviously are particularly dangerous legally. They include, for example, arrests, charges of criminal conduct and allegations of official misconduct by *individuals.* Some aren't so obvious. For example, society today demands racial equality, so writing a seemingly innocent story about a *company* discriminating in hiring might be considered defamatory. It's also obvious that strong-willed, wealthy individuals might be more inclined to sue for libel (libel law has been called the "rich man's revenge"). But not so obvious is that you can get into big trouble by publishing a libelous statement about a *group.* Write, for example, that a small group of impoverished members of a nearly bankrupt church are morally degenerate, and any single member of the congregation can bring suit against you. *Lesson:* Examine your writing from every possible angle, looking for not-so-obvious danger signs.

Beware of Stories Charging Criminal Misconduct

Now, what should you do if you get a furious complaint about a story you wrote?

What to Do Until Your Lawyer Arrives

Be professional and courteous if contacted by someone offended by one of your stories. Take full details of the complaint. *But listen only.* Don't comment on rights or wrongs in the story. *Never* acknowledge a story might be libelous. Libel law is complex and a story that might appear to be libelous in fact might not be. *Never* talk to a complainant's lawyer. Make it a rule: Only lawyers talk to lawyers when lawsuit talk is in the air. What you *say* about a story after its publication can be damaging legally.

It's possible you could be served with a subpoena (a court order to perform) directing you to turn over notes, appear in court to testify, and so forth. Sometimes reporters are subpoenaed to testify not about what they have written but, rather, what they have learned about an event at issue in a lawsuit having nothing to do with libel or the newspaper. Immediately consult your editor before responding to a subpoena. Most newspapers vigorously fight subpoenas that could lead to outsider intervention in the news-gathering process. But if finally ordered to testify you may have to do so or possibly face contempt-of-court charges.

Immediately Reveal All to Your Editor

Avoid the temptation (and it's very strong) of trying to handle a threatened lawsuit yourself. You might think you can "talk down" an angry complainant, or perhaps set things right by quietly doing another story—and your editor won't even know. Reporters can dig themselves into deep legal trouble by trying such do-it-yourself remedies. Don't attempt it. Listen, take the facts, immediately reveal all to your editor.

When "lawsuit" is even implied, it's time for your editor to call in your newspaper's lawyer. Be entirely forthcoming with your editor and lawyer. Again, the temptation may be to withhold embarrassing facts about how you reported or wrote the contested story. It's a very natural instinct to protect your own reputation (and job). But when lawsuit is threatened your attorney needs *all* the facts to fashion the best possible defense.

Any retraction or other corrective action should be taken only in full consultation with your newspaper's lawyer. A hastily done correction sometimes can be judged to have reiterated or confirmed a libel, and state laws vary on how and when corrective action should be taken.

Many newspapers carry libel insurance that covers employees. Newspapers and insurance companies almost always defend employees in a libel suit because self-interest is at stake: If employees defend themselves independently and are found guilty, the newspapers also are in legal jeopardy. There have been cases, however, of newspapers settling out of court and leaving employees to fashion their own defense.

Settling out of court is attractive to some newspapers and insurance companies that want to avoid going before juries that might be prejudiced against the media. In view of the track record of juries harshly finding against the media in recent years, settling can seem warranted.

However, libel suits proliferated at such an alarming rate in the 1980s that some newspapers announced they would make no out-of-court settlements and would fight every suit—even filing countersuits against plaintiffs *and* attorneys for any baseless legal action.

Libel Law and the "Chilling Effect"

The stiffening resistance to libel suits stems, in part, from realization that media foes and powerful officials sometimes try to use libel law to stifle aggressive investigative reporting. This is called the "chilling effect."

Even *threat* of a lawsuit can have chilling effect.

Retired Executive Editor Ben Bradlee of the *Washington Post*, who directed some of the most aggressive and courageous reporting in America, acknowledges an editor must think twice if a reporter says, "I've got a great story and it'll cost you only a million dollars to defend in court."

Leading editors resist the "chill" and report the news as their judgment dictates it must be reported. Certainly nothing in this chapter is designed to "chill" your reportorial ardor as you launch your newswriter career. Nevertheless, it is only prudent to be alert to legal ramifications of the job. So although your first defense against libel is journalistic—being fair, accurate, balanced—you also must grasp fundamentals of the law to be an effective newswriter.

ADDITIONAL ISSUES IN PRESS LAW

Although they may not immediately involve you, in your first newswriting job, other issues are important in press law.

Free Press/Fair Trial

Sometimes the First Amendment is perceived as clashing with the Sixth Amendment guarantee that criminal defendants will receive speedy and public trial by impartial juries and the Fourteenth Amendment guarantee of due process under the law for everyone. Mostly, this conflict arises in belief that news coverage can prejudice juries and prevent fair trial. Judges sometimes close courtrooms or issue "gag orders" prohibiting reporting of certain details in criminal trials. Generally, the U.S. Supreme Court gives preferred status to the First Amendment and strikes down gag orders. But *pre*trial proceedings sometimes are closed, a serious problem for reporters because so many criminal proceedings are concluded in pretrial plea bargaining. Some newspapers equip reporters with short statements to read, respectfully requesting that a judge not close a court session until a newspaper attorney can be summoned. Your editor will provide guidance on what your newspaper does in event of a gag order.

"Gag Orders" and You

"Sunshine" Laws

Both federal and state laws require certain government meetings and records to be open. Most states have laws specifically requiring advance notice of meetings, complete with time and place. Letting the sun shine on public business is the mission of every journalist. But for some reason, even the nicest people, when elected to a school board or city council, often want to conduct public business behind closed doors. If you are prevented from covering public business, protest and call your editor. On the federal level and in most states, sunshine laws provide legal remedies. Freedom of information laws guarantee access to public records in most states. Your state press association can advise on your state's sunshine and freedom of information laws.

Check Your State's "Sunshine Laws"

Shield Laws

Some states have laws shielding reporters from being forced to divulge the identity of sources, to turn over notes, or to testify in court or before administrative or legislative bodies. Such laws support reporters' contentions that there should be legal recognition of their confidential relationship with sources comparable to the societal recognition that members of the clergy should not be forced to divulge what transpires with their parishioners or that physicians can keep confidential their relationship with patients. State shield laws for reporters vary widely, however, and are open to interpretation. Even though New Jersey had a shield law, a reporter there went to jail for refusing to turn over notes subpoenaed in a murder trial. In 1990, the California Supreme Court ruled that, even though that state has a shield law, reporters can be compelled to testify in criminal cases when their testimony is essential to an accused's defense. Check your editor or state press association for laws in your state.

"Shield Laws" Aren't Foolproof

Misappropriation

If you use a person's name, photo, or likeness for commercial gain, without permission, you can be liable for substantial damages. This problem arises mostly in advertising, endorsements, and non-news products. Using names or photos in *news*

In some states, these reporters interviewing Barry Goldwater, long-time power in the Republican Party, could be forced by a judge to turn over their notes for use in a lawsuit. In other states, "shield laws" protect reporters against being forced to turn over notes or to reveal sources.

(AP photo
used with permission)

coverage generally is protected. Don't release to anyone else, for commercial exploitation, materials you have collected in your news reporting duties.

Trademarks

Use Generic Terms for Trade Names

Companies spend millions of dollars—sometimes billions—to develop commercial value in trade names. Some, such as Coca-Cola or Pepsi, become more valuable than all the buildings and other physical assets a company owns. So, you can expect stiff protest if you misuse trade names, particularly if you use them in lower case as generally descriptive words. If a trade name becomes generically used it may slip into the public domain for any company to exploit (as happened with "aspirin" and "nylon"). And enormous value to the originating company is lost. So use generic terms such as "soft drink" and "copying machine" unless you use Coca-Cola and Xerox properly. If you receive a complaint over misuse of a trade name give it to your editor for relay to the newspaper's attorney for formal response.

Copyright

Owners of writings and photographs have rights to them, particularly the right to be paid for their use, that are protected by federal copyright statutes. *Information in those materials cannot be copyrighted*—neither can ideas, theories, news. But the *manner of expression,* the arrangement of words, sentences—the writing—can be. Under the doctrine of "fair use," you may use limited portions of someone else's writing in, for example, a book review or news article. When copyright infringement is charged, a test is whether usage hurt the commercial value of the work. If so, you might be open to claim for damages. Questions of copyright normally concern use of literary works, music (including lyrics), dramatic works, photos, graphics, sound recordings, audiovisuals, and so forth.

Cameras and Courts

The U.S. Supreme Court leaves to state courts the decision of whether to permit news photography during trials. The Supreme Court holds that the First Amendment does not give photographers automatic access and that the Sixth Amendment guarantee of fair trial does not automatically bar photographers or cameras from the courtroom. Generally, judges who permit photographs in their courtrooms insist on use of certain equipment and procedures designed to prevent disruption of proceedings.

Questions of *ethics* that arise in such issues will be discussed in the next chapter.

SUMMARY CHECKLIST

- ☐ Reflecting wider societal suspicion of the media, juries found against newspapers in three out of four libel cases that went to trial in 1980–1986.

- ☐ Most judgments against newspapers are overturned or dramatically reduced by appeals courts, but legal costs alone can run into millions of dollars for newspapers that are sued.

- ☐ A newswriter's first defense against libel is reporting and writing accurately, fairly, with balance and, certainly, without malice.

- ☐ The First Amendment gives newswriters strong protection in covering public officials and figures but doesn't free them from liability in civil actions for defamation.

- ☐ Defamation is communication that harms the reputation of a person or business by exposing either to dislike, hatred, ridicule or disgrace.

- ☐ Libel is writing, pictures, cartoons or another tangible medium that injures one's reputation. Slander arises from injury to reputation through the spoken word.

- ☐ To be libelous, a statement must harm reputation, be published and identify a specific person.

- ☐ Provable truth is the only absolute defense against libel action.

- ☐ Another important defense is absolute privilege, which protects participants in public and official proceedings and most public records. Qualified privilege extends protection to the media if they report accurately, fairly and without malice defamatory statements from public and official proceedings and public records.

☐ In *New York Times Co.* vs. *Sullivan,* the U.S. Supreme Court ruled that public officials must prove malice to recover damages for defamatory falsehoods in coverage of their official conduct.

☐ In *Associated Press* vs. *Walker,* the Supreme Court extended its *Times* vs. *Sullivan* ruling to public figures. Subsequent rulings left vague the definition of public figure.

☐ A person's right to privacy is well established in U.S. law. Consider whether there is current newsworthiness in what you are writing about private individuals.

☐ If threatened with a libel suit, make no comment about the contested story. Take full details of the complaint, then consult your editor and newspaper's attorney.

RECOMMENDED READING

For the non-lawyer newswriter, the libel manual in *The Associated Press Stylebook* is must reading.

For excellent treatment of media law see Kent Middleton and William Chamberlin, *Law of Public Communication* 2nd ed. (White Plains, N.Y.: Longman, 1991), and Ralph L. Holsinger, *Media Law* (New York: Random House, 1987).

Current issues in media law are covered particularly well by *presstime,* the American Newspaper Publisher Association's monthly. Note also *WJR, Editor & Publisher* and, for daily newspaper coverage, *The New York Times* and *The Wall Street Journal*

NOTES

1. For details on these cases, see, in order, the following: Michael deCourcy Hinds, "Philadelphia Paper Assessed $34 million for Libel," *The New York Times*, national edition, May 4, 1990, p. A-1; Amy Dockser Marcus and Wade Lambert, "Magazine Is Sued by Ex-Husband on Story of Child-Visitation Fight," *The Wall Street Journal*, Jan. 25, 1990, p. B6; Amy Dockser, "Wayne Newton's NBC Libel Suit Returning to Trial," *The Wall Street Journal*, Oct. 19, 1988, p. B8.
2. Randall Bezanson and Gilbert Cranberg, "Punitive Damages: Muzzled Press?", The *New York Times*, June 13, 1988, p. A19.
3. "Reporting Says Media Faring Better in Libel Suits," *Broadcasting,* Sept. 11, 1989, p. 133.
4. Landmark cases are discussed in AP's libel manual. Also see Kent Middleton and William Chamberlin, *Law of Public Communication* (White Plains, N.Y.: Longman, 1991).
5. The *Washington Post,* "Deskbook on Style," 2nd ed. Thomas W. Lippman, ed. (New York: McGraw-Hill, 1989).

Exercise 9–1   Questions About Libel—I

1. Define defamation.

_____

_____

_____

2. What is libel?

_____

_____

_____

3. What is slander?

_____

_____

_____

4. What constitutes publication of a libel?

_____

_____

_____

5. What is the only absolute defense against libel?

_____

_____

_____

6. Define absolute privilege.

_____

_____

_____

_____

7. Define qualified privilege.

_____

_____

_____

_____

8. Do reporters have qualified privilege if they report a police chief's statement that a person was arrested on, say, a burglary charge?

_____

_____

_____

_____

9. Describe the use of "neutral reportage" in defense against libel suits.

_____

_____

_____

_____

10. Under the "provable truth" defense in a libel case is it necessary for a reporter to be able to prove allegations made by news sources?

_____

_____

_____

_____

Exercise 9–2   Questions About Libel—II

1. In *New York Times Co.* vs. *Sullivan*, the U.S. Supreme Court ruled that public officials must prove what to recover damages for defamatory falsehoods in coverage of their official conduct?

_____

_____

_____

2. Describe what officials must do to prove malice under the *New York Times Co.* vs. *Sullivan* ruling by the U.S. Supreme Court.

_____

_____

_____

3. In *Associated Press* vs. *Walker*, the Supreme Court extended its *New York Times Co.* vs. *Sullivan* ruling to public._____

4. Describe the Supreme Court's definition of Walker as a "public figure" under the *Associated Press* vs. *Walker* ruling.

_____

_____

_____

5. What distinction did the Supreme Court draw between AP's conduct in the Walker case and the *Saturday Evening Post's* conduct on the Butts story?

_____

_____

_____

6. What is the distinction between civil and criminal libel charges?

_____

_____

_____

7. What legal principle underlies a person's claim to privacy?

_____

_____

_____

8. How does "current newsworthiness" affect the privacy issue?

_____

_____

_____

9. Define "falsity" in its legal sense.

_____

_____

_____

10. What is a defense against a charge of holding someone in "false light"?

_____

_____

_____

_____

Exercise 9–3   Dangerous Words and Phrases

Underline in the following examples all words and phrases that are judgmental or dangerous from a legal point of view.

1. A West Side meat packing firm notorious for adulteration of products was charged Wednesday with five counts of endangering public health.

2. An adulterer wanted in three states on charges of child abuse was arrested Friday.

3. The firm was thought to be bankrupt long before the Internal Revenue Service subpoenaed its records. The president was charged with tax evasion.

4. Men in the unit said the officer was a coward and couldn't explain why he received a medal. They claimed he was a drunkard, too.

5. The district attorney charged her with blackmail, and a well-informed source told reporters she was guilty of bribery as well.

6. "This guy is a confidence man," one source said. Police Chief Fred Smith said he was arrested on five charges of buying votes.

7. It was revealed Wednesday that the bank president was charged 25 years ago with drunken driving.

8. A police source said Smith probably was a member of the American Nazi party long before he was charged with blackmail.

9. Rocco Ricco, a well-known gangster chief, went on trial today on 16 charges of blackmail. What's not well known is that he's a drug addict.

10. The Republican candidate charged that his Democratic opponent was arrested as a peeping Tom while a teenager and is incapable of understanding high finance.

Exercise 9–4   Eliminating Danger

Rewrite the following to eliminate potentially dangerous language.

1. She is extremely popular in social circles but known as something of a scandalmonger and friend of the homeless.

_____

_____

2. Police said he is wanted in Texas on bank robbery charges and is considered by police to be a shyster lawyer.

_____

_____

3. During the Senate debate, he said from the floor that his opponent was a "sneak." He told reporters at the press club that night he meant his opponent had sold his influence.

_____

_____

4. In a heated moment, the defense attorney shouted that the witness was a "stool pigeon." The prosecutor, in turn, shouted that the defense was proceeding unethically. When court adjourned, the defense attorney told reporters the witness was a secret FBI informer.

_____

_____

5. He attempted suicide and neighbors called police. Detective Fred Smith said he was despondent over a failed marriage and was found bleeding from a head wound. A note was in his hand.

_____

_____

6. While in school, she was an unmarried mother of a boy and girl.

_____

_____

7. The university fired the professor on a charge of plagiarism. Colleagues said that was the second time he was guilty of unprofessional conduct.

_____

_____

8. Acme Construction Co. closed its doors last night. It was found unworthy of credit and a banking source said the company might reopen on Monday.

_____

_____

9. Banks announced they withdrew credit from Acme shortly before it closed its doors. A banking source said Eastern Bank Inc. was the villain in the piece and moved first.

_____

_____

10. Environmentalists said Acme discharged toxic chemicals into the river. The Environmental Protection Agency charged Acme with noise pollution.

_____

_____

Exercise 9–5   Writing Libel-Free Copy

Write five paragraphs from the following details. Be certain your copy is fair, balanced, accurate, and free of legally dangerous material.

1. His name is Fred Smith III. He is 54. His address is 316 N. Maple Ave. He is charged with cocaine possession. He was arrested at home this morning. County police made the arrest. Smith is said to be an addict and drunkard.

_____

_____

_____

_____

_____

_____

_____

_____

_____

2. Police said they found incriminating materials in Smith's home. They said they seized 14 ounces of a powdery substance. One thing they found was an address book. Sgt. Will Jones said it listed cocaine delivery points.

_____

_____

_____

_____

_____

_____

_____

_____

_____

_____

_____

_____

3. Smith was booked on three charges of drug possession, then jailed. One source said Smith also will be charged with distribution. Smith retained Jason Smooth, a criminal attorney well-known for defending drug dealers and other unsavory characters.

_____

_____

_____

_____

_____

_____

4. The Greene County Commission is investigating charges against the sheriff. He is Fred Smith, Jr., 62, who has been sheriff for 19 years. Commission Chairman Ned Jones told a press conference he suspects the sheriff misused county vehicles. Smith didn't return three telephone calls to his office and hasn't commented on the investigation.

_____

_____

_____

_____

_____

_____

_____

5. Wilson Friendly is elected president of the chamber of commerce. He is 64 and chairman of East Bank Inc. Friendly was elected today. He is active in community affairs and is known among friends as a "southern charmer" with a keen eye for the ladies and a liking for bourbon and water.

_____

_____

_____

_____

_____

_____

_____

Chapter Ten

A Personal Code of Ethics

No professional newswriter's tool chest is complete without a personal code of journalistic ethics.

Note the use of *personal*. Some newspapers have ethics codes, but often they take a *corporate* stance designed primarily to protect the newspaper's image and marketplace position, not to solve ethical problems you might face personally.

Professional and journalistic societies also have codes, but they represent a broad consensus among editors nationwide. Often they state ethical principles in terms so general that they give little guidance to individual newswriters trying to answer specific troubling questions: Was my handling of that story ethical? Unethical? What is my personal stand on ethics? What is my view of right and wrong?

Like questions of press law, ethical issues can arise the first day you touch a keyboard. *Un*like law, however, ethics offers no long list of court rulings you can apply as precedent in search for answers. Ethics takes you frequently into uncharted waters of personal judgment and personal definition of right and wrong.

Developing a personal sense of ethics is a long process. Just as it will take years to fashion your personal, distinctive writing style, so will it take years to create your personal ethical framework for writing.

Thus, this chapter may not provide answers to all your intensely personal questions of journalistic ethics. However, it will touch on important ethical questions you should consider carefully during your march toward professionalism in newswriting.

ETHICS: THE QUANDARY

Imagine yourself in your first newsroom job, working on a relatively minor assignment: updating the mayor's biographical sketch.

The mayor was elected four years ago on an anti-crime platform and has waged war on crime ever since. She is seeking reelection with the nickname "Mrs. Clean," and she woos crime-weary voters with the slogan "Sweep our streets clean." Senior reporters covering the campaign need updated background on the mayor. Also, your newspaper, like many, keeps undated biographical sketches on leading personalities that can be used quickly in writing obituaries.

You dig into the files and talk to people around town as you research the mayor's life. Then, a shocker: Someone anonymously mails you photocopies of court records showing "Mrs. Clean" was convicted and jailed twice in a distant city 20 years ago for operating a house of prostitution.

The mayor appears to have lived a blameless life since arriving in town 15 years ago. She's married, has two children, and enjoys a fine reputation for being active in performing good works in the community.

What to do?

Well, draw up a checklist:

**Create Your Own Ethical
Checklist**

1. Obviously you must check the accuracy of the information you received.
2. You must apply standards of news judgment we looked at in Chapter 1: The mayor certainly is news to your newspaper's audience (or "market"). A story about her would have deep impact on a large number of people. She is prominent. Coverage of her would be timely. And, politics is conflict, another factor in judging news.
3. Think of the *writing* job you could do on this one, how you could draw word pictures discussed in Chapter 2. Is this *your* Big Story? Your way out of cub ranks and into the front rank with senior reporters?
4. Tick off legal implications discussed in Chapter 9: The mayor is a public official. She thrusts herself into the public limelight. If the story were published and she sued, she would have to prove actual malice. Your newspaper's attorney would check the story before publication. But you probably could make a strong case that there is "current newsworthiness" in the sinful past of a woman running for public office on an anti-sin platform.

From a news and legal standpoint, then, it appears you *could* do the story.

But *should* you?

Check your own emotions: Do you feel revulsion at digging into Madam Mayor's background? Do you admire her for bouncing back from a shady past to lead a "good" life? Or, do you see her as a willing participant in the rough and tumble of politics and, therefore, fair game?

You must consult your editor, of course. But wait! What is the editor's stance on such ethical issues? Indeed, does the *newspaper* have a code of ethics that applies to this case?

What happens if *you* decide that whatever her past, the mayor is a good person, entitled to privacy on what happened so long ago—but your boss decides this is news and should be published?

If ordered, will you write the story? After all, you're in the business of selling newspapers, and, you *are* being paid to write what the paper wants to publish. Are you a "newswriter for hire"?

Will You Quit Over Ethics?

Or will you object? And if you do object, how strenuously? If pressed to the wall, will you quit?

In just this manner, for journalists, ethics moves from leisurely, theoretical discussion into the harsh reality of making tough judgment calls. And they are calls that must be made very quickly in a busy newsroom and without much firm historical guidance on what to do.

ETHICS: THE BEGINNINGS

It's not that ethics hasn't been discussed by many people for a very long time. Recorded ethical debate extends back nearly 2,500 years. Before he died in Athens in 399 B.C., Socrates discussed the concepts of "good" and "justice." His student, Plato, who died in 347 B.C., discussed the notion of good existing, despite how a society might conduct itself at the moment. Plato's student, Aristotle, spoke of the individual's responsibility for acting with virtue—even if the price included forsaking happiness, and making sacrifices.

Imagine those heavy thinkers advising you on the story about the mayor: Socrates would draw you into looking inward, considering deeply the justice of revealing her secret past. Plato might urge you to seek good, even if those around you—including your editor—don't recognize it. For certain, Aristotle would say that your editor's sense of ethics aside, you have a personal responsibility to do the right thing, even at heavy cost. Aristotle probably would advise sacrificing your job if your editor ordered you to proceed in a manner you regard as unethical.

Your Personal Responsibility to Do Right

In this way the mainstream of ethical thought descends through the generations to your keyboard today. Libraries have been written about that mainstream, and definitive discussion of ethics in this or any other single book is impossible. However, high points crucial to a journalist can be identified.

Development of Judeo-Christian ethics loaded enormous responsibility on the individual for interpreting God's will—including the Ten Commandments—and doing the right thing. It's not much of a leap from that concept to believing that whatever your editor says, whatever your newspaper's code of ethics holds, you are ultimately responsible, as a principled journalist, for doing what is right. And *you* must figure out what "right" is.

In the 17th century there appeared the then-revolutionary notion (Thomas Hobbes, 1588–1679, was an early advocate) that the people, not sovereign rulers, possess true power. It follows that to wield power the people must be informed—thus the fundamental concept today in American journalism that the media have a special societal role of placing before the people the information they need for considered use of democratic power.

The People Must Be Informed

John Milton (1608–1674) wrote of the "open marketplace of ideas" where truth would survive while false and unsound ideas would be vanquished if all were permitted to freely express ideas. Not many journalists today quote his *Areopagitica,* a defense of press freedom, published in 1644, but we follow Milton's advice by insisting that our primary role is placing *facts* before readers (and viewers) and trusting them to ascertain *truth*.

In the 18th and 19th centuries, three philosophers contributed mightily to the mainstream: David Hume (1711–1776) argued that usefulness—"utility"—is the measure of value for any ethical principle. Justice serves the good of humanity; justice is utilitarian. Immanuel Kant (1724–1804) held the individual responsible for freely and rationally reasoning out what is good. Kant argued that rational intention—the will to be moral—determined the moral worth of an act. John Stuart Mill (1806–1873) interpreted Hume's *utilitarianism* to mean ethical conduct should aim at general well-being for the greatest number of people. Would Mill favor revealing the mayor's background? Publication would invade her privacy and perhaps destroy her career, but would publication serve the well-being of the greatest number of people (the voters)?

Utilitarianism in Ethics

By the late 17th century, the press (itself dating from Johann Gutenberg's popularization of movable type in the 15th century) was developing within a philosophical context. We term it *libertarianism*—trusting in the people's ability to make intelligent decisions and find truth if sufficient information is available in a free press operating in a free society. Implicit in libertarianism is rejection of any attempt by government or other institutions to censor news or restrict press freedom. That includes rejecting responsibility even to the public. The libertarian press regarded itself as a provider of information and entertainment (and, later, advertising), which would serve the political and economic systems while making a profit.

Libertarianism: Trust the People

Out of that basic desire for freedom came the First Amendment to the U.S. Constitution, passed by Congress in 1789 and ratified by three-fourths of the states in 1791 ("Congress shall make no law . . . abridging the freedom of speech, or of the press . . .").

Objectivity Arrives in American Journalism

By the late 19th century, the concept of *objectivity* was spreading through American journalism. As an ideal to strive for, objectivity is central to much in American journalism today. True objectivity probably cannot be achieved, but the ideal requires reporters to avoid activist involvement in the news, to keep their views out of their writing, and to strive to present all sides of issues with balance and as dispassionately as possible.

ASNE's First Statement of Ideals

By the early 20th century, a sense of community conscience began to stir newspapers. Many journalists accepted responsibility to society as a corollary to press freedom. This thinking flowered in 1923 when the American Society of Newspaper Editors (ASNE), founded a year earlier, adopted the "Canons of Journalism," a statement of ideals—that newspapers should serve the public, stay independent of special interests, and be truthful, sincere, accurate. The Canons, a strong *moral force* throughout American journalism, stood until 1975, when supplanted by the society's "Statement of Principles" (see the sidebar below).

Codes Exert *Only* Moral Force

Note that ASNE's principles—and codes of other journalistic organizations—exert moral force *only*. None of the codes have the machinery for defining ethical transgressions by members or for punishment or expulsion for infractions. Law and medicine do have self-regulating machinery and thus are accorded the label "profession" by society. Some social commentators say the media will be a "trade," not a "profession," until they adopt self-regulating machinery. Many journalists, however, fear even voluntary self-regulation would serve as precedent for government or court imposition of mandatory rules—contrary to the First Amendment.

Social Responsibility of Press

In the 1940s, the concept of the press having *social responsibility* came under wide discussion among editors and publishers. Consequently, you'll find in many newsrooms today a sense of mission among journalists who feel they must serve their newspapers' business interests, of course, but also have important responsibilities to the public. It's a guiding principle behind much of the journalism that probes, pushes, shines light in dark corners on behalf of the journalist's ultimate constituency—the reading public.

People's Right to Know Arises

The *people's right to know,* a crowbar reporters use to pry open doors hiding the people's business, entered the journalistic mainstream after World War II. It was

Statement of Principles
American Society of Newspaper Editors

PREAMBLE

The First Amendment, protecting freedom of expression from abridgment by any law, guarantees to the people through their press a constitutional right, and thereby places on newspaper people a particular responsibility.

Thus journalism demands of its practitioners not only industry and knowledge but also the pursuit of a standard of integrity proportionate to the journalist's singular obligation.

To this end the American Society of Newspaper Editors sets forth this Statement of Principles as a standard encouraging the highest ethical and professional performance.

ARTICLE I: RESPONSIBILITY

The primary purpose of gathering and distributing news and opinion is to serve the general welfare by informing the people and enabling them to make judgments on the issues of the time. Newspapermen and women who abuse the power of their professional role for selfish motives or unworthy purposes are faithless to that public trust.

The American press was made free not just to inform or just to serve as a forum for debate but also to bring an independent scrutiny to bear on the forces of power in the society, including the conduct of official power at all levels of government.

ARTICLE II: FREEDOM OF THE PRESS

Freedom of the press belongs to the people. It must be defended against encroachment or assault from any quarter, public or private.

Journalists must be constantly alert to see that the public's business is conducted in public. They must be vigilant against all who would exploit the press for selfish purposes.

ARTICLE III: INDEPENDENCE

Journalists must avoid impropriety and the appearance of impropriety as well as any conflict of interest or the appearance of conflict. They should neither accept anything nor pursue any activity that might compromise or seem to compromise their integrity.

ARTICLE IV: TRUTH AND ACCURACY

Good faith with the reader is the foundation of good journalism. Every effort must be made to assure that the news content is accurate, free from bias and in context, and that all sides are presented fairly. Editorials, analytical articles and commentary should be held to the same standards of accuracy with respect to facts as news reports.

Significant errors of fact, as well as errors of omission, should be corrected promptly and prominently.

ARTICLE V: IMPARTIALITY

To be impartial does not require the press to be unquestioning or to refrain from editorial expression. Sound practice, however, demands a clear distinction for the reader between news reports and opinion. Articles that contain opinion or personal interpretation should be clearly identified.

ARTICLE VI: FAIR PLAY

Journalists should respect the rights of people involved in the news, observe the common standards of decency and stand accountable to the public for the fairness and accuracy of their news reports.

Persons publicly accused should be given the earliest opportunity to respond.

Pledges of confidentiality to news sources must be honored at all costs, and therefore should not be given lightly. Unless there is clear and pressing need to maintain confidences, sources of information should be identified.

These principles are intended to preserve, protect and strengthen the bond of trust and respect between American journalists and the American people, a bond that is essential to sustain the grant of freedom entrusted to both by the nation's founders.

(This statement of Principles was adopted by the ASNE Board of Directors on Oct. 23, 1975; it supplants the 1923 "Canons of Journalism.")

popularized by the general manager of The Associated Press, Kent Cooper, who wielded it against censorship and barriers to free flow of information around the world. The concept of "people's right to know" isn't in the U.S. Constitution, incidentally. Nevertheless, it is firmly fixed in the minds of many as an inalienable right of the people. So is the belief that the press is the people's surrogate and plays a crucial "watchdog" role in our democracy as the *Fourth Estate,* along with the legislative, judicial, and executive branches.

Fourth Estate Watchdogs

You have just had a quick look at some historical factors influencing industry thinking about ethics today. But what gets first priority when you start assembling a personal code of ethics? Arguably, as we discussed in Chapter 7, building a personal attitude toward the ideal of objectivity comes first.[1] (Note the sidebar below for one professional's look at how choice of language can affect objectivity.)

Now, let's look closely at ethical considerations you confront when structuring an individual news story.

A Professional's View:

Secrets of Journalese

Suppose you are a fair-minded journalist and you wish to point out that Senator Forbush is a clod. Do you type "Forbush, the well-known incompetent"? Not at all. You simply write that the poor fellow's reputation is "still dogged by doubts about his competence." Or, if you feel he ought to be indicted, depict him as "haunted by allegations," which, as a dutiful and thorough reporter, you are obliged to dig up and embellish.

These are everyday triumphs of journalese, the secret tongue of reporters and pundits. This little-known, ill-fated, oft-hyphenated language slashes through the full patina of mundane objectivity and lets readers know what you really think.

Thus does John Leo, writing in *U. S. News & World Report,* introduce his readers to getting "the hang of journalese."

Tongue in cheek, Leo translates journalese:

actress-model (means "bimbo")
womanizer (lecher)
freewheeling (crooked)
agreeable (wimpy)
volatile (deranged)
well-known (tiresome)
self-proclaimed (grotesquely uppity)

Leo adds: "One of the richest veins in journalese is the proliferating set of terms that mean 'guilty.' These include 'scandal-plagued,' 'embattled,' 'reputed'. . . ."[2]

Writing with Honesty

It's possible to write a story whose individual components are accurate yet leave false impressions in readers' minds.

Writers who do so intentionally are unprincipled propagandists, and we need not waste space here condemning them. We must discuss, however, how you can *un*intentionally create false impressions with writing that, on its face, seems accurate—but isn't.

Unintentionally dishonest writing stems mostly from *the sin of omission*—failing to include material essential to structural honesty within the story itself and failing to provide readers with full, balanced information needed for proper understanding.

The Sin of Omission

The sin of omission stems primarily from two factors:

• Lazy reporters fail to collect and relay essential facts.

• Space limitations of newspapers and magazines and the time constraints of broadcast media make it impossible to shovel everything into a story—and judgment errors are made in deciding what goes in and what doesn't.

Note this example:

Honest	Dishonest
The White House said today the U.S. economy will be strong for the first half of the year but probably will fall off sharply in the second half. A spokesman told reporters. . . .	The White House said today the U.S. economy will be strong for the first half of the year. A spokesman told reporters. . . .

Obviously, leaving the bad news out of the example above commits the sin of omission. The dishonest paragraph, though true as far as it goes, leaves a decidedly incorrect impression in readers' minds.

We can't fix the dishonest example above if we include the White House's bad news but hold it for the 15th paragraph. Newswriters assign degrees of importance or emphasis to various elements of a news story by where they position them. First paragraph (or "lead") positioning signals readers that "this is most important." Positioning deep in a story signals "less important."

For even highly experienced newswriters, deciding which facts are essential and where they should be placed in a news story can be a difficult process—if honest writing is the goal, as it must be.

Fact Placement a Difficult Process

The difficulty increases when you select quotes and position them in a news story. Consider the challenge of listening to perhaps thousands of words in a speech, then selecting for quotation, say, 50 or 75 words—all you have room for in a story that your editor limits to 300 words total! Skillful use of quotes is so important to the integrity of a news story that we'll spend much more time on them later in the book. For now, add their ethical use to your list of concerns in honest newswriting.

Writing honestly requires you to be open with your readers, *to level with them.* Two especially troublesome factors are examined next.

Identification of Sources

You haven't done your job properly if your writing is sprinkled with "an informed source said" or "according to an informant who did not want to be identified." Research shows that readers deeply distrust "informed source" writing; thus you owe it to readers to reveal as precisely as possible the identity *and* credentials of

Provide Sources' Identity and Credentials

your sources and also how knowledgeable and authoritative the sources are about the issue at hand. Of course, many critically important news stories never would get into print if we didn't sometimes permit sources to go "off the record" and speak anonymously. When that is necessary, strive for language that will establish the source's credentials. "A source close to the mayor and knowledgeable about city finances" is much better than "informed source."

Explaining Apparent Lapses

Explain Apparent Lapses in Your Reporting

To be effective, newswriting must anticipate questions likely to arise in readers' minds, then answer them *or* explain why they cannot be answered. For example, if you must grant anonymity to a source, explain why: "The source asked not to be identified for fear of losing his job." If the source is charging financial irregularity in the mayor's office, your readers will wonder what the mayor's response is. So, if you try but fail to reach the mayor for comment, say so—with precision: "Despite six telephone calls to her office and home, the mayor could not be reached for comment." If you reach her and she won't comment, say that too: "The mayor, reached at her home, declined comment." Any apparent lapse in your reporting should be explained.

For example, don't let your readers wonder why in, say, a story about a mysterious death you can't pin down all the facts: "The coroner said he couldn't determine cause of death until an autopsy was completed. That would take several hours," he said. It's especially important that you level with your readers on methods of newsgathering if they are pertinent to how your story is put together. For instance, don't quote "press reports." Tell your readers your press sources were *The New York Times*, *Washington Post*, *Time* magazine, or whatever. And explain why you are quoting them: "Those three publications alone were permitted to send correspondents to the scene."

YOU, ETHICS AND COURAGE

You'll find treading the ethical path in newswriting isn't easy. It often demands courage and self-discipline and, sometimes, sacrifice. Every year, journalists die in pursuit of news. Some go to jail rather than sacrifice principle. Others make ethical stands that cost them their jobs and the economic security of their families. And every principled journalist sometime in a career will walk away from a Big Story because writing it simply wouldn't be the proper thing to do. (See the sidebar on p. 283 for one foreign correspondent's view of courage in reporting.)

Beginning newswriters often don't meet such dramatic tests of courage early in their careers. But challenges sometimes do arrive early in more subtle form.

Beware Temptation of "Hyping" a Story

For example, it's almost certain that on occasion (not too frequently, we hope) you will be "beaten" by competing reporters. They will have facts or a story "angle" more attractive than yours—perhaps an exclusive story, a "scoop" or a "beat." Beware the temptation (it can get very strong) to push your story beyond its facts, to strive for impact that your story doesn't merit. That's called "hyping" a story, and it's dishonest.

A newswriter lives in an intensely competitive media world. It's embarrassing to be beaten. If you are, your editor might scream for a "matcher"—a story matching the competition's. Get one if you can. If you can't, stand firm. It takes courage, but don't go with a story that plays loosely with the facts or is overwritten.

Avoid the "Herd Effect"

Maintaining independent news judgment can come under heavy pressure from the so-called herd effect. That's the tendency of reporters to follow the lead of certain high-profile, experienced journalists and prestigious newspapers—*The New York Times*, *The Wall Street Journal*, *Washington Post*, among them. If any of

A Professional's View:
Pursuing Truth with Courage

Finding the truth in news is difficult even for veteran newswriters. Here, George Melloan, for more than 30 years a Wall Street Journal *reporter, editor, and foreign correspondent, discusses how complex the search for truth is.*

The challenge the press faces now and will face in the future is to convey to readers and viewers something called truth.

Some people think that is simple. I don't think it is simple at all. Trying to get to the truth of things is very difficult and it will become more difficult as more of what we cover involves greater complexity, which will be the case in the years to come.

At least as important, telling truths sometimes requires courage. Men and women have been martyred throughout time for telling truths. Indeed, that still happens in some parts of today's world.

A reporter working in the United States and other free societies faces little physical risk for truthfulness. But that, in a sense, raises the level of obligation. In unfree societies, the press is not taken very seriously. People find out things by informal means to the extent that they find out things at all.

But in free societies, readers assume that reporters are trying to provide them with truths. Reporters who violate that trust have nothing to blame other than their own lack of effort or integrity.

Doing the job properly not only requires hard work but frequent self-examination: Am I telling this story honestly or am I putting a spin on it? Am I influenced by a desire to be popular among my colleagues or with my editors or publisher? Have I been lazy in my reporting? Am I motivated by a desire to "get" someone I don't like? Have I become a partisan in the conflict I'm covering? Are my ambitions and the competitive pressures applied by the business organization I represent causing me to exaggerate relatively minor events or fall prey to headline-grabbing sources with sensational charges or claims to make?

In short, am I making an effort to be intellectually honest?[3]

George Melloan

those fronts a story and with positioning and headline size signals it is important, journalists nationwide tend to scramble for matchers. Coolly examine your own news judgment if your story is moving contrary to the herd's (after all, you might be wrong). Then do what your conscience and professionalism dictate.

Heavy pressure can build on your news judgment in less recognizable ways. For example, let's say you are covering a proposal that voters approve tax increases to build a new hospital. Doctors, nurses, political leaders, bankers—all might tell you the hospital must be built. But don't let the glowing comments blind you to other sides of the issue. Report other points of view. Stay neutral—hard to do when "good guys" are urging you to help do "good work."

Sometimes you must summon the courage to defy authority. If the city council wants to close its doors to consider the hospital plan, you must push, politely but firmly, to open those doors. As surrogate of the people, you may have to insist the sheriff open arrest records that should be in the public domain. And confrontations of that sort can be difficult, especially for beginning newswriters.

Hold If You Doubt Your Story

Doing the right thing sometimes requires you to resist your superiors. The mechanical demands of the media—the deadline need to go *now* with a news story—can lead your editor to demand a story before you think it's ready for publication. If it comes to that, if you feel your story still is unsubstantiated, still weakly reported, *hold*. Learning when to hold back is part of becoming a professional.

We've now looked at ethics in writing individual news stories. Let's take a slightly wider view.

SPECIAL PROBLEM AREAS IN ETHICS

Ethics clearly is a major part of the professional context for newswriting. In establishing that context for your own career you'll find your professionalism measured, in part, by how you grapple with certain special problem areas.

Truth vs. Fact

Who Is to Judge Truth?

Is it enough for a journalist to find and report fact? We've seen how straightforward but unbalanced and unthinking reporting of facts can create untruthful journalism. History's every demagogue, when written about objectively and dispassionately, could manipulate the media as a propaganda tool. Reporting the facts of what Hitler or Stalin said was one thing; reporting the truth another. But what is truth for the beginning newswriter covering, say, a school board fight or a sewer commission debate? Who, after all, is to judge truth? Perhaps middle ground for the newswriter lies in a career context of painstaking research and reporting, careful and balanced writing, and enough background and interpretation to translate for the reader the complexities of such questions as why the board or commission is in an uproar. The danger, of course, is that for the unwary newswriter "interpretation" easily can slide into personal opinion—and that must be avoided.

Conflict of Interest

Avoid Even Perception of Conflict of Interest

It's obviously unethical to permit personal self-interest to influence your reporting and writing. You shouldn't write about General Motors at all, let alone favorably, if you own GM stock. Many newspapers will forbid you to write about any auto companies if you own auto stock. But how far must a journalist go not only in avoiding conflict of interest but also in avoiding public *perception* that conflict exists? Should you avoid, for example, serving on the board of education if assigned to the education beat? Yes. But should you eschew *any* involvement in politics or local government? Where is the line between the reporter's obligation as a citizen to participate in democratic government and the reporter's obligation as an objective journalist to avoid conflict of interest? The *Washington Post* requires employees to "make every reasonable effort to be free of obligation to news sources and to special interests." Its "Standards and Ethics" states, "Our private behavior as well as our professional behavior must not bring discredit to our profession or to *The Post.*" That includes refusing gifts or favors, free tickets to movies, the theater or sports events, refusing free trips or preferential treatment. Many newspapers have similar policies, and you'll do well to embark on your newswriter career determined to avoid *any* act that could create true or perceived conflict of interest.

Privacy

Privacy: Often a Tough Call

One of the most difficult judgment calls you'll make in newswriting is deciding where an individual's right to privacy ends and the public's right to know begins.

Often, your news sense will tell you the most intimate details of a person's private life are news—and common sense will tell you that revealing these details will inflict unspeakable agony on that person. Does the public *really* need to know an entertainer is a closet homosexual and his fatal disease is AIDS? Balance the need to inform the public against the wife's private horror should you decide to report the "hotel" where the town's leading banker had a fatal heart attack really is a house of prostitution. Many newspapers base such difficult judgments on precise definition of the public's "need to know." The banker, a private person, might be allowed to die in a hotel; a politician, a public figure, and especially one who presumes to be president of the United States and leader of the Free Western World, might not.

In revealing Gary Hart's extramarital sex life in 1987, the *Miami Herald* decided the man who wanted to be president had no private life and, furthermore, that his personal conduct had direct bearing on his capabilities as a public official. Thus ended Hart's run for the Democratic nomination.

Good Taste and Sensationalism

How much gory detail is needed to tell a story? When does gore become sensationalism? That's a judgment call you'll make throughout your career, starting when you decide which type publication you want to work for. If you choose a small-town "family" newspaper, you will filter out of your writing much of the blood and thunder you witness as a reporter. If you choose to work for a sensational supermarket tabloid, you will opt for quite another approach. Thus, the character of your reading audience—its likes, dislikes, customs and preferences—at times answers questions of good taste. When in doubt, many professionals use the same yardstick they take to vulgarity or obscenity: Use detail central to the meaning of an *important* story; don't use detail merely for shock value. For many journalists, the instinct is to protect reader sensibilities. Sometimes that means defaulting in reporting responsibilities.

Don't Shock Just to Shock

For example, when AIDS erupted in the United States many journalists couldn't bring themselves to write details of why homosexual men were a high-risk group. (It's because exchange of semen during anal intercourse can transmit the disease.) That protected reader sensibilities—but also permitted near panic to develop as people speculated whether AIDS could be contracted through the air we breathe, from a handshake or by sitting next to someone on a bus. Sometimes unpleasant details are necessary in important stories.

Reporting Technique

You change the world around you when you arrive on the scene with a reporter's notebook and pen. Your very presence *makes news*. Your questions can lead people to say and do things they wouldn't say and do otherwise. Thus, the personal approach you are developing to ethics in newswriting must be expanded to cover how you will conduct yourself as a reporter.

Adversarial relationships have been built between many reporters and institutions they cover, particularly government at all levels. In building your reportorial techniques, you'll have to decide what your personal relationship will be with news sources. Like it or not, much important news wouldn't see light of day unless tough, aggressive reporters tugged it free from bureaucratic secrecy.

Adversarial Relationships Develop News

News sleuth techniques are practiced by some reporters who disguise their identities or, even, masquerade under false identities in search of news. Some use hidden cameras or tape recorders. You'll have to decide whether to use such devices. Sentiment seems to be building in the profession against such techniques, yet many important stories have been broken by reporters who use them.

In building a personal approach to ethics you have a partner—the newspaper that employs you. Let's look at how you must relate to its stance on ethical issues.

YOU AND YOUR EMPLOYER'S ETHICS

Ethical Codes Are Controversial

To get—and hold—a job at most newspapers today you must "mesh" with your employer's stance on critical issues of ethics and social responsibility.

At some newspapers, ethical standards have not been written down. Some editors maintain that complicated ethical issues cannot be covered in any single desk manual and that boiling them down to a manageable document would produce little more than sweeping generalities of little practical guidance in making tough, day-to-day judgment calls. Some editors fear that even voluntarily written codes could serve as precedent for legislatures or judges tempted to establish mandatory standards of behavior for all media—a threat to First Amendment freedoms.

At newspapers without written codes, your guidance on ethical issues will come from various sources: the paper itself, its reporting techniques and writing styles; your editors' guidance during indoctrination and training; editing that your copy receives; conversation with other staffers.

Traditionally, a newsroom's approach to ethics was transmitted to successive generations of beginning reporters through just such informal means. Today, however, newspapers increasingly are writing formal codes—and requiring adherence to them as a condition of employment. Not even the strongest supporters of written codes argue they are definitive or answer every ethical dilemma you might face. Codes, nevertheless, do set *ethical tone* and do establish a corporate attitude toward some of the most critical questions of principle you will face. The sidebar on p. 287 reproduces one leading newspaper's code. Let's look at the *Washington Post*'s code.

CONDITION OF EMPLOYMENT In its first three paragraphs, the *Washington Post*'s code pledges that paper to aggressive but fair pursuit of truth *and* requires its reporters to be similarly pledged. Conforming to certain ethical as well as journalistic standards is a condition of employment at the *Post* (and many other newspapers).

CONFLICT OF INTEREST Avoiding even the *appearance* of conflict of interest is essential to the *Post*'s marketplace position as a dispassionate, even-handed source of news and information. That, in turn, requires reporters not only to avoid obvious conflict of interest—free gifts, tickets and so forth—but also to shun involvement, even in off-hours, in community or political affairs. Note that employees are even required to discuss with their supervisors any involvement by their family members that might "compromise our integrity."

THE REPORTER'S ROLE Cover the news; don't make it—or you cannot work for the *Post*. And wear your journalist's label. No masquerading as cops or anyone else.

Watergate Changed Attribution Rules

ATTRIBUTION OF SOURCES The *Post* drew heavy criticism for sometimes relying on unidentified sources during its reporting of the Watergate scandal that toppled President Richard Nixon. The *Post*'s policy of attribution of sources that was developed since Watergate is a model you could well follow.

FAIRNESS Nothing is more central to a code of ethics than fairness. Note that the *Post* emphasizes completeness in reporting, balanced structuring of a news story, leveling with the reader, and even-handed use of language as means of ensuring fairness.

Other sections of the *Post*'s code similarly direct staffers to conform to certain ethical standards in their reporting and writing. These are realities of daily journalism today to keep in mind as we turn, in Part 5, to deeper exploration of professional newswriting.

Issues and Challenges:
The Washington Post's Code

Retired Executive Editor Benjamin C. Bradlee of the Washington Post *encountered many of the ethical quandaries confronting young newswriters today. For his own staff, Bradlee wrote the "Standards and Ethics" reproduced with his permission below. Note how one of the most highly respected editors of our time first outlined his newspaper's journalistic mission, then structured an ethical framework for his editors and reporters who must accomplish that mission.*

The *Washington Post* is pledged to an aggressive, responsible and fair pursuit of the truth without fear of any special interest, and with favor to none.

Washington Post reporters and editors are pledged to approach every assignment with the fairness of open minds and without prior judgment. The search of opposing views must be routine. Comment from persons accused or challenged in stories must be included. The motives of those who press their views upon us must routinely be examined, and it must be recognized that those motives can be noble or ignoble, obvious or ulterior.

We fully recognize that the power we have inherited as the dominant morning newspaper in the capital of the free world carries with it special responsibilities:

- to listen to the voiceless.
- to avoid any and all acts of arrogance.
- to face the public politely and candidly.

CONFLICT OF INTEREST

This newspaper is pledged to avoid conflict of interest or the appearance of conflict of interest, wherever and whenever possible. We have adopted stringent policies on these issues, conscious that they may be more restrictive than is customary in the world of private business. In particular:

- We pay our own way.
- We accept no gifts from news sources. We accept no free trips. We neither seek nor accept preferential treatment that might be rendered because of the position we hold. Exceptions to the no-gift rule are few and obvious—invitations to meals, for example, may be accepted when they are occasional and innocent, but not when they're repeated and their purpose is deliberately calculating. Free admission to any event that is not free to the public is prohibited. The only exception is for seats not sold to the public, as in a press box. Whenever possible, arrangements will be made to pay for such seats.
- We work for no one except the *Washington Post* without permission from supervisors. Many outside activities and jobs are incompatible with the proper performance of work on an independent newspaper. Connections with government are among the most objectionable. To avoid real or apparent conflicts of interest in the coverage of business and the financial markets, all members of the Business and Financial staff are required to disclose their financial holdings and investments to the assistant managing editor in charge

of the section. The potential for conflict, however, is not limited to members of the Business and Financial staff. All reporters and editors, wherever they may work, are required to disclose to their department head any financial interests that might be in conflict or give the appearance of a conflict in their reporting or editing duties. Department heads will make their own financial disclosures to the managing editor. We free-lance for no one and accept no speaking engagements without permission from department heads. Permission to free-lance will be granted only if *The Post* has no interest in the story and only if it is to appear in a medium that does not compete with *The Post.* It is important that no freelance assignments and no honoraria be accepted that might in any way be interpreted as disguised gratuities.

- We make every reasonable effort to be free of obligation to news sources and to special interests. We must be wary of entanglements with those whose positions render them likely to subjects of journalistic interest and examination. Our private behavior as well as our professional behavior must not bring discredit to our profession or to *The Post.*

- We avoid active involvement in any partisan causes—politics, community affairs, social action, demonstration—that could compromise or seem to compromise our ability to report and edit fairly. Relatives cannot fairly be made subject to *Post* rules, but it should be recognized that their employment or their involvement in causes can at least appear to compromise our integrity. The business and professional ties of traditional family members or other members of your household must be disclosed to department heads.

THE REPORTER'S ROLE

Although it has become increasingly difficult for this newspaper and for the press generally to do since Watergate, reporters should make every effort to remain in the audience, to be the stagehand rather than the star, to report the news, not to make the news.

In gathering news, reporters will not misrepresent their identity. They will not identify themselves as police officers, physicians or anything other than journalists.

ERRORS

This newspaper is pledged to minimize the number of errors we make and to correct those that occur. Accuracy is our goal; candor is our defense. Persons who call errors to our attention must be accorded a respectful hearing.

ATTRIBUTION OF SOURCES

The *Washington Post* is pledged to disclose the source of all information when at all possible. When we agree to protect a source's identity, that identity will not be made known to anyone outside *The Post.*

Before any information is accepted without full attribution, reporters must make every reasonable effort to get it on the record. If that is not possible, reporters should consider seeking the information elsewhere. If that in turn is not possible, reporters should request an on-the-record reason for concealing the source's identity and should include the reason in the story.

In any case, some kind of identification is almost always possible—by department or by position, for example—and should be reported.

No pseudonyms are to be used.

However, the *Washington Post* will not knowingly disclose the identities of U.S. intelligence agents, except under highly unusual circumstances, which must be weighed by the senior editors.

PLAGIARISM AND CREDIT

Attribution of material from other newspapers and other media must be total. Plagiarism is one of journalism's unforgivable sins. It is the policy of this newspaper to give credit to other publications that develop exclusive stories worthy of coverage by *The Post*.

FAIRNESS

Reporters and editors of *The Post* are committed to fairness. While arguments about objectivity are endless, the concept of fairness is something that editors and reporters can easily understand and pursue. Fairness results from a few simple practices:

- No story is fair if it omits facts of major importance or significance. Fairness includes completeness.
- No story is fair if it includes essentially irrelevant information at the expense of significant facts. Fairness includes relevance.
- No story is fair if it consciously or unconsciously misleads or even deceives the reader. Fairness includes honesty—leveling with the reader.
- No story is fair if reporters hide their biases or emotions behind such subtly pejorative words as "refused," "despite," "quietly," "admit" and "massive." Fairness requires straightforwardness ahead of flashiness.

OPINION

On this newspaper, the separation of news columns from the editorial and opposite-editorial pages is solemn and complete. This separation is intended to serve the reader, who is entitled to the facts in the news columns and to opinions on the editorial and "op-ed" pages. But nothing in this separation of functions is intended to eliminate from the news column honest, in-depth reporting, or analysis or commentary when plainly labeled.

THE NATIONAL AND COMMUNITY INTEREST

The *Washington Post* is vitally concerned with the national interest and with the community interest. We believe these interests are best served by the widest possible dissemination of information. The claim of national interest by a federal official does not automatically equate with the national interest. The claim of community interest by a local official does not automatically equate with the community interest.

TASTE

The *Washington Post* as a newspaper respects taste and decency, understanding that society's concepts of taste and decency are constantly changing. A word offensive to the last generation can be part of the next generation's common vocabulary. But we shall avoid prurience. We shall avoid profanities and obscenities unless their use is so essential to a story of significance that its meaning is lost without them. In no case shall obscenities be used without the approval of the executive editor or the managing editor or his deputy.

THE POST'S PRINCIPLES

After Eugene Meyer bought the *Washington Post* in 1933 and began the family ownership that continues today, he published "These Principles":

The First mission of a newspaper is to tell the truth as nearly as the truth may be ascertained.

The newspaper shall tell all the truth so far as it can learn it, concerning the important affairs of America and the world.

As a disseminator of the news, the paper shall observe the decencies that are obligatory upon a private gentleman.

What it prints shall be fit reading for the young as well as for the old.

The newspaper's duty is to its readers and to the public at large, and not to the private interest of the owner.

In the pursuit of truth, the newspaper shall be prepared to make sacrifices of its material fortunes, if such course be necessary for the public good. The newspaper shall not be the ally of any special interest, but shall be fair and free and wholesome in its outlook on public affairs and public men.   Benjamin C. Bradlee

"These principles" are re-endorsed herewith.

SUMMARY CHECKLIST

- [ ] Ethics has been debated for 2,500 years. Socrates discussed the concepts of "good" and "justice" before he died in Athens in 399 B.C.

- [ ] Plato suggested good exists, despite how a society might conduct itself at the moment. Aristotle defined the individual's responsibility for acting with virtue, making sacrifices to do so, if necessary.

- [ ] In the late 16th century, there emerged the concept of the people, not sovereigns, wielding power—thus the journalists' role today of providing the citizenry with information necessary for considered use of power.

- [ ] John Milton (1608–1674) wrote of the "open marketplace of ideas," leading to today's emphasis in the media of placing facts before the people and trusting them to ascertain truth.

- [ ] Objectivity, an ideal central to American journalism today, arose in the late 19th century. By the early 20th century, newspapers were developing a strong sense of responsibility as a corollary of their power. By the mid-1940s, that was defined as *social responsibility.*

- [ ] *News*writers make a commitment to strive for facts, keeping their personal views out of their reporting and presenting issues as objectively as possible. *Advocacy* journalism requires wearing the label "advocate."

- [ ] Writing with honesty requires completeness of reporting to ensure that all sides of an issue are provided to the readers.

- [ ] Unidentified sources must be used only sparingly and when necessary; honest writing requires establishing the identity and authoritativeness of all sources.

- [ ] Courage will be needed to resist pressures that tend to force you into unethical writing. Beware the "herd effect" on your independent news judgment.

☐ Special ethical problems include the unresolved question of whether your obligation is to provide facts or truth, and the often troubling decision of whether to invade a person's privacy on behalf of the "public's right to know."

☐ As a condition of employment, many newspapers require employees' adherence to company policies on avoiding conflict of interest and other ethical issues.

RECOMMENDED READING

Ethics in both the newsroom and in the business side of the media, in addition to the role of the media in society, are explored in Conrad C. Fink, *Media Ethics in the Newsroom and Beyond* (New York: McGraw-Hill, 1988). Also note Clifford G. Christians and Kim B. Rotzoll, *Media Ethics, Cases and Moral Reasoning* (White Plains, N.Y.: Longman, 1991), and John L. Hulteng, *The Messenger's Motives: Ethical Problems of the News Media* 2d ed. (Englewood Cliffs, N.J.: Prentice-Hall, 1985).

For history of ethical thought, see Robert C. Solomon, *Morality and the Good Life* (New York: McGraw-Hill, 1984) and Alasdair MacIntyre, *A Short History of Ethics* (New York: Macmillan, 1966).

A detailed manual of ethics and procedures in broadcast journalism is in *CBS News Standards, a Policy Manual*, CBS Inc., 51 W. 52nd St., New York, NY 10020. It is representative of policy manuals published by other TV networks.

Timely coverage of current ethical issues is provided in *WJR, Editor & Publisher, presstime,* and *Broadcasting.* Most publicly owned media companies include in their annual reports statements of corporate philosophy and social responsibilities.

NOTES

1. History of the American press is surveyed in Michael Emery and Edwin Emery, *The Press and America,* 6th ed. (Englewood Cliffs, N.J.: Prentice Hall, 1988).
2. John Leo, "Reading Between the Hyphens," *U.S. News and World Report,* May 21, 1990, p. 23.
3. Letter to author, June 11, 1988.

Exercise 10–1   Ethical History and Journalism Today

In one paragraph for each question below, describe lessons you feel journalists today must draw from ethical princi-ples stated in this exercise. Be certain to write in clear, correct sentences that conform to AP style.

1. For journalists today, what meaning is in Plato's discussion of good existing, despite how a society might conduct itself at the moment?

_____

_____

_____

2. Describe the meaning for journalists in Aristotle's position on the individual's responsibility for acting with virtue.

_____

_____

_____

3. Thomas Hobbes wrote that the people, not sovereign rulers, possess true power. How does that mesh with your view of a journalist's responsibilities?

_____

_____

_____

4. In terms of reporting and writing today, what meaning is in John Milton's reference to the "open marketplace of ideas"?

_____

_____

_____

5. Describe the meaning for journalists in the interpretation of *utilitarianism* set forth by David Hume and John Stuart Mill.

_____

_____

_____

6. Describe *libertarianism* as a philosophy in newspapers.

_____

_____

_____

_____

7. Define *objectivity* as an ideal.

_____

_____

_____

_____

_____

8. What were the "Canons of Journalism"?

_____

_____

_____

_____

_____

9. Of what relevance today is the concept, developed in the 1940s, that the press has *social responsibility*?

_____

_____

_____

_____

10. What is the origin of the concept of "people's right to know"?

_____

_____

_____

_____

Exercise 10–2   Writing with Honesty

Answer each of the questions below in one paragraph. Check your spelling, adhere to AP style, and use precision in your language:

1. What do you believe "sin of omission," as used in our textbook, means?

_____

_____

_____

2. The text says the sin of omission stems primarily from two factors. What are they?

_____

_____

_____

3. In terms of leveling with readers, what is a danger in using "informed sources"?

_____

_____

_____

4. Give two examples of how writers must explain apparent lapses in stories.

_____

_____

_____

5. What is the "herd effect" in journalism?

_____

_____

_____

_____

6. The text argues there is "middle ground" between those who argue the journalist's mission is to collect facts and those who argue it is to ascertain truth. What is that middle ground?

_____

_____

_____

_____

7. Describe the danger in permitting conflicts of interest to influence a journalist's performance.

_____

_____

_____

_____

8. The text says questions of privacy vs. public interest can plague journalists. What do you understand that to mean?

_____

_____

_____

_____

9. What is one danger in filtering out gory details from news stories on subjects crucial to the public?

_____

_____

_____

_____

10. The text refers to "news sleuth" techniques. What are they?

_____

_____

_____

_____

Exercise 10–3 Newspaper Codes of Ethics

Writing in correct AP style, answer each of the following questions in a single paragraph.

1. Give two reasons why some editors believe newspapers should not have written codes of ethics.

_____

_____

_____

2. In general, what is accomplished by editors who do write formal codes of ethics?

_____

_____

_____

3. Is pledging conformity to a code of ethics a condition of employment at the *Washington Post*?

_____

_____

_____

4. Discuss the *Washington Post*'s policy on conflict of interest.

_____

_____

_____

5. Discuss the principal elements of the *Washington Post*'s statement on *fairness*.

_____

_____

_____

_____

Exercise 10–4   Word Alert

The following underlined words can create bias in a reader's mind. Suggest for each a word more "neutral" in meaning.

1. He showed <u>abnormal</u> zeal for political intrigue.

_____

2. Her remark <u>betrayed</u> her cold, unfeeling personality.

_____

3. His thinking was <u>chaotic.</u>

_____

4. "Their position is unfair," he <u>argued.</u>

_____

5. They <u>flaunted</u> their wealth at every opportunity.

_____

6. She, however, was a person of <u>humble</u> finances.

_____

7. He had a <u>cocky</u> air about him.

_____

8. She <u>smirked</u> when told the bill she supported had passed.

_____

9. "Hurry," he <u>snapped.</u>

_____

10. Police <u>ransacked</u> the house during the drug raid.

_____

11. "There is much more to come out," he <u>admitted.</u>

_____

12. He <u>harped</u> on his ideas every day.

_____

13. He took a <u>tough</u> stance on the issue.

_____

14. "I'll win in the end," she said <u>arrogantly.</u>

_____

15. "Not if I can help it," he <u>thundered.</u>

_____

Exercise 10–5   Self-Examination

Write about 200 words on your personal feelings, attitudes, (and, yes) prejudices that might influence your news-writing. On which subjects would you have to be especially alert to ensure objective and dispassionate writing? Do you feel so strongly about some subjects that you could not cover them dispassionately? Which are they? Throughout, adhere to AP style. Use newswriting hints from earlier chapters in striving for clear, precise use of language.

Exercise 10–6   Enforcement of Ethics

Examine the American Society of Newspaper Editors' "Statement of Principles" reproduced in this chapter. In about 200 words, discuss whether ASNE and other professional journalists' groups should (1) define precisely what is ethical or unethical in reporting and writing, and (2) construct self-regulating machinery under which journalists would be obliged to adhere to such standards or be expelled from journalism. Make sure your writing conforms to AP style and is correct in spelling, grammar, and sentence structure.

Part 5

Beginning with Basic Stories

By progressing this far in this book you have equipped yourself with basic skills of reporting and newswriting. You have read examples of professional writing, and you have worked classroom exercises. You have even studied the legal and ethical context of newswriting.

Now you are ready to get started reporting and writing for real.

In Part 5, we will suggest ways to obtain hands-on experience working for newspapers while still in school and thus boost yourself toward professionalism. Importantly, this could lead to a job after graduation.

Editors put premiums on graduates who work on newspapers and publish while in school. Experience outside the classroom shows commitment to journalism, desire to succeed and willingness to work hard. Editors know that covering news for real, then writing it under deadline pressure, is the best way to develop not only news values and judgment but also the writing skills and self-confidence so crucial to professionalism.

In Chapter 11 we will examine basic stories that, for starters, you can volunteer to cover for publications on or off campus: *speeches, seminars,* and *debates,* plus *meetings* and *news conferences.* We will also look at how to do *reaction stories* on news events that develop locally or afar.

In Chapter 12 we will turn to covering *basic economic* and *business news* stories. These stories are on front pages and in newscasts everywhere, nearly every day, and you'll draw assignments to cover them early in your career in campus journalism and, certainly, as a professional.

Science news is everyday fare for newswriters, too, and in Chapter 13 we will look at how you can get started—now—in that news sector.

Sports writing is serious business for every news organization, and in Chapter 14 we shall study how you can begin developing skills for writing the specialized stories demanded these days by leading sports editors.

Professional newswriters use many writing devices to focus the news. We'll look at some in Chapter 15: *newsfeatures, sidebars, profiles,* and *obituaries.* We'll also study how to write news stories about *public opinion polls,* and how to handle stories that will be illustrated by *graphics.*

I encourage you to write for publication on campus or off as you study the chapters ahead. As you do that it's important to realize *every* professional has been right where you are now: young, inexperienced, perhaps a little unsure of yourself or, even, scared to death about venturing from the cocoon of the classroom into the "real world" of newspapering. You can conquer any self-doubt you might feel, just as they did.

Also, more people out there are willing to help you than you might realize. There's a tradition in newspapering of spotting young talent (that's you) and helping it get started in journalism. Oh, sure, you may get rebuffed occasionally when offering stories for publication. But more often, editors will be glad you asked them for an assist.

So, let's *get started*.

Chapter Eleven

Getting Hands-on Experience

Your best chance for reporting and writing experience is with student-run weekly or daily newspapers. Often they are desperate for help, and they have two things you need: ink and newsprint.

Newspapers and magazines published in laboratory courses also can provide an excellent start, under an instructor's supervision, in reporting, writing and editing. Working on yearbooks, annual publications, newsletters, and other forms of written communication can also be valuable.

Student-run newspapers have a staff hierarchy through which you can climb if you're talented and willing to work hard. Generally there are two ways to make contact and step up on the first rung of the hierarchy:

1. At least one student editor will be assigned to recruit and train beginning reporters. Find out who that is and make contact. Often, story assignments are given to any aspiring reporter who asks. Sometimes as many as 15 or 20 story ideas will be posted on an assignment board. Take your pick.

2. Study the newspaper's content, find holes in its coverage, and suggest to the editor stories you can do to fill those holes. Many student-run papers are so short-handed that they don't fully cover the campus or all the interests of their readers. You'll find some campus papers don't regularly cover entire schools or departments. The sciences, agriculture, and forestry are among those sometimes covered inadequately. Most campus papers publish calendars of upcoming events. Volunteer to cover those that appeal to you.

You also should contact off-campus newspapers. Small or medium-size dailies and weeklies frequently need part-time help in general assignment and sports reporting. Ask particularly about covering village or county government in areas distant from the city of publication. Smaller papers often want to cover far-flung areas but don't have sufficient full-time staff. Nearby metropolitan dailies often hire students as part-time campus stringers, and those jobs can lead to full-time employment after graduation. The "state editor" normally arranges such coverage but *always* make contact as high in the newsroom as you can—preferably with the managing editor. Find out who does the hiring, then contact that person.

Go about all this intelligently. You know from earlier chapters, for example, that editors of afternoon papers are on deadline from 10 a.m. or so until after noon.

Don't drop in unannounced for a chat at that busy time. And don't try to visit editors of a morning paper at 8 a.m. Many don't start work until mid-afternoon. Always telephone or write ahead for an appointment. After you've made personal contact, you can coordinate by telephone much more easily.

Now let's look at how to select and write basic stories that will get you started with editors, on campus or off.

THE SPEECH STORY

Covering a speech is a splendid way to ease into the challenge of reporting and writing accurately—and for real. You'll normally have enough notice so you can obtain background on speaker and subject. Often an advanced text will be available and you'll have to take notes only when the speaker departs from it. Many speeches have only one or, at most, a few central themes, so your difficulty will be minimized in finding the news and focusing on it in your lead.

Campus public information offices issue notices of upcoming speeches. Many regularly publish events calendars. Check announcements on departmental or school bulletin boards.

Seek Story Ideas on Front Pages

Covering just any speech won't do. Remember news definitions in Chapter 1, and volunteer to cover speeches close to the news mainstreams on your campus or in town. Front pages of newspapers themselves will give you clues. For example, newspapers everywhere cover the following subjects, and you can catch an editor's attention by volunteering to cover speeches on almost any aspect of them:

environment	U.S. foreign policy	rock music
spending in education	oil/Middle East	big-time athletes
gay rights	the economy	personal health
women's rights	crime and violence	Soviet Union
black history/culture	drinking laws	filmmaking
AIDS		

Your greatest challenge in writing a speech story is to:

Search *Throughout* Speech for Lead

1. Search through everything the speaker says and find for your lead the topic of greatest news value *to your readers* (even if the speaker emphasizes something else), but also

2. Reflect accurately the central thrust of the speech and major points the speaker is trying to make. That's especially difficult when you must summarize, sometimes in just several hundred words, speeches that run into thousands of words.

Start a speech story as you do most other types of stories. Fix firmly in your mind two factors:

1. What is the single most important element for the lead? Sometimes it is deep in a speech and isn't flagged by the speaker as being particularly important. You must search for the lead within the context of the day's news flow and what you know is of compelling interest to your readers.

Give Your Readers the Speaker's Credentials

2. Determine the speaker's authoritative credentials and how you will position them in your story to answer that question all readers ask, "Why should I read a story about what this person says?"

Note the following example:

Charlotte-Mecklenburg Schools Supt. Peter Relic thinks school children shouldn't watch television before dinner and should learn more patriotic songs.

"No child should watch any of that garbage between 3 and 5:30 p.m. . . . with its mindless disregard of human sexuality," Relic said.

And though the Pledge of Allegiance is still recited in schools, emphasis on patriotic songs and honoring the flag began to decrease in the 1960s, Relic said.

"Many children don't know how to sing 'America the Beautiful,'" he said. "We have slipped very badly."

Relic spoke to about 100 First Union Corp. employees during a lunchtime seminar.

The monthly seminars began in February in answer to a Charlotte Chamber of Commerce call for business involvement in public schools, said First Union's community relations director Judy Allison. . . .

In his talk, Relic outlined a dozen ways parents could help their children. They included. . . . *John Minter, "Parents Urged to Sing, Hug, Turn Off TV,"* Charlotte Observer, *June 14, 1990, p. C-1*

In considering the example above, note first that the lead is written to emphasize the speaker's credentials. Superintendent Relic is an important educator in Charlotte, N.C. Many readers are familiar with his name. This story *begins* with a ring of authority.

Second, the lead contains two themes from the speech (TV, songs). The writer reached down in the speech to find them and give the lead punch. Do *not* write this type of lead:

A Charlotte educator spoke yesterday to about 100 First Union Corp. employees.

That a speech was given is not news; the news is what the speaker said.

Third, both elements in the lead are quickly backed up with full quotes (second and third paragraphs). Full quotes strengthen a speech story.

Fourth, the forum for the speech is reserved to the fifth paragraph. Precisely where this speech was given is not news for a lead. But where and to whom the speech was given must be in the story.

Fifth, in the sixth paragraph, the writer answers the obvious question, Why did Relic speak at First Union? This adds for the reader a valuable context for understanding the speech.

Sixth, with smooth transition ("In his talk, Relic outlined . . ."), the writer swings readers away from "housekeeping details" and back into specific points made in the speech.

Seventh, note how cleanly and directly the writer of the article leads readers through the two main elements selected as most newsworthy (TV, songs). When you write your first few speech stories you may feel panic over trying to sort out newsworthy material hidden in thousands of words. Stay cool. Apply your news judgment to the speech's various elements and write in lean, calm language, as did the *Observer*'s reporter. With experience, you'll be able to quickly spot the news lead in a speech.

Sometimes *audience reaction* to a speech can be newsworthy—even as important as the speech itself. A United Press International (UPI) correspondent decided that was the case in this example:

Audience Reaction Can Be News

Issues and Challenges

One of the toughest challenges beginning newswriters face is learning to write rapidly, yet accurately and clearly, under deadline pressure. In working on basic stories described in this chapter, keep these hints in mind:

Assign news priorities early. As you report the story, by listening to a speech or interviewing a source, *assign priorities to news elements as they develop.* When an obviously important angle emerges, say to yourself, "Ah! *That* is the lead." Move that angle to No. 2 priority if a more important one develops later.

When the speech or interview ends, you should have fixed firmly in mind the three or four most important news angles. You may find it difficult to juggle talking and listening with keeping a changing list of news priorities in your mind. But with practice it will become second nature.

"Write" your lead in your head. Dictate the lead to yourself while traveling back to the newsroom. Dictate several approaches. Dictating aloud works best (even if it may draw stares from passersby). *Listen* to the rhythm of your language. Your ear will signal if your lead gets too long or convoluted. (Another signal: If you must draw three breaths to get through your first sentence, your lead is too long.)

Incidentally, you can fashion a learning game out of "writing" in your head. On drives or walks, for example, imagine a set of circumstances—a plane crash up ahead, a talk with a personality in the news—and dictate leads to yourself. Keep dictating until you find one that communicates the news clearly and with punch. Practicing when not under pressure makes it much easier to do it for real, on assignment.

Talk out your story. If you sit at your keyboard and the lead still eludes you, talk over the story with a colleague or editor. Don't be reluctant to approach a senior reporter and say, "I'm having a little trouble with a story . . . can you help me?"

Mention what you regard as the most important news angles and the writing approaches you've been thinking about. Often, merely talking about your story will clarify which lead you should choose and how you should structure your writing.

Start writing. Don't sit staring at the keyboard waiting for the muse to move. Ignore your notes for a moment and start writing what naturally flows through your mind. Key elements of the story often will float to the top *if* you avoid forcing your writing.

When you've written four or five paragraphs, consider: Is that the lead and story structure you want? If so, use your notes to flesh out the story with facts and quotes.

Stay cool. In the news business, your job is to report accurately and write quickly. Professionals can't afford the panic of "writer's block" or temper tantrums (no kicking over chairs or shouting aloud). The commotion of the newsroom—telephones ringing, people rushing about—is simply background music to wordsmiths. Learn to concentrate so intently that noise and distractions are shut out of your mind.

Write and rewrite. If time permits, write and rewrite until you have done your very best. Then, think of something else for several minutes. If your story still looks good when you return to it, turn it over to your editor.

SAN FRANCISCO—Catcalls and whistles nearly drove federal Health Secretary Louis Sullivan from the stage yesterday during a speech wrapping up the Sixth International AIDS Conference.

Sullivan, straining to be heard over the shouts of hundreds of protesters angered by the Bush administration's AIDS policy, pleaded that scientists and activists "stand together" in the fight against the killer disease.

"No more words. We want action," chanted the demonstrators, who were blocked from the stage by a line of police.

Sullivan dodged wads of paper hurled at him and pleaded over the din: "Let us not turn our frustration into theater. The AIDS epidemic can divide us or it can unite us.

"Let us stand together, united in a common cause."

Sullivan's speech was delayed 10 minutes by the activists, who called on the 10,000 convention delegates to turn their backs on the top health policy-maker in the nation. . . .

UPI dispatch for afternoon papers of June 25, 1990

Note above how deftly the UPI writer emphasizes audience reaction, yet weaves in the forum (AIDS conference, first paragraph), the speaker's main point ("stand together," second paragraph), full quotes from the speaker (fourth and fifth paragraphs), and defines the speaker's credentials ("top health policy-maker," sixth paragraph). This is a story fair to the facts of the audience reaction but also fair to the speaker.

Below, note a writer's decision that the *targets* of a speech and its *central theme* are more important than the speaker's name or credentials:

MOBILE, Ala.—The nation's governors were urged Monday to consider boot camps for drug offenders as a lower-cost alternative to traditional prisons.

"To try to treat drug addicts in a prison setting is a mistake," New York state corrections commissioner Thomas Coughlin told a committee at the National Governors' Association conference.

"We have a different type of prison population now—a population addicted to drugs," Coughlin said.

Said Nevada Gov. Bob Miller: "I

like the boot camp philosophy . . . if we are, in fact, simply warehousing the bulk of our prisoners."

The USA's prison population has climbed 113% in a decade, prompting the governors to search for options to handling the increase.

Thirteen states have military-style boot camps, where prisoners encounter discipline measures and hard labor.

In New York, a "shock incarceration" program treats drug offenders and forces them to reconsider their ways. . . .

Note above these factors:

First, the lead tightly summarizes the main thrust of the speech and focuses on the target audience (governors).

Second, a full quote in the second paragraph backs up the lead. Importantly, the speaker's title and name of the conference, both long and cumbersome, are held to the second paragraph. No need in this example to junk up the lead with either. (Obviously, if President Bush were the speaker, both his name and title would need to be in the lead.)

Back up Lead with Quotes

Third, the writer neatly swings into audience reaction (Gov. Miller's comment, fourth paragraph). In this example such comment is mandatory because of the lead's focus on the audience.

Fourth, in the fifth paragraph, the writer superbly inserts essential background on the prison population and why governors are discussing it. Make sure your speech stories have similar "housekeeping" background.

Fifth, in the seventh paragraph, with "In New York" as transition, the writer swings readers back to the speech itself.

Three more paragraphs (which we don't have room to reproduce) are devoted to the speech and governors' comments. Then, the writer takes readers to other salient points raised during the conference:

Also Monday:
• Democratic governors were circulating a letter. . . .
• Governors expressed concern over proposed cuts in National Guard troops. . . .

• The White House rejected a plan from the governors. . . . *Mark Hatfield, "Boot Camp for Drug Offenders Is Pushed," USA Today, July 31, 1990, p. A-3*

THE SEMINAR/DEBATE STORY

You'll have many opportunities to cover seminars or debates on campus. Many produce excellent stories attractive to editors.

Writing about a seminar or debate is more complicated than writing a speech story. First, your lead generally must capture any consensus that develops in the discussion or, conversely, point up conflict that arises. Second, instead of pulling readers through a single central theme made by a single speaker, in writing a seminar or debate story you've got to keep straight several speakers and their multiple viewpoints.

Below is an example of how you can write when speakers arrive at a consensus:

Members of an advisory health board warned yesterday of impending conflict and confusion as state officials, who are already two months behind schedule, move to provide expanded services for low-income pregnant women.

"Potentially this is going to be very chaotic," said Dorothy Mann of the Family Planning Council of Southeastern Pennsylvania.

Mann and other members of the advisory committee for the Health-

Pass program made the comments during a discussion of Healthy Beginnings Plus, a program designed to provide a wide array of new services to pregnant women. . . .

"I think we need to do some fast thinking. We have to make some decisions," said Richard Weishaupt of Community Legal Services.

Michael Brown, a state official said. . . . *Walter F. Roche Jr., "Panel Sounds Alarm Over Prenatal Program," Philadelphia Inquirer, June 15, 1990, p. B-6*

Keep "Housekeeping" Detail High

Note above how, after summarizing panel consensus in the lead, the writer quickly uses a full quote (second paragraph) to back up the lead. The third paragraph is "housekeeping" detail on where the discussion took place. The writer then moves to quote from other panelists, further supporting his lead.

Below is an example of how you can cover a debate when it yields differences, not consensus:

TALLAHASSEE—After praising each other and calling themselves old pals, Democratic gubernatorial candidates Lawton Chiles and Bill Nelson landed punch after punch Thursday in their first debate.

Whether the issue was abortion, voting records in Congress or campaign tactics, each man held nothing back.

Chiles, who is limiting his contributions to $100, challenged Nelson to quit airing campaign advertisements and save his money for the general election. Nelson countered that Chiles is dodging debates and trying to protect his advantage as a better-known candidate.

"Mama didn't raise no fool," Chiles replied. "I'm not gonna allow you to. . . ." *Tim Nickens, "Old Pals' Debate Turns a Bit Bitter," Miami Herald, June 1, 1990, p. A-1*

There is nice contrast in the lead above: "old pals" land "punch after punch." The second paragraph illustrates the breadth of conflict by listing some of the issues the candidates argued over. But note how the third paragraph singles out one of the most important arguments (campaign contributions). A debate often yields many differences. Help your readers along by highlighting the most important. Note, also, the colorful quote in the fourth paragraph. It catches the spirit of debate.

THE MEETING STORY

Covering meetings escalates the difficulty of writing because you generally must handle a complex cast of characters and many issues, not the single or several issues of a speech or panel discussion.

The biggest trap in covering meetings is to treat the meeting itself as news, instead of focusing on *news generated by the meeting.* For example, you're not going to catch readers with this:

Focus on News Generated by Meeting

Los Angeles police met Monday for two hours with representatives of the Nation of Islam.

Now note how a pro fleshes out a meeting story with news:

Los Angeles police officials and representatives of the Nation of Islam met Monday and agreed to a continuing dialogue designed to ease tension between the two sides.

The two-hour meeting, called historic by some participants, grew indirectly from a violent clash earlier this month between Muslims and police officers. . . . *Andrea Ford, "Muslims, Police Hold Peace Talks to Ease Hostilities," Los Angeles Times, Jan. 23, 1990, p. B-1*

Here's a meeting story that never mentions "meeting" in the first paragraph:

BATON ROUGE, La.—Louisiana lawmakers yesterday took a significant step toward passing the nation's strictest state abortion law.

After five hours of debate, the Louisiana House of Representatives voted 74–27 to approve a bill that would ban all abortions except to save the life of the woman.

The bill will now move to the Senate, where it is expected to pass.

State Rep. Louis "Woody" Jenkins, a Democrat from Baton Rouge and author of the bill, told lawmakers that he was proud of Louisiana's anti-abortion stance.

"Louisiana has always stood for the right to life, and I presume we will continue to do so," Jenkins said minutes before the vote. . . .

The bill would make it a criminal offense for anyone to perform an abortion, subjecting the person to 10 years of hard labor. . . .

Supporters of abortion rights were dismayed over the bill's passage, say-ing the resulting law would be a breach of privacy.

"Woody Jenkins and his lot should not be allowed to force their morality on the people of this state," said Marie Ashby, president of the Louisiana Coalition for Reproductive Freedom. . . . *Tanya Barrientos, "Louisiana House Approves Bill Outlawing Nearly All Abortions,"* Philadelphia Inquirer, June 15, 1990, p. A-3

Issues and Challenges

For beginning newswriters, the most important assignments aren't politics in Washington, war in the Persian Gulf, or famine in Africa. Most important are speeches at Rotary, school board meetings, and other basic local stories.

You must do well on such beginner stories to win more coveted assignments. Do poorly and you won't have a future in journalism. Yet many beginners, their eyes on distant news horizons, tend to forget that the most important story in the world is the one in their hands. Beware! Don't "kiss off" that basic local story.

Here is a checklist for use in spotting any holes in each story you write:

Accuracy. Is *every* detail accurate? Are names spelled correctly? How about ages, addresses, occupations? Is your story *accurate in its totality?* Does it truthfully report the event your covered?

Fairness and balance. Is your story dispassionate? Does it report all sides of a controversy, give all parties opportunity to comment?

Local. Did you find the local angle and highlight its importance for your local readers? Do you relate even a distant event to local interests?

People. Have you gotten people into your story? Remember that school board meetings are about educating *children;* police blotter statistics are not about murder or robbery—they're about *people* who are murderers and the murdered, robbers and the robbed.

Enterprise. Does your story go beyond the obvious, beyond "He said . . . she said . . . they said"? Does your writing underscore truly meaningful developments beneath the surface?

Drama. If there is drama in the event you covered does your writing highlight it? Check particularly whether you've covered the impact on people. (Beware that you haven't "hyped" your story with drama that isn't truly there.)

Humor. If you've found a "brite," be sure to share it with your readers. Too much news is doom and gloom.

Judgment. Have you applied professional news judgment to reporting and writing this story? Do you emphasize meaningful elements, or have you written trivia? Does the basic news value of your story warrant the coverage you've given it?

Taste. Definitions of taste vary. So check whether your story is aimed properly at *your* audience and *its* sense of decency and taste.

Writing. Check once more: Have you done your very best writing job? Check your grammar, sentence construction, word choice. Is your story clean, concise, readable? *If not, rewrite!*

Note above three factors:

First, the writer sifts through all arguments raised by all sides during the controversy and delivers, in just 15 words, a superbly taut lead summarizing the most important meaning of the news. Not until the second paragraph is there mention of the meeting or its process ("five hours of debate").

Second, many meeting stories raise the question, "What's next?" In her third paragraph, the *Inquirer*'s Barrientos answers (the bill now moves to the Senate). Note she uses just 14 words to do so and thus doesn't let her description of the mechanical process of future legislative action in Louisiana slow down the immediacy of her news story.

Third, the writer quickly gives readers representative quotations from both sides of the abortion controversy (Jenkins and Ashby).

Always Quote Both Sides

As in writing speech stories, you'll find sometimes that *audience reaction* to a meeting is the lead:

GRAND PRAIRIE—About 200 angry neighborhood residents jammed City Hall Tuesday night to try to stop the City Council from approving a State Highway 161 route that would cut through a popular park and eliminate more than 120 homes.

Despite the debate, which has dominated the past few council meetings, the council voted 7–2 to approve a resolution recommending the route to the Texas Department of Highways and Public Transportation. . . . *David Nather, "GP Crowd Blasts City Plan to Wipe Out Popular Park, 120 Homes for Street,"* Dallas Morning News, *March 21, 1990, p. A-25*

The writer above does a good job of tying together, in the first and second paragraphs, the two central points: protest and council vote. Could you improve on that? (How about making the lead read ". . . Tuesday night and tried *unsuccessfully* to stop . . ."?)

THE REPORT STORY

Written reports circulate throughout your campus in great numbers. Find one with news, write it well—and you'll have a fine offering for an editor, on or off campus.

As in writing speech stories, the key is to search a report for *news* and focus on that. An example:

AUGUSTA—Highway deaths in Maine were down for the first six months of this year, but showed an alarming increase in July, when 32 people were killed in accidents, the Bureau of Highway Safety reported Wednesday.

Richard E. Perkins, director of the bureau, said. . . . *"Highway Fatalities Up in July,"* Bangor (Me.) Daily News, *Aug. 9, 1990, p. 7*

In writing from a report be certain to state clearly the authoritative credentials behind it. In the example above, the authoritative credentials (Bureau of Highway Safety) are obvious to readers.

Provide Report's Authoritativeness

Note in the example below how the writer refers to "scientists" in his lead and lets that stand as the source for three paragraphs but, in the fourth, states specifically what credentials are behind the report on marijuana:

Scientists said yesterday they have isolated specific "ports of entry" in the brain for the active ingredient in marijuana, a finding that may lead to new therapeutic drugs stripped of the weed's intoxicating effects.

The discovery also suggests that among the many systems of chemical messengers in the brain, there must be one that employs a marijuana-like substance.

Scientists trying to explain the mysterious effects of marijuana (or specifically "cannabis," its active ingredient) had long searched for structures on brain cells to which cannabis molecules could link up and enter the cells.

In today's issue of the journal Nature, researchers from the National Institute of Mental Health say. . . .
Richard Saltus, "Scientists Crack Marijuana's Mystery," Boston Globe, *Aug. 9, 1990, p. 68*

THE NEWS CONFERENCE STORY

News conferences often are scheduled without much notice—and you can turn that to your advantage if off-campus newspapers can't get a staffer reporter on the scene quickly enough. When you learn that one is scheduled to deal with important news, telephone nearby editors with an offer to cover it.

Two factors in covering news conferences:

Explain Motives Behind Press Conference

1. You must lead with *news,* not the process of the conference, just as in writing speeches, reports, or any other type story.
2. You must explain carefully that the news developed in a news conference and, insofar as possible, what motives were behind calling reporters in.

Here, the motives are clear:

The FBI yesterday announced a drug education program that will target elementary and junior high school students in Colorado and Wyoming.

The Drug Demand Reduction Program, developed after a year of research, will feature current and re-tired agents, former drug addicts and professional athletes as speakers, said Bob Pence, FBI spokesman in Colorado. . . . *Tony Pugh, "FBI to Take Drug Education to Schools,"* Denver (Colo.) Rocky Mountain News, *Jan. 18, 1990, p. 25*

Below, a writer wisely takes pains in his second paragraph to inform readers precisely why the news conference was called:

RALEIGH—North Carolina's 500 cities and 100 counties will back a "moderate" statewide tax increase if it averts a reduction in state money to local governments, officials said Wednesday.

Representatives of the N.C. League of Municipalities and the N.C. Association of County Commissioners held a news conference objecting to a Senate plan that would cut $23.4 million in reimbursements paid to cities and counties. . . .
F. Alan Boyce, Associated Press dispatch for afternoon papers on June 14, 1990.

Note the writers above don't report in their leads that a news conference was held. In most news conference stories, the precise forum can be left for elaboration in later paragraphs.

Important: Don't go to a news conference simply to listen, then run to the keyboard. Ask, probe, question. Don't take at face value much that's said or handed out. And also follow up speeches, reports, and debates with questions. Remember you're a reporter, not a stenographer.

THE REACTION STORY

This category of news story gives you unlimited opportunity to display initiative and make a name for yourself in a hurry.

There are on your campus experts in many subjects. Some engage in scholarly research in everything from Soviet policy in the Middle East to plant diseases. They are authoritative sources for comment and analysis on news stories that break every day. Their *reaction* to distant events can make fine news copy.

Consult Experts on Campus

For example, the media made great effort to locate knowledgeable U.S. sources after Iraq's invasion of Kuwait in 1990. The second-day, or reaction, story was the meaning of that invasion for Middle Eastern politics, international availability of oil, U.S. interests in the Persian Gulf, the political impact on the Bush administration—the list is endless. It's likely that on your campus at the time were scholars with firsthand knowledge of the Middle East and its ways. Quick interviews with them would have made a newsworthy story.

Many universities publish names of experts on their faculties and their research specialties of interest to reporters. The University of Georgia's information office, for example, gives reporters the names (and home telephone numbers) of experts willing to comment on news developments in politics, government and world affairs.

When you spot news developments breaking on front pages or TV newscasts, move quickly! Telephone editors and volunteer to interview a campus expert or do a roundup of reaction from several experts.[1] What follows are examples of how you can spot news developments and link them to on-campus experts available for interviewing.

INTERNATIONAL NEWS DEVELOPMENTS Almost every day, somewhere in the world, there is news of war or peace, famine or feast, with impact on U.S. interests. Seek analysis and opinion from professors in world studies, political science, geography. Contact visiting faculty members or students from foreign countries in the news.

React Quickly to Foreign News

ECONOMIC NEWS Figures are announced regularly in Washington on employment, consumer spending, wholesale and retail prices, and other economic indicators—and all are important signals of economic things to come. But how to read the signals for readers? Contact professors in economics, the business school, or other relevant departments. Bet on it: Somewhere on campus, somebody knows the meaning behind a $5 per barrel increase in the price of Texas crude oil. As close as your telephone is someone who knows the effect of rising interest rates on availability of home mortgages in your town.

Develop Business School Sources

LEGAL NEWS U.S. Supreme Court rulings, new laws passed in Washington, your state legislature, and in other states can have profound impact on your community. Expert analysis of their meaning is as close as your law school. Scholars there watch court decisions extremely carefully and probably will have analyzed their meaning even before you contact them.

Contact Law School, Too

HEALTH NEWS Personal health is an important news sector for your readers. Reports from afar about new diseases, new cures, new preventive measures—all can be interpreted locally by physicians in your medical school or health center. When

Health Center Is Valuable Source

writing for a campus audience, watch particularly for news concerning sexually transmitted diseases, drug or alcohol addiction, and other developments of interest to students.

Those are just four categories of reaction stories you can do from your campus. Others will jump to mind if you look closely at this morning's front pages or tonight's TV news. Remember that in Chapter 1 the definition of news was that it be *timely*. Volunteering a reaction story today on a news break of this morning or last night has the best chance of catching an editor's attention. Reaction on a news break of a week or month ago is far less compelling.

When approaching a newspaper with a story idea also remember to consider carefully the audience it serves. For example, a narrow story on, say, campus parking regulations could be of major interest to student readers of a campus publication. Off-campus readers of a distant daily probably wouldn't be interested. But you *could* interest off-campus editors in stories about, say, student drinking or drug habits, crime on campus, major speeches by recognized experts, research reports, and so forth.

In the next chapter we'll look at ways to do basic stories in other special news sectors.

SUMMARY CHECKLIST

☐ Student-run campus publications and those published in laboratory courses are your best chance for obtaining hands-on experience.

☐ Covering speech stories is an excellent way to ease into reporting and writing for real. Search the speech for the single most important news element and focus your lead on that. State for readers the speaker's credentials.

☐ Seminars and debates can provide excellent stories. Make sure your lead captures any consensus or conflict that arises.

☐ In covering meetings you must handle an often complex cast of characters and several news elements. Beware: The meeting itself generally is not news; what develops *in* the meeting can be.

☐ In covering written or oral reports, focus on the single most important news elements, as in covering speeches. Report fully the credentials of the person or organization releasing the report.

☐ News conferences are held by persons with motives for calling in reporters. Make sure you inform your readers what those motives are.

☐ The reaction story involves obtaining comment and opinion from campus experts on distant news breaks in many subjects—world affairs, economics, politics. This type story permits you unlimited opportunity to display initiative and make a name for yourself.

RECOMMENDED READING

The New York Times and other major newspapers publish full texts of important speeches and press conferences by the U.S. president and other figures. It's excellent practice to find the lead in the text, write your own story—then compare your effort with that of *Times* writers. Do the same when watching televised press conferences and speeches.

George A. Hough's *News Writing*, 4th ed. (Boston: Houghton Mifflin, 1988) is strong on writing the basic speech story. See p. 243 *et seq.*

Two periodicals with excellent and continuing coverage of writing basics applicable to beginners are The Associated Press Managing Editors *News* and the American Society of Newspaper Editors *Bulletin*.

NOTES

1. If you're working for a campus newspaper with access to an AP or UPI wire you can spot news developments as quickly as they break. "Watching the wire" is a good habit to develop.

Exercise 11–1   Volunteering Stories–I

Check two issues of your campus newspaper (or another paper designated by your instructor) and compare its coverage with your understanding of your school, its administrative structure, how it operates, and news you know to be developing. Then suggest below five story ideas you could volunteer to the newspaper's editor. Pay particular attention to schools or departments not regularly covered in addition to issues (drinking, academic honesty, drugs, etc.) you think are not being covered adequately. For each story idea, write one paragraph outlining how you would approach reporting the story (including sources).

Exercise 11–2 Volunteering Stories–II

Think deeply about your school and how it is (or isn't) covered by off-campus newspapers. Below, write five story ideas you would volunteer to the editor of an off-campus newspaper your instructor will designate. Remember that in arranging coverage of campus issues for a non-campus audience, the editor needs reporting and writing that fully backgrounds issues that would need no explanation for student readers. "Step back" from your story ideas, in other words, and consider (1) whether they are pertinent for an off-campus audience and (2) how you would write them for distant readers. For each idea, describe in one paragraph how you would approach the story and sources you would seek.

Exercise 11–3   Covering a Speech

This morning (Dec. 20, 1989), President Bush spoke to the nation from the White House at 7 a.m. For an afternoon paper today, write about 300 words from these excerpts from the speech transcript:

Fellow citizens, last night I ordered U.S. military forces to Panama. No President takes such action lightly. This morning, I want to tell you what I did and why I did it.

For nearly two years, the United States, nations of Latin America and the Caribbean have worked together to resolve the crisis in Panama. The goals of the United States have been to safeguard the lives of Americans, to defend democracy in Panama, to combat drug trafficking and to protect the integrity of the Panama Canal Treaty. Many attempts have been made to resolve this crisis through diplomacy and negotiations. All were rejected by the dictator of Panama, Gen. Manuel Noriega, an indicted drug trafficker.

Last Friday, Noriega declared his military dictatorship to be in a state of war with the United States and publicly threatened the lives of Americans in Panama. The very next day forces under his command shot and killed an unarmed American serviceman, wounded another, arrested and brutally beat a third American serviceman and then brutally interrogated his wife, threatening her with sexual abuse. That was enough.

General Noriega's reckless threats and attacks upon Americans in Panama created an imminent danger to the 35,000 American citizens in Panama. As President, I have no higher obligation than to safeguard the lives of American citizens. And that is why I directed our armed forces to protect the lives of American citizens in Panama, and to bring General Noriega to justice in the United States. I contacted the bipartisan leadership of Congress last night and informed them of this decision, and after taking this action, I also talked with leaders in Latin America, the Caribbean, and those of other U.S. allies.

At this moment, U.S. forces, including forces deployed from the United States last night, are engaged in action in Panama. The United States intends to withdraw the forces newly deployed to Panama as quickly as possible. All forces have conducted themselves courageously and selflessly, and as Commander in Chief, I salute everyone of them and thank them on behalf of our country.

Tragically, some Americans have lost their lives in defense of their fellow citizens, in defense of democracy, and my heart goes out to their families. We also regret and mourn the loss of innocent Panamanians.

Exercise 11–4   Writing from a Report

In Kansas City, Mo., on Thursday the board of directors of the National Education Association, the nation's largest teachers union, issued an important report on providing early childhood services. From this information and details that follow, write 200 words on the report. Write for Friday morning papers. Follow AP style, of course.

The teachers union said day care, meals and health screening should be provided by public schools for preschool, kindergarten and elementary school children. The union's board approved a committee report that said this and also said such early childhood services should come from public schools. The report said public schools should be the primary provider of such services. The report also said all children should have equal access to such services and that the services should be universal, that they should cost the child's family little or nothing. Now, most day care or preschool programs are offered by private or non-profit organizations. The Head Start program is an exception. Head Start provides services for needy youngsters 3 to 5 years old. Services include education meals and health screening. But only a small percentage of children are served by the program. The committee report said changes in American families and the labor force in partly prompted its recommendations. Also, it cited increases in preschool population, changes in demographics of poverty and the changing ethnic composition of the preschool population. The recommendations were made during NEA's annual meeting.

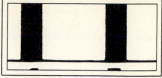

Chapter Twelve

Writing About Dollars With Sense

Just a few years ago your introduction to professional newswriting might have consisted primarily of learning to write inverted pyramid leads and stories on speeches, car accidents and other simple issues. On your first job in many newspapers, you might have rattled around in a newsroom apprenticeship for some time without writing anything very complicated.

No longer.

Today, you must prepare to arrive on your first job understanding complex issues in the news. And even in small-town journalism you'll be expected to possess precision techniques for writing basic stories in economics and business and other specialty topics once assigned mostly to experienced reporters.

Today's front pages reflect the change: Economics and business are everyday fare for modern journalists because they are of compelling importance in the lives of our readers, listeners and viewers. There's another reason you'll be expected to perform at a higher technical level than perhaps did many beginning newswriters before you: Soaring costs and competitive pressures make it difficult for all media to maintain profit levels. In the newsroom, that means beginners get a shorter grace period before being expected to "come up to speed" and produce front-page stories on any subject.

Therefore, it's important that we now turn to writing basic stories in specialty news sectors. It's part of my fundamental effort to help you prepare for entering a newsroom equipped to handle virtually any story assignment.

I start here with fundamental approaches to covering economic, business and financial news. It's the hottest specialty topic in news today and offers wonderful career opportunities.

ECONOMIC AND BUSINESS NEWS HAS POCKETBOOK IMPACT

All media require beginning newswriters to understand at least the basics of economics and business. Why? Consider the following:

• When Iraq invaded Kuwait in 1990, prices jumped at corner gas stations across America scarcely hours later.

• When *any* news development affects the cost of buying a home or going to college, it affects millions of Americans, for whom those two items are the largest financial investments they'll ever make.

• When hundreds of savings and loans (S&L) institutions collapsed in the late 1980s and early 1990s, *every* American taxpayer—and future taxpayer—could look forward to coughing up thousands of dollars more in taxes to bail out S&L depositors.

Those are examples of why developments in economics and business, even if distant and seemingly esoteric, get high-priority handling by the media today: They strike directly into the pocketbooks of our readers, viewers, and listeners.[1]

In studying this news specialty note these factors:

There's No Mystery in Business News

1. Don't worry (as many beginners do, unfortunately) that some impenetrable mystery surrounds economic and business news. Methodically apply to this news the same news definition and values you studied in Chapter 1. What impact does this news have on your audience? Does it meet standards of timeliness and proximity? Reflect on its real meaning. Then, write it clearly and simply.

Need for Accuracy Is Paramount

2. Double—triple—everything you learned about the need to be accurate. We're dealing here with people's money, not a football score or wedding announcement. Misspell Alice's name in her wedding story and you've made a serious error; give her erroneous information that leads her to make a disastrous investment and you've committed journalistic sin.

Translate All Business Jargon

3. Approach every economic or business story as a *translator*. Explain even the most complex development in language your readers can understand. Never write anything *you* don't understand. Never use jargon without explaining it. Never report a news development without seeking authoritative sources who can place its meaning in understandable context. And *always* go beyond the superficial "what" into the "real what." For example, don't report your city council approves, say, a new civic center without explaining its cost, how funding will be raised, and the impact of all that on local taxes.[2]

Avoid Any Conflict of Interest

4. Beware improper attempts to influence what you write. Money—lots of it—moves on news. It also moves on unconfirmed reports, rumors, distortions and lies. Unprincipled people can make fortunes by influencing reporters to write something that, say, sparks selling or buying on stock and commodity markets. Even in small-town journalism what you write can have far-reaching consequences. Write, for example, an unconfirmed report of a new shopping center being planned for outside town and you can affect real estate prices throughout town. Probe the motives of everyone who provides you information. Suspect anyone who feeds you information and demands anonymity. Always obtain balancing comment, particularly from anyone whose financial interests might be harmed by a news story. And, of course, avoid any conflict of interest between your personal investments and what you report. Discuss with your editor any real estate you own or other holdings that might be construed as influencing your writing.[3]

New Career Opportunities in Business News

5. Have fun covering economics and business. It's exciting news that commands front-page display and has influential and devoted readers. Reporters who can handle it well are in great demand by leading newspapers, often at salaries higher than those paid general-assignment reporters. New career opportunities are opening: City, state and regional daily and weekly business newspapers are mushrooming; business magazines are spreading, even to medium-sized cities; newsletters of all sorts are hiring writers; huge staffs of business writers are employed by news services, including AP, Dow Jones, Reuters and others that serve private subscribers, such as banks, brokerage houses and commodities dealers, as well as the media.

Obviously, discussing all ramifications of such a broad area of news requires a

Issues and Challenges:
Ethical Considerations in Business News

News often has direct impact on how business is conducted. Stock prices can rise on good news, fall on bad news. Favorable stories can help companies flourish; unfavorable stories can harm them seriously.

This tight cause-and-effect relationship between news and business activity raises special ethical issues that many news organizations address in policies that employees are required to follow.

Dow Jones & Company, Inc., publisher of *The Wall Street Journal* and other newspapers, has a detailed "Conflicts of Interest Policy" covering reporting and writing of economic, business, and financial news. Employees cannot use, for their own or another person's financial gain, "confidential information obtained in connection with Dow Jones employment until such information has been made available to the public. . . . "

The Dow Jones policy means, for example, that reporters cannot buy or sell stocks in anticipation of, say, a story to be published in the *Journal* that will cause a company's stock price to rise or fall. Enormous profits could be made by using such "inside information" to invest in stocks even just minutes ahead of the public.

Dow Jones also requires employees to "bend over backwards to avoid any action, no matter how well-intended, that could provide grounds for suspicion" that they unethically are using inside information on *advertising* that the *Journal* will publish. Many companies use advertising to announce developments that affect stock prices.

Dow Jones also requires employees to avoid any suspicion that they are "beholden to brokers or any other group we cover or advertisers. Such indebtedness could arise through acceptance of favors, gifts or payments for performing writing assignments or other services for them."

The American Society of Newspaper Editors, a leading professional organization, cautions journalists in its "Statement of Principles" to "avoid impropriety and the appearance of impropriety as well as any conflict of interest or the appearance of conflict. They should neither accept anything nor pursue any activity that might compromise or seem to compromise their integrity."

The Society of Professional Journalists is explicit in its "Code of Ethics": "Journalists must be free of obligation to any interest other than the public's right to know the truth." The code adds: "Gifts, favors, free travel, special treatment or privileges can compromise the integrity of journalists and their employers. Nothing of value should be accepted."

The Associated Press Managing Editors, an association of newspapers that are members of AP, uses its "Code of Ethics" to warn business news writers: "Financial investments by staff members or other outside business interests that could conflict with the newspaper's ability to report the news or that would create the impression of such conflict should be avoided."

Business news offers reporters splendid opportunities for in-depth writing on subjects of compelling interest to readers. Note the three in-depth local stories on the front page of this *Tulsa* (Okla.) *World* business section.

(Used with permission of *Tulsa World*)

book (or *several*) in itself. So, we'll concentrate here on three sectors where you likely will start covering basic stories for a local audience:

• Interpreting *economic indicators* from Washington and elsewhere on major or "macro" economic developments, then writing the local angle.

• Writing *personal finance* stories from a local perspective on cost of living, real estate prices, and so forth.

• Writing *local business* stories, particularly "company news," on local firms and business personalities.

Reading Distant Signals for Local Impact

No one can predict accurately the economic future, obviously, and trying to isn't your job as a reporter. It *is* your job to report *economic indicators* your readers can use in making financial decisions that will affect their own futures.

In part based on economic news they read, business executives decide this is—or isn't—a good time to build that new factory or hire more workers. Private individuals decide to buy a car or home or take a Caribbean vacation—or bank the money against stormy times ahead.

Whether in business or not, readers of economic and business news search for signals of what the future holds. Here are some economic indicators issued regularly by the federal government, and some hints on how you can write meaningful local news stories about them:

Localize Federal Economic Indicators

Gross National Product (GNP)

This *growth* indicator, issued by the Bureau of Economic Analysis in the Department of Commerce, measures in dollars and percentages the nation's total output of all goods and services. Gross national product (GNP) includes consumer spending, business investment in plant and equipment, housing, the balance of exports and imports, and purchases by federal, state and local governments. The GNP figures are issued about two weeks after the end of each quarter, and you will find them reported by news services, national newspapers and magazines and TV.

In sum, GNP figures reflect whether the nation's total business activity is increasing, decreasing or holding steady—and as a local business writer you can create important stories by comparing local business trends with national ups or downs.

For example, interviews with your town's business leaders—bankers, company executives, retail merchants—will reveal local indications of whether business activity is following national trends. You'll not be able to match your local findings exactly with components of the GNP released in Washington, so don't try to arrive at some "local GNP" figure. But you've got a story—and a good one—whatever your local interviews yield: It's *news* that local leaders say Main Street business is matching the pace of national activity, is behind it or ahead of it.

What Local Business Leaders Say Is News

Note below how a *Chicago Tribune* writer adapts one federal economic indicator for local readers in Illinois and the Midwest:

The U.S. economy has lost its drive, downshifting into a slower pace with manufacturing levels nearly flat and real estate construction and sales running behind 1989's, the Federal Reserve said Wednesday.

The slowdown is mirrored in most of Illinois and its neighboring states, said the Fed's so-called "Beige Book" update on the economy. The five-state Midwest region has a sluggish economy with mixed conditions, the report said. . . . *Stephen Franklin, "Feds 'Beige Book' Colors the Economic Outlook Blue," Chicago Tribune, Aug. 9, 1990, p. 1, Section 3*

In subsequent paragraphs of the story above, the *Tribune* writer quotes a University of Illinois economist on the local outlook, and reports on local real estate and other business activity. National economic figures issued in faraway Washington *thus become an important local story.*[4]

Beware Business Community Optimism

Warning: Business people often make optimistic statements, whether or not facts support a rosy view. Many feel happy talk creates good business, and poor-mouthing ruins it. Thus, your interviews must push beyond generalities and obtain *facts*— exactly how many cars are being sold locally, precisely how home prices are moving, whether—in solid dollar figures and percentages—retail sales in fact are up or down.

Consumer Price Index (CPI)

The consumer price index measures price changes on a "market basket" of goods and services, including food, transportation, clothing, housing, fuel. Each month the Bureau of Labor Statistics prices the same items (nearly 400) in urban areas nationwide. Results are reported urgently by news services, national newspapers and TV. Localize them by writing your own "market basket" story. Select, say, 20 or 25 supermarket items that reflect consumption habits in your area, then report how local prices moved. Housing costs, including rent, are a heavy component of the federal CPI. Periodic stories on local housing costs will give your readers important indicators of local economic conditions. Track other consumer items important to your particular audience—heating oil prices in cold-weather sections of the country, for example.

Unemployment Rate

The Labor Department reports, normally on the first Friday of each month, the size of the nation's civilian work force and the number of people unemployed. For one week, the department's researchers canvass thousands of households for the work status of anyone 16 years old and over. Counted as unemployed are those who did not work in the survey week but who in the prior four weeks tried to find a job by registering with employment agencies or writing job applications. Individuals temporarily laid off also are counted as unemployed. Counted as employed are those who worked for pay for one or more hours in the survey week.

Like all broad-based economic indicators, the unemployment rate is controversial. Some critics say it understates unemployment because it doesn't report on unemployed people who have given up looking for work. Nevertheless, you can localize the story by reporting the work force situation in your town. State employment services break down their figures by county. Most maintain offices in county seats and other towns, where you can interview local employment officials. Watch also

Classified Ads Are an Important Barometer

the employment section of your newspaper's classified advertising. It is an important local barometer of job availability and wage levels. Tracking work force numbers and wages at local factories or other employers is another way of measuring important local trends.

Housing Starts

This is a monthly measurement by the Commerce Department of housing starts—when ground is broken—for privately owned housing units. Each month's figures include starts for single-family housing, and buildings with two and more units. Housing starts are a key economic indicator because construction responds quickly to movement in interest rates and other economic activity. If times turn tough, housing starts often are delayed, and construction under way is halted. In good times, construction mushrooms. Localize this story by surveying construction activity in your town. Check construction company owners. Sometimes a builder's association has valuable data. Other good sources are real estate brokers and officials of banks or savings and loans associations that finance housing. Also check city and county

Survey Local Home Construction

clerks for numbers of construction permits issued. By tracking them over a period of months you can establish meaningful trends.

Index of Industrial Production
Each month the Federal Reserve Board issues the index of industrial production, reflecting production by factories, mines and electric and gas utilities nationwide. Among its components are production figures for cars, appliances, food, clothing. Opportunities for localizing this story are numerous: If you're in a car manufacturing town, for example, compare local auto production with nationwide figures. Look for similar local angles in other industrial sectors.

TRACKING AND INTERPRETING INDICATORS

Many economic indicators are easily available in national and regional newspapers. *The New York Times* and *The Wall Street Journal* are gold mines of information that will lead you to significant local stories. You can monitor in the *Times,* for example, prices of orange juice and eggs or hogs in Omaha. Just check commodities coverage in the business section. The *Journal* reports daily on prices paid for pork bellies, milk products, lard, and many other commodities.

You'll note every commodity mentioned in the preceding paragraph is of crucial interest to farm families and small-town readers whose local economy is farm-based. I wrote that paragraph with that information to make a point: It's crucial to *follow through* when you spot important changes in one of the economic indicators we've been discussing. If you're reporting for a newspaper in rural Indiana—hog country—and you see pork prices falling, jump on the story. If you are reporting in upstate New York or Wisconsin—dairy country—and you see milk product prices dropping, move quickly. And the story is *not* only pork or milk prices; rather, it's the economic status of farmers just outside your town. Sit down in their living room with a farm couple. Walk their fields with them. Reduce those distant economic signals on pork and milk prices to stories on the fears and hopes, dreams and nightmares, of *real people* struggling financially. That's the way to translate macroeconomic signals for your readers.

Again, the Real Story Is People

Below is a story about unemployment in Los Angeles. Note how the writer humanizes the lead *by focusing on a real person, not a statistic.* Bureau of Labor figures that tell the broader story are held to subsequent paragraphs.

For 24 years, for half her life, [Jane Smith] has worked at an AT&T service center in the City of Commerce.

"I never had to worry about what tomorrow will bring," she said.

She does now.

[Smith], a metal fabrication technician, is about to become a casualty of AT&T's seemingly endless campaign of "downsizing," an annual exercise the corporation performs in an effort to remain competitive in the post-divestiture world of telecommunications. . . . *Bob Baker, "'Downsizing' Strains AT&T Employees," Los Angeles Times, April 19, 1990, p. D-1*

In researching the story below, an *Atlanta Constitution* writer spotted a distant economic indicator—a Gallup Organization poll—showing that a growing number of Americans are squeezed between increasing financial responsibilities and diminishing job opportunities. Heavy stuff? Not when localized and expressed in *human* terms:

With a son in college, an aging parent needing help and retirement approaching, [Betty and Fred Smith] are facing the triple whammy.

"We had planned to retire in the next three years, but we've found that it is no longer possible," said [Mrs. Smith], 52. "Our financial responsibilities seem to be increasing every year."

The North Fulton couple is feeling the financial squeeze faced by a growing number of families nationwide, according to a survey by the Gallup Organization released Wednesday. . . . *Charles Haddad, "Baby Boomers Feel Money Squeeze,"* Atlanta Constitution, *June 14, 1990, p. D-1*

WRITING PERSONAL FINANCE STORIES

Little you write will take you closer to your readers than news stories affecting their personal pocketbooks. But where to find those stories? Look in your own pocketbook.

For example, what personal financial concerns do you have as a student? Getting a part-time job or loan? Limiting your expenses? If you're writing for a campus publication most of your readers share those concerns. They want to know where jobs are available and what the pay is, how to get a loan, and how to control their expenses. Give them guidance and you'll have avid readers.

Report News Readers Can Use

That is the core of personal finance journalism: delivering operative information readers can use to improve their income, control their expenses and prepare for a secure financial future.

Here are beginner approaches to doing that in campus journalism and, later, as a professional newswriter:

Job Availability

Most schools have employment bureaus or placement offices that coordinate job offerings by employers around campus. Do a story on jobs currently available—the types of jobs, hours, pay. Is job counseling available? When? Where? At what cost? Off campus, state employment offices and local employment agencies can provide detailed information. Don't forget to look for *indicators:* Compare today's available jobs and wages with those over the past three or four years, and give your readers trends.

Loan Availability

For many students and non-students alike, availability of loans is of crucial importance. For student readers, do a story on loans available through both school and off-campus sources. School loan officers (often working in the student affairs office) can provide details on government and other available funds. Don't overlook scholarships and grants. Many thousands of dollars often are available—and sometimes not even requested. Off campus, interview bank loan officers. For both student and non-student audiences, certain information must be in your story: Who is eligible for loans and under what terms? How much can be borrowed? What interest is charged? (Be sure to compare interest rates on various forms of loans.) How quickly must loans be repaid, and what are penalties for defaulting? For many of your readers, requesting a loan will be a new experience. So, walk them gently through the process.

Walk Readers Gently Through Finance Stories

Establishing Credit

Many readers don't understand the importance of establishing good credit rating or, if they do, how to go about it. Many undergraduates, for example, don't realize that bouncing checks at a local bar or defaulting on a student loan can impair severely their ability in later life to get credit—to borrow money for a car or home. This presents you with superb opportunity for a how-to-do-it story of great significance. Interview business school professors, bank officers and officials of a local credit rating bureau, an institution that in many cities serves local merchants as a clearinghouse on credit problems. For readers on campus or off, first establish in your interviews the need each person has for sound credit rating and, second, how that can be established.

Reading Leases

How many undergraduates know the traps that can be hidden in apartment leases? So few that if you do a story on how to find the traps you'll have a real bell-ringer. Some schools have housing officers who can shed light on what to look for in a lease. You also can interview local lawyers or real estate agents. Focus your story where many students get trapped: They unknowingly commit to 12 months rent for an apartment they need for only nine; they overlook restrictions on people who can share the apartment, and often neglect to determine whether "key money" or a deposit is refundable, and whether they are responsible for damage to the apartment. Write your story to take readers through a lease step-by-step.

How to Buy a Car

It's a dream of many students to buy a car immediately upon graduation. It's also a trap for those who don't understand how to get the best buy under favorable terms. Talk to business school professors, car dealers and, especially, bank officials about car loans. Points to make: The car's price sticker is only the *starting point* for negotiating a purchase. Searching for the best interest level and terms on a car loan is crucial. Maintenance and insurance contracts can cost the unwary a bundle. This is another perfect "service" story to do now, for a campus publication, and later, as a professional.

The ideas above are just a few for getting started in writing personal finance stories, a news category so important that newspapers today devote major resources to covering it. Many papers publish special "personal finance" sections or magazine inserts. Favorite subjects are how to handle your taxes, manage your money, buy homes and cars, how to shop for best mortgage and loan terms, how to find best credit card terms, how to plan your children's college expenses or plan your retirement.

Always, the best writers focus on real people, then go into elaborate how-to-do-it detail. Note:

How-to-Do-It Detail Is Crucial

Home buyers looking for the best mortgage deal sometimes have to have the doggedness of a detective.

And the guts of a poker player.

Just ask [Jane Smith] of Lawrenceville.

"From August through November, I checked daily on the mortgage rates," said [Mrs. Smith], who moved into a new house with her husband, [Dick], in December.

She was checking not only for her own family but for potential buyers of the home the [Smiths] were selling. "I sold our other house myself. I had to be more aware of interest rates because the potential buyers were not

up on the markets. I needed to know that to help them."

People considering the purchase of a new home this year will probably need the same fortitude.

That's because mortgage rates, after spending several months in single digits, crept over 10 percent in January. The higher rates are coupled with an overabundance of homes for sale in Atlanta, which makes it tougher for people who need to sell one home before buying another.

And when they do sell one home, they have to sort through scores of rates to find the best deal on the new mortgage.

Provide Readers with Solutions

Stories such as the one above must go beyond describing the problem to *provide readers with solutions*. This story goes on to quote an authoritative source on how to get the best mortgage rates. Note the clear, understandable language that makes this story a perfect how-to-do-it piece:

So where are rates currently in Atlanta?

Mortgage rates Thursday were hovering in the 10 percent to 10.25 percent range—with no points—said Robert S. Cannon, senior vice president of residential lending at Home Federal of Atlanta. Points refers to the up-front fee charged by lenders. A point is 1 percent of the loan.

By paying points, a borrower could get a rate below 10 percent.

Assuming a 10 percent rate without points, if a borrower wanted a rate of 9.75 percent, he would have to pay 1 point, or $1,000, on a $100,000 loan, Mr. Cannon said. For $3,000 or 3 points, the borrower could get a loan at 9.5 percent.   *James A. Mallory, "Tracking Down the Lowest Mortgage Rate,"* Atlanta Constitution, *Feb. 2, 1990, p. E-1*

Note how this *San Francisco Chronicle* writer addresses solutions by looking ahead to give her readers information crucial to their home-buying plans:

Slowing increases in home prices coupled with the stabilization of mortgage rates may give more homebuyers the chance to purchase a home in the 1990s.

But that doesn't mean home prices in the Bay Area will fall as they have in other parts of the country or that the first-time homebuyers will get more house for his money, say housing experts willing to hazard a guess about the trends of the next decade.

What it does mean is that the size of starter homes will probably shrink and the go-go home price appreciation of 25 percent annually over the past few years will slow to between 5 percent and 10 percent. That should give first-time homebuyers a fighting chance at mustering up a down-payment in the next few years. . . .
Laura Evenson, "1990s May Benefit Homebuyers," San Francisco Chronicle, *Dec. 29, 1989, p. C-1*

COVERING LOCAL COMPANIES

Covering local companies is a coveted assignment on many newspapers because it can yield what every dedicated journalist is after: meaningful stories with page-one impact on readers' lives.

Consider the following: Jobs offered by factories, banks and financial institutions, retail stores and other Main Street companies drive the local economy. Their paychecks are mostly spent locally and fuel business activity. Taxes they pay support local government and schools. How they act as "good citizens" is important to the local environment and quality of life.

Broadly, you can take two beginner's approaches to company news.

Report Business for Lay Readers

First, you can report local business news significant to the general economy and everyone who lives in it. A challenge here is learning what company news is important to a wider audience and how to extract it from business people who speak their own jargon-filled language. Then you must translate for non-business readers.

Report Business for Experts

Second, you can report within the business community for the community itself—

what's called "company-to-company news" of interest to business executives, investors and others who follow, with a high degree of expertise, what's happening to local companies.

Here's a reporter who went into the business community for a story that, when properly translated, is crucial to a wide reader audience in the San Francisco Bay Area.

Bay Area businesses are optimistic when it comes to office hiring plans for the coming year.

Twenty-two percent of San Francisco and Peninsula businesses expect to need more office employees in the first half of 1990--more than triple the number planning to hire a year ago—according to a poll conducted for Thomas Temporaries, a personnel agency based in Irvine.

Last year, only 7 percent of businesses in San Francisco, San Mateo and San Bruno had plans to hire more staff in the first six months of the year.

East Bay employers also report a dramatic rise in hiring projections, according to the survey of 1,500 executives across the state. . . . *Jamie Beckett, "Many Area Firms Planning to Boost Hiring Next Year," San Francisco Chronicle, Dec. 27, 1989, p. C-1*

Note above several points essential to this type of reporting. First, the lead is short (16 words) and addresses clearly the single point about hiring optimism—and that's the bottom line interest for non-business readers. Second (in the second paragraph), the story explicitly states the source (poll). Third, the story provides an economic indicator—a trend—by mentioning (second paragraph) 22 percent of businesses and comparing that (third paragraph) with 7 percent last year.

Below, the same writer combines a distant news event with local interviews in a story for *both* a wider general audience of consumers and the business community itself:

Freezing temperatures that destroyed crops in the Gulf Coast states may bring some California farmers higher prices, while consumers here pay more for oranges, grapefruit and orange juice, farm experts predicted yesterday.

The cold devastated the citrus crop in Florida and Texas. . . .

California growers say they already are seeing an increased demand for their navel-orange crop, which reached near-record levels this year.

"When the freeze hit in Florida, the phones started ringing off the hook in California with calls by brokers looking for oranges to fill the void," said a spokesman for the California Farm Bureau. California produces 26 percent of the nation's oranges.

A few growers already are receiving high prices. In some cases, wholesale prices jumped 50c to about $8.50 per 40–pound box, according to the Farm Bureau.

Consumer prices for oranges already have jumped by as much as 12c a pound, farm officials said. . . . *Jamie Beckett, "California Feeling Effects of Freeze," San Francisco Chronicle, Dec. 30, 1989, p. B-1*

Above, note how quickly (fifth and sixth paragraphs) the writer presents precise figures on the impact this news has on prices for *both* the growers and consumers of oranges. This type of reporting must trace a development through to its *impact on your readers' pocketbooks.*

Highlight Story's Pocketbook Impact

Wordsmiths at Work

One key to successful business news writing is finding a local angle, a human element or the drama of big money and highlighting that with clarity in your story. Below are examples of professionals who succeed at that.

Catching the Drama of Big Money

IRVING, Texas—Among the casual shoppers in Aisle 3 of the Tom Thumb supermarket one recent Thursday morning, Louis V. Gerstner Jr. stands out. He is wearing a suit. He is accompanied by a young executive with a clipboard. And he is thinking of spending, say, $200 million.

Mr. Gerstner, chief executive officer of RJR Nabisco Holdings Inc., is scouting for small, food-company acquisition candidates. Bread, cakes, cereals, spices and a dozen other categories all draw a look.

When Mr. Gerstner is intrigued by what he sees on the shelf, he lingers a moment to engage his strategy chief, Stephen Wilson, in rapid-fire dialogue about profit margins and market share. When Mr. Gerstner is unimpressed, he walks on, forcing Mr. Wilson to abandon all talk of that acquisition idea, flip ahead in his notes and start afresh.

This is the new RJR: A no-nonsense, impatient company where top-level strategy meetings are sometimes held on the linoleum aisles of supermarkets. Bureaucracy, flamboyant spending and intra-company rivalries are out. Teamwork, urgency and a Japanese-style fixation on quality are in. . . .   George Anders, "Old Flamboyance Is Out as Louis Gerstner Remakes RJR Nabisco," *The Wall Street Journal,* March 21, 1991, p. 1

Highlighting the People Angle

Last summer, [Fred Smith] of Alexandria opened his telephone bill and made a horrifying discovery: One of his children had called a 900-number "gab line" and run up a tab of more than $1,000.

"I was shocked and outraged with my children," [Smith] said, but as he thought about what had happened he became even more incensed with a telephone system that left him unprotected when his children responded to the blandishments of "gab line" or "true confession line" purveyors. These lines offer callers a chance to talk to other kids or someone who provides a sympathetic ear—or in some cases will talk dirty with the caller.

[Smith] is not alone. Last week, he was among a group of consumer and regulatory officials calling on Congress to enact new legislation to protect telephone users from abusive and sometimes downright fraudulent uses of 900-number service. . . .   Albert B. Crenshaw, "900 Lines Are Ringing Up A Number of Complaints," *Washington Post,* March 3, 1991, p. H3

Emphasizing the Local Angle

The potential opportunities in rebuilding war-torn Kuwait already are whetting the appetites of many Pacific Northwest companies.

Though they are headquartered halfway around the world from the little nation where everything from infrastructure—roads, sewers, electrical lines—to commerical and residental buildings needs to be replaced, Seattle-area business wants to be involved. . . .   Polly Lane and Tom Brown, "Local Companies Look Mideast," *Seattle Times,* March 1, 1991, p. F1

APPLYING A LIGHT WRITING TOUCH

Successful professionals seize every opportunity to write in a light, featurish style that makes a business story just plain good reading. Note this example:

> Given the recession and a national obsession with dieting, [Fred Smith's] latest venture might seem, well, adventuresome.
>
> [Smith], who for 15 years has operated a well-known restaurant bearing his name at Front and South Streets, is getting into the canned-food business.
>
> Under a separate entity [Smith Foods], he is marketing four items from his restaurant menu, all with a thick Irish brogue.
>
> They aren't cheap, costing from $3 to $4 a can. "We can't compete with Campbell's," he said.
>
> They don't wear the label *lite*. While it seems every new food product these days promises to make the consumer svelte, if not immortal, [Smith's] canned soups—Irish potato, Galway Bay seafood chowder and Dublin Bay Lobster Bisque—aren't recommended for snacking on the way to the health club. Nor is the fourth item, Irish stew.
>
> "There's a lot of calories in these," he acknowledges.
>
> And, he hopes a lot of profits. . . .   Anthony R. Wood, "This Restauranteur Has a Soup Course Straight From Can," *Philadelphia Inquirer,* March 12, 1991, p. C-1

Below, a writer's coverage of construction companies follows through to their impact on quality of life in Seattle:

> From Greenwood to Queen Anne Hill to West Seattle, all across Seattle, an apartment construction boom is changing the face of neighborhood business districts.
>
> One-story storefronts and older houses used as offices are disappearing, replaced by three- and four-story apartment buildings with offices or shops offering sandwiches, video rentals and mailing services at street level.
>
> Chased out of residential zones over the past two years by increasingly strict controls on the size of apartment buildings, developers are turning to the neighborhood commercial strips where larger projects still can be built. . . .   *Dick Lilly, "Mixed-Use Buildings a Mixed Blessing,"* Seattle Times, *Dec. 26, 1989, p. B-1*

Incidentally, the story above was considered so important by *Seattle Times* editors that they gave it virtually the entire front page of the paper's "Today" section. The story ran several thousand words, with a large photo, a map showing construction locations and a sidebar story that listed new buildings address-by-address. We're not discussing here a type of writing that editors hide among the classified ads. The impact of business on quality of life is big news that gets major display.

Now, consider the *reporting logic* and *writing techniques* of the three previous examples on covering local companies. Note they reflect the same news values and judgments you take to any story. There is no special mystery to this type of writing. You need not be a financial genius. Just use sound reporting techniques and basic writing skills!

You've got to shift gears a bit, however, in covering company-to-company news in the business and investment community for readers in that community itself. In this writing you must make two basic assumptions.

First, your readers have a higher degree of expertise than does a general audience. That means your job of translating jargon will be easier. It also means even a slight error in your writing will be caught.

Business Readers Want Facts, Accuracy Foremost

Second, readers within the business community aren't seeking particularly colorful writing. They want *facts*, straightforward and unadorned. It matters not to them that the sky was dark and stormy the day General Motors announced year-end financial results.

That is, covering company-to-company news *does* require special training. A minor in business and several courses in accounting are good first steps for a career in this advanced form of business journalism. So, for our purposes I'll discuss just a few beginner stories you can write as you edge into this specialized field.

THE EARNINGS REPORT

This is the most basic—and important—company news story. In effect, it is a "report card" on the financial performance of publicly owned companies—those whose stock is traded on stock exchanges. By law, publicly owned companies must divulge four times annually, at the end of each quarter, certain information the Securities and Exchange Commission, a federal regulatory body, considers essential to investors who might want to buy, sell or hold the stock. (Privately owned companies need not divulge results this way.)

If you've never studied accounting, your first step in covering this type of story should be to learn how to read a financial report. A basic (and, thus excellent) explanation is in "How to Read a Financial Report," available from any local office of the brokerage firm Merril Lynch, Pierce, Fenner & Smith, Inc., or its headquarters at P.O. Box 30441, New Brunswick, N.J., 08989–0441.[5]

Your second step should be to focus narrowly on what this type story is designed to do: report in sparse, direct language the key information business executives and investors need to understand how well (or poorly) the company performed in the preceding three-month period or, in the case of an *annual report,* the preceding year. Most essential are earnings (or profit), total sales (or revenue)—and whether both were up or down from a previous period.

Below, a *Baltimore Sun* writer presents those essentials in minimum wordage:

Westinghouse Electric Corp. reported a 30 percent gain in fourth-quarter earnings yesterday, marking the company's 26th consecutive quarter of improved profits.

For all of 1989, the diversified manufacturing and service company earned $922 million ($6.31 a share) on total sales of $12.8 billion, a gain of 12 percent over the previous year.

The company's Electronic Systems Group, Maryland's largest private employer in manufacturing, posted higher revenues for the fourth quarter, but they were unchanged for the year. The group's operating profit was even for the quarter and up slightly for the year. . . .

During 1988, the Electronic Systems Group reported a 7 percent increase in sales and a 17 percent improvement in operating profits. Mr. Jones said yesterday that the group posted an operating profit of $262.7 million in 1988 "and we're saying this was up slightly" for 1989. . . .

Ted Shelsby, "Westinghouse Made 30% Gain in 4th Quarter," Baltimore Sun, Jan. 18, 1990, p. B-1

Report Company's Profit Perfurmancce

Let's discuss the *Baltimore Sun* story above:

Lead paragraph: Earnings—profits—were up 30 percent in the period October–December (fourth quarter). That's the key information in this story because profit reflects total sales of goods and services minus the cost of labor, materials, rents, and other expenses. Profit is the primary goal of this company, so a 30 percent gain is significant. Any investor would be impressed with that in addition to the company's record of profit for 26 consecutive quarters. That doesn't mean future profits will increase—but it signals the company is well managed.

Second paragraph: Note the brief description ("diversified") of the company. An earnings report should mention goods or services sold. For all of 1989, profit and total sales are reported. That's not the lead because previous quarterly reports told readers of profits in the three quarters before October–December. What happened in the last three months is the news. Expressing profit in per-share terms ($6.31) is another way of signaling readers on how well the company is doing. (In the previous year, it was $5.66.) Comparing results with those of the same period a year earlier is essential in this type of writing.

Third paragraph: Here, the *Baltimore Sun* writer localizes the story on this international diversified company by focusing on its Maryland operations. Do as the pros do: Find the local angle.

Fourth paragraph: The new information here is "operating profit"—profit from the company's normal business of selling goods and services. It does *not* include profit from financial investments, interest on bank deposits, and so forth. Essentially, operating profit measures company performance in its mainline business but does not reflect its total performance.

Most newspapers also publish "earnings digests" that present the most essential information in graphic form. Below is the *Baltimore Sun's* digest for Westinghouse:

Three months ended 12/31/89

	Revenue	Net	Share
1989	$3,651,000,000	$270,000,000	$1.85
1988	$3,648,000,000	$208,000,000	$1.43
% change	+0.1	+29.8	+29.4

Year ended 12/31/89

	Revenue	Net	Share
1989	$12,844,000,000	$922,000,000	$6.31
1988	$12,500,000,000	$823,000,000	$5.66
% change	+2.8	+12.0	+11.5

Note above how quickly you can absorb the revenue (total sales) and net (profit) figures for both the fourth quarter ended December 31, 1989, and the full year 1989. Also note results are expressed in both dollars and percentages. Like the earnings story, the earnings digest is structured for quick comprehension. You can practice analyzing company results by reading earnings stories and digests. You'll find scores of them in business sections several weeks after each quarter ends.

THE "NEW COMPANY" STORY

New companies that open for business in town are big news. For business readers, they can be competitors or opportunities for new business relationships. For your general audience, they can be new places to shop. For all readers, a well-written "new company" story can be an intriguing tale of risk-taking by local entrepreneurs. An example:

> When people talk about starting a small business on a shoestring, they may be thinking of entrepreneurs like Leslie Cowley and Jane Niehuser.
>
> The two women opened Watermark Press, a commercial printing shop, in March 1989. Cowley handles sales, and Niehaser does the printing on two small offset presses. Most of their business is letterheads, envelopes, brochures and leaflets, and newspaper advertising inserts.
>
> If that sounds simple, it isn't. *Jim Kadera, "Fledgling Business Making Mark on Portland Printing Scene," Portland Sunday Oregonian, April 1, 1990, p. D-1*

In the story above, writer Kadera goes on to describe how the two women started a successful business with money borrowed from their parents and scrounged used equipment. The story has business *and* human interest importance.

New Businesses Are News

(If you doubt new businesses are news, attend the next grand opening of a new shopping center or supermarket in your town. Seeing the crowds that turn out can help you understand how your readers define news. Readers don't believe news all comes from Washington or from politicians.)

THE COMPANY "SITUATIONER"

Even as a beginner, you can easily spot your town's important companies. They employ the most people and have the largest payrolls. That makes them crucial to all your readers, in and out of the business community.

Make a name for yourself: Identify important companies and track their performance through occasional stories on their current situation. Below, the *Oregonian*'s Jim Kadera does such a "situationer." (Note the light touch in the lead!)

> STAYTON—There are no small potatoes at Norpac Foods Inc.
>
> Oregon's largest farmer-owned food processor ends the 1980s with two years of unusually strong sales. The Williamette Valley cooperative shipped $220 million of fruit and vegetables in 1989, up more than 20 percent from $180 million in 1988. Sales were $155 million in 1987.
>
> "In the last two years, drought in the Midwest helped Oregon," said Art Christiansen, president and general manager. "We took advantage of higher demand and prices.
>
> "We go into next year with balanced inventories. If there are no bumper crops, they could stay balanced in 1990. . . ." *Jim Kadera, "Norpac Foods Ends 1980s Strongly," Portland Sunday Oregonian, Dec. 31, 1989, p. C-1*

Precision Reporting Is Essential

Above, note two points: First, the story is strongly reported with dollar and percentage specifics (second paragraph). Cute lead aside, precision reporting makes this story. Second, the writer (fourth paragraph) throws the story ahead with the president's quote on the outlook for the upcoming year (in this case 1990). For readers of business news, what happened last year is important. But it's history. What they're trying to figure out is what's going to happen *next* year. Good reporting helps them make informed predictions.

Incidentally, writer Kadera dominated page one of the *Sunday Oregonian's* business section with the Norpac Foods situationer above. Not a bad showcase for a byline in a paper with more than 413,000 circulation.

THE HERO (OR GOAT) STORY

Like all human endeavors, business has its heroes or goats, winners or losers. Readers love stories about winners. They read with morbid fascination about high and mighty people who turn out to be losers.

It's the same with companies. You'll find avid readers for stories about companies that do well—or poorly. Especially popular are stories about turnarounds—loser companies that become winners. This story about a turnaround and the business hero who engineered it dominated the *Los Angeles Times* business section:

It owned a foreclosed bordello, a mine that produced a Kitty Litter-like gravel for cats and a collection of securities and loans that at one point were worth a staggering $3 billion less than their original value.

In short, American Savings, once the nation's largest savings and loan, up until the end of 1988 was the thrift industry's equivalent of a huge toxic waste dump. It was a mess in need of a mind-boggling clean-up job, with nasty surprises lurking everywhere.

What a difference a year and a $1.7 billion bailout make. A little more than one year after the Stockton-based savings and loan was sold by regulators to Texas billionaire Robert M. Bass, American is not only in the black, it's returning the kind of profit that most savings and loan executives dream about. . . .

American's turn-around is partly a tribute to the hard work and drastic cost cutting of Chief Executive Mario J. Antoci, a well-respected manager who. . . .   *James Bates, "The Renaissance of American Savings & Loan,"* Los Angeles Times, *Feb. 5, 1990, p. D-1*

Who said business news is dull?

SUMMARY CHECKLIST

☐ Economic and business news is a high-priority item in the media because it strikes directly into reader, listener and viewer pocketbooks.

☐ No impenetrable mystery surrounds business news. Use the same news definitions, values and writing skills applied to any other type of news.

☐ Double—triple—your efforts to be accurate. Giving readers erroneous information on which they make bad investments is a journalistic sin. Translate jargon, and beware attempts by some to influence what you write. Money moves on business news.

☐ You can write meaningful stories by localizing national economic indicators. Among them: gross national product, a measurement of the nation's goods and services; consumer price index, a federal report on prices of a "market basket" of goods and services; unemployment rate, monthly federal figures on size of civilian work force and number of unemployed; housing starts, a key indicator of new construction of privately owned housing units; index of industrial production, which measures monthly output of factories, mines, and electric and gas utilities nationwide.

☐ Personal finance stories take you close to reader pocketbooks. Do stories for campus readers on your own financial concerns: How to get part-time jobs. How to obtain student loans, and establish good credit rating. How to find hidden traps in apartment leases. How to buy a car.

☐ Humanize personal finance stories by focusing on real people and—always—go beyond describing the problem to provide readers with solutions.

☐ Covering local companies can yield meaningful stories with page-one impact on readers' lives. Broadly, you can cover local business for a wider, general audience, or write company-to-company news for expert readers within the business community itself.

☐ Basic business stories for beginners include the *earnings report,* a report card on a company's financial performance; the *new company* story on a business newly opened in your town; the *situationer,* or periodic report on a particularly important company, and the *hero* (*or* goat) story on winners and losers in business.

RECOMMENDED READING

Reading *The Wall Street Journal* daily is a must (and, when you get into it, a *delightful* must) for anyone preparing to cover business news. The *Journal* (200 Liberty St., New York, N.Y., 10281) publishes an Educational Edition that explains in basic language how to read and understand its economic and financial data. Also see Richard Saul Wurman, Alan Siegel and Kenneth Morris, *The Wall Street Journal: Guide to Understanding Money and Markets* (New York: Access Press, 1989).

Business sections of *The New York Times*, *Los Angeles Times, Chicago Tribune* and other metropolitan papers can be extremely educational if you read them regularly.

Forbes, Business Week and *Fortune* are among national business magazines that are highly readable and informative. Depending on your locale or the business news specialty that interests you, many specialized "trade" publications are available. For example, if writing aviation business news appeals to you, read *Aviation Week & Space Technology.* Similar "niche" magazines are available in farming, banking, auto production and so forth.

Ask your school librarian for a list of basic information sources for business students. Among them will be business dictionaries, glossaries and directories in addition to other standard reference works and publications.

Also see Louis M. Kohlmeier Jr., Jon G. Udell and Laird B. Anderson, *Reporting on Business and the Economy* (Englewood Cliffs, N.J.: Prentice-Hall, 1981), and Donald Kirsch, *Financial and Economic Journalism* (New York: New York University Press, 1978).

NOTES

1. Attesting to the importance of this news, The Associated Press devotes an entire section in its *Stylebook and Libel Manual* (pp. 253–264) to business guidelines and style. It's a good starting point for any beginning writer.

2. Excellent glossaries invaluable in this translating process are published by AP (in its *Stylebook)* and by Dow Jones & Company.

3. I discuss some of these ethical problems, particularly in the relationship of journalists with advertising and public relations, in *Media Ethics: In the Newsroom and Beyond* (New York: McGraw-Hill, 1988). Also see John L. Hulteng, *The Messenger's Motives,* 2d ed. (Englewood Cliffs, N.J.: Prentice-Hall, 1985), and H. Eugene Goodwin, *Groping for Ethics in Journalism,* 2d ed. (Ames: Iowa State University Press, 1987).

4. The *Tribune* regards itself as a Midwest regional newspaper and its periodic roundups on Midwest economic developments are excellent how-to-do-it illustrations for beginning reporters. Others that do superb regional economic reporting include the *Boston Globe* on the Northeast; *Dallas Morning News,* Texas and the Southwest; *Los Angeles Times*, California and the West; *Seattle Times*, Northwest.

5. See AP's *Stylebook*, Revised Edition (1987), pp. 252–253, for detailed discussion of the necessary components of an earnings story.

Exercise 12–1   Localizing Economic Indicators

For each economic indicator below write two ideas of about 75 words each on how you could write localized stories. Mention individuals you would interview.

Gross National Product

_____

_____

_____

_____

_____

_____

_____

_____

_____

_____

_____

Consumer Price Index

_____

_____

_____

_____

_____

_____

_____

_____

_____

_____

_____

Unemployment Rate

Housing Starts

Exercise 12–2   Following Through to Real People

The text mentioned the need to follow through on economic and business news stories to find "real people." It gave an example of interviewing hog farmers in Indiana on a drop in pork prices. In about 50 words each, write a story idea on how you would follow through on these developments:

Drought strikes corn crop

_____

_____

_____

_____

_____

_____

_____

_____

_____

_____

_____

_____

Auto sales plummet nationwide

_____

_____

_____

_____

_____

_____

_____

_____

_____

_____

_____

_____

Unemployment soars in industrial production

_____
_____
_____
_____
_____
_____
_____
_____
_____
_____
_____
_____

Personal bankruptcies increase dramatically

_____
_____
_____
_____
_____
_____
_____
_____
_____
_____
_____
_____
_____

Exercise 12–3   Consumer Prices Rise

Write about 150–200 words from the following facts. Use a Washington dateline. Follow AP style. Write for this afternoon's paper.

This information was released today by the Labor Department. It's the consumer price index. It shows that last month, consumer prices shot up 1.1 percent. The department said today that increase reflected sharp increases in fuel and food costs. Those increases were lingering from December's record cold weather. The 1.1 percent increase was the biggest monthly gain in 7½ years. The index is the government's primary gauge of inflation at the retail level. The 1.1 percent increase was seasonally adjusted. It was the largest since June 1982. The increase then was also 1.1 percent. Last year, the steepest gain was in April. The increase then was 0.7 percent.

Exercise 12–4   Following Through

Write for today's Seattle Times *about 200 words from the following facts. Because the* Times *is a regional daily, the statewide impact of the following should be your lead. But follow through, not later than your second paragraph, on the meaning—in dollars and cents—for residential users of U S West telephone service in Seattle.*

This is from a decision yesterday by the Washington State Utilities and Transportation Commission. There are three members on the commission. It approved a plan that would cut U S West's phone rates in the state. The cut could be $65 million. The plan would dramatically change the way the company is regulated. Under the plan, if it goes through, monthly rates for residents would drop to $10.75. That's in Seattle. They now are at $11.50. Rates for business would change too. For those with five or more lines, rates would drop to $42.25 from the present $47.10. Per month. If a business has fewer than five lines its rates would drop from $35.10 to $28.20 That's also per month. The decision yesterday by the commission was roundly criticized. By competitors of U S West, and by consumer advocates. Some big-business users of the company, U S West Communications Inc., were also critical. They were against the commission on grounds it allowed U S West to give with one hand and take away with the other. U S West is the state's largest phone company.

Exercise 12–5   Fuel Price Increase Story

Any increase in airline and shipping rates is big news in San Francisco. Write for the San Francisco Chronicle *about 150–200 words from the following:*

Fuel prices increased recently. And that is translating into bad news. It's translating into higher airline fares. Shipping rates are going up too. Economists warn inflation could be fueled by the increase in fuel prices. Northwest Airlines is increasing prices next Wednesday. It will add $6 to the price of tickets for all U.S. flights. That's $6 for *each* way. International ticket prices might go up too. And soon. Northwest will seek to add to the price of international tickets its so-called fuel surcharge. That would be the first in the airline industry since 1987. Meanwhile, more news: Continental Airlines announced an increase in ticket prices starting next Wednesday. The increase is 4 percent. Across the board. The increase is designed, Continental says, to offset what it calls "soaring fuel costs." Fuel costs at Continental have risen. They rose 43 percent in the fourth quarter of 1989. The price is 71 cents a gallon. It was 49.6 cents in the fourth quarter a year earlier. Starting today, other airlines are expected to follow suit with similar increases.

Exercise 12–6   Earnings Report

Write a brief story—three or four paragraphs—from the following. Use an Atlanta dateline. Write for Wednesday afternoon papers.

Southern Co. has headquarters in Atlanta. It is the parent company of Georgia Power Co., Savannah Electric Co., Gulf Power Co., Alabama Power Co., and Mississippi Power Co. Most people know that. Its president is Edward L. Addison. On Wednesday, Southern Co. reported earnings for the first 11 months of this year. Earnings for the 11 months were $804 million. That's $21 million over earnings last year for the same period, the first 11 months. Addison put it this way: Earnings represented $2.55 a share. That's up 3 cents a share more than in the same period last year.

Chapter Thirteen

Writing Science News

As a reporter today, you will write science news. One way or another, whether or not you choose to specialize in science, you will be given assignments that involve writing it. All reporters are.

That reflects two realities in journalism: First, some aspect of science is pivotal in much "general" news reporting. City council reporters encounter it in government moves on toxic waste, garbage, air pollution and in the broader story on societal concerns over the environment. Reporters covering police, business, sports, education—all find science thrusting itself into their reporting.

Second, editors nationwide in both print and television increasingly insist their staffs go beyond simply picking up science news that pops willy-nilly into the spotlight. They want reporters to act aggressively in seeking out important scientific news, then expertly translating it in meaningful terms for readers and viewers whose lives are affected by it.

Major newspapers publish full-fledged science sections staffed by highly qualified writers—physicians to report health news, for example, or trained chemists or other specialists to cover the environment, agriculture, space, oceanic exploration, nuclear power and many other subjects that bear on how well we live and, literally, how we die.

But even small dailies develop general-assignment reporters skilled in writing local science stories at least part-time. For magazines, science is major news, and not only for the likes of *Science* or *New England Journal of Medicine,* which specialize in the subject. On TV, science no longer is relegated principally to public-television documentaries. Noting all major networks now do in-depth science reporting, *The Wall Street Journal* says, "It isn't just the result of Hollywood producers with beach houses finding they can't jump into the ocean for a backyard swim because of raw sewage. The environmental crisis is truly heating up. . . . People are increasingly aware there's a hole in the ozone, too much garbage and that the planet's climate is heating up."[1]

We turn to science news with two motives: First, to give each of you, whatever your career goals in journalism, a few hints on developing beginner's capability in covering this important news sector. We'll discuss ways you can start, now, in campus journalism, trying your hand at it. Second, we hope to encourage any of you with scientific bent to explore long-term careers in this rewarding specialty. Few news sectors bear so directly, with as much meaning, on the lives of your readers or listeners. And, editors in all media put a premium on writers who can translate that meaning with accurate reporting and clear writing.

352

BEGINNING WITH BASIC STORIES

This chapter discusses writing science news broadly defined to concentrate on two sectors frequently on front pages—the *environment* and *personal health*.

SPECIAL RESPONSIBILITIES IN WRITING SCIENCE

The woman, sobbing and pleading, was telephoning AP's Chicago bureau from somewhere in Canada: She had seen a newspaper report from Chicago of a new "cure" for cancer.

Was it available for her husband? He was near death, in terrible pain. "Please help me," she cried. "Please, please. . . ."

That was *1958*. The cancer "cure," like many others since, didn't pan out, of course. The woman's hopes, and the hopes of perhaps millions, were raised, then broken, by researchers who were well-meaning but entirely too optimistic about their findings—*and by reporters who let themselves get swept along by that optimism.*

It goes without saying that, yes, in reporting science news you apply the same news definitions and values you do to any news. *But* in writing science news, which can affect readers so dramatically, you have special responsibilities.

Accuracy First

As in economic and business news, you must redouble your efforts to be accurate, authoritative and *cautious* in reporting and writing science news. Note how cautiously a *Los Angeles Times* writer handles an *apparent* major medical advance:

In a major advance toward understanding why women are more vulnerable to the effects of alcohol than men, researchers reported today that women appear to have significantly lower amounts of a stomach enzyme that breaks down some of the intoxicant before it circulates through the body.

The report by researchers from the University School of Medicine in Trieste, Italy, and the Veterans Affairs Medical Center, Bronx, N.Y., also may help explain why women who drink heavily suffer more liver damage than men and why consumption of even small amounts of alcohol during pregnancy can cause serious birth defects.

If the results are confirmed in other studies, health and government officials may need to consider sex differences when defining safe levels of drinking for driving motor vehicles

and other activities that demand high degrees of attention or coordination.

"The stomach represents a protective barrier against the penetration of alcohol into the body," said Dr. Charles S. Lieber, director of the Alcohol Research and Treatment Center at the Bronx center and the senior author of the study, published in today's New England Journal of Medicine.

The study of 20 men and 23 women shows "that the stomach plays a significant (protective) role in the metabolism of alcohol in men and a less significant and perhaps even negligible role in women," said R. Albert L. Jones, a liver and metabolism expert at the Veterans Administration Medical Center in San Francisco. . . .

Robert Steinbrook, "Research Links Enzyme to Alcohol's Effect on Women," Los Angeles Times, Jan. 11, 1990, p. A-1

Don't Oversell Your Story

Let's examine the story above.

The lead: Note the L.A. *Times* reporter carefully avoids overselling the story. He writes of "major advance *toward understanding*" (not a "breakthrough," not a "cure"). He writes that women "appear" to have lower amounts of the enzyme. Attribution ("researchers") is clear.

Second paragraph: The writer states explicitly who did the research and again is careful in describing its meaning (it "may help explain . . .").

Third paragraph: In science writing, it isn't enough to coyly slide in low-key qualifiers ("researchers said" or "studies appear to show"). Use explicit qualifiers your readers can't miss, such as, "If the results are confirmed in other studies. . . ."

Fourth paragraph: Attribution is by name, title, and medical affiliation of the senior author, and the authoritative journal that published the study is named. *Always* cite authoritative sources in science reporting.

Authoritative Sources Are Essential

Fifth paragraph: The L.A. *Times* writer goes to an independent—and nearby—medical authority (Dr. Jones of San Francisco) for another interpretation of the study. Localize science stories. Importantly, the writer mentions precisely how many persons (20 men, 23 women) were studied. That permits readers to deduce for themselves the magnitude of the research.

Later in this story, a classic of responsible, balanced science writing, reporter Steinbrook adds another qualifier: *New England Journal of Medicine* editorially "called for further study, cautioning that 'firm proof' . . . is lacking and other factors may be operative."

Incidentally, the *Los Angeles Times* gave prominent *front-page* display to the science story above. As with much specialty reporting, we're discussing here a news sector so highly regarded by editors—and readers—that writers are rewarded with major display for well-done stories on important topics. (Salaries often are higher than those of general-assignment reporters, too.)

Develop Expert Sources

For a full-time career in science news you'll need special training—a science minor, at minimum. But academic training cannot equip you with adequate background in all of the many science specialties you'll encounter as a reporter. So, as in all reporting, developing sources—well-placed human sources—is crucial. It's not that written reports, studies, and scientific journals aren't available. The problem is there are too many and you need help from expert sources in locating (and understanding) what's truly important. For example, at the Sixth International AIDS Conference in San Francisco in June 1990, *3,000* research papers were presented.[2]

You Need Access to Scientific Circles

Gaining access to scientific circles, then the confidence of experts, can be difficult. Many bankers, lawyers and sources of other specialty news have experience in explaining things to nonexperts—bankers to clients, lawyers to juries and so forth. With scientists, however, you often must penetrate a closed circle of experts who spend their professional lives talking and writing in highly technical language for other experts. Additionally, many scientists feel reporters are superficial, too quick to popularize science news and that in the process they sometimes neglect the facts. Proceed slowly and carefully. Learn to talk the language of science. Show respect for science.

Above all, develop a reputation as an authoritative, accurate reporter. Then you can penetrate that closed circle.

In covering science, you can use any writing style and story structure you've studied in this book. For example, you can write in sparse, concise language and let the facts tell the story, or you can let your imagination flow as you reach for a catchy lead.

The *USA Today* writer below chooses to write in simple, direct language and get out of the way and let the facts tell the story.

The chances of a woman getting breast cancer in her lifetime just increased to 1 in 9, new figures from the American Cancer Society show.

That's the second increase in lifetime odds since 1987, when the chances rose from 1 in 11 to 1 in 10.

In 1940, it was 1 in 20.

The steady increase in rates is due in part to better detection through self breast exams, more routine breast exams by doctors and increas- ing use of mammography, says Dr. Gerald Dodd, ACS president.

And as more women live longer, the rate increases—risk is highest for women older than 50. Risk factors:

- Family history of breast cancer.
- Never having children.
- Having a first child after age 30.

A possible risk: dietary fat. . . .

Tim Friend, "New Breast Cancer Odds: 1–in–9 Risk," USA Today, Jan. 25–27, 1991, p. A-1

Note how the writer below chooses to write a lead you cannot refuse to read:

Just when you thought it was safe to procreate, the population bomb is back. Two decades ago, mainstream economists brushed aside the vision of a future chronically short of food and fuel. Now some are having second thoughts, prompted by new con- cerns about possible global warming and other strains imposed by population and economic growth on the planet's ecology. *Peter Passell, "Economists Start to Fret Again About Population," The New York Times, Dec. 18, 1990, p. C-1*

Issues and Challenges:
The Need For Healthy Skepticism

The wonders of science—and they are many—can be dazzling. Learned scientists and technocrats sometimes can speak with a certainty and sense of authority that can overwhelm the nonexpert. Don't be awed. Don't get wrapped up in the "gee whiz" of it all. Retain a healthy skepticism. Probe, push, ask, seek corroborating comment—just as you do in any news sector.

Looking back, many of your predecessors in science reporting agree they were dazzled—and lost their sense of balance—on important stories. For example, the National Aeronautics and Space Administration for years surrounded itself in an aura of technical invincibility that few reporters penetrated—until, that is, the spaceship Challenger exploded over Cape Canaveral in 1986, starting a series of NASA failures. Some reporters assigned to NASA in those days acknowledge they were caught up in public-relations glitz and didn't take to this science story the discerning judgments routinely applied to other types of news.

Also, beware any story revealing scientists have discovered the "oldest" of anything, or that the "most distant" reaches of space have been photographed, or that the "final breakthrough" has been achieved. The horizons of science are expanding so rapidly that tomorrow—or no later than the day after tomorrow—a new "oldest" or "most distant" will be announced in a study that achieves the ultimate "final breakthrough."

Translate!

Nowhere in journalism must you spend more time trying to understand complex developments and to find ways to translate their meaning into terms readers comprehend. No function is more important for you as a science writer than serving as translator—a bridge of understanding—between expert source and nonexpert reader.

Note below how a writer avoids the technical term for a disease and, instead, uses its popular name as she eases readers into a complicated scientific development:

After three years of struggling to overcome frustrating technical snags and red herrings, scientists have isolated the gene that causes the disfiguring and sometimes fatal condition known as Elephant Man's disease.

The discovery of the gene for the disease, neurofibromatosis, is the first for a hereditary disease of the nervous system, said Dr. Allan E. Rubenstein, medical director for the National Neurofibromatosis Foundation. The organization helped finance and coordinate the research leading to the new finding.

The gene had been among the big-game quarry of molecular biologists, both because the illness is one of the most common hereditary diseases, afflicting one in 4,000 people worldwide with varying severity, and because scientists believe studying the gene will yield insights into the biology of the brain and the nervous system, the targets of the disease.

"In my view, this is the single most exciting discovery in neurogenetics that has ever taken place," Dr. Rubenstein said. . . . *Natalie Angier, "Scientists Discover the Gene in a Nervous System Disease,"* The New York Times, *July 13, 1990, p. A-1*

Military affairs reporting is a news specialty that requires "translating" jargon into terms readers understand. Theresa Humphrey, AP correspondent in Dover, Del., covers Dover Air Force Base, home of giant Galaxy C-5A cargo planes.

(AP photo
used with permission)

**Turn Science News into
Readable Stories**

Note above that the writer's fundamental success in translating is turning a scientifically complex, somewhat esoteric development into a darned good page-one thriller about a hunt for "big-game quarry." Later, she introduces—and, of course, defines—scientific terms.

Also above note (second paragraph) that the writer explains who financed the study. That's important because in science news, as in all reporting, you will encounter individuals and institutions who have their own motives for announcing research results. If someone announces a study showing cigarette smoking is good for you, your readers deserve to know whether it was financed by the American

Seek Independent Corroboration

Tobacco Institute—and, further, whether there is *independent* corroboration from other authoritative scientific sources.

Sometimes, translating requires just a few words:

A *Los Angeles Times* writer reports doctors use genetically altered cells as an "internal Band-Aid" to repair injured arteries.

A *Wall Street Journal* writer describes a medical technique as "an artery-opening procedure called angioplasty."

An *Orange County* (Calif.) *Register* writer explains cholesterol "is a white, waxy substance that flows through the bloodstream in tiny particles and sticks to artery walls like Elmer's glue, clogging arteries."

Write to Capture the Magic of Science

Let's say you've got 10 minutes over breakfast for your morning paper before rushing to class. Would you like to spend those precious minutes reading about the Pasadena-based Planetary Society, a grass-roots organization dedicated to promoting the exploration of space?

No? Well how about the following?

Hey, E.T., if you have been hiding somewhere in the southern sky, the jig may be about up.

The Planetary Society, which has been looking for you in the northern sky for several years now with no success, is shipping a truckload of equipment to Argentina to carry out the search for the first time from the Southern Hemisphere. And if you would just beam out a radio message to Earth sometime soon now, it would save everybody a lot of time.

The Pasadena-based Planetary Society, a grass-roots organization dedicated to promoting the exploration of space, is investing about $200,000 in the expansion of its search for extraterrestrial intelligence in hopes that some folks out there on some other planet in some other solar system may be interested in letting earthlings know they are there. . . .
Lee Dye, "E.T. Hunters to Seek Signs of Life in Southern Skies," Los Angeles Times, Feb. 5, 1990, p. B-3

Capture the Magic of Science

There *is* magic in science and you can capture it in your writing. You *must*. If you don't, editors won't give you adequate display, readers won't read you—and you fail in pulling in an audience, essential in all news writing. Below is a writer who succeeds. Stop reading (if you can) after the second paragraph:

Ah, romance. Can any sight be as sweet as a pair of mallard ducks gliding gracefully across a pond, male by female, seemingly inseparable? Or better yet, two cygnet swans, which, as biologists have always told us, remain coupled for life, their necks and fates lovingly intertwined.

Coupled for life, with just a bit of

adultery, cuckoldry and gang rape on the side.

Alas for sentiment and the greeting card industry, biologists lately have discovered that, in the animal kingdom, there is almost no such thing as monogamy. In a burst of new studies that are destroying many of the most deeply cherished notions about the animal mating habits, researchers report that even among species assumed to have faithful tendencies and to need a strong pair bond to rear their young infidelity is rampant. . . .   *Natalie Angier, "Mating for Life? It's Not for the Birds or the Bees,"* The New York Times, *Aug. 21, 1990, p. C-1*

Note above it was the good, gray *New York Times,* the "newspaper of record," that found room—amid war, peace, famine and feast in the tumultuous summer of 1990—for a story on gang rape in the animal kingdom. The story took nearly the entire front page of the *Times*'s science section in addition to almost a full inside page, and undoubtedly drew thousands of readers all the way to the end with its combination of strong, detailed scientific reporting and superb writing.

It's not only in big-city journalism that such writing opportunities present themselves. Stewart Craig, who combined study of chemistry and journalism in college, was hired out of school as a science writer by the *Augusta* (Ga.) *Chronicle and Herald,* a morning-afternoon combination with 79,000 total circulation. Note his writing touch:

When Dr. Ramon Pumarejo goes to work every morning, he pulls up to a hospital surrounded by barbed wire and armed guards.

To get to his office, he passes by more guards and through locked doors and gates. His footsteps echo in hallways monitored by a camera.

Security is tight—it has to be. Because this is medicine behind bars, and the patients Dr. Pumarego treats are criminals: thieves, killers, child molesters and psychos. They are the dregs of society, forgotten and unwanted, but the state is obligated to keep them healthy. . . .   *Stewart Craig, "Highly Guarded Operations,"* Augusta Herald, *Feb. 5, 1990, p. A-1*

GETTING STARTED IN SCIENCE NEWS

You have many opportunities for writing science news while still in school and adding beginner skills in this specialty to others you eventually will offer potential employers. Or, you even can start moving now toward a full-time career in science reporting.

We will discuss four broad areas of science writing where you can develop beginner skills: (1) localizing distant news developments, (2) writing science news generated on campus, (3) covering personal health issues, (4) reporting environmental news.

Localizing Distant Science News

Virtually *every* scientific development anywhere has a local angle and almost every campus or community has experts you can interview to develop it.

For example, consider the message to E.T. in the *Los Angeles Times* story above. Campus astronomers can comment:

University astronomers reacted with excitement today to a plan to search for extraterrestrial intelligence in the sky above the Southern Hemisphere.

Dr. John Jones of Our College said in an interview. . . .

Or, think of local angles you can develop on, say, a new report about cigarette smoking:

• University health officials add their warnings to students who smoke. Student smoking is up/down.

• University health service offers stop-smoking counseling. (Sit in on sessions and write first-person.)

• University has (or tightens) anti-smoking regulations in campus buildings.

• Community bars/restaurants do (don't) have nonsmoking areas. City council does (doesn't) consider municipal approach to anti-smoking campaign.

And, if you're in a tobacco-producing area:

• University agriculture professors say tobacco farmers could switch to other crops.

• Business school professors discuss tobacco's importance in state's overall economy.

Professional science writers quickly jump on local angles of national stories. When the March of Dimes Birth Defects Foundation announced a national campaign against infant mortality, the *Los Angeles Times* front-paged the local angle and got to the national campaign only in the sixth paragraph:

Infant deaths and the number of babies born underweight in Los Angeles County are rising dramatically, according to the latest county statistics. Experts trace the trend—which is most striking among blacks—to increasing drug use and shortages of obstetric and prenatal care. . . .

In hopes of addressing those problems, the March of Dimes Birth Defects Foundation announced. . . .
Janny Scott, "Rise in Infant Deaths Laid to Drugs, Prenatal Neglect," Los Angeles Times, Feb. 3, 1990, p. A-1

Campus Scientists Are Superb News Sources

Familiarize yourself with the campus scientific community—which departments and experts are available—and then watch the distant news "horizon" for science stories you can localize. (Incidentally, if you're waiting for *me* to suggest ways of localizing *The New York Times* story on gang rape in the animal kingdom, forget it! Use your imagination.)

Writing Science News Generated on Campus

Whatever the size of your school, or where it is, it generates important science news you can cover. Consider:

• Most large universities, particularly state universities, have scientific research under way in many subjects. Often, it is not covered regularly in campus journalism or by nearby dailies that report other campus news.

Cover Your Campus Community's Science Stories

• Even if you attend, say, a small liberal arts school without a large science faculty or research program, your school is a "community" in itself, with the problems of any community in personal health, garbage, toxic wastes and so forth. Each of these problems is news.

Obviously your best options for writing beginner science stories are in covering your school's science departments and research. For starters, check which departments are science-oriented. The University of Georgia, a state university, has colleges of agriculture, pharmacy, forest resources and veterinary medicine. Many universities have medical and engineering schools on campus, excellent sources of science stories.

Also check out research service units. For example, Georgia has them in applied isotope studies, biological resources, computational quantum chemistry, environmental biotechnology, plant cellular and molecular biology and other research disciplines.

State universities have continuing education and extension services staffed by experts in everything from commercial fishing to rice growing. Extension service headquarters on campus can give you a list for adding to your source book.

Next, check your university administration or school "fact book" for which research efforts receive state and federal aid or industry and foundation support. Most schools publish dollar figures—and they can lead you directly to major stories.

For example, start "from the top down" by interviewing your school's vice president for research (or other appropriate officials) for a story on the overall research budget and activity. Compare this year's with last year's. Familiarize yourself with the broad picture of science and research on campus.

Examine Your School's Research Activity

Then, start going after more focused stories. For example, the University of Georgia's vice president for research publishes figures showing that in 1988–1989, campus scientists received $53 million in research grants and contracts from 19 federal departments, the United Nations, private industry and foundations. The U.S. Department of Energy awarded $10,011,128. The inquiring science reporter wants to know: Why? For what uses? Here's another: $22,029 from the National Security Agency. What in the world is that all about?

In just that manner you can start reporting campus science stories—and building a reputation for yourself as a reporter with specialized skills.

Writing Personal Health News

Think for a moment about your campus friends and classmates.

Do you know anyone who worries constantly about being too fat or too thin? Have any friends been showing dangerous stress from the academic and social pressures of college life?

Do you know anyone who smokes or drinks too much or uses drugs? Are any of your friends sexually promiscuous?

If your answer is yes to any of the above you're well launched toward formulating story ideas for covering personal health issues on campus. It's a thrilling news sector that's expanding rapidly in American journalism. And it offers special reward: knowing readers can use your stories as guidelines to better living. It also offers special challenge: You must go well beyond where much newswriting stops—with description of the problem—and discuss, as well, how your readers can seek solutions.

Writing Health News Has Special Rewards

Your writing should follow three steps:

First, your story should *define the problem* from official records or through interviews with authoritative sources. For example, it's likely an important (but often unreported) story on your campus is eating disorders among students, particularly young women. Bulimia, an insatiable hunger, and anorexia, a rejection of food, strike thousands. Sources who can describe the problem's extent are in your school's health center, personal counseling department, medical college, local hospitals and clinics, in addition to city, county, and state health departments.

Second, your story should quote authoritative sources on *how to recognize* the health problem. This involves writing, sometimes in considerable detail, what experts say are warning signs—what doctors say, for example, are indications of eating disorders. Your challenge is to give readers operative information for analyzing their own behavior or a friend's.

Third, and always, your story should quote authoritative sources on *what to do* about the problem. This primarily involves writing where and how to get expert help—complete with addresses, telephone numbers, hours help is available, and at what cost.

Always Report Where to Get Help

Following those three steps, you can write meaningful stories on personal health developments on your campus. Here are a few ideas for getting started:

• The incidence of sexually transmitted diseases on campus. Expert advice on how to avoid them.

• Drinking and drug problems. How to recognize when you do have a problem—and where and how to get help.

• Skin care. Particularly, how to guard against cancer-causing exposure to too much sun. Dangers of tanning salons.

• Do-it-yourself diet programs. Dangers of shedding weight without medical guidance.

• Body care during strenuous physical activity. (*The New York Times* published a detailed two-part series written by its superb personal health reporter, Jane Brody, on how to buy proper athletic shoes and care for your feet when engaging in sports!)[3]

Write Health News Calmly, with Balance

You must exercise extreme care in writing personal health news. Readers often take very seriously—and personally—what they read about their health. Don't cause panic. Stick to facts and quote authoritative sources. Write in language and tone that are calm and balanced. That doesn't mean you can't write bright copy. Note how a *Los Angeles Times* writer opens a major piece on depression:

It afflicts one person in five at some time in their lives, leaving them feeling more than just the occasional blues that can descend on everyone, even, say, during the just past holiday.

For some, it's like a constant veil over experience, a shadow that never darkens but never lifts.

For others, it's an even grimmer, socially stigmatizing concern that lingers and often worsens with time.

Depression.

"The pain is unrelenting, and what makes the condition intolerable is the foreknowledge that no remedy will come—not in a day, an hour, a month or a minute. It is hopelessness even more than pain that crushes the soul," author William Styron wrote in December's Vanity Fair, describing his own struggles with depression and his downward spiral to near suicide four years ago.

But a new generation of psychotherapeutic drugs—as well as new short-term approaches to psychotherapy—make it unnecessary for people to endure depression without hope, experts say.

Still, even this optimism must be tempered by the continued limits in treatment: Drugs and psychotherapy can take weeks to give relief; patients and doctors sometimes give up on therapies too early; and depressions often recur. . . . *Linda Roach Monroe, "New Weapons in the Assault on Depression," Los Angeles Times, Jan. 2, 1990, p. E-1*

Note these points in the example above:

1. The lead neatly defines the problem (depression afflicts one person in five) in calm language.

2. In both the lead and fifth paragraph, the writer "pegs" the story to two recent developments: the just-past Christmas and New Year's holidays, when many people feel depressed, and an article by a well-known victim of depression, author William Styron. Watch news from afar for similar "pegs" on which you can hang local campus stories.

3. Quickly, in the sixth and seventh paragraphs, the story quotes experts on the good news and bad news in treating depression. This story is *balanced* in its early stages, before the writer goes into new drugs and psychotherapies being used to treat the illness.

Writing Environmental News

Few news sectors in recent years soared more quickly to prominence—and controversy. The environment and what we're doing (or not doing) to protect it is *hot* news, and many newspapers assign full-time reporters to cover it.

In writing environmental news, your special concern is determining which of many controversial issues is truly important, then finding objective, dispassionate sources who can help you fashion balanced coverage.

Many deeper issues are being fought out by strongly committed people under the heading "environment." What appears to be a battle over, say, saving pine trees might, in fact, be a struggle between big business developers and back-to-mother-earth activists. Or, arguments over sea birds dying in an oil spill may have their roots in bitter controversy over whether the United States is going to develop domestic oil production or continue dependent on foreign imports.

So, approach environmental reporting carefully. On campus, you can edge into it two ways:

Approach Environmental News Carefully

• Faculty experts and local officials of, say, the U.S. Environmental Protection Agency or state and county departments can be interviewed for local angles on distant news developments. Build a source book on local experts available for comment on environmental news.

• Cover environmental issues generated by your school "community." You will find most national issues—waste disposal, air and noise pollution, asbestos disposal and others—are being thrashed out locally.

SUMMARY CHECKLIST

☐ Science news dramatically affects readers' lives, and writing it carries special responsibilities for being accurate and quoting authoritative sources.

☐ Because science is so varied, you'll need well-placed sources, despite whatever academic training you might have in one sector of science. A problem is the huge amount of data available. Sources can help you locate the most important developments.

☐ Nowhere in journalism must you spend more time trying to understand the news than searching for ways to translate it in terms readers comprehend.

☐ Translating science news requires imaginative writing; sometimes just a few words will help readers—as in describing genetically altered cells as an "internal Band-Aid" used to repair injured arteries.

☐ To get started in science news, interview faculty members or other campus experts who can help you localize a distant scientific development.

☐   Personal health issues on campus open many opportunities for science writing. Think first of the health concerns your friends and classmates have, then develop stories that address them.

☐   To start writing environmental news, interview campus experts to localize developments elsewhere. But also cover issues peculiar to your own school, such as air and noise pollution or asbestos removal.

RECOMMENDED READING

Superbly reported and written science news appears regularly in *The New York Times* and *Los Angeles Times*. Both papers display news judgment and reporting techniques any beginning science writer should emulate.

If you have a science specialty in mind, read regularly the trade journals and periodicals that cover it. Your school librarian or the reference desk of your science library can help you locate pertinent publications. Start building the in-depth, "vertical" expertise you'll need in science writing.

For helpful guidance in environmental reporting, see *Chemicals, The Press, and the Public*, published by the National Safety Council's Environmental Health Center, 1050 17th St., N.W., Suite 770, Washington, D.C., 20036.

NOTES

1. Meg Cox, "TV Is Giving Star Status to Environment," *The Wall Street Journal,* Oct. 3, 1989, p. B-1.
2. Philip J. Hilts, "3,000 Papers at AIDS Gathering Point to Gains and Frustrations," *The New York Times*, June 26, 1990, p. C-11.
3. Jane E. Brody, "Personal Health," *The New York Times*, July 15, 1987, p. C-8.

Exercise 13–1   Localizing Science Stories

For each science story below write two ideas of about 75 words each on how you would localize the stories. Mention on-campus experts you would interview and news angles you would take.

Research indicates AIDS is spreading among heterosexuals.

_____

_____

_____

_____

_____

_____

_____

_____

_____

_____

_____

Sun exposure is a cause of skin cancer.

_____

_____

_____

_____

_____

_____

_____

_____

_____

_____

_____

_____

Bulimia strikes many teenage girls.

Exercise 13–2 Special Responsibilities

Read a major science story in The New York Times *or* Los Angeles Times *(or another newspaper your instructor designates) and examine how well (or poorly) it meets the special responsibilities science writers have for accuracy, balance, and authoritativeness. Write your findings in about 250 words, being careful to address the major points about responsibility made in the text. And, of course, write in AP style.*

Exercise 13–3   Translating Science

Study one example of science writing in a newspaper of your choosing (or one your instructor designates) that properly translates for readers all scientific or technical terms. Study another that doesn't. Then, write below, in about 100 words each, (1) how the writers did or did not do the proper translating job, and (2) how you would have done it.

_____

_____

_____

_____

_____

_____

_____

_____

_____

_____

_____

_____

_____

_____

_____

_____

_____

_____

_____

_____

_____

_____

_____

_____

Exercise 13–4   Oat Bran Story

Write about 150 words from facts below.

Dr. Frank Sacks said there's nothing special about oat bran. He is a heart specialist. At Harvard and Brigham and Women's Hospital in Boston. He was the lead researcher for a study published today in the *New England Journal of Medicine*. The researchers, in a study published today, said oat bran has no inherent cholesterol-lowering effect. No such effect despite all the hoopla and commercialization. Some critics were skeptical, saying the sample was too small to draw conclusions. So they were skeptical of the findings. But Dr. Sacks said there's nothing special about oat bran. This is his quote: "If you like it, fine, eat it. . . . You could just as well eat other [low-fat, low-cholesterol] food like wheat or fruit to lower cholesterol."

_____

_____

_____

_____

_____

_____

_____

_____

_____

_____

_____

_____

_____

_____

_____

_____

_____

_____

_____

_____

Exercise 13–5   Lead and Learning Story

Write 150–200 words from facts below.

A major study was published today. It was headed by a pioneer lead researcher, Dr. Herbert Needleman. He and his colleagues published the report in the *New England Journal of Medicine*. Needleman's study is the first to follow children who were exposed to relatively low levels of lead, most likely from paint, household dust and air pollution—to follow them to adulthood. The study shows learning and behavioral problems triggered by childhood exposure to lead persist in adulthood. This indicates the damage is permanent. The report comes at a time when readers are discovering that lead impairs intellectual ability, even when exposure is at levels widely found in American children and commonly believed to be harmless. This is a quote from Needleman and his colleagues in the *Journal* article: "Exposure to lead, even in children who remain asymptomatic, may have an important and enduring effect on [their] success in life."

Chapter Fourteen

Sports Writing: More Than Fun and Games

For millions of readers, sports news is as important as any business news or science story. For hundreds of newspapers, courting those readers is so important that they spend more money covering sports than either business or science.

Thus, in turning to sports writing in this chapter, we discuss how to get started in a newswriting specialty that's among the most important in journalism today.

Sports writing—like sports itself—is changing rapidly. Leading papers require writers to possess a much higher sense of professionalism than ever before. Amateurs seeking only a job that provides free game tickets need not apply. Sports writers must have strong technical skills in reporting and writing, intimate knowledge of the sports they cover and a balanced, objective view of a national obsession that has become not only big news but also very big business—on college and even prep, as well as professional, levels. For the media and writers alike, sports writing today is more than fun and games. Careful, precise reporting is in. Boosterism—backing the home team regardless—is out.

Because sports writing is an enormously broad field, we will deal principally with three areas: *news values and judgments* in writing sports, hints on *how professionals write,* and a few suggestions on *how you can get started,* now, in sports writing.

Incidentally, a big push is under way to get more women and minorities into sports writing, and not only to cover minor sports. Top jobs covering major league and college sports are open, as are spots as editors and columnists, to all who possess the talent.

WHAT'S NEW(S) IN SPORTS WRITING?

In simpler, bygone days, sports writers essentially covered games, then wrote who won. No longer. Today, major emphasis is also on what happens *off the field*—in drug-testing clinics, contract negotiations, player's strikes, courtrooms.

Time was, many sports writers engaged in "boosterism"—rooting openly, frankly for the home team through one-sided reporting. It was an era of white hats (local team) and black hats (visitors). Today, that's a sign of amateurism in sports writing, and although it dies hard, boosterism is being balanced on better papers by hard, discerning investigative reporting that exposes the hometown team's faults as well.

In recent memory, many sports writers cooperated in a conspiracy of silence that

The Conspiracy of Silence Is Ended

left tawdry aspects of the sports world unreported. National sports heroes were created through one-dimensional portraits drawn of athletes whose off-field lives were less than savory. Today, the sexual habits, drug use, gambling addiction of even the greatest athletes are considered news—and news to be published.

Note, for example, a study by Mead Data Central, a company that sells access to computerized news stories from hundreds of newspapers and news services. Mead analyzed baseball coverage in the 1980s by more than 400 publications. It found most articles were written about these developments:

1. Drug abuse (6,071 articles)
2. Contracts and salary arbitration (2,459)
3. Labor strikes (2,196)
4. Corked bats and other illegalities (1,601)
5. George Steinbrenner, controversial owner of the New York Yankees (1,592)
6. Racism (1,381)
7. Gambling by baseball hero Pete Rose (1,364)
8. Bo Jackson, a football and baseball star (1,083)
9. Installation of lighting for night games in Chicago's Wrigley Field, a departure from one of the traditions many sports fans guard zealously (773)
10. Pete Rose's pursuit of Ty Cobb's batting record (578)

Of the 10 most heavily covered stories in the decade, only items 8 and 10 are pure on-field baseball stories.[1]

Note the skills that sports writers needed to cover the Top 10 stories:

* ability to handle scientific data (drug abuse and testing),

* business sense (contract negotiations, labor strikes),

* knowledge of the law and legal process (Rose's trial and imprisonment).

Participatory Sports Are Big News

But the definition of what's news in sports writing today covers much more than even that, of course. Sports pages are going far beyond the standard fare of football, baseball, basketball, boxing, horse racing. Participatory sports, such as tennis, jogging, hunting and fishing, are major news stories, sometimes in the most unexpected places: *The New York Times*, winner of many Pulitzer Prizes for its foreign and Washington coverage, takes readers wading in the predawn mist of upstate New York trout streams or into chilly duck hunting marshes along the Mississippi in some of the best outdoor coverage published anywhere. And *The Wall Street Journal* prints graceful essays on many aspects of sports.

Strong coverage is developing in sports of regional and local interest. Stock car racing is front-page news in sections of the country. Ice fishing and snowmobile racing are important in some, scuba diving and surfing in others.

Whatever your personal interests or sports skills, it's likely that somewhere a newspaper, magazine or TV or radio station offers career opportunity as a sports writer—*if,* that is, you understand that the definition of what's news in sports today requires you to go deeper into a story than who won or lost.

DIG BELOW THE SURFACE

Dramatic changes are under way in sports writing. For example, pure "what" stories—what happened, simply who won—no longer suffice. In many sports pages, you must hunt for this type of once-prevalent lead:

Sports sections challenge writers to present a combination menu: in-depth, analytical writing plus box scores and other statistics that sports fans love. Note the variety of sports covered on the front page of this *Tulsa* (Okla.) *World* sports section.

(*World* photo
used with permission)

SAN DIEGO—Tom Pagnozzi's tie-breaking double sparked a three-run ninth inning as the St. Louis Cardinals defeated San Diego 4–1 and sent the Padres to their eighth loss in nine games. *"Cardinals Win 4–1, Add to Padres' Woes," USA Today, July 6, 1990, p. C-5*

More frequently, you'll see this type of lead—a combination of *what* happened and *why* it happened:

CLEVELAND—The only thing worse than mud is half-frozen mud. Buffalo kicker Scott Norwood wiped out on a critical extra point today, teammate Ronnie Harmon muffed a last-second touchdown because of moist hands and the Bills wasted quarterback Jim Kelly's grandest day since the U.S. Football League, 34–30.

The triumphant Cleveland Browns, who merrily advance to next week's AFC Championship, barely survived another game-closing drive, and Coach Bud Carson chastised his defense afterward. "It was embarrassing," he said. "It was poor defense. I don't think I've been around a poorer defense." *Tom Friend, "Browns Outlast Bills,"* Washington Post, *Jan. 7, 1990, p. C-1*

Write Analytically to Combat TV

The strong trend toward analytical writing, even on hard news stories, is caused by competition from television and, to a lesser extent, radio. Fact is, newspaper readers often already saw or heard the entire game broadcast or, at least, know the score or saw game highlights on the evening news or morning shows.

That doesn't mean sports readership of newspapers is diminishing. To the contrary, it's increasing. Many people want to read about what they saw—whether that be a car accident or televised sports event. Sports readers look particularly for analysis of how and why the game came out as it did.

Note how the writer below *assumes* his readers know the final score, and delays even mentioning it until the fourth paragraph:

PORTLAND, Ore.—Sometimes great success must be preceded by miserable failure. Byron Scott, the Lakers' shooting guard, saw one jump shot clang off the rim and his next miss altogether in the first minute of overtime against the Portland Trail Blazers Tuesday night.

He had the failure part down cold. Success would have to wait.

Normally, in such circumstances, Scott might defer to Magic Johnson. But Johnson had fouled out in regulation, so Scott had no choice but to keep shooting and hope for better results.

Maybe only slightly daunted, Scott then made two jump shots, one a three-pointer, in overtime to lift the Lakers past the Trail Blazers, 121–119 in the battle for first place in the Pacific Division. . . . *Sam McManis, "Lakers Spin Extra Magic in Overtime,"* Los Angeles Times, *Feb. 7, 1990, p. C-1*

Write for Knowledgeable Fans

Imagine a Laker fan who watched the game reading the third paragraph above and thinking, "Yeah, I agree. If we'd had Magic in there. . . ." That's the link—discerning writer to knowledgeable fan—the *Times*'s McManis strives for in his writing.

It should be emphasized that the story above is from the *Los Angeles Times*, a *morning* paper, and thus was the first *written* account available to Laker fans in Los Angeles the morning after the game. But note the story is written almost as if for an *afternoon* paper, with what in other types of news we would call a second-day lead. In sports writing, you must assume much of the time that TV or radio was there first and that your lead must take a second-day, interpretive approach.

Look at it this way: If you are assigned to write for tomorrow morning's paper the game your college football team is playing this afternoon, you'll look pretty silly if you fashion a lead something like this:

Our Old Fashion Blue Devils defeated the Young Upstarts of Their University 14–0 yesterday before 10,987 in Field Stadium.

Issues and Challenges

A principal challenge in sports writing today is how to attract and hold readers who watch sports on television. The Associated Press Managing Editors, an associa-tion of executives from AP member newspapers, asked leading writers for their views. Below are excerpts from the responses of three top professionals.

Give Sports Fans a Reason to Read

I would say to the writer that, you have to understand that the reader already knows the score, the key plays, etc.—I mean, he has television, doesn't he? It's up to you to find a way to dramatize the event, get an angle, interview the in-teresting individual. You have a responsibility not to bore the reader with a re-cital of facts he already knows. Give him a reason to look forward to the paper. Find the fascinating, if obscure, fact. And have writers who can present it entertainingly. . . .

I think sports pages can lure readers back to newspapers and away from getting all their information from television. It's an opportunity as well as a responsibility. Just remember, you read to be informed and entertained. If you've already been informed when you open the paper, what's left?   Jim Mur-ray, who won a Pulitzer Prize for his *Los Angeles Times* sports column

More Legwork, Less Lunching

I'd like to see a little more poetry in the sports news pages, and a little less punditry, a little more legwork and little less lunching (I remember a number of years ago a sports editor who never missed a freeload and was called "Sir Lunchalot"), a little more humor and a little less of those grim statistics, a little more anger at injustice (such as the private golf clubs that get tax write-offs and are hosts to national tournaments) and a little less acceptance of the status quo.

In the end, I'd like to see the sports pages mirror the news pages on hard-hitting social issues, but keep the balance that sports, regardless of the huge business it has become, owes its existence to the fact that it was meant to enter-tain us, to divert us, to give us pleasure.   Ira Berkow, sports columnist, *The New York Times*

Cover Sports as News

When I pick up a sports section, I want to read the day's news. I want the reporters to be reporters and tell me what the hell happened and why it happened and what it means—and I want it in the first three paragraphs.

Instead, I am forced to endure yet another writing exercise. Clearly, from my reading of sports pages, there are many of us who need the exercise, but my advice is to get the exercise in the privacy of our homes, not on the pages deliv-ered to our readers' breakfast tables.

Much of this alleged "writing" is committed at the direction of sports edi-tors who either have forgotten what news is or never knew. These editors give their "writers" the license to be cute, to be clever, to wander through six para-graphs before even giving the poor reader the score of the game. The assumption seems to be that the game was on TV and everybody knows the score by morn-ing. The truth of life is more complicated than that. The truth is, even if we knew the score last night, we've forgotten it by morning—and even if we remem-ber the damned score, we still want to be told in an orderly and sensible fashion how that score came to be. Hey, we've got more important things to do than puzzle out an unfathomable sports story. We've got to make coffee, for one.
Dave Kindred, sports columnist for the now-defunct *National*[2]

Most everybody in town who wasn't at the game itself would have heard about it—in the barber shop, over a beer, at the supermarket—by the time your account was published!

Expect even more television competition ahead. ABC, CBS and NBC together are paying the National Football League $2.7 *billion* for increased TV broadcast rights in 1990–1994.[3] National TV coverage of golf, tennis, horse and auto racing, and other sports is increasing. Regionally and, importantly, even locally, the burgeoning growth of cable-TV means more televised coverage of college and, also, prep sports. Scores and highlights are available from an increasingly wide array of telephone and electronic services.

Start practicing now to write every sports story with an explanatory dimension that carries your account beyond what TV offers.

Avoid Reaching Too Far for Unique Twist

Of course, as in any writing that stretches way out, you can go too far in trying to put a unique twist on a sports story. In a column for readers of the *Washington Post,* the newspaper's ombudsman, or reader representative, Richard Harwood, complains about "gibberish" in too much *Post* writing. He adds:

On the subject of gibberish, why are Post sports writers apparently forbidden in all but rare cases to report in the first paragraph of their stories the score of the games they cover? Instead of scores we get this: "Ledell Eackles has about 9 years 11 months 29 days and 45 minutes before he can have a decade like 'Saturday Night Live' comedian Al Franken did." That was the warm-up lyric on a story about a basketball game. . . .[4]

HOW THE PROS WRITE IT

Great sports writing—and much is around these days—is marked by three major characteristics:

1. Highly professional writers possess *expert knowledge of the sport* they're covering. They are as expert in their trade as Washington correspondents or business writers in theirs. They are long-time, serious students of sports.

2. The best writers have wonderful, *free-flowing* styles. Some of the most colorful, punchy writing in many newspapers is in sports. There is some feeling that sports writers as a group develop more readable styles than other journalists because they learn their trade as youngsters under editors whose departmental guidelines are less restrictive than, say, those of city or foreign editors. *However,* the best writers don't forget that the good old Five W's and How still must guide all newspaper writing. It's good to be colorful and entertaining in your writing, but it's mandatory that you transmit *essential information.*

Always Remember Five W's and How

3. Great sports writers develop *intimate relationships with readers.* In no other form of newspaper journalism do writers generally achieve quite the same contact with readers that sports writers do. Few others build quite the same loyalty to their bylines. Successful writer-columnists (and the line between the two is blurred in much sports writing) can pull in thousands of readers who follow them personally each day.

The best professional sports writers, like the best in all forms of news, are highly skilled in weaving in the essential Five W's and How. Writers who cover night games face severe deadline pressure for next morning's paper. So they must write quickly and clearly, or they don't last long on the job. The AP, which covers all major sporting events, has writers particularly adept at this. Note:

MINNEAPOLIS—Ron Karkovice hit an inside-the-park grand slam in the fourth inning to lead the White Sox past the Minnesota Twins, 4–3, today and end Chicago's five-game losing streak.

Chicago loaded the bases against David West (7–9) with one out in the fourth on Phil Bradley's single, Ivan Calderon's double and Frank Thomas' walk.

Karkovice then lined a pitch over the glove of the Twins shortstop Greg Gagne. The ball rolled to the fence be- tween the left fielder, Dan Gladden, and the center fielder, John Moses.

Moses slipped at the base of the fence and tossed the ball to Gladden. Gladden, who was looking toward the infield, missed it and the ball rolled away.

It was the second career grand slam for Karkovice and only the second inside-the-park grand slam in the majors this season. Luis Polinia of the California Angels hit one Aug. 14 against the Yankees. . . .   *AP dispatch for morning papers of August 31, 1990*

To meet morning newspaper deadlines, writers of night games must fashion stories such as the one above in only minutes. Generally, there is no time for rewriting or polishing.

And, as I've stated repeatedly in this book, when you're on deadline and rushed, don't try to be too fancy. Fall back on a clean, straight Five W's and How lead plus direct narrative of the salient news development that gives your story a central theme.

When Rushed, Use Direct Narrative Structure

Read again the Minneapolis story above. Note all Five W's and How are in the first paragraph, along with the big play of the game—Karkovice's homerun with the bases loaded. Many sports editors, overwhelmed with copy, particularly on busy sports weekends, publish one-paragraph briefs on such games. The AP lead paragraph could be used in that manner.

After the lead paragraph, the AP writer opens the central theme of the story with a four-paragraph narrative about that homerun. With line scores or box scores (statistical summaries of the game), sports fans can read the five paragraphs above and "dope out" the contest.

The following essentials, with the Five W's and How, must be in a *well-done* sports story:

1. *Key plays, turning points in the game, or remarkable individual or team performances, and factors (weather, injuries) that influence them.* The Karkovice homerun in Minneapolis is an example of focus on a key play.

Note Key Plays

2. *A statistical context for the* game. Note the second paragraph above refers to "David West (7–9)." That means West, a pitcher, previously won 7 games and lost 9. That's important statistical background for reader-fans who, in this story, are being "set up" for the feud between pitcher and batter. Note the fifth paragraph places the homerun within the context of performance by other batters. As in all reporting, *do your homework,* and study league, team, and individual star statistics *before* going to a game.

Provide Statistical Context

3. *What star performers did (or didn't) do.* Reader-fans follow stars closely. How they perform is news. Of the many thousands of sports stories transmit-

To save time, AP sportswriters Harry Atkins (left) and Chuck Melvin write their coverage of a National Basketball Association game on a portable computer, then use a telephone to "dump" their stories into a distant central computer for transmission to newspapers. The entire process is complete before fans leave the arena.

(AP photo
used with permission)

ted by the AP in 1990, the following—which focuses on a star's performance—was selected by the Associated Press Sports Editors organization as the year's best:

MILWAUKEE (AP)—Nolan Ryan, a pitcher defined by great numbers, finally got the number that defines great pitchers. Ryan won his 300th game Tuesday night, reaching the milestone in his second try and ensuring his place in history as the Texas Rangers beat the Milwaukee Brewers 11–3. *Ben Walker, AP New York baseball writer*

Search for *Meaningful* Quotes

4. *Quotes from players and coaches.* Seek in postgame interviews *meaningful* quotes on key decisions, strategies, team performance—nuances that will lift your writing above the pedestrian "this team won, that team lost."

5. *A look-ahead angle.* There's always a next game, a next season. And how today's game fits into all that is important to reader-fans. Does a win (or loss) today set a team up for a win (or loss) next weekend? Do injuries (or lack of) improve the team's chances for the rest of the season? Do winning (or losing) strategies and performances on the field today portend well (or ill) for the future?

6. *A wider, off-field dimension.* Not all news breaks on the field or court. Substitutes on the bench, trainers in the lockerroom, fans in the stands—all can yield important and interesting stories.

Hunt for Off-Field News

Communicating essentials such as those above and *simultaneously* weaving in a deeper dimension of expert knowledge is the mark of the very best sports writers. Note below how Frank Litsky of *The New York Times* displays in just a few words his grasp of nuances of football. These are excerpts from a story about the New York Giants in training camp (his writing's extra-analytical dimension is in italics):

In the first two preseason games, Morris carried 13 times for 31 yards, Anderson 11 times for 21 yards. *Some of those carries came behind young and unsophisticated offensive linemen.* [Knowledgeable sports readers understand runners need experienced blockers to be successful]. . . .

Aaron Emanuel or Lee Rouson. Emanuel, a rookie, seemed headed for a job until he was sidelined by a pinched nerve in the neck. That opens the door for the veteran Rouson, *because a team that uses a two-back offense much of the time needs a backup fullback.* . . .

That leaves room for perhaps one other running back. Someone must start at tail-back until Parcells is convinced that Hampton *can handle blitz pickups.* The main candidates are Morris and Anderson, and Anderson seems to have the edge *because he has also been the team's short-yardage runner.* Frank Litsky, *"After Jets Tonight, Will There Be a Tomorrow?," The New York Times, Aug 25, 1990, p. 43*

Note above some terms ("unsophisticated offensive linemen" and "blitz pickups") aren't translated for readers unfamiliar with football. Much sports writing assumes fairly expert knowledge by readers. It's an assumption permitted in sports writing (unlike in, say, business writing) because sports readers generally are dedicated followers—students, even—of such esoterica.

Below, can you spot the "insider's" touch an expert writer displays in communicating with expert readers?

There were a couple of anxious moments for the 49ers in yesterday's regular-season-ending, 26–0 victory over the Chicago Bears.

In the first quarter, Joe Montana threw a pass and then was hit hard to the ground by defensive tackle Steve McMichael.

In the second quarter, Jerry Rice dropped a pass and then was slammed by corner-back David Tate and hit by two other Bears, pinball-style.

First, Montana, and later, Rice, were slow getting up. But they got up, none the worse for wear, and stayed in the game. . . .

They survived without injuries and beat Chicago without much difficulty in a lethargic final tuneup before the playoffs. . . . Ira Miller, *"49ers Rout Bears; Playoffs Next," San Francisco Chronicle, Dec. 25, 1989, p. C-1*

The expert-to-expert touch in the story above is the writer's concentration on two stars—Montana and Rice—surviving unhurt so they can compete in the playoffs. The victory over Chicago and the one-sided score are secondary, and only an unsophisticated writer would concentrate on them. Note also how the central theme of the story (Montana and Rice) fulfills the "look-ahead" requirement. At this point in the season, the Bears game is irrelevant—except for how it influences San Francisco's chances in the playoffs ahead.

KEEP YOUR FOCUS ON PEOPLE

The drama in sports is, above all, about people—their competition against each other, against time, record books, the limits of human endurance. The best sports writing stays narrowly focused on the people factor.

Focus on People

For example, auto racing involves, obviously, cars, their engineering, pit crews and other *technical* factors, as well as drivers. But note below how competition between two men, not cars, makes this account come alive:

The hurt of losing the Indianapolis 500 on the next-to-last lap never will be totally erased, but Al Unser Jr. scrubbed away a little of it Sunday when he held off Emerson Fittipaldi—the man who beat him at Indy—to win the Toyota Grand Prix of Long Beach.

A record crowd of 86,500 watched a nose-to-tail race between the youthful Unser and the veteran Fittipaldi over the final 20 laps of the 95-lap race on the seashore streets of Long Beach.

For a time, it appeared as if Long Beach could have the same scenario as Indianapolis a year ago as Fittipaldi, the 43-year-old former world Formula One champion in the red and white No. 1 Penske-Chevy, pulled within striking distance of Unser, 28. . . . *Shav Glick, "Unser Keeps Fittipaldi Behind Him This Time," Los Angeles Times, April 23, 1990, p. C-1*

Note below that the writing focus on a single individual turns what could be a routine look-ahead lead into a winner:

PALO ALTO, Calif.—If there was a statistic for heart, hustle and floor burns, Traci Thirdgill would have no peer.

That is something fans and foes of the University of Washington women's basketball team have learned the past 3½ seasons and what they will be reminded of again tonight in Maples Pavilion.

There, the Husky senior will be a defensive thorn in a bed of offensive roses when the seventh-ranked Huskies face the second-ranked Stanford Cardinals.

Thirdgill will be the one flying out of bounds in pursuit of a loose ball. She'll be the one absorbing charges. She'll be the one chirping and chirping at a rival who dared to quit dribbling before passing. . . . *Dick Rockne, "Heart of the Defense," Seattle Times, Jan. 11, 1990, p. E-1*

Compare the above lead with this one:

PALO ALTO, Calif.—The seventh-ranked University of Washington women's basketball team faces the second-ranked Stanford Cardinals tonight.

As they say in sports, it's no contest. The lead that focuses on a person wins.

However, there is danger in stretching for a dramatic "people factor" as a news peg. Your writing can get skewed away from the fundamental news of an event. For example, you decide whether the following properly focuses on the *real news*. This is a *Baltimore Sun* dispatch published by the *San Francisco Chronicle* on the front page of its sports section as the primary account of the 1990 Rose Bowl game:

Don't Overlook the Fundamental News

PASADENA—It ended with one last tantrum, the granddaddy of them all, Bo ranting and raving, throwing his notes to the ground as another Rose Bowl exploded in his face. How else would Bo Schembechler leave the scene?

"It's pretty ironic, isn't it?" Schembechler would say later.

Well, yes. A disputed holding call on a fake punt—imagine, old, conservative Bo trying to win his last game on a trick play—turned the ball over to USC, which went 75 yards in a final drive to beat Michigan, 17–10, yesterday.

"It's the most unbelievable call I've ever seen, and it happened in my last game," said Schembechler, whose Michigan team slipped to 10–2, dropping it out of contention for the national championship.

And Schembechler, whose retirement took effect after the game, slipped to 2–8 in the Rose Bowl. . . .

The end came when Ricky Ervins, who gained 126 yards on 30 carries, ran 14 yards for a touchdown with 1 minute, 10 seconds to play, breaking a tie and Bo's heart. *Mike Littwin, Baltimore Sun dispatch for Jan. 2, 1990*

Critics would say the story above, in focusing on a temper tantrum, subordinates the real news—the game itself—too severely. But wait! How many tens of millions saw the televised outcome or heard the score well before the *Chronicle* hit the streets? For how many was Bo Schembechler one of football's all-time greats? And, how many were intrigued by that tantrum (shown on TV) and the official's call that sparked it?

Did the *Sun*'s Littwin miss the news story—or focus on it superbly? You make the call.

Focusing on people coverage inevitably brings sports writers to describe conflict between individual stars in what, after all, are competitive sports. When *truly* competitive situations arise they make "great copy":

Conflict Between Stars Is News

EDMONTON, Canada—What does it take to stop the greatest hockey player in the world?

The Shadow knows.

Left wing Esa Tikkanen's primary mission in head-to-head meetings has been to guard Gretzky and upset his game: Stay on his back. Keep a stick

in his face. Deny him the puck. Make a general nuisance of himself.

It's become the Great One against The Grate One. Tikkanen's tactics could get on anyone's nerves. . . . *Steve Springer, "Kings Got Licked, Gretzky Tikked," Los Angeles Times, April 20, 1990, p. C-1*

Unfortunately, a serious danger exists in sports writing's focus on individual stars: It tends to set up phony competition between players. Come a doldrum in training camp news, and "feuds" between players, or players and coaches, break out all over. Undiscerning focus on the "people factor" also can establish phony heroes—make national icons of people who, after all, are news only because they can run faster than most, jump higher, or hit balls better. For years, baseball writers idolized Pete Rose. Then, to everyone's shock, this:

Don't Create Phony Heroes

MARION, Ill.—Pete Rose, No. 14 in his fame, is No. 01832061 in his shame.

Baseball's all-time hits leader became a prisoner Wednesday when he entered a minimum-security camp next to the federal penitentiary to begin a five-month sentence for cheating on his income taxes. . . . *AP dispatch for Aug. 9, 1990*

ALWAYS REMEMBER THE DOLLAR FACTOR

Boxer Mike Tyson earned an estimated $28.6 million in 1990 for hitting other people and, more rarely, getting hit himself on occasion.

Jack Nicklaus pulled in $8.6 million, mostly for hitting golf balls; Boris Becker, $7.2 million for hitting tennis balls.

In calculating those figures, *Forbes* magazine puts 1990 income of the world's 30 highest-paid athletes at about $230 million and comments that one-third comes "from pitching products not from hitting balls."[5]

Two thoughts to consider:

• If people are the drama of sports, money is the fuel that drives the giant corporate sports machine you'll be covering. Salaries, endorsement fees and the businesses that feed off fans make sports today Big Business. Even at the college level, millions of dollars are at stake.

• If it weren't for what sports writers report, the machine—for all its drama and money—would starve from lack of publicity and, eventually, public interest.

None of this means sports are any less important news. After all, business news is about pursuit of profit. Covering war, international economic rivalry, the competition of nations—real news in anyone's book—is about self-interest, too. But the money and self-interest behind big-time sports *do* mean you shouldn't kid yourself (and, thus, your readers) about what it is you're reporting from the sidelines.

Honest Sports Writing Spotlights Economic Issues

One key to honest sports writing is straight news treatment of economic issues—writing, say, a player's demand for millions or an owner's lockout as just more labor-management conflict, not as an unacceptable, evil infringement on the Great American Dream, baseball's opening day.

Note this hard-nosed treatment:

NEW YORK—Major League baseball players and owners ended a bitter 32–day lockout, but they left the 1990 season in disarray, local economies crimped and millions of fans disgusted.

After a final marathon meeting, the players and owners signed a collective bargaining agreement early yesterday morning, ending baseball's seventh work shut-down in 18 years. . . . *Mark Robichaux, "Major League Baseball Players, Owners Reach Accord, But the Damage Remains," The Wall Street Journal, March 20, 1990, p. A-6*

You can keep the commercialism of sports in perspective for your readers by asking the right questions. When baseball's Kirby Puckett won a $3 million contract, AP's John Nelson asked him flat out if he was worth it. Puckett replied, "Am I worth it? I don't know. But I know one thing. If they [the owners] didn't have it to give to you, you sure wouldn't get it." Nelson then wrote a story detailing the profits made by some owners and the enormous values of their franchises.[6]

Beware Being Manipulated

Beware: Protagonists in the economic struggle surrounding big-time sports habitually attempt to negotiate through the media. Stars call news conferences to announce they're unhappy with their contract and won't go to training camp. Owners call in reporters to reply that other players are being considered for the holdouts' positions. All that is news, of course. But you've got to write it in a way that prevents you (and your reader-fans) from being manipulated. The best way is to describe what's happening in a frank and open manner. Note below how a writer does that and—among other things—reveals fascinating insights into professional football:

FLORHAM PARK, N.J.—Bill Parcells is either convinced that one of his four defensive holdouts will not play this season or the coach of the Giants is making an attempt to put pressure on someone through the news media.

Lawrence Taylor, Mark Collins, Erik Howard and Leonard Marshall are the four players missing from training camp with 19 days left before the Giants open their season.

"I don't want this to be a headline," Parcells said in discussing the holdouts today in his daily meeting with reporters. "But there is one particular case I don't think anything will get done."

"I just feel there is one case where I'm going to have to play without the guy," Parcells said. . . . *Alex Yannis, "Suspense Over Giants' Holdouts Continues," The New York Times, Aug. 22, 1990, p. D-23*

You can't change the fact that coaches and players use the media to put pressure on each other, as Parcells seemed to be doing in the account above. But you *can* level with readers about what's going on—and with that kind of honest writing you'll thread your way successfully through the pressures of covering Big Business sports.

GETTING STARTED IN SPORTS WRITING

You'll find even entry-level sports writing jobs highly competitive at newspapers both on campus and off. But there are ways you can obtain crucial hands-on experience in sports writing.

At on-campus publications, sports staffs often are preoccupied with football—which pays the way for most college-level athletic programs—along with basketball and baseball. Volunteer ideas for covering campus sports that go unreported:

Secondary sports. At many schools there is no regular, in-depth coverage of swimming, wrestling, tennis, volleyball, gymnastics. Pick one that interests you, become an expert in its nuances, and suggest to the sports editor you can plug a hole in the paper's coverage.

Start by Covering Secondary Sports on Campus

Features. Before every game, yards of tape are used on players' ankles. Anonymous trainers and junior coaches work with athletes on injuries, body strength, academic performance. Who are these unsung performers? How many yards of tape? Is all this crucial to a win-loss record? How do athletes stay in shape during off-season? What year-round work preoccupies, say, the football coaching staff? Features can offer interesting insights into on-campus sports—and they are among hundreds that sports writers often don't have time to do.

The economics of sports. Ever see in your campus paper a story on, say, what a home game means to local merchants, hotels, restaurants? How much money flows into town during a football weekend? What is the cost of athletics—coaches' salaries, equipment, travel—and what comes in through ticket sales and other revenue? How much is given in athletic scholarships? How much last year and the year before? These, too, are stories often unreported in campus journalism.

Intramural sports. By far, more students participate in intramural athletics than in the Big Three—varsity football, basketball, baseball. But few intramural programs are reported regularly. Suggest to the sports editor that you take on the task. It's a great way to ease into handling statistics, game reports, interviews and all the other challenges in sports writing.

With off-campus newspapers, two broad areas are open for obtaining hands-on experience.

1. Most daily editors, like their on-campus brethren, don't have sufficient staff to cover *all* campus athletics. The same ideas we developed above for on-campus publications can be offered to daily sports editors—covering secondary sports, writing features, and so forth. Importantly, many sports editors retain stringers on campus for story tips, interview arrangements and to help with play-spotting and keeping statistics on game day. You'll hew wood and haul water in this work, but it'll get you started—and will give you contacts among professional writers.

Volunteer to Cover Prep Sports

2. For most dailies, an underdeveloped area of coverage is prep sports. Sports editors cannot cover regularly even a fraction of high school games, let alone Little League or other "junior" contests, yet reader interest is very strong at this level. In the family scrapbook, next to Alice's wedding announcement, is a clipping reporting she was high scorer in a girl's basketball game. Next to that is a clipping of brother Billy's touchdown. Newspaper strategists push sports editors to get those stories—and local names, lots of names—into the paper. They boost circulation. This is where you can come in: Volunteer to cover, if even for only a couple of nights weekly, prep games in the newspaper's circulation territory, or to take scores by telephone. Becoming "Our Little League correspondent" is a start toward becoming a professional sports writer.

Two hints on volunteering attractive story ideas:

First, don't offer (as so many undergraduates do) to "do a column" or a "think piece." Those are coveted tasks assigned to experienced writers on off-campus newspapers. Stick to the Five W's and How on spot-news stories, then stretch a bit later. And *write short.* Newspapers don't have yards of news hole for the secondary college or prep sports you'll be covering.

Second, watch for off-field stories that regular sports writers don't have time to cover. Chris Decherd, a University of Georgia undergraduate, did that after volunteering to cover prep sports for the *Athens* (Ga.) *Daily News.* He quickly won front-page display in the sports section with this story on a local high school star:

Never has [Fred Smith] gone as long without picking up a basketball.

It's been more than a month since the former Cedar Shoals High School star held the sphere with which he can work near magic.

It's not his choice. He's been in Clarke County Jail since Dec. 20. Games often end there.

[Smith] is charged with burglary and theft by shop-lifting, according to Clarke County jail records. [Smith] says he's innocent.

"Wrong place, wrong time," he says. . . .   *Chris Decherd, "Fallen Star," Athens (Ga.) Daily News, Jan. 22, 1990, p. B-2*

STAY FRESH AND BALANCED

As you launch into sports writing, there are several factors to bear in mind.

Avoid Cliches and Boosterism

First, "cliche-itis" (a feverish urge to write in trite, hackneyed language) is an *occupational hazard* (that's a cliche) in sports writing. When you stretch for a colorful phrase and one comes to mind too easily (because you've read it elsewhere so many times), try again. *Stay fresh.* Read the great sports writers. They don't copy anybody. You just *know* Jim Murray of the *Los Angeles Times* was original in describing a jockey: "Eddie Arcaro came down the lane like a Cossack running down peasants." And Chris Dufresne, his *Times stablemate* (another sports cliche; don't use it), was alone in describing quarterback Phil Simms as "fire-hydrant slow."[7] That originality is partly why Murray and Dufresne are writing for one of the best sports sections in the country.

Second, wonderful camaraderie warms many locker rooms, and you may feel tempted to "get on the team" (isn't that everyone's childhood desire?). Careful. That's boosterism sneaking up on you. *Remember:* You are a *reporter* who happens to be on sports, not a public relations cheerleader. In professional sportswriting there still isn't enough hard-hitting reporting. Significantly, the only two Pulitzer Prizes for investigative sports reporting went to *general assignment*—not sports—writers. (They were writers at the *Macon* (Ga.) *Telegraph & News* for investigating football abuses at the University of Georgia and Georgia Tech, and at the *Lexington* (Ky.) *Herald-Leader* for a probe of basketball at the University of Kentucky.)

Third, keep sports in perspective. These are games you're reporting, not the Fate of the Western World. Look for the humor in it all, and when you find it, *write it*. That's what Frederick C. Klein of *The Wall Street Journal* did:

NEW ORLEANS—Oscar Wilde, who said everything better than anyone else, called fox hunting "the unspeakable in full pursuit of the uneatable." What we have here during Super Bowl Hype Week, with 2,000–odd (and I do mean odd) news types chasing stories from 90 football players and a score or so coaches, might be called the insatiable pursuing the inarticulate. . . .   *Frederick C. Klein, "May the Glibbest Team Win,"* The Wall Street Journal, *Jan. 26, 1990, p. A-13*

SUMMARY CHECKLIST

☐ Sports news today is broadly defined to include many off-field developments, including contract negotiations and player strikes.

☐ Boosterism, one-sided reporting that roots openly for the home team, is a sign of amateurism, and sports writers increasingly are looking at the tawdry side of sports (and sports heroes), as well as reporting the glory of sports.

☐ Sports pages increasingly are covering nontraditional, participatory sports, such as fishing, hunting, jogging, tennis.

☐ Successful sports reporting requires going below the surface "what" of a development and finding "why" and "how" angles.

☐ A strong trend toward analytical writing is caused by competition from TV and radio. Many sports readers watched the event or know the score and highlights before a newspaper account hits the streets.

☐ Great sports writing is characterized by *expert knowledge* of the game, *free-flowing writing style,* and an ability to create *intimate contact* with readers. As in no other form of news writing, sports writers can build reader loyalty to their bylines.

☐ Sports writing first must communicate essential information—the Five W's and How. Other essentials are key plays or turning points in a game, statistics, how stars performed, meaningful quotes from players and coaches, and a look-ahead to the next game, the next season.

☐ Great writers simultaneously display expert knowledge of the game. After all, they're writing largely for *expert readers*.

☐ Sports drama is about people, and the best sports writing focuses on people, their competition against each other and the record books.

☐ Always remember, however, that sports is Big Business, and straight, hard-nosed reporting of its business aspects is required.

☐ To get started in sports writing, volunteer to cover often-neglected secondary or intramural sports for campus papers. For off-campus papers, volunteer to serve as a campus stringer or to cover off-campus prep sports.

☐ Finally, a warning: Avoid cliches, a danger in sports writing; don't "get on the team," a form of boosterism, and keep sports in perspective. These are games you're covering.

RECOMMENDED READING

The best way to uncover "how-to-do-it" hints in sports writing is to read "how it was done" by professional writers in the best sports sections of the nation's newspapers. A partial list: *Boston Globe*, all three New York newspapers (*Times, Post, News*), *Washington Post, Philadelphia Inquirer, Atlanta Journal and Constitution, Orlando Sentinel, Miami Herald, Dallas News, Chicago Tribune, Los Angeles Times, Seattle Times, USA Today.* And do yourself a favor: Read, as often as you can, Jim Murray in the *Los Angeles Times* and Frederick C. Klein in *The Wall Street Journal*.

Fine writing is in *The Sporting News,* St. Louis, Mo. (which also publishes an annual of best sports stories), *The National,* and *Sports Illustrated.* Frank Deford, formerly of *Sports Illustrated* and editor of the now-defunct *National,* is one of the best sports writers of our era.

To develop the required expert knowledge of sports, study game statistics ("agate," in newspaper parlance) found in all major newspapers. The "Sports Guidelines and Style" section of AP's *Stylebook* (pp. 236–251) will help you decipher them.

NOTES

1. Robert McG. Thomas Jr., "Sports World Specials," *The New York Times*, Sept. 11, 1989. The study was conducted by Suzanne Quigley for Mead's company newsletter, "Nexis News Monitor."
2. "Associated Press Managing Editors 1990 Report," pp. 17–19.
3. "NFL: More Games, Cable, Revenue," *Broadcasting,* Aug. 13, 1990, Special Report, 35.
4. Richard Harwood, "Gibberish of the Year," *Washington Post*, Dec. 31, 1989, p. C-6.
5. Peter Newcomb and Christopher Palmeri, "Throw a Tantrum, Sign a Contract," *Forbes,* Aug. 20, 1990, p. 68.
6. John Nelson, AP dispatch for Dec. 31, 1989.
7. Jim Murray, "Horses Are Losing Their Best Friend," *Los Angeles Times*, Feb. 1, 1990, p. S-1., and Chris Dufresne, "Simms Isn't Styling, Just Smiling," *Los Angeles Times,* Jan. 4, 1990, p. C-1.

Exercise 14–1   Developing Story Ideas

Review sports coverage in your campus newspaper (or another paper your instructor designates), and write, in about 75 words each, three story ideas you could volunteer to the editor. State the sports area (secondary varsity or intramural sports, for example) you would cover, the stories you would report, in addition to sources you would approach and writing angles you would take.

_____

_____

_____

_____

_____

_____

_____

_____

_____

_____

_____

_____

_____

_____

_____

_____

_____

_____

_____

_____

_____

_____

Exercise 14–2   Localizing Sports Stories

Select sports stories from USA Today, The New York Times, *or* Los Angeles Times *(or other newspapers your instructor designates) and write, in about 75 words each, three ideas on how you would localize the stories. Be sure to pick stories truly applicable to your campus (for example, on athletic scholarships, graduation rates for varsity athletes, drug-testing, and so forth).*

Exercise 14–3   Writing Baseball Leads

From the following facts write a straight Five W's and How story of about 200 words for this morning's paper.

Use a Montreal dateline. This is about a game between the Montreal Expos and the Houston Astros. The score was a rout. It was 11–0 in Montreal's favor. It was a four-hit shutout last night. Mark Gardner of Montreal pitched it. Montreal's Dave Martinez hit a two-run homer. That lifted Montreal to a win. Of its last 20 games away from the Astrodome in its home town, the Houston team has lost 19. The Astros, last in the National League West, lost their fifth in a row in Montreal. That dropped them to 10 wins and 31 losses on the road. Pitcher Gardner, who has won five and lost four, walked four batters. He struck out 11. That was his high for the season. The game was his second shutout. And, it was the second complete game he pitched. Mike Scott pitched for Houston. His record is six wins and eight losses. He gave up eight runs on seven hits and six walks in 3–2/3 innings. And he then lost his first game in Montreal since 1982. He pitched for the New York Mets that year. Scott had won seven in a row in Montreal. He now has a career record of 8–2 there.

Exercise 14–4   Writing Football Leads

Write 150–200 words from the following facts. Include a look-ahead angle on the Notre Dame team awaiting final ratings in competition for the national championship.

Use a Miami dateline. Notre Dame's football team defeated No. 1 Colorado. That was last night. In the Orange Bowl. The score was 21–6. In winning, the Notre Dame Irish topped the nation's only unbeaten team. That staked out Notre Dame's claim to its second straight national championship. The Irish season record is 12 wins and one loss. They were ranked fourth in the nation. They played nine bowl teams this season. They beat eight. The only mar on their perfection was a loss to Miami of Florida. The loss was 27–10. It ended Notre Dame's 23-game winning streak. There are no undefeated teams remaining in the race for the national championship. Now the Irish must await the final ratings. They will be released this afternoon. The Irish have hopes of becoming the first repeat champion since Texas. That was in 1969–1970. Notre Dame Coach Lou Holtz delivered this quote: "I don't know what more you can do but beat the No. 1 team by 15 points. I think we're No. 1. We were No. 1 all year. We played with pressure. We played nine bowl games." Early in the game, the Colorado team—nicknamed the Buffaloes—had chances to take control of the game. The Buffaloes have 11 wins and one loss. They blew three first-half scoring chances. That allowed Notre Dame to stay in the game.

Chapter Fifteen

Devices for Focusing the News

Your beginner's arsenal of newswriting techniques must contain more than the basic approaches to hard news we've been discussing in this book. Examine carefully this morning's newspaper on tonight's TV news and you'll see why: Professional newswriters use a wide variety of devices to focus the news—to examine it from different perspectives, to illuminate for readers its increasing complexities.

In this chapter we'll study some of those devices and suggest ways that you can employ them effectively. *Master* them and you'll be on your way to becoming a well-rounded newswriter.

We'll look first at *newsfeatures, sidebars* and *profiles*. These writing forms offer wonderful, creative writing opportunities. However, it's important to remember a newspaper's basic mission is communicating *news,* and this book's central thrust is *news*writing. So although newsfeatures and sidebars can be used to amuse or entertain readers, we'll concentrate on using them to deliver operative news and information.

Finally, we'll discuss three other devices that focus the news: *obituaries, polls,* and *graphics.* The first device is an old standby that's being written in new, interesting ways. Polls and graphics are used extensively throughout the newspaper industry, and you've got to understand both to be a complete newswriter.

NEWSFEATURES: SOMETIMES A WRITER'S BEST FRIEND

Do you know that drug pushers work the streets with small bags of cocaine hidden in their clothing? And that police officers battle every night to catch them?

Of course you do. So do your readers. You—and they—have read about it many times.

Well, if assigned to cover the narcotics battle on the streets of, say, Seattle, how would you write it? How about the following?

> Each night, Seattle police officers cruise the city's streets, watching for drug pushers who ply their trade with small bags of cocaine hidden in their clothing.

Nah! That's not news! Besides, the writing is deadly dull; been used a thousand times, and your job is to _pull in readers,_ not drive them away.

How about the following?

> It's a cold, foggy night, and scantily clad prostitutes are strutting in front of the bars on South Cloverdale Street in South Seattle. But the state trooper ignores the hookers.
>
> Instead, he guns his motor, taking off after a white Ford. The nervous-looking driver has merely turned left without signaling, but the trooper's gut tells him the Ford spells trouble.
>
> The car pulls over and the trooper asks to see a driver's license.
>
> No license? He's under arrest.
>
> But as the driver climbs out of his car, he starts touching his groin. The trooper looks down and sees a plastic bag hanging out of the man's blue sweat pants.
>
> "What you got down there?" the trooper asks.
>
> "Nothing, just a pager," the man replies. But beads of sweat pop out on his forehead, and the pupils of his eyes dart back and forth. The trooper touches the man's chest, over the heart. It is beating rapidly.
>
> He pats the man down, finding a pager.
>
> He also finds, in the plastic bag, an ounce of cocaine.
>
> Trooper Todd Lunquist has an instinct for drugs. . . . _Christy Scattarella, "Troopers Attack Drug Traffic,"_ Seattle Times, _Dec. 26, 1989, p. B-1_

The story above is a _newsfeature_—a basic, hard-news story written with a featurish touch. Newsfeatures can be lengthy, stand-alone stories designed to treat a significant news development in considerable detail, but only once and not as part of ongoing coverage. However, they're also effective when designed to focus on one aspect of a wider and continuing news development—the drug problem in Seattle, for example.

Newsfeatures Let You Stretch for Creative Horizons

For you as a newswriter, newsfeatures are a way to show imagination, to reach for creative horizons, to tell a story from a different viewpoint with new, exciting approaches.

For readers, newsfeatures offer change of pace, from lean, hard-hitting and essentially straightforward news stories to word pictures that evoke images and pleasurable reading. Newsfeatures can transport readers into the "cold, foggy night," and let them ride beside a trooper gunning down the highway after a drug pusher in a white Ford.

Newsfeatures also are vehicles for gently leading readers into news dimensions that are secondary but, nevertheless, fascinating. For example, coverage of the communist world in 1990 necessarily dealt primarily with tumult in the Soviet Union and Eastern Europe. But with a newsfeature, this writer relayed an intriguing angle from New York City:

> NEW YORK—Anonymous in a city of limousines, a chauffeur-driven Chevrolet sedan arrives each morning at a weathered, seven-story building in Manhattan's Chelsea section.
>
> The old man who emerges, a rumpled figure in cardigan sweater and knit tie, ambles inside, passing knots of aged workers, then rides a shuddering elevator to the top floor.

Once inside his wood-veneer vault of an office, Gus Hall, the patriarch of American communism, renews his lifelong struggle with capitalism under the frozen glare of Marx and Lenin. . . .

U.S. party chairman for 30 years, longer than any living world Communist leader, the 79-year-old Hall has never wavered from the official line. Undaunted by his shrunken ranks of American Communists, the ceaseless scrutiny of FBI agents and his party's slow fade from public enemy to historical relic, Hall always has been able to turn to the Eastern Bloc for ideological consistency.

Now, as epic turmoil in the communist world alters the party line almost daily, Hall and his fellow functionaries show signs of ideological whiplash. . . . *Stephen Braun, "Gus Hall: Never Say Capitalism," Los Angeles Times, Feb. 6, 1990, p. A-1*

You also can use newsfeatures to focus with laser-beam precision on a crucial element of a diffuse, multifaceted social issue, yet avoid leading with the deadening statistics and technical jargon that so often drive readers away from hard-news approaches to such stories. For example, the role of women in our society has been covered for years in its many dimensions in broad, sweeping terms. Below, a writer uses a newsfeature to focus on one aspect of the story—one that came into focus during the U.S. intervention in Panama—in graphic, understandable terms:

Use Newsfeatures to Focus on Social Issues

PANAMA CITY, Panama—When snipers drove by and fired at 2nd Lt. Sioban Ledwith in the first days of the American invasion, she did the same thing the male soldiers around her did.

"We all ducked down, we all pulled weapons and we shot," she said.

In Panama, war is not just for the guys.

Women are guarding roadblocks, charging enemy positions and patrolling sniper-infested city streets, their hands clutching M-60 machine guns and M-16 automatic rifles as tightly as any male soldier. . . . *John Monk, Knight-Ridder Newspapers dispatch for morning papers, Dec. 30, 1989*

Above all, you can use newsfeatures to write creatively, to *soar* in your writing, to lift your readers away from the mundane and pedestrian:

PASADENA, Calif.—Out in the twilight of the solar system, far from the warmth of the Sun and the vitality of Earth, Voyager 2 cruised tonight over the cold blue clouds of Neptune, its cameras snapping pictures and its sensors gathering data on the composition and dynamic forces of the giant planet.

The rendezvous was the culmination of the most far-ranging exploration of the planets in the 32–year history of the space age.

"This is it," Dr. Edward C. Stone, the chief project scientist, said at a news conference here at the Jet Propulsion Laboratory. "This is the 24 hours we've been waiting for." *John Noble Wilford, "Passing Neptune, Voyager Climaxes a 12-Year Mission," The New York Times, Aug. 25, 1989, p. A-1*

In sum, here are some hints on writing newsfeatures:

1. They are second only to straight, hard-news stories as effective vehicles for explaining the news. They aren't features on Michael Jackson or frog-jumping contests (see sidebar on p. 392 for the fun you can have with those!). Newsfeatures are *news* stories with featurish twists. Sometimes they have a *today time element* (Voyager 2).

Use Newsfeatures to Explain News

2. Newsfeatures are effective in every news category—general news, business, science, sports—if written in *timely fashion*. That is, newsfeatures published

Keep Newsfeatures Timely

Wordsmiths at Work

These are facts about American newspapers:

1. Space in them is so tight that newsrooms can become competitive cockpits, with writers scratching and clawing to get some space for their stories.

2. They are so dominated by *bad* news—war, famine, murder and mayhem—that editors grasp at *good* news, lunge at *funny* news.

Out of that chemistry you can fashion opportunity to get your byline in print *if* you develop a keen reporter's eye for light stories—"brites," in newspaper parlance—and a writer's knack for capturing them in words.

In a time of awful news at home and abroad—the year 1990—the writers below won major display in important papers because they could lay a featurish writing touch on bright spots in an otherwise dismal world picture:

WASHINGTON—Picture this: Michael Jackson in chrome-plated boots Thursday, standing shoulder to shoulder with George Bush in the White House Rose Garden and the president talking about—what else—U.S.–Soviet relations.

President Bush, in a navy business suit, was posing for a photo with the mega-entertainer, who wore a saucy black drum major's costume, the eye-popping boots and an air of inscrutability masked by his sun shades.

It was, it is, hard to come by an explanation of precisely what the star was doing at the White House. But he had asked for a meeting with Mr. Bush, and the president said, "Bad!"—or words to that effect.

This had to be the Most Bizarre Moment in the Bush presidency. . . .
Ellen Warren, Knight-Ridder Newspapers dispatch for April 6, 1990

SANDERSVILLE, Ga.—Holy guano, Batman!

Hundreds of bats have infested the walls and crawl spaces of the lunchroom at T. J. Elder Primary School here, giving its students and teachers a peculiar case of Batmania.

For more than a week they have been forced to eat breakfast and lunch at a nearby community center, partly out of health worries, but mostly because of the staggering stench of the animals' droppings. . . .   David Goldman, "Being Driven Batty," *Atlanta Constitution,* Feb. 9, 1990, p. E-1

SAN FRANCISCO—Jumpin' jimminy! Can it be? Is someone really trying to slip a ringer into the celebrated jumping frog contest of Calaveras County?

Contest organizers said Monday that a Seattle man, a professional importer of exotic animals, has created a "super frog crisis" by trying to enter three eight-pound Goliath frogs in the whimsical contest made famous by Mark Twain.

"It would be like racing draft horses against thoroughbreds," complained Diane Baumann of the 39th District Agricultural Assn., which runs the annual contest as part of the Calaveras County Fair in May. "It's just not fair. . . ."
Mark A. Stein, "Frog Jump Contest in Crises Over Extra-Large Leapers," *Los Angeles Times,* Jan. 9, 1990, p. A-1

SAN FRANCISCO—State fish and game wardens Wednesday hopped into the fight over a Seattle man's plan to enter eight-pound Goliath frogs in Calaveras County's whimsical frog-jumping contest, saying the African amphibians are not welcome in California.

The policy flip-flop—contest organizers said game wardens originally said the frogs could legally be brought into the state for display—came after some wardens expressed fears that the giant, sharp-toothed frogs might run amok in the wild. . . .   Mark A. Stein, "State Jumps into Calaveras' Fray on Goliath Frogs," *Los Angeles Times,* Jan. 11, 1990, p. A-3

NEW YORK—In a glaring example of poor planning, a robbery suspect found himself hanging upside down from a fence today, his pants at his ankles, with 20 police officers waiting on the other side, pistols drawn.

The fence just happened to lead into the backyard of the 32nd Precinct station house in Harlem. . . .   Dennis Hevesi, "Caught Dangling with His Pants Up," *The New York Times,* March 2, 1990, p. A-1

You can even get on one of the most prestigious editorial pages in America, that of the *Wall Street Journal,* with a little humor, as did the anonymous author of this brite:

For those who think life is often nasty and brutish, consider what folks argue about in Shaw, Miss. A judge in Shaw has just fined the town's fire chief $100 for making faces at the aldermen. The mayor testified that the chief "stuck his hands in his ears and said, 'Oooh-oooh.'" To all this the fire chief replied, "If I was wrong, I'd apologize. But I'm not wrong. I was right. I won't apologize." How come we never encounter this sort of thing at congressional hearings?   "Stress in Shaw," *The Wall Street Journal,* Feb. 7, 1990, p. A-18

soon after a hard-news event help explain different aspects of that event if readers in their own minds can tie the two together (as the newsfeature on American communist leader Gus Hall tied to earlier stories on the collapse of communism in Eastern Europe).

3. Many writing approaches can be used. Anecdotal introductions work well (state trooper and drug pusher). So do narrative structures and chronological organization.

Anecdotal Leads Work Well

4. Newsfeatures are perfect for focusing on the "people factor" (woman soldier in Panama). Draw a word picture of a single individual and use that to pull readers into your wider story. The statistics and technical jargon that often must be positioned high in a straight news story can be woven in lower in newsfeatures—a big advantage in achieving readability.

Focus on "People" Factor

5. Many newsfeatures run long and are used in Sunday editions. Weekend readers have more time for their newspapers and can be tempted into pleasurable but time-consuming reading they often avoid during their busy workweek. But newsfeatures don't need to be long. Short, punchy approaches can be extremely effective.

6. Shoot for *front page* with newsfeatures. Each example we studied was displayed on page one, or the front pages of important sections.

SIDEBARS: HIGHLIGHTING IMPORTANT ANGLES

Sidebars are close cousins of the newsfeature. They illuminate and explain various elements of a main story. However, although newsfeatures are effective if published within days or even weeks of the main story, sidebars are published the same day and often beside the main story (thus "sidebar").

When Big Stories Break, Hunt for Sidebars

Sidebars are best for highlighting important story angles that otherwise would be buried in the main story's thousands of words. Editors display sidebars in adjacent columns or pages to present readers with a "package" of stories on an important development.

For example, on Jan. 21, 1990, the *Washington Post* led its front page with one of the most important local stories in years:

U.S. Attorney Jay B. Stephens, setting the stage for a possible plea bargain agreement on D.C. Mayor Marion Barry's crack cocaine charge, suggested yesterday that he would look favorably on Barry resigning when deciding how to proceed with the ongoing federal investigation into the mayor's activities. . . . *R.H. Melton and Michael York, "Pressure Increases for Barry to Resign," Washington Post, Jan. 21, 1990, p. A-1*

On that same front page, the *Post* published these sidebars:

"Damn right, I feel vindicated," a former FBI agent said Friday. "We all do. If you had a party and invited all the guys who worked these Barry cases since the 1970s, you'd have to book a big room. Maybe we'll have it at the Vista."

There won't be any parties—it's against bureau procedure on decorum—but for the FBI agents who blunted their swords on Marion Barry over the years, the mayor's arrest Thursday at the Vista International Hotel presents an odd, stunning and satisfying culmination of a long battle. . . . *Bill Dedman, "Years of Toil Pay Off for FBI"*

He has conducted his life in a spectacular arc, the rise and fall of a public man.

He was Marion Barry, a little boy who rode the tail of his mother's gunnysack down cotton rows in Mississippi.

Then he was Marion Barry the upward-bound graduate student, a master's degree in one hand, his other hand clenched to fight the early battles of the civil rights movement.

Reaching his peak, he was Marion Barry the brash, in-your-face mayor of Washington, who bristled with hard-earned power wrestled from tired old elites who had learned not to underestimate this street-smart pol.

And finally, he was Marion Barry on Friday, eyeing a distant horizon as he walked to his arraignment through the throng, a man squinting to see his way past ruin. . . . *Arthur S. Brisbane and Milton Coleman, "A Success Story Takes Tragic Turn"*

Mayor Marion Barry, the defendant: a high-flying black leader turned tragic figure, another statistic.

The very thought of it has left many black city residents reeling with hurt and anger, embarrassment and confusion. . . . *Lynn Duke, "Many Blacks Feel They Themselves Have Been Stung by Barry's Derailment"*

Note the subjects of those sidebars: FBI angle, profile of the mayor, black community reaction. Each is important, but would get only a paragraph or two in the main story. All that makes the three stories perfect for sidebars.

Inside the *same edition,* the *Post* published other sidebars: a commentator's column on Barry's political style; a look at administrators running the city in Barry's absence; Barry's advisers recommended resignation; the impact on District children; the woman who gathered evidence against Barry for the FBI; a chronology of Barry's career; drug treatment for VIPs; how European papers played the Barry case; an opinion page examination of how Washington suffered from the scandal; plus an editorial, many photos and an editorial cartoon.

USA Today uses a front-page sidebar ("Female Fliers Braving") to highlight an important news angle acccompanying the lead story ("U.S. Bombing Runs"). The left-hand column, "Newsline," alerts readers to other sidebars inside.

(Gannett photo
used with permission)

Note *Post* editors thought through the many dimensions of the Barry scandal, then ordered sidebars to illuminate readers on each. In big league newspapering, editors *go for it* when a major story breaks. When *you* see a big one break, hunt around its periphery for sidebar ideas that can get your byline on the front page.

PROFILES FOR AN IN-DEPTH LOOK

What do people gossip about most? Other people. That's why profiles are one of your best writing tools for luring readers deeply into a story. People love to read "inside" stuff about people.

But, as with all newswriting devices we're studying in this chapter, profiles in the hands of a writing pro can accomplish serious purpose: They communicate *news* extraordinarily well, even when seemingly structured to flit lightly across serious subjects.

For example, read the following and decide what it's *really* about:

Some things she just plain hates: The term First Lady.

Comparisons of her popularity with George's.

Self-analysis.

Media scrutiny of her health.

Some things she clearly loves: Being the wife of the president.

George's popularity.

Talking about her dog and her grandkids.

Sharing the White House with the world.

Beneficiary, like her husband, of life's luckier rolls of the dice, Barbara Bush is who she is and couldn't be happier about it. If the White House was a hardship post for some who lived there, it is not one for her.

"I really think if you can be depressed in this job, then boy, you're really going to be depressed in real life," she says with that flair she has for plain speaking.

Unchanged by her year in the fishbowl, she is also unscathed. Her approval rating is among the highest of any president's wife at the end of the first year and higher still than her husband's. It is a bittersweet compliment that slightly embarrasses her. . . .

Donnie Radcliffe, "Barbara Bush & Her Freshman Year," Washington Post, Jan. 21, 1990, p. F-1[1]

What's the above story all about? A nice, white-haired lady who lives at 1600 Pennsylvania Ave., in Washington, D.C.? No. It's about a *political phenomenon,* a major force in the White House and, thus, American politics—about a woman who (the story later points out) is President Bush's "not-so-secret weapon on the campaign trail."

Now compare the writing approach above with this:

After one year in the White House, Barbara Bush has proven to be a political phenomenon and a major force in American politics.

Profiles Entice Readers into Your Story

Which version would *you* read? Precisely. The profile is the choice most readers would make, and that's the wonderful thing about personality profiles: They entice readers in, lure them through sometimes thousands of light, readable words and, at the end, leave them with an important *message,* which, if written in the Five W's and How fashion, would turn them off.

OBITUARIES: NEWS STORIES ABOUT DEATH

How do readers weigh the importance of obituaries in relation to news about business and finance, fashion and lifestyle features, movie reviews, and political opinion columns? Obituaries are regarded as more important.

What news category draws most reader complaints about inaccurate writing? Obituaries.

Newspaper Advertising Bureau (NAB) research shows 50 percent of readers "usually read" obits, more than any category named above. Nine percent placed obits among their three favorite information categories.[2] It doesn't take a survey to reveal reader sensitivity about obits. Generations of editors who have received angry telephone calls about inaccuracies know that.

Obits Are Heavily Read

All to say that, as everyone knows, obits are important, and have been fixtures in newspapers for a long time. However, there is *news* about obits: In the best papers, they are written these days to go far beyond dull recitation of facts about a dead person. And that's why we include obits in this chapter's treatment of writing devices so useful for focusing the news: They often are almost like newsfeatures or personality profiles that, simply, make good reading.

Of course, basic (and *accurate*) information is required in obits:

Basic, Accurate Information Required in Obits

- full name, age, address, occupation and achievements of the deceased;

- time and cause of death, survivors, birthplace;

- clubs, organizations, or other memberships; time and place when public can view the body;

- the funeral service and burial.

Note below that type of detail in an obituary published by a small-town newspaper:

Joseph Allen Young, 27, of Bowdon, died March 15 from injuries sustained in an automobile accident.

He was born in Carroll County April 30, 1963, son of Joe L. and Myric Marlow Young. He was a lifelong resident of this area, a member of Rock Springs Baptist Church, and was a landscaper at West Georgia College.

Survivors include his wife, Mrs. Pam Jeter Young of Carrollton; sons, Amos and Will Young, both of Carrollton. . . .

Here, the obituary lists the full names of *10* other relatives, including great-grandmother and great-grandfather. In small towns, people want *all* the names. Note how the obituary concludes:

Services will be today at 2 p.m. from the Antioch Baptist Church with Rev. H. T. Henderson officiating. Music by the church choir under the direction of Mrs. Linda Cater. Pallbearers will be Chris Noles, Mills Lane, Phil Foster, Joe McCormick, Bobby Patterson, Dennis Rowland, Mike Knowles and Jay Grizzard. Internment in the church cemetery.

Rainwater-West Funeral Home and Chapel of Bowdon in charge of arrangements. *"Deaths,"* Carrollton (Ga.) Times-Georgian, *March 16, 1991, p. 3*

Wordsmiths at Work

To write profiles that effectively communicate important information you must make personalities *come alive* for readers. That means developing a shrewd reportorial eye for detail that will fashion portraits readers can "see." Note how the professionals below do it:

This is from a profile of a 1960s student activist who now teaches at UCLA:

> At 5-foot-11 and 180 pounds, the graying researcher with wire-rim glasses looks as if he could have been a college running back. He dressed casually for an interview in a plaid sports shirt open at the collar, a blue v-neck sweater and green cotton pants. He slouched with his hands in his pockets or touched his cheek to ponder questions.   Garby Libman, "'60s Radical Puts Past Behind Him," *Los Angeles Times,* Jan. 30, 1990, p. E-1

Catching *mannerisms* helps pull readers along, as in a profile of U.S. Rep. Henry Waxman, known as a masterful political fund-raiser:

> It's a brisk March day in Washington, and as he swivels behind his desk, Henry Arnold Waxman looks more like a movie mogul than a member of Congress. Short, balding and mustachioed, he works the phones smoothly, like a Hollywood agent booking high-priced talent.
>
> "Can we get Streisand?" he asks one caller. "I think I can reach Norman Lear if we want to," he tells another. "What about Meryl Streep? Try to get her on the phone. Maybe we could get her on board, too. . . . "   Josh Getlin, "What Makes Henry Tick?," *Los Angeles Times,* April 25, 1990, p. E-1

And, what does the following reference to clothing and TV tell readers about a former U.S. attorney general now active in human rights causes?

> For a man who hasn't owned a car in 17 years, doesn't watch television and still wears bell-bottom pants, Ramsey Clark has always managed to keep up with the times.   Josh Getlin, "Loner of the Left," *Los Angeles Times,* Feb. 18, 1990, p. E-1

In sum, personality profiles are strongest when tied to current news events (for example, focusing on Barbara Bush at the end of her husband's first year in office, an event widely covered). Profiles attract readers, and thus communicate important information, when written with plenty of personal, colorful detail—age, weight, speech, habits, mannerisms, clothing.

Profiles also are effective on subjects other than people. Here's the catchy intro on a profile of a *town:*

> Beverly Hills is a small town really, just five square miles of wide streets and tall trees and, it seems, a jewelry store on every corner. Beauty shops outnumber booksellers 534 to eight. It is easier to find a psychiatrist than a gas station.   David Farrell, "Town That Tells Time on Rolex," *Los Angeles Times,* Jan. 28, 1990, p. A-1

A *Seattle Times* writer won *front-page display* by profiling a *dog:*

> Pounder's rags-to-riches career as a narcotics dog reached its zenith this week when, nostrils flaring, he jumped atop a washing machine and sat down.
>
> The golden retriever then leaned over and put his nose on the back of the adjacent clothes dryer in the hallway of a North Seattle home. Police officers turned the dryer around and Pounder "hit on the source," says his handler, Officer Gary Kuenzi.
>
> Pounder slapped the back of the dryer with a paw and sat down on the floor. That final seating was his signal that he was as close to drugs as he could get.
>
> Pounder had hit pay dirt—seven kilos of cocaine with what police are saying is a street value of about $4 million, and heroin worth $2,990. For that, he got his beloved tennis-ball reward.
>
> "He loves that ball, and when he gets it we play a little tug of war," Kuenzi said. "Then I let him chew around". . . .   Julie Emery, "Dogged Pursuit Led to Big Cocaine Stash," *Seattle Times*, Jan. 13, 1990, p. A-1

But what makes obits *news?* Mostly it's the dead person's lifetime achievements or reputation. And that, of course, means you take to obit writing the same news values and judgments you apply to other forms of news.

Note how the following obit focuses on a principal achievement—and reads almost like a hard-news story on, say, a promotion or award.

Alden Whitman, a retired reporter for *The New York Times* who pioneered the use of interviews of notable people to personalize and energize their obituaries, died yesterday at the Hotel de Paris in Monte Carlo. He was 76 years old and lived in Southampton, L.I.

He died of a stroke, his wife, Joan, said. The Whitmans were in Monte Carlo for a 70th birthday celebration for Craig Claiborne, the food writer.

For many years, newspapers and broadcasters have compiled advance obituaries of noteworthy people to capture their achievements fairly and accurately, in the event that they die close to production deadline.

But it was Mr. Whitman and *The Times,* under the leadership of A.M. Rosenthal, then metropolitan editor, who initiated and published a personalized approach and style to obituary writing by interviewing the subjects in advance of their deaths.

From 1964 to 1976, when he retired, Mr. Whitman wrote hundreds of advance obituaries. To perfect them, he traveled around the world to speak informally with leaders in all endeavors.

Besides notability, his criteria for interviews included whether a person could illuminate himself beyond information available from other sources and whether the subject could express himself with introspection and perspective. . . .   *"Alden Whitman, 76, a Reporter for Obituaries in The Times, Dies," The New York Times, Sept. 5, 1990, p. D-3*

The obit above, incidentally, not only goes on to outline other nice things about Whitman but also recounts some of his darker moments, including his acknowledgement in 1956 to having been a member of the Communist Party, and his conviction twice for contempt of Congress when he refused to identify other members of the Party.

Like any personality profile, obits on prominent persons should tell the *complete* story. Whitman himself said in 1980 that obits should be "a lively expression of personality and character as well as a conscientious exposition of the main facts in a person's life. A good obit has all the characteristics of a well-focused snapshot, the fuller the length the better. If the snapshot is clear, the viewer gets a quick fix on the subject, his attainments, his shortcomings and his times."[3]

Sometimes a person's death is news not so much because of outstanding achievement but, rather, because he or she is remembered widely. An example:

Alan Hale Jr., a veteran character actor best remembered as the blundering but likable skipper of a charter boat that for three television seasons during the 1960s was shipwrecked on "Gilligan's Island," has died of cancer.

Hale, who was 68, had been undergoing treatment for cancer of the thymus for about a year before he died Tuesday evening at St. Vincent Medical Center, his wife, Naomi, said.

The actor had been admitted to the medical center about four weeks ago and was undergoing chemotherapy and radiation treatments, a hospital spokeswoman said. The thymus is a gland-like structure that helps in the body's immune function, she said.

"During the last two weeks, it became quite painful for him," Mrs. Hale said. "He fought very hard until he died. His mind was very clear, it was just that his body couldn't fight back any more...." *John H. Lee, "Alan Hale Jr., 68; Skipper on TV's 'Gilligan's Island,'" Los Angeles Times, Jan. 4, 1990, p. A-26*

Obits Are *News* Stories

Note above the detailed coverage of Hale's struggle against death (including quote from his widow) and the explicit statement of cause of death: cancer. That is *news story treatment* of death and very unlike how obits were written traditionally. Cancer used to be a "long illness." Dying was "passing away." Euphemisms were hallmarks of obits. Today, many newspapers are reporting cause of death, including AIDS. For homosexuals, survivors include "long-time companion."

For *local* obits, many small-town newspapers are much more circumspect, however, particularly if the dead person was not prominent. Most newspapers have policy statements on approaching funeral homes and survivors for information, and on what details are to be included in obits.

POLLS AND MAKING NEWS

To set the scene:

1. Virtually all newspapers and TV networks regularly report results of opinion polls. Many operate their own.
2. It's impossible for individual reporters to conduct valid "man-on-the-street" polls without possessing precise understanding of scientific polling techniques, as well as considerable time and money to do the job correctly.
3. Whether done on the street or scientifically, polling is under attack by some news executives and ethicists as *making news,* rather than reporting it. Polling, they say, *creates* opinion and, if reported improperly, can be very misleading.

We turn, therefore, to polling in this introduction to newswriting not to suggest you try your hand at it but, simply, to caution that when you eventually get involved in it (as you likely will) you should keep several things in mind:

Informal sampling of opinion is a valid journalistic technique *if* readers are informed clearly of its limitations. For example, if tuition is increased at your school, it would be valid to include in your news story a random sampling of student reaction encountered in dorms, the library, student union, and so forth. *However,* your story should *not* report, on the strength of, say, 10 interviews, something like, "The student body was furious over the increase." Your story should be explicit: "Ten students interviewed at random said. . .," or "Students contacted in an informal sampling of campus opinion said. . . ."

Handle Informal Sampling Carefully

Formal sampling by legitimate polling firms must also be handled carefully. In writing the results, for example, you should describe the *credentials* of both the sponsoring and polling organizations (as you would *any* news source) so your readers can decide for themselves what motives are behind the polling. Poll results, like press handouts and research reports, can be issued for partisan purposes. Also, you should explain to readers how the polling was conducted. Often that can be woven into the body of your story. Many newspapers choose to publish an explanatory sidebar like this one on a poll published Jan. 19, 1990, in *The Wall Street Journal* on how Americans view the economy:

Tell Readers How Polling Was Done

How Poll Was Conducted

The Wall Street Journal/NBC News poll was based on nationwide telephone interviews of 1,510 registered voters, conducted Saturday through Tuesday by the polling organization of Peter Hart and Robert Teeter.

The sample was drawn from 315 randomly selected geographic points in the continental U.S. Each region of the country was represented in proportion to its population. Households were selected by a method that gave all telephone numbers, listed and unlisted, an equal chance of being included. One registered voter, at least 18 years of age, was selected from each household by a procedure designed to reflect the number of males and females in the population. Results of the survey were minimally weighed by age to ensure that the poll accurately reflects registered voters nationwide.

Chances are 19 in 20 that if all registered voters in the U.S. had been surveyed using the same questionnaire, the finding would differ from these poll results by no more than 2.6 percentage points in either direction. The margin of error for subgroups would be larger.

Being Graphics Literate

We've discussed rapid changes under way in how news is defined. Changing equally fast is *how news is displayed.*

Editors today display *combinations* of writing, photos, color layout and detailed graphics to achieve a total presentation that assists reader comprehension of a news development.

Be Graphics "Literate"

Only in recent years has newspaper production technology permitted the kind of colorful, razzle-dazzle layout you see in many newspapers. From electronic writing and editing in the newsroom to new high-speed precision presses in the backshop, a technological revolution has changed the way we do things.

Simultaneously, new thinking has emerged in newsrooms. Editors increasingly feel, as predecessor generations of editors did not, that a news story—in a long gray column of type—is only part of what's required to communicate with readers. Making the newspaper visually appealing now is also seen as part of effective communication.

All of that—new thinking, new technology—came together with the launch, in 1982, of *USA Today* by Gannett Co. Inc. The national daily combined satellite

The importance of graphics is illustrated by this *Detroit News* front page, which uses only a headline and huge graphic to announce the beginning of the Persion Gulf War.

(Gannett Photo used with permission)

technology with some of the newspaper industry's most innovative newsroom thinking to produce an entirely new approach to communicating via newsprint. One effect was immediate circulation success for *USA Today* (although the paper has been a big money loser). Readers—and research proves this—enjoy color, photos that are big and bold and graphics. Another effect was that newspapers everywhere plunged into color and graphics.

Your first newsroom job may not place you at the center of creating such total presentations. But you likely *will* be part of a team that puts them together, either as a reporter, writer or beginning copy editor. Thus, it's important that you understand how graphics fit into the total newsroom effort. Frank Hawkins Jr., vice president of Knight-Ridder, Inc., one of the nation's leading newspaper companies, says all reporters must be "graphics literate."

Graphics are created by The AP, by Knight-Ridder and other news services, and are delivered by wire and expedited mail. For local stories, graphics are created by newspaper staff artists. News service and staff artists alike put high premium on fast delivery of graphics that help explain spot-news stories—a written account with a graphic beside it.

As a beginning reporter you may be called on to provide information for graphics. If you cover an accident, a fire or disaster you may have to describe the scene to an artist who creates a graphic to accompany your story.

As always in *news* work, the mission is to deliver *information*.

SUMMARY CHECKLIST

☐ Newsfeatures are basic hard-news stories written with a featurish touch. For newswriters, they are a way to tell a story with new, exciting approaches. For readers, newsfeatures offer pleasurable change of pace from hard-hitting, straightforward news stories.

☐ Newsfeatures permit the highlighting of interesting but secondary stories or the focusing on a single element of a diffuse, multifaceted story.

☐ Above all, newsfeatures are a chance to let your writing soar, to lift readers away from the mundane.

☐ Sidebars are close cousins of newsfeatures and can be used effectively to explain various elements of a main news story. Unlike newsfeatures, which can be published within days or even weeks of the main news event, sidebars are published the same day, usually beside the main story.

☐ By presenting details of individuals' lives, personality profiles entice readers deep into stories and leave them with important messages.

☐ Profiles must make personalities come alive through writing that catches color details, mannerisms, even what clothes an individual wears.

☐ Profiles are strongest when tied to current news events. Profiles can be done effectively on things other than people—towns, even.

☐ Obituaries are important to readers, who watch them carefully for inaccuracies.

☐ Although basic information such as names, addresses, time and cause of death must be included, many obits today are written as news stories about death. They need not be dull.

☐ Virtually all newspapers and TV networks broadcast polling results. But polling is attacked by some critics as making news rather than reporting it. "Man-on-the-street" polling is unscientific but can be used with validity if readers know random sampling is involved.

☐ By using graphics, photos and color layout, in addition to news stories, editors today display total presentations that effectively explain complex news developments. All journalists must be "graphics literate."

RECOMMENDED READING

The weekly "AP Newsfeatures Report," issued with the *AP Log,* lists stories written for the news service's excellent AP Newsfeatures Department and always discusses in detail at least one major newsfeature done by an AP writer. This provides a fine weekly check on how the pros are approaching newsfeature writing.

Sunday newspapers often publish excellent newsfeatures. Strong entries can be found in the *Los Angeles Times, Chicago Tribune*, *Milwaukee Journal, Boston Globe* and other metropolitan papers. Helpful writing hints are in Edward Jay Friedlander and John Lee, *Feature Writing for Newspapers & Magazines* (New York: Harper & Row, 1988).

Reporting and research methodology are discussed in Philip Meyer, *Precision Journalism* (Bloomington: Indiana University Press, 1973). Also see G. Cleveland Wilhoit and David H. Weaver, *Newsroom Guide to Polls and Surveys* (Washington, D.C.: American Newspaper Publishers Association, 1980).

NOTES

1. This piece appeared in the *Washington Post*'s Style section, where excellent writing is published frequently. The section stays close to hard news, which strengthens its newsfeature presentations.
2. The NAB study is, "News and Newspaper Reading Habits," a 1988 study by the Readership Task Force of the bureau. This and other matters relating to obits are discussed in C. David Rambo, "Obits Provide Lifelong Reading Appeal," *presstime,* June 1990, p. 46.
3. Whitman made this statement in the introduction to the second of two collections of his writings, *Come to Judgment,* published in 1980 by Viking Press.

Exercise 15–1   Newsfeature Story Ideas—I

In about 75 words each, write three story ideas for newsfeatures on subjects close to hard news that have developed on your campus or in a nearby town in recent weeks. Each story must be tied tightly enough to a major news event so readers will see it as an elaboration or explanation of the event—much as readers saw the Barbara Bush story as one aspect of her husband's first anniversary in the White House.

Exercise 15–2   Newsfeature Story Ideas-II

With your instructor's approval of your story idea, write a newsfeature that addresses a hard-news subject of compelling interest to students of your school. Do this in about 500 words. Suggested topic areas: cost of education, cost of living off campus, drugs or drinking, crime on campus. Use an anecdotal approach, perhaps focusing on one person's experience in one of those topic areas. Before launching this project, refresh yourself on the text's "hints on writing newsfeatures."

Exercise 15–3   Writing Sidebars

The scenario for this exercise: A vicious wave of cold weather has swept through your area. People died from exposure; cars failed to start; plumbing froze and burst; livestock and pets were threatened. All that is wrapped up in the lead story planned for your newspaper's front page tomorrow morning. Now, write a sidebar—a how-to-do-it story—that gives readers hints on how to dress, how to spot symptoms of frostbite and hypothermia, how to help victims of both, how to care for homes, cars and pets. Your sources can include weather service and health service officials, plumbers, auto mechanics—anyone involved in caring for people and things threatened by extreme cold.

Exercise 15–4   Writing Obits

Write an obituary from the following facts:

This man's name was Richard Haughton Livesey. He lived in Upper Providence, Delaware County, just outside Philadelphia (you're writing for the *Philadelphia Daily News*). He was a State Farm Insurance agent and a former manager for Sun Oil Co. He died Monday. Livesey worked 30 years for Sun Oil and retired as manager of the boilermakers' department. That was in 1971, when he retired. He had been a State Farm agent concurrently, since 1950. He settled in Delaware County after coming to the United States. That was in 1922. He came from England. Livesey was a member of the George W. Bartram Lodge 298, F & AM, and the LuLu Temple Shrine. He had been captain of the Sun Oil retirees bowling league. His wife is Mary Fayette DuVal Livesey. They were married 55 years. Other survivors include Nancy DuVal Livesey, his daughter. And a son, Richard Haughton Livesey III, and a brother, Charles Haughton Livesey. There will be private funeral services and burial. Contributions may be made to the charity of the donor's choice. No cause of death was given. Livesey was 78.

Part 6

Writing for Broadcast

Broadcast newswriting is loaded with excitement that comes from working with media—radio and television—which, if used properly, have extraordinary capabilities for capturing audiences, stirring their imaginations, communicating with them. Broadcast far outstrips print journalism in ability to entertain or deliver dramatic, gut impact.

A major challenge in broadcast newswriting is using wisely that ability to entertain or dramatize, and still provide your audience the news it *needs,* in sufficient detail and meaningful context, along with entertainment or a punch in the gut. Radio and TV are primarily entertainment media and they devote fewer resources—including air time—to informing than to entertaining. In that environment, it's not easy for the broadcast newswriter to inform audiences of all the day's compelling issues.

Rewarding careers await those of you who succeed in broadcast. But be prepared for intense competition. All news jobs are competitive, of course, but there is an added complication in radio and TV: Most small and medium-size stations (where entry-level jobs are available) don't hire full-time newswriters. They combine newswriting with other tasks, such as producing—a job that involves pulling an entire news-gathering effort together, much as an editor does in print journalism. Of course, you may be hired as on-air "talent," with the job of reporting and reading as well as writing the news. Even in smaller cities ("markets," in industry parlance), that function can offer considerable career satisfaction. Listeners and viewers identify much more closely with broadcast anchors than readers do with bylines in print journalism. At larger stations and networks, news directors hire full-time newswriters and pay them well. Those writers are mostly anonymous and must learn to write for the delivery style of others.

News values and judgments you developed earlier in this book are central to effective broadcast newswriting. So are basic print writing skills. News in broadcast still is news, and the best way to write it is, as in print, with simple and clear language. However, broadcast and print newswriting do differ, so we'll examine in this chapter several areas where radio and TV require a different approach:

- Your broadcast audience and its news needs. Understanding them is essential.
- Writing in broadcast style, with proper pace and rhythm. It requires special touch.
- Preparing broadcast copy. It's handled in unique ways.

We'll also look at how broadcast pros handle the newswriting challenges of radio and TV.

Chapter Sixteen

You and Your Broadcast Audience

Radio and television command huge audiences for their entertainment programming. Sitcoms, game shows, movies and sports entertainment are TV's principal attractions. Music and talk shows are radio's. The popularity—and, thus, financial success—of networks and major stations is reflected in audience measurements ("ratings"), which rise or fall mostly on such entertainment programming.

In both radio and TV, therefore, news is second to entertainment in the corporate "pecking order" when air time, money and other resources are dispensed. (Demonstrating this, the CBS-owned flagship in New York City, WCBS, moved the network's star anchor, Dan Rather, from 7 p.m. to the less-attractive 6:30 p.m. time slot to make way for a game show that would increase station advertising revenue by $5 million annually.) Within broadcast newsrooms, the entertainment factor in news has a much higher priority than in newspapers, whose principal offering is hard news. TV newswriting tends to emphasize human interest—dramatic, whimsical, amusing stories—and deal less effectively with in-depth, issue-oriented stories. One goal in TV newswriting is making information palatable to viewers who seek from that medium a fast glimpse of the news—not lengthy, detailed coverage. At some stations, wooing the audience extends to writing in conversational style and mindless "happy talk"—news delivered in chatty, informal ways that are presumed to be entertaining and thus make information easy to digest.

The *technical* challenges in effectively reaching your broadcast audience are formidable. In radio you're writing for the ear with a mix that often includes sound ("actualties") other than the news reader's voice. For TV you're writing in a mix of sound, movement, color and, above all, pictures, as well as words. In both media, you're doing all that within cruel time limitations. You don't have many column inches to explain for your audience even stories of top importance; you have *seconds*. Broadcast tends to make a trade-off: dramatic impact on an audience for shallow treatment. The time constraints heighten your challenge of meeting your audience's news *needs* (as contrasted with entertainment-oriented *desires*) without the luxury of detailed, analytical writing that goes in-depth to explain complicated issues.

In Radio, Write for the Ear

In TV, Write for Sound, Movement, Pictures

Obviously, effective newswriting requires precise understanding of your audience and its demographics—age, income, education and so forth. Writers at *The New York Times,* which serves educated and affluent readers, take in-depth, analytical writing approaches very different from writing at the fast-paced, racy tabloid *New York Daily News,* a paper beloved by the subway crowd. *The writing is different because the audiences are different.*

In broadcast writing, understanding your audience must guide you in selecting which stories to cover, how to structure your writing and, even, the vocabulary you use. Three factors are of paramount importance:

First, Understand Your Audience

1. The entertainment package offered by broadcast stations serves to carve out audiences of distinct characteristics. In radio, these audience "niches" can be narrow: Rock music stations attract young listeners, for example. "Golden Oldies" programming pulls in older folks. You can see the importance of all this in the news story selection process: You'd probably be mistaken to lead your newscast at a Golden Oldies station with news on Mick Jagger's latest album. You could be right on target, however, with a new development on Social Security!

2. Serving your audience effectively can be terribly difficult because you are writing in *aural* style—that is, for the ear, not eye (even in TV news most information is absorbed through hearing). In print journalism, your readers can absorb information at a time and place of their choosing—early or late, whichever is convenient; over coffee or in bed, at the office or on a bus. And, importantly, they can absorb it *at their own pace.* They can read, then reread, rapidly or slowly, and control completely the circumstances under which they receive and "process" your information. Not so in broadcast news. Viewers or listeners must have their sets on at a time of *your* choosing, even if that's inconvenient. The audience must catch details as news readers proceed at a pace of their choosing. There are no re-runs on the 6 p.m. news. Your writing must communicate effectively the first time around.

No Second Chance in Broadcast Writing

3. In broadcast writing you can't use question marks, quotes, exclamation points and other typographical devices so effective in print writing. And, because your listeners are distant and anonymous, you can't use a smile, shrug, sneer or lifted eyebrow—all effective in emphasizing a point in that other form of aural communication, one-on-one conversation. Further, you can't see whether your listeners are smiling or sneering, either, so you can't "adjust" your delivery style in mid-sentence or mid-paragraph, as you might in conversation with a friend.

Writing in Broadcast Style

Picture the leading network TV news anchors reading the news: Dan Rather of CBS leans toward the camera with an intense, penetrating stare. He reads the news with a bang-bang, staccato style. Tom Brokaw of NBC, much more relaxed, comes on sounding like the Midwestern small-town native he is. Peter Jennings of ABC is polished, urbane, a bit reserved. What you *see* are three distinctly different on-camera styles.

But listen closely to all three and you can *hear* many commonalities in the words they are reading: informal language patterns; short, understandable sentences; lots of transition words; simple vocabularies with strong emphasis on descriptive, forceful words; the active voice; contractions, and, above all, writing *and* reading that deal out information at a pace designed to ease listening and understanding.

Use Short Sentences, Simple Words

Issues and Challenges

Broadcast newswriters who strive to do a professional, principled job of communicating news are under great pressure from several directions.

They frequently lack sufficient air time or other resources necessary for substantive treatment of complex issues. One researcher found the average "sound bite" or actuality on network TV newscasts averaged 9.8 seconds during a period in 1988. That compared with 42.3 seconds in 1968. Hitting at the news with glancing blows that last just a few seconds doesn't communicate very meaningfully.[1]

Preoccupation with making news engaging—entertaining, even—means ever-increasing use of stylish video, quick movement, color, snap, crackle, pop. That, in turn, means *images,* not issues, often are communicated, leaving viewers without substantive depth of information needed today to be informed.

Students of broadcast writing would do well to set career goals of learning to use the enormous strengths of radio and TV to more telling effect. Tony Verna, executive producer-director for Turner Broadcasting System, provided this guidance: "Style without substance is a formula for failure."[2]

Critics often charge that TV news presents *shallow coverage without meaningful perspective,* is *too "show biz," intrusive and invades the privacy of people in the news.* A leading professional organization, The Radio/Television News Directors Association, addresses those charges in its "Code of Broadcast News Ethics," calling on its members to accept these standards:

Article Two (which addresses shallowness)

Broadcast news presentations shall be designed not only to offer timely and accurate information, but also to present it in the light of relevant circumstances that give it meaning and perspective.

This standard means that news reports, when clarity demands it, will be laid against pertinent factual background; that factors such as race, creed, nationality or prior status will be reported only when they are relevant; that comment or subjective content will be properly identified; and that errors in fact will be promptly acknowledged and corrected.

Article Three (sensationalism)

Broadcast journalists shall seek to select materials for newscast solely on their evaluation of its merits as news.

This standard means that news will be selected on the criteria of significance, community and regional relevance, appropriate human interest, and service to defined audiences. It excludes sensationalism or misleading emphasis in any form; subservience to external or "interested" efforts to influence news selection and presentation, whether from within the broadcasting industry or from without. It requires that such terms as "bulletin" and "flash" be used only when the character of the news justifies them; that bombastic or misleading descriptions of newsroom facilities and personnel be rejected, along with undue use of sound and visual effects; and that promotional or publicity material be sharply scrutinized before use and identified by source or otherwise when broadcast.

Article Four (privacy)

Broadcast journalists shall at all times display humane respect for the dignity, privacy and the well-being of persons with whom the news deals.

Those stylistic factors should influence *your* broadcast writing. Let's examine an example:

They're on the way—about 300 Americans and 100 Britons, who'd been trapped in Kuwait by Iraq's invasion, left Iraq's capital today for home. A jumbo jet, chartered by the U.S. and Britain, is handling the transport. And a U.S. diplomat in Baghdad hopes for two more flights this week. But, even at that, there will be a lot of westerners left. An estimated seven-thousand, not all of them Americans, were trapped by the war. And the Iraquis are keeping an unknown number of western men as human shields at vital installations.

Ira Dreyfuss, AP broadcast wire dispatch for radio and TV stations on Sept. 12,1990[3]

First, the story above was No. 1 in a series of stories transmitted by AP on the most compelling news development of the day—the Persian Gulf crisis. Yet, the story contains just 93 words. In a broadcast news story, you often are limited to wordage about equivalent to the first and second paragraph of a newspaper story.

Write for "Rip and Read" Anchors

Second, the story is written for "rip-and-read" news anchors who, literally, often rip copy off the AP machine and read it, as is, on air. The story is clean, free of errors and ready for airing. In broadcast newswriting, put nothing on paper that will cause you (or an anchor) to stumble on air—no misspellings, jumbled sentences, confusing editing, and, certainly, no jokes or comments in bad taste. If it's on paper—even in a marginal comment—it might be read on air. Note also that because the story is written for the ear not eye, it contains a stylistic feature unique to broadcast writing ("seven-thousand"). Some news readers prefer copy to be all upper case, which makes it easier to read.

Follow Normal Conversational Patterns

Third, note the informal language. "They're on the way" is a "warm-up" (or "throwaway") line that, in effect, says to listeners, "Tune in for this, folks." The contractions ("they're," "who'd") follow normal *conversational* patterns. Listen carefully to friends talking and note how, probably without thinking, they use "warm-up" language, contractions and other informal speech patterns to communicate effectively.

Fourth, note the short sentences—six that average 14.6 words. Write that way and you'll achieve two things: You (or your news anchor) won't have to gulp for air trying to read a single sentence and, importantly, your listeners will have a better chance of comprehending your meaning.

Fifth, transition words tie the sentences together in a simple, comprehensive package for the listener's ear. Three sentences open with transition words (one "but" and two "ands").

Use Active Voice, Forceful Words

Sixth, an active voice and forceful, colorful words help create a picture in the listener's mind: "they're on the way . . . is handling . . . trapped (twice) . . . human shields." Note, incidentally, my reference to listener, singular, not listeners, plural. Many broadcast writers feel you can build a personalized link—an intimacy—into your writing if you imagine you are writing for a single person, a friend or relative, and "talk" to that person alone.

Seventh, note the sacrifices that the AP writer makes in meeting the broadcast requirement for brevity: The story answers who (Americans, Britons), what (leaving), where (Baghdad), when (today), how (jumbo jet), but fails to explore *why*.

You Often Must Sacrifice Depth

The story has none of the explanatory depth or analytical detail that are the strength of newspaper and magazine reporting. Not even the entire series of AP broadcast stories on the Persian Gulf came close to matching the detail possible in a single

A Professional's View:
Writing Hints from a Broadcast Pro

Jackie Crosby Legge was co-winner of a Pulitzer Prize for investigative reporting at the Macon (Ga.) Telegraph and News *before turning to broadcast. Below, she provides hints on writing for television.*

The hardest thing about making the transition from print to television reporting is this: I've had to develop the discipline to *stop* writing—to be silent and let the pictures and natural sound of the story unwind without killing it with unnecessary words.

Writing coaches call this "loose writing," and it is one of the most challenging tasks of television reporting. Writing loose means you have to select the most powerful, creative and compelling words. It means you don't waste time saying with words what the pictures say better. Television writers use words to help set the scene, to make the transition between thoughts and to explain a complicated process. Unlike print, you've got the benefit of pictures that can help people relive the story. If your writing is loose, you can let viewers *experience* what happened—not just watch it.

Loose writing can also help you pace your stories better. Today's viewers are eager to reach for the remote control if your story starts dragging or if they get confused by complicated writing. Viewers can't listen to paragraph after paragraph of descriptive narration. They need short, snappy sentences that are carefully woven between the natural sound of the story and quick, strong interviews.

I've also had to learn to write conversationally. There's a big difference between writing to be read and writing to be heard. Television viewers don't have the chance to go back and reread something they didn't catch the first time around. You need to make sure they hear and understand everything you tell them. You have to tell your story in a logical way. You have to use simple sentences so viewers don't get lost. You have to use language they understand.

Importantly, you must learn how to write complicated stories that can be told in 90 seconds. I still approach television stories the same way I did as a newspaper reporter. I spend the same amount of time researching my subject and setting up interviews. The biggest difference is that many of the facts I uncover won't make it into my copy. I've had to learn to prioritize facts—and throw away everything that isn't essential. I've had to learn to make sure every word I write contributes to the story. In many ways, this has made me a more disciplined writer. I'm more focused and direct, even though I often feel frustrated by the lack of depth in a daily newscast. I think it's the old newspaper reporter in me who enjoys working on longer news reports (longer in this business means two or three minutes) and the occasional half-hour documentary.

I think the following really underscores the difference between television and print. It comes from Frank N. Magid Associates of Marion, Iowa, a television consulting firm. It's called the Producer's Creed: "Newspapers and magazines reach emotion through the intellect. Television reaches intellect through emotion."

Jackie Crosby Legge, special projects producer, KSTP-TV, Minneapolis

Writer-producer Jackie Crosby Legge of KSTP-TV, Minneapolis, with cameraman Russ Brown. Coordination between writer and photographer must be close in TV news.

(Chris Meltvedt photo used with permission of KSTP-TV)

column of newspaper writing. But the broadcaster's mission of providing brief treatment of the news for quick comprehension was served. (See the sidebar for other hints, by a TV and newspaper pro, on writing for broadcast.)

Let's examine in greater detail a few crucial factors in broadcast writing.

Sentence Structure

Straightforward, subject-verb-object sentences are most effective in broadcast. Opening with lengthy, convoluted modifying phrases or clauses almost invariably confuse listeners. For example:

NO:
Fifty-five-year-old, Harvard-educated, gray-haired Fred Smith was appointed president of our university today.

YES:
Our university has a new president today. He is Fred Smith, fifty-five. The new president was educated at Harvard.

OR:
Fred Smith is the new president of our university. The fifty-five-year-old Harvard graduate was appointed today.

Writer-producer Legge edits a special project with Senior Editor Joe Guion for KSTP-TV, Minneapolis.

(Chris Meltvedt photo used with permission of KSTP-TV)

You'll lose listeners if you break up sentences with subordinate clauses:

Avoid Subordinate Clauses

NO:
President Bush, who quoted from an army private, is getting high marks for his speech to Congress last night.

YES:
President Bush is getting high marks for his speech to Congress last night. In his speech, Bush quoted from an army private. . . .

As in print writing, there's danger of a dull sameness settling over your broadcast writing if you get too simplistic—particularly if you string together nothing but subject-verb-object sentences. You should break up the monotony. Read the following aloud and note how the writer provides you with opportunities to vary your delivery style:

Iranian spiritual leader Ali Khamenei (kah-may′ -nee) says Moslems who die fighting the U.S. presence in the Gulf region will go to heaven. The call is another apparent sign of Iran's willingness to let bygones be bygones after its eight-year war with Iraq—with hatred of the U.S. being the common theme. Yesterday, Tehran reportedly agreed to give Iraq food and medicine in exchange for oil and cash. If that happens, it could punch holes in the U.N. embargo aimed at forcing Iraq out of Kuwait. *Ira Dreyfuss, AP dispatch, Sept. 12, 1990*

In the above, note these points:

The *pronouncer* "(kay-may′ -nee)" is a device for helping the news reader through unfamiliar words. Use one on any word that might cause an on-air flub.

Using the *dash* (. . . "with Iraq—with hatred" . . .) is a signal to the news reader to change tone of voice or pause to add special emphasis to the material that follows. The anchor can't underline words for emphasis. But pauses, tone of voice, volume—all can be used to make a point. You also can use ellipses to signal when to lend special emphasis to material that follows . . . like this!

Story Structure

Because most broadcast writing is short and punchy, you'll not often face all the structural problems you do in lengthy print writing. In broadcast, stories in the 90- to 150-word range are most common. Occasionally, however, you'll need to write longer, and story structure then becomes a challenge. Because they cannot slow the pace of the story or ask for a rerun, listeners will be lost unless you lead them carefully through any switches in time elements, persons being quoted, or references to geography.

In handing chronology, write step-by-step when you can:

> Police gave these details: First, the gunman entered the bank. Second, a teller tripped a silent alarm. Then, two patrol cars arrived at the main street entrance. . . .
> Yesterday, almost the same sequence occurred in a bank stick-up in suburban Washington. . . .

In the example above, the listener is taken through the chronology in logical steps. "Yesterday," as a transition into the second paragraph, enables the listener to switch time elements. That second paragraph wouldn't work as well if it read, "Almost the same sequence occurred in a bank stick-up in suburban Washington yesterday. . . ."

Be sure to signal listeners clearly when you're switching persons being quoted:

> President Bush says he is. . . .
> White House spokesman Marlin Fitzwater says the president intends the message to mean. . . .

You can use similar transitions in switching geography:

> In Moscow, Soviet officials say the president's message. . . .
> In London, the reception is better for Bush's speech. British officials say. . . .

As in any form of newswriting, it's important to structure your story so listeners can keep complex issues straight. It's difficult for many listeners, for example, to keep straight what the lineup is in the Middle East. An AP writer helps them: "One report from Egypt—which sides with the United States—is that. . . ."

Attribution

Tight attribution to authoritative sources is as important in broadcast writing as in print journalism. Your special challenge lies in inserting it in the story, yet avoiding cumbersome structure that offends the ear. Example:

NO:	YES:
Charles Bowsher, head of the General Accounting Office, a congressional agency, says that in one year the federal government will be spending more for interest on its debt than it does on defense.	In one year, the federal government will be spending more for interest on its debt than it does on defense. That's the estimate from the head of the General Accounting Office. The congressional agency says. . . .

Other ways of inserting attribution:

> President Bush said today—and I quote—"Iraq must withdraw from Kuwait."
>
> President Bush said—quote—"Iraq must withdraw from Kuwait."
>
> President Bush said—in his words—"Iraq must withdraw from Kuwait."

In each example above, the dashes alert the news reader that a brief pause or even minor change in tone or pace will emphasize for listeners the quotation that follows—much as a printed dash catches readers' eyes.

Parceling It Out

You may not be aware of it, but student audiences have superb techniques for signaling whether they're being given too much information too quickly or, conversely, whether lectures are slow and boring. Experienced lecturers adjust their pace and the complexity of their information in accordance with, for example, frantic note-taking and frowns (meaning, "Too much, too fast") or vacant stares out the window (signaling, "Tell a joke . . . throw chalk . . . do something, fast!"). Unfortunately, in broadcast newswriting you can't see such audience signals (although sometimes it seems you can *hear* sets being turned off across the nation).

Your Listeners Aren't Reporters

Your writing, therefore, must assume your listeners can accept and "process" information only at a pace considerably slower than yours. After all, most listeners don't have professional experience in sifting, absorbing, and understanding breaking news. They don't spend their days listening, reading and talking news, as reporters do.

Carefully parcel out information in your writing. Don't always jam all essential facts into the first sentence, as you might in a newspaper lead. At times, open with a "throwaway" line to catch their attention, then deliver one bit of essential information . . . delay a bit, then deliver another . . . then, another. Note this story:

President Bush has a message for Iraq—special delivery, on Iraqi TV, if Iraq sticks by its word and airs it. Aides say he taped a forthright, eight-minute explanation of why the United States is building its forces in the Persian Gulf. U.S. officials won't say exactly what's in it—they say Iraqis should find out first. But White House spokesman Marlin Fitzwater says Bush stood by his position that America has no quarrel with the Iraqi people—just their leader. *AP dispatch for Sept. 12, 1990*

Above, the opening "throwaway" line with its "special delivery" play on words is a nicely crafted way of warming up the listening audience. The real news in the story is in the last sentence quote from a White House spokesman, and by the time the writer delivers it, listeners are ready to absorb it. Note also that the writer uses dashes to signal the news reader to pause or change tone to lend emphasis to material at three points in the story.

Other Writing Considerations

PERSONAL PRONOUNS It's considered bad form for writers to always inject themselves into news stories. Sometimes, however, you *should* strive in broadcast to achieve the special intimacy that comes from using personal pronouns. The goal is to join each listener individually in *talking* about the news—even though you really are delivering it to a mass audience of anonymous listeners. Note the difference:

Strive for Intimacy with Listeners

NO:	YES:
A fire in a one-hundred-year-old warehouse here on the south side is out of control. . . .	I'm here on the south side where, as you can see, the fire in this old warehouse is out of control. . . .

In the preferred version above, each viewer is invited to "come along" to the fire. On radio, you can accomplish that with, "As you can hear in the background, flames are roaring. . . ." Or, "You can hear sirens of more fire trucks arriving. . . ."

More examples of achieving intimacy with personal pronouns:

> "*We've* got tough economic times ahead . . . that's the prediction for *us* from . . ."
> "*Our* fuel oil bills are going up . . . that's the bad news for *us* out of the Persian Gulf today . . ."
> "If *you're* worried about inflation . . . *I've* got good news . . ."

Avoid Homophones

HOMOPHONES The ear can err where the eye doesn't. For example, you can read this sentence and immediately spot the different meanings of "heir," "air," "error," and "err." But pity the *listener* trying to figure out which meaning an anchor intends when news copy includes such *homophones*—words that sound alike but carry different meanings. Here are others to avoid:

sex/sect	to/too/two	aisle/isle
council/counsel	wear/where	tee/tea
pray/prey	reign/rein/rain	threw/through
capital/capitol		

REDUNDANCIES In print newswriting, you can summarize in your lead a story's salient points, then return to them with elaborating detail in subsequent paragraphs. The inverted-pyramid structure in fact is based on ever-expanding explanation of the lead's Five W's and How. In broadcast, you don't have time for either wasted wordage or much repetition.

Mercilessly Edit Your Copy Down

First, be merciless in editing your copy down to bare essentials. Make it "told reporters" for "appeared before reporters at a morning news conference." "The government in Washington released an official statement announcing today that . . ." can be edited down to, "The administration announced today. . . ."

Second, don't waste precious air time saying the same thing twice—unless you must repeat for clarity or to ensure crucial information has been communicated. For example: "A tornado warning is out for Jackson County—that's Jackson County. . . ." Or, you can conclude a story with a "kicker" to ensure that listeners caught an important fact. For example, you can close a story about the death of a prominent person with, ". . . Fred Smith . . . dead at 90."

NUMBERS Round them off ("about 2–thousand") or write them as you speak them:

- nine-dollars and fifty-cents (not $9.50)
- 18-hundred and five (not 1,805)
- in the year 19-hundred (not in 1900)

Spell Out Most Abbreviations

ABBREVIATIONS As in print, use only those abbreviations likely to be immediately understood: FBI, CIA, NASA. Spell out most: mister, missus, general, lieutenant (Not Mr., Mrs., Gen., Lt.)

PUNCTUATION Most rules for print writing are valid for broadcast writing—except that you must make common-sense adjustments for punctuation that is heard, not read. For example:

- Make it 56-year-old Fred Smith, not, Fred Smith, 56.

- For reading ease, make it F-B-I and C-I-A.

- Acronyms should be enclosed in quotes: "NASA," "NATO."

IDENTIFICATIONS Usage differs from print writing style:

NO:	YES:
Fred Smith, museum director, said. . . .	Museum director Fred Smith said. . . .

If titles are long, insert them after the name, as in print:

> Fred Smith, associate director of the museum for Indian exhibits, said. . . .

Sometimes you can delay precise identification:

> Word today that inflation threatens the nation. Alan Greenspan told a news conference in Washington that inflation's a real threat. Greenspan is chairman of the Federal Reserve, which monitors economic activity.

Note above that the third sentence repeats Greenspan's name for listeners who might have missed it while listening to the second sentence.

PREPARING BROADCAST COPY

Broadcast copy—"script" or "continuity," in industry parlance—needs special preparation as you weave your words together with pictures and sound.

In radio, taped sound from a cassette or cartridge can lend great impact to a news story. Letting an anchor quote President Bush is one thing; providing Bush's own voice is much more dramatic. A radio script should be prepared along these lines:

> BUSH (story slug)
> 9/16 (date)
> 8 a.m. (time)
> smith (writer's name)
> More trouble over the Persian Gulf today . . . President Bush told reporters Iraq again is defying world opinion.
> CART:BUSH
> TIME:19
> OUT: we will not back down.
> Earlier, a White House spokesman said. . . .

In the example above, "CART" identifies one of several cartridges containing prerecorded sound—or "sound bites"—to be used in this newscast. TIME shows the excerpt runs for 19 seconds. OUT alerts the news anchor that "we will not back down" are Bush's last words. After they are spoken, the anchor must resume reading the news.

Broadcast news reporters aren't shy about pushing forward to obtain pictures and sound for a story on actor/comedian Dan Aykroyd on film location in Long Beach, Calif.

(AP photo used with permission)

Preparing a TV package of prerecorded audio and visual news is more complicated, of course, because pictures, as well as sound, must be woven into a script. Here is the first page of a script written by Jackie Crosby Legge, special projects producer for KSTP-TV, Minneapolis:

MINNESOTA REPORT—CORPO-
RATE SCHOOLS
1-25-90 10 P.M.//LEGGE//2:39
PAGE ONE

ELAINE FINLEY ON CAMERA 00:32:13:09—00:32:26 #2 START TO COVER WITH B-ROLL OF LITTLE ONES GETTING OFF BUS AND GOING INTO SCHOOL; CAPTURE SHOT OF SCHOOL NAME KIDS IN HALL-WAY W/BOOK	"WE'RE NOT CREATING MAGIC HERE, NOT AT ALL. WE'RE CRE-ATING AN ENVIRONMENT IN WHICH CHILDREN CAN LEARN AND BE SUCCESSFUL IN THEIR LEARNING AND CAN ALSO BE HAPPY." (:13) (NAT BREAK, KIDS READING) (:20)
KIDS PLAYING WITH BUNNY (RANDALL TRACK)	SOME MIGHT ARGUE THAT IT *IS* MAGIC. THAT IN THE MIDST OF ONE OF THE POOREST, MOST CRIME-RIDDEN AREAS IN WEST CHICAGO, YOUNG CHILDREN AND THEIR FAMI-LIES ARE FINDING HOPE. (:09)

| SHOTS OF BLIGHTED AREA OUT OF SCHOOLBUS WINDOW KIDS SOT UNDER VIDEO #7 00:34:29:20

 00:45:44:24 | "WE BE SEEING DOPE DEALERS AND PROSTITUTES . . . PEOPLE BE DRINKING WHISKEY AND STUFF." (:09)

 "IT'S JUST BAD, BECAUSE EVERY TIME WE BE RIDING THE SCHOOL BUS, WE BE SEEING PEOPLE GET SHOT OR THEY GET HURT OR THEY HAVE TO CALL AN AMBULANCE TO PICK THEM UP." (:12) |
| (ANGELA TRACK) PAN FROM BAR ACROSS STREET TO SLOW ZOOM INSIDE CLASSROOM; KINDERGARTNERS | WITH FAILURE IN EVIDENCE EVERYWHERE, THE SCHOOL'S PHILOSOPHY IS SUCCESS. THERE ARE NO GRADEBOOKS OR REPORT CARDS. CHILDREN HERE ARE GROUPED ACCORDING TO SKILL, NOT . . . [4] |

Note above that each segment is timed precisely, down to fractions of seconds. Writing exactly to time available is a major challenge in this form of TV newswriting—a "reporter-packaged" story that ties prerecorded segments of a reporter's voice to video. A routine "stand-up" of a correspondent reporting from, say, the White

Segments Must Be Timed Precisely

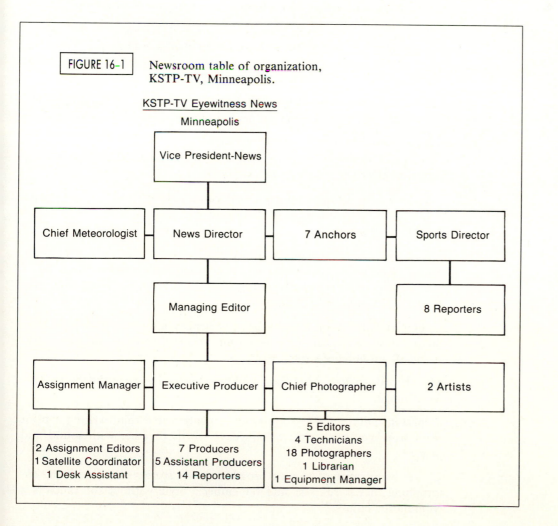

FIGURE 16–1 Newsroom table of organization, KSTP-TV, Minneapolis.

House lawn would not be timed so precisely. But toward the end of the newscast, the anchor (perhaps aided by writers off-camera) would juggle news items and lengths to ensure the show ends on time.

In the script above, writing to both pictures and sound is challenging. The script opens (see left-hand column) with a reporter, Elaine Finley, on camera. In exactly 13 seconds, the video switches to a "B-roll"—background tape—showing children getting off a bus. The reporter, meanwhile, is narrating the script (right-hand column).

When the script moves (left-hand column) to "shots of blighted area," TV viewers will hear children talking. That's signaled by "kids SOT (sound on tape) under video."

Obviously, producing a successful TV news show is a team effort involving many persons. (See accompanying diagram for how the newsroom of KSTP-TV is organized.)

SUMMARY CHECKLIST

☐ Newswriting in TV and radio offers the excitement of working with media that capture huge audiences, stir their imagination and, if used properly, communicate extremely effectively.

☐ A challenge in newswriting is using wisely the broadcast media's ability to entertain and dramatize, and simultaneously provide listeners and viewers with the news they *need*.

☐ Because they are principally entertainment media, radio and TV sometimes give news departments No. 2 priority when passing out air time, money and other resources.

☐ Technical challenges in effective broadcast newswriting are formidable because you must write for the ear with a mix of words and sound and, in TV, pictures, as well.

☐ Understanding your audience—its age, income, interests and so forth—is crucial to effective broadcast newswriting.

☐ Unlike readers, TV and radio listeners cannot absorb and "process" news at a pace of their choosing. Writers must parcel out information in manageable portions.

☐ Effective newswriting requires informal language patterns; short, understandable sentences; use of transition words; simple vocabularies; use of contractions, and, above all, writing that deals out information at a pace designed for easy understanding.

☐ Straightforward, subject-verb-object sentences often are most effective. But a dull sameness can settle over your writing if you are consistently too simplistic in sentence structure.

☐ Most broadcast stories are short and punchy. Many are in the 90- to 150-word range.

☐ Preparing radio and TV copy is more complicated than writing a print news story because scripts must weave words together with sound and pictures.

☐ Under the pressure of keeping broadcast news stories short and being entertaining, newswriters should remember: "Style without substance is a formula for failure."

RECOMMENDED READING

Two excellent approaches to newswriting are Mervin Block, *Writing Broadcast News* (Washington, D.C.: Broadcasting Book Division, 1989), and Roger L. Walters, *Broadcast Writing* (New York: Random House, 1988).

For a broader view, see Richard D. Yoakam and Charles F. Cremer, *ENG: Television News and The New Technology* (New York: Random House, 1985).

Broadcasting magazine carries valuable news-oriented commentary plus excellent career information for beginning newswriters.

NOTES

1. Richard Rosen, "For Overloaded Eyes and Ears, Bite Makes Right," *The New York Times*, June 10, 1990, p. H-31.
2. Tony Verna, "Monday Memo," *Broadcasting,* April 16, 1990, p. 30.
3. The AP serves more than 6,000 radio and TV stations with a wide variety of news, audio, and photo services.
4. I am indebted to Jackie Crosby Legge for providing material for this chapter.

Exercise 16–1　Newscast Content

Analyze tonight's broadcast of CBS Evening News (or another TV newscast your instructor designates). Write below, in about 200 words, your feelings about the news show's professionalism, whether the stories selected for broadcast were appropriate and the effectiveness of the newscast in communicating the day's important news. Address such points as number of stories covered, time devoted to each and whether you think the depth and detail of treatment were adequate. Discuss, also, whether you feel CBS writers and producers achieved the correct "mix" of words with sound and pictures. Were video and text properly balanced or was the newscast weighted toward entertaining, if not particularly informative, use of video?

Exercise 16–2   Writing for Broadcast—I

Write a broadcast version of each story on the front page of today's New York Times *(or another newspaper your instructor designates). Use no more than 150 words for the day's top news story, about 80-90 maximum for others on the front page. Be certain to write in broadcast style, complete with "throw away" lines for openers. Read your copy aloud and edit down or rewrite to shorten any sentences that are too long for comfortable reading. Include pronouncers for any names that might give an anchor difficulty on the air.*

This exercise will test your ability to capture the essential details of a story in the limited wordage available in broadcast newswriting.

Exercise 16–3 Writing for Broadcast—II

Write the following story in broadcast style for an Atlanta radio station. Limit yourself to 90 words.

Even without a record-breaking summer heat wave, average temperatures for the first eight months of 1990 were the warmest ever recorded, the National Weather Service reported Thursday.

The agency's Climate Analysis Center said the temperature for six states regarded as the Southeast by meteorologists averaged 66.5 degrees through the end of August—two degrees above normal.

Although the higher temperatures were most pronounced in the Southeast, the country as a whole shared in the warmer weather. Average temperatures across the nation have been about one degree above normal during the first two-thirds of the year.

But not since the agency started maintaining records in 1895 has the Southeast been so warm, said David Miskus, editor of the Climate Bulletin.

Exercise 16–4 Writing for Broadcast—III

Write the following for a Boston radio station on September 21. Write a story that can be read in no more than 30 seconds.

BOSTON—Roger Clemens, side-lined since Sept. 4 by severe tendinitis in his right shoulder, was given a medical OK Thursday to rejoin the Boston Red Sox.

Dr. Arthur Pappas, the team physician and an orthopedic specialist, told the Red Sox "he's ready to pitch."

Clemens, who has missed three scheduled starts, was given clearance to return to action after being examined by Pappas at the University of Massachusetts Medical Center in Worcester.

The Red Sox said Clemens will rejoin the team in New York today and pitch against the Yankees Sunday.

_____

_____

_____

_____

_____

_____

_____

_____

_____

_____

_____

_____

_____

_____

_____

_____

_____

_____

_____

_____

_____

_____

_____

Part 7
Writing for Public Relations

It can be argued that public relations writing—a form of *persuasive* communication—isn't a legitimate topic for a book dedicated to *news*writing. After all, PR writers often must pursue goals that differ dramatically from the newswriter's goals we've studied in this book.

In PR, the goal is not always objective reporting, balanced writing, or dispassionate revelation of facts. Rather, the goal is to shift the audience's thinking into directions beneficial to a cause, to cajole, to *sell* an idea, principle, product, service, institution or personality. In happiest of circumstances, PR writers labor for "good" causes in which they believe (the Red Cross, a leading corporation and so forth). Sometimes, however, PR writers use their skills in less constructive ways (explaining, for example, why cigarettes still have a place in our society).

Why, then, even discuss persuasive writing if at times its values are so inconsistent with those of principled newswriting? Three reasons:

First, fascinating, rewarding—and thoroughly legitimate—careers are available for writers as advocates of causes. Drop the "newswriter" label and openly assume the role of "advocate," and you can have a principled career in the commercial marketplace of ideas, which includes public relations and its sister craft, advertising.

Second, many PR practitioners are trying to raise the standards of their industry above methods that in the past sometimes gave the term "PR" a connotation less than ethical. Many practitioners today say, for example, that effective PR writing, like the best newswriting, is factual. That is, although a PR writer's ultimate mission is to serve the best interests of employer or client (not necessarily the public), it *is* possible to find PR jobs with companies whose policies are to be honest with the public and the media—to tell the truth about oil spills, not attempt to cover them up; to compete for public favor by being straightforward, not by being devious.

Third, the *technical* characteristics of good PR writing are remarkably similar to those of good newswriting. This book's examples of effective language use, writing strong and direct sentences, structuring stories carefully—all are applicable to PR writing.

Thus, we turn in Chapter 17 to PR writing for those of you attracted to legitimate advocacy writing in the commercial marketplace. We'll concentrate on how to direct your writing skills into forms appropriate for public relations and how to make your writing attractive to the media through which you must reach your ultimate constituency, the public.

Chapter Seventeen

The Public Relations Industry

Thousands of people are employed throughout the United States in public relations activities. For college graduates seeking to join them, the ability to write well is the admission ticket. And, of the many skills required for long-range success in PR careers, strength in writing is the most important.[1]

THE ROLE THAT WRITING PLAYS IN PUBLIC RELATIONS

Public Affairs

This involves working in government or politics, for example, as a press secretary or information specialist. Duties include researching and analyzing opinion among reporters and editors and assessing the public mood, then helping formulate and carry out PR policies in a campaign designed to influence both the media and public. The PR practitioner then helps analyze the campaign's impact and adjust future relations with the media and public to achieve desired results. It's a never-ending, circular process of researching, recommending policies, executing PR programs, monitoring results and, again, recommending policy adjustments. In every step, clear, direct writing that communicates effectively is crucial. In public affairs PR you can expect to draft speeches, write newsletters, formulate news releases for print and broadcast media, write and produce videoscripts and, even, draft correspondence for your employer.

Public Affairs PR Involves Policy Formulation

Corporate Public Relations

In this PR sector you have two major responsibilities: Helping represent your company to the external media and public and, second, conducting internal communication programs for employees. Externally, your primary constituencies can be the local community, investors, Wall Street analysts, plus print and broadcast media through which your message often is distributed. Your basic mission is "image building" to assist the corporation in its principal goal of making a profit. Among tasks are arranging news conferences, responding to reporters' queries, writing news releases and setting up "photo opportunities." Additionally, as a practitioner you write annual reports, magazines, newsletters and other material for the public and shareholders in the company. Internally, you use company magazines, newsletters and

Working with Internal and External Constituencies

other forms of written and video communication to transmit top management's thinking and directives to employees.[2]

Association and Institutional Public Relations

Trade Associations Need Writers

Trade associations, labor unions, social and religious groups, colleges and universities—all employ writers to help get their message across to their public, donors and investors. A citrus growers' association, for example, uses many forms of written and video communication to help sell citrus products to the general public. The association's own members are kept in touch with association affairs through internal newsletters and correspondence.

Publicity

Publicity Seeks Free Access to Media

Broadly, this involves positioning a product, service, cause, idea or personality as *newsworthy* enough to gain free access to the media, contrasted with access through paid advertising. In corporate PR, this can include writing news releases on, say, a new airplane or auto. In institutional PR, you might arrange news conferences for a university's football stars, or write news releases covering research on campus that the media will consider legitimate news. Publicity also covers acting as PR agent for film stars or singers. Shady practices employed by some Hollywood publicists in the past are responsible in great measure for the negative connotation "PR" carries among many editors and reporters.

THE MESSAGE, MEDIA AND YOU

Structuring your PR writing approach to achieve desired results differs considerably from laying down a strategy to inform and enlighten through reporting and writing a news story. In public relations, eight factors are essential to consider before you start writing.

Refine the Desired Message

The message. What viewpoints must your writing communicate? What ideas, principles or facts does your employer want transmitted?

Select Your Precise Objective

The objective. What end result is desired? Simply *informing* the reader, viewer or listener isn't enough in public relations. Do you want to change people's minds? Influence them to take action? What action? To buy your firm's product? Approve your firm's action? Donate money?

Decide Exactly Which Audience to Target

The audience. Ultimately, you must reach the general public or a tightly focused segment of it. For example, is your PR effort designed to sway widespread public support for, say, timber company operations? Or to focus narrowly on countering objections from a small group of environmentalists actively opposing timber cutting?

Select Medium Best Suited to Reach Audience

The medium. Which medium best reaches your targeted audience? For example, TV reaches huge audiences. Newspapers and magazines reach smaller audiences, but readers generally are better educated and have higher incomes than TV viewers. It's essential in PR writing to understand the strengths and weaknesses of all media, including direct mail, newsletters, and other forms of written, visual and aural communication.

Writing Should Focus on Key Ideas

Key ideas or *"the angle."* You must decide which key ideas will communicate the desired message. For example, can you create a climate of public acceptance for timbering by writing about the size of company payrolls and their value to the local economy? If so, your key ideas should include a great deal of such statistical material—and print is your best medium. It's easier for your audience to absorb facts and figures through reading. However, your key idea might be that timber companies plant trees to replace those cut down. Television coverage of tree planting or wildlife flourishing in areas that have been cut probably will best transmit that mes-

Issues and Challenges

Early in their careers, PR newswriters must resolve a fundamental question: Where does their allegiance lie—with employer or public—as they generate, shape, and handle information that ultimately appears in news media.

Under the best circumstances, PR writers don't face conflict between their employers' interests and the public's. Enlightened companies, after all, follow PR policies of openness, truth and *service to the public.*

As candid PR practitioners acknowledge, however, some companies place service to the public well behind service to the corporation, and they use PR skills to dodge the truth—or lie outright. In government PR, numerous examples abound of practitioners manipulating the media with unethical methods.

All this is of more than passing interest to our society. The public relations industry is huge and powerful. By some estimates, more than 100,000 people are engaged in PR nationwide, handling 40 percent or more of the information that eventually appears in the news media.[3]

In an attempt to give PR practitioners ethical guidelines and engender a spirit of professionalism, the Public Relations Society of America (PRSA) formulated a "Code of Professional Standards for The Practice of Public Relations." Excerpts from the code illustrate the PRSA stand on the employer vs. public question:

> Members of the Public Relations Society of America base their professional principles on the fundamental value and dignity of the individual, holding that the free exercise of human rights, especially freedom of speech, freedom of assembly and freedom of the press, is essential to the practice of public relations.
>
> In serving the interests of clients and employers, we dedicate ourselves to the goals of better communication, understanding and cooperation among the diverse individuals, groups and institutions of society, and of equal opportunity of employment in the public relations profession.
>
> We pledge:
>
> To conduct ourselves professionally, with truth, accuracy, fairness and responsibility to the public. . . .

Articles of the Code (in part)

> These articles have been adopted by the Public Relations Society of America to promote and maintain high standards of public service and ethical conduct among its members.
>
> 1. A member shall deal fairly with clients or employers, past and present, or potential, with fellow practitioners and the general public.
>
> 2. A member shall conduct his or her professional life in accord with the public interest.
>
> 3. A member shall adhere to truth and accuracy and to generally accepted standards of good taste. . . .
>
> * * *
>
> 6. A member shall not engage in any practice which tends to corrupt the integrity of channels of communication or the processes of government.
>
> 7. A member shall not intentionally communicate false or misleading information and is obliged to use care to avoid communication of false or misleading information.
>
> 8. A member shall be prepared to identify publicly the name of the client or employer on whose behalf any public communication is made.
>
> 9. A member shall not make use of any individual or organization purporting to serve or represent an announced cause, or purporting to be independent or unbiased, but actually serving an undisclosed special or private interest of a member, client, or employer.

sage. The most important key idea gives you the "angle" for your writing—the element you will highlight. It's the PR version of the news "peg."

The tool. You have communication tools other than *news releases* for print media and *video tapes* for TV. *Backgrounders* (fact-filled memos) can be written to provide reporters with details they weave into their own stories. *Publishable articles* or *editorials* can be written for newspapers and magazines. Print media with small staffs, particularly weekly newspapers, often use such articles as written. *Direct mail* bypasses the media and goes directly to the public. So do *fliers*. *Paid advertisements* use the media to reach the public. If you represent the right "cause," you can write *public service announcements*. Broadcast stations often use them free of charge ("Contribute to the Red Cross . . . it's a good cause . . .").

Format. Public relations writing must be structured precisely to meet the format and style specifications of the media you've targeted. A news release that violates *Associated Press Stylebook* guidelines probably will end up in a newspaper's wastepaper basket. More broadly, you must know how the target medium defines news and its standards for writing and presenting it. You must approach the challenge of getting into print or onto the air just as a staff writer would—by writing to standards established by editors. They decide what gets into print or on the air—and for that reason are called "gatekeepers."

Tone. In general, your writing and its tone must lead editors to recognize you have legitimate news that will interest their readers, viewers or listeners. Newspapers receive thousands of news releases. Public relations practitioners constantly are pressing for what editors regard as "free" space or air time. Generations of editors grow up regarding PR as less than savory and practitioners as people to be avoided. So your writing tone should strive to establish a relationship of mutual benefit: Editors get valuable information for their audiences, you and your employer get access to those audiences.

GENERAL WRITING GUIDELINES

Whatever form of PR writing you do, the following guidelines will help you communicate effectively:

Use your news instincts. Insofar as possible, bring to PR writing the same instincts and techniques you use in newswriting. Write to stress what is new in the development you are reporting, what is different and unusual. Write in timely fashion for media that regard *now* as news, yesterday as history. Look for a local angle that will appeal to local newspapers, magazines or broadcast editors. Structuring a release to emphasize a local personality or local development increases enormously your chance of attracting a gatekeeper's attention.

Be accurate and credible. If you issue inaccurate releases or, worse, try to lie, stonewall or evade the truth in your writing you will (1) ensure that your releases land on newsroom "kill" hooks and (2) build for yourself a *lasting* reputation as a PR writer who cannot be trusted. Reconcile yourself to the reality that many reporters and editors mistrust PR writers anyway; give them actual reason to mistrust you and you might as well seek another line of work.

Translate. To communicate your PR message your writing must break down complex issues and technical jargon into language that readers, viewers and listeners can understand. Some PR writers forget that responsibility because they, unlike reporters, spend their days concentrating on a single subject, a single corporation, a single university—and begin to use jargon. For example, educators understand what is meant by the so-called gap year in high school graduation rates. But the writer of the University of Georgia release reproduced as Figure 17.1 on p. 437 translated that into terms that editors—and their readers—can understand easily.

Check and double-check. Once a news release goes into a reporter's hands or into the postal system en route to a newspaper you lose control over how it is used.

Many PR Tools Are Available

Write in Target Media's Style, Format

Emphasize Legitimate News in Your Writing

Use Newswriter Instincts in PR Writing

Build a Reputation of Trust

Jargon—a Special Danger

FIGURE 17-1

Week of Sept. 24, 1990
Writer: Tom Jackson, 404/542-3354
Contact: Dwight Douglas, 404/542-8223

UGA ANTICIPATES ANOTHER RECORD ENROLLMENT

Record Enrollment Expected As UGA Begins Fall Quarter

ATHENS, Ga. — The University of Georgia opened the 1990-91 academic year this month expecting more than 28,000 students to enroll, the seventh consecutive fall quarter to establish a record enrollment.

Preliminary figures from Dr. Dwight Douglas, vice president for student affairs, predict enrollment to exceed by 600 students the previous record 27,448 set last fall. Final enrollment figures will not be available until early October.

The increase comes primarily in the number of transfer students, up more than 300 from a year ago, and in the number of freshmen.

"In a time of severe budget constraints we have tried to keep enrollment relatively constant in recent years, but a number of factors have continued the upward pressure," Douglas said.

Freshmen entrance requirements have been tightened, which last year resulted in a freshman class of 3,106, somewhat smaller than the target size of 3,350. But Douglas estimates that this year the number of freshmen will be very near the target, for a complicated reason.

"This is the so-called 'gap' year in Georgia," Douglas explained. Twelve years ago, the state changed the birthdate for entrance to first grade from Jan. 1 to Sept. 1, resulting in a smaller than usual class graduating this year from Georgia's high schools.

"With the state's pool of high school graduates this year down a hefty 12 percent, our applications declined only 8 percent and we again received a strong pool of well-qualified students. The result is that we're going over a pretty deep pothole with hardly a bump," Douglas said.

Two years of tighter freshman entrance requirements also have increased the number of transfer applications, as students originally unable to gain admission to the university as freshmen establish successful records at other institutions, qualifying them for transfer to the Athens campus, he said.

A strong enrollment increase also is developing in the graduate school, which will add approximately 100 students.

Applications are expected to rebound for fall '91 as the "gap" in high school graduates passes.

"We are going to have to control enrollment to an even greater degree in the future," said university President Charles B. Knapp. "As more and more of the state's brightest students choose UGA, we could easily exceed 30,000 students in the near future, but with the current state budget situation we just cannot afford to do that. The university has not been able to keep pace in terms of capital facilities. We have some serious catching up to do there before we allow enrollment to grow further."

Knapp said the university admissions committee will consider options available to control enrollment, including increased admission standards for transfer students and further increases in freshman entrance requirements.

-30-

(Used with permission of UGA News Bureau)

And you can't recall it. Before letting go, check and double-check: Does it say precisely what you want to say? Is it clear and understandable? Does it answer all obvious questions a reporter might have? Importantly, does it say—or imply—anything you *don't* want said?

In sum, effective persuasive writing must raise in the minds of readers, viewers or listeners a need or concern or interest *that stirs determination to act.* Further, persuasive writing should outline, clearly and logically, *suggested courses of action.* For example, PR writing should not only explain what a charitable organization is but also create in the audience an interest in supporting it—by sending in a check; persuasive writing not only should inform the public about Corporation XYZ but also motivate the audience to support it economically or politically.

Above All, You Must Stir Action

That goal of changing minds and stirring action along predetermined lines is principally how persuasive writing in PR is distinguished from newswriting.

Writing Careers in Public Relations

Public Affairs

Public affairs PR writing isn't newswriting. Like all PR writing, it is aimed at communicating a special viewpoint and persuading an audience to act in a predetermined manner. However, many technical similarities exist between newswriting and public affairs PR writing—and it's an area of public relations where you may be able to get hands-on experience while still in school. So, let's examine public affairs PR writing as a PR sector offering career options.

College News Bureaus Offer Careers

One active dimension of public affairs PR is college and university information services. Most schools have a news bureau or public information office whose mission is to report on-campus developments and communicate to the public through the media. The overall PR thrust is to develop public support that, in turn, aids fund-raising efforts. That requires, obviously, careful selectivity in what information is volunteered to the media and public. Simply, many campus news bureaus volunteer lots of "good" news to the media and provide information on "bad" news only when asked.

With those conditions in mind, examine in Figure 17–2 on p. 439 a "menu" of stories offered to newspapers by the University of Georgia's Office of Public Information. News bureau writers, many of them jounalism student interns, report on a wide variety of topics—enrollments, campus meetings and seminars, sports and so forth. A package of stories is mailed weekly to daily and weekly newspapers throughout the state.

You'll note, of course, the "good" news emphasis in the University of Georgia news release—enrollments that are up, not down; athletes who star in the classroom, not those who flunk out. Nevertheless, much of the news bureau's writing is straightforward and provides excellent practice for students. Figure 17–1 on p. 437 is an example of straightforward writing in public affairs PR.

Best PR Writing Is Straightforward

Note the enrollment news release is straightforward treatment of the same Five W's and How essential to a news story. The PR "angle" is subtle: Enrollment is up, even though the state's pool of high school graduates is down. The message to readers is that things are perking along nicely at the University of Georgia—so nicely that they might consider sending their children to Athens (Georgia, that is) or forwarding a check to support expansion of Georgia's capstone state university. *The best PR writing is straightforward and devoid of hype.*

Note also the mechanical aspects of the news release: The writing conforms to AP style and thus is easy for editors to prepare for publication. Presenting the release in newspaper-like column widths aids editors in estimating space needed to publish the story. Effective PR writing removes all possible obstacles that might lead "gatekeeper" editors to discard the story. Names and telephone numbers of both the writer and a university contact are listed so reporters easily can reach sources in the university administration with follow-up questions. Also, the university's news bureau suggests a headline with the slug, "UGA Anticipates Another Record Enrollment." The release even concludes with "-30-," the traditional newsroom way of writing "the end." This release *looks* professional, which lends it credibility.

Eliminate Possible "Gatekeeper" Objections

Some PR releases are issued with an "embargo" stating they cannot be published or aired until some future time. An embargo might read, "For Release at 10 a.m., September 19" or "Advance for Publication on Thursday, March 17." If the release contains "hot" news, some editor somewhere likely will break the embargo and

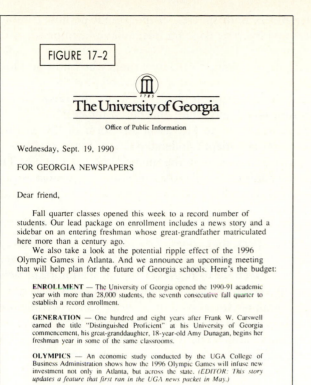

FIGURE 17-2

The University of Georgia

Office of Public Information

Wednesday, Sept. 19, 1990

FOR GEORGIA NEWSPAPERS

Dear friend,

Fall quarter classes opened this week to a record number of students. Our lead package on enrollment includes a news story and a sidebar on an entering freshman whose great-grandfather matriculated here more than a century ago.

We also take a look at the potential ripple effect of the 1996 Olympic Games in Atlanta. And we announce an upcoming meeting that will help plan for the future of Georgia schools. Here's the budget:

ENROLLMENT — The University of Georgia opened the 1990-91 academic year with more than 28,000 students, the seventh consecutive fall quarter to establish a record enrollment.

GENERATION — One hundred and eight years after Frank W. Carswell earned the title "Distinguished Proficient" at his University of Georgia commencement, his great-granddaughter, 18-year-old Amy Dunagan, begins her freshman year in some of the same classrooms.

OLYMPICS — An economic study conducted by the UGA College of Business Administration shows how the 1996 Olympic Games will infuse new investment not only in Atlanta, but across the state. *(EDITOR: This story updates a feature that first ran in the UGA news packet in May.)*

EDUCATION — The 21st Century Consortium for Educational Improvement in Georgia convenes a meeting Oct. 5-6 in Athens to seek recommendations for school improvement from educators, parents and business people.

"ISSUES IN EDUCATION" — Georgia schools must recognize cultural differences if they hope to reach all students, writes science education professor Mary Atwater. *"Issues" is a weekly editorial column written by faculty in the UGA College of Education.*

SPORTS — Alec Kessler, UGA's all-time leading basketball scorer and a first-round selection in the NBA draft, has been named the 1989-90 GTE Academic All-American of the Year in a vote of the 1,500-member College Sports Information Directors of America.

BRIEFS — A page of news briefs and filler items.

Thanks,

Tom Hallman
Manager, UGA News Bureau

Alumni House • Athens Georgia 30602 • (404) 542-3354
An Equal Opportunity/Affirmative Action Institution

(Used with permission
of UGA News Bureau)

print or broadcast the release. And when one editor breaks the embargo, others by tradition are free to use the release immediately. It's best to issue press releases "For Immediate Use" or, as in the example above, without any directive on use—which means the release is for immediate use. (One form of writing often issued under an embargo, however, is advance texts of speeches. They frequently are provided to reporters covering speeches to ease the problem of catching the speaker's exact words.)

Corporate PR

Corporate public relations offers attractive (and, often, highly paid) careers for students who can develop strong technical skills in writing *and* deep understanding of how business and corporations operate.

For those who develop strengths in both spheres, corporate PR permits combining a writing career with a personal interest. For example, aviation companies offer exciting careers for individuals who are both strong PR writers and airplane buffs; major automakers have huge PR departments staffed by writers who know and love automobiles; companies dealing in agriculture need writers who know the difference between a Holstein and a Hereford (the former is black and white and raised mainly for milk production; the Hereford is red and white and raised for beef).

In Corporate PR You Must Understand Business

Writing versatility is required in corporate PR, as in any form of PR writing. However, another basic requirement is in-depth understanding of business. Note in Figure 17–3 below how the writer of a release on the financial performance of The New York Times Co. had to understand precisely what information is most important to Wall Street investors and others who want to judge how well the company is doing.

As the release indicates, media companies offer PR careers for media "buffs"—people who understand how newspapers, magazines and radio and TV stations operate. Note also that the writer's "lead" is hardly a model of punchy, colorful writing. The lead, however, *is* crafted carefully to highlight the most important news elements in the company's announcement and handle facts and figures with precision. Obviously the precision techniques we studied in Chapter 12 for writing economic, business and financial news are applicable to corporate PR writing.

A major in journalism or public relations and a strong minor in business would be excellent college preparation for work in this sector of public relations.

FIGURE 17–3

News About The New York Times Company

229 West 43d Street, New York, NY 10036

For release: Immediately
For further information: Nancy Nielsen (212) 556-7078

NEW YORK TIMES COMPANY ASSESSES
1989 EARNINGS AND 1990 OUTLOOK

New York, Jan. 18 -- The New York Times Company said today it expects record earnings per share in a range of $3.35 to $3.40 for 1989. This includes a gain of $2.46 per share from the sale of its cable television system. This gain plus $.06 per share earned from cable operations prior to the sale date will be reported as discontinued operations in the Company's 1989 results. Reported earnings from continuing operations for 1989 are expected to be in the range of $.83 to $.88 per share.

    In 1988 the Company reported earnings from continuing operations of $2.00 per share. The decline in 1989 earnings from continuing operations was primarily attributable to a weakness in the New York region's economy, which affected advertising linage at The New York Times, and to the following three previously announced factors:

    - a charge of $.57 per share for a valuation reserve against the Company's investment in its Forest Products Group and for costs primarily associated with voluntary union staff reductions at The New York Times,

(Used with permission of *The New York Times*)

Summary Checklist

☐ Writing skills are crucial in every sector of public relations work—in public affairs, corporate public relations, association and institutional PR, and publicity.

☐ Public affairs PR involves working in government or politics, for example, as a press secretary or information specialist.

☐ Corporate PR has two responsibilities: representing your company to the external media and public and, secondly, conducting internal communication programs for employees.

☐ Association and institutional PR involves working for trade associations, labor unions, social and religious groups, colleges.

☐ Publicity broadly involves positioning a product, service, cause, idea or personality as newsworthy enough to gain free access to the media (as contrasted with access through paid advertising).

☐ PR writing requires considering the *message* or viewpoint you need to communicate; an *objective* such as influencing the thinking of your audience; the *medium* best suited to reach your *targeted audience;* a *key idea* or "angle" your writing should use.

☐ Other factors to consider in PR writing: which *tool* to use (news release, backgrounder, direct mail and so forth); how to *format* what you write so it meets editors' standards; how to achieve a *writing tone* that signals, "This is legitimate news."

☐ The best PR writing meets the Five W's and How goals of good newswriting and is straightforward and devoid of hype.

☐ Use your *news* instincts in PR writing. Look for a local angle that will interest editors. Always be accurate and credible. Be sure to translate jargon into language editors and readers can understand. And, always, check and double-check your writing for inaccuracies before giving it to editors.

RECOMMENDED READING

Two excellent surveys of public relations are: Scott M. Cutlip, Allen G. Center and Glen W. Broom, *Effective Public Relations,* 6th ed. (Englewood Cliffs, N.J.: Prentice-Hall, 1985), and Dennis L. Wilcox, Phillip H. Ault, and Warren K. Agee, *Public Relations: Strategies and Tactics* (New York: Harper & Row, 1986).

A survey of the industry and an inside look at Burson-Marsteller, one of the world's largest PR agencies, is in Conrad Fink, *Inside the Media* (White Plains, N.Y.: Longman, 1990).

Excellent PR writing hints are in Thomas Bivins, *Handbook for Public Relations Writing* (Lincolnwood, Ill.: NTC Business Books, 1989), and Kerry Tucker and Doris Derelian, *Public Relations Writing* (Englewood Cliffs, N.J.: Prentice-Hall, 1989).

Current developments in public relations are covered by *PR News, Communication World* (published by the International Association of Business Communicators), *Public Relations Journal* and *pr reporter.*

NOTES

1. Public relations professionals repeatedly list "ability to write" as the No. 1 trait required for success in the field. See Scott M. Cutlip, Allen G. Center and Glen W. Broom, *Effective Public Relations,* 6th ed. (Englewood Cliffs, N.J.: Prentice-Hall, 1985), p. 73.

2. A first-rate training program for entry-level employees in corporate PR, at Caterpillar Inc., is described by C.A. Williams, the company's manager of college relations and recruitment, in Conrad Fink, *Inside the Media* (White Plains, N.Y.: Longman, 1990), p. 324.

3. Cutlip, Center and Broom, *Effective Public Relations,* op. cit., p. 429. The estimate of 100,000 is from Allen H. Center and Frank H. Walsh, *Public Relations Practices,* 3rd ed. (Englewood Cliffs, N.J.: Prentice-Hall, 1985), p. 7.

Exercise 17–1   Writing Releases—I

Interview officers of the campus chapter of the Society for Professional Journalists (or another organization your instructor designates) and write a news release advocating student membership in the group. Use persuasive writing skills to put forward the group's strengths and what it offers students who join. Find a news angle likely to attract editors and *write, insofar as possible, in a straightforward, balanced manner. A news peg might be a current membership drive by the group or a forthcoming program or featured speaker. Write this release in about 300 words, following directives in Chapter 17 on format. Write in AP style.*

Name **Course** **Date**

Exercise 17–2 Writing Releases—II

Interview the dean or director of your school or department and write a news release on current student enrollment. Write from an advocate's viewpoint, as you would if employed by your college's news bureau or information office. If enrollment is up, emphasize that. If it's down, find a way to write that in the best possible light. Write in AP style and in accordance with standard press release format. Write this release in about 300 words.

444

Exercise 17–3   Writing Releases—III

From the facts below, write a news release for issuance by the University of Georgia Office of Public Information. Seek a standard news peg for your "lead" and structure the story, in AP style and tone, for publication by newspapers in Georgia. Write about 200 words.

This is a fact sheet from the university's research office. It's from Dr. Michael Moriarty. He's associate vice president for research. This refers to funding for research for the university from both private and federal sources. It actually reached a record level in 1990 of $57.4 million. That's according to the research office. Moriarty said, "This increase in awards is significant because it comes at a time of heightened competition for research funding, particularly at the federal level." The total was above the 1989 total—up 8.1 percent from $53.1 million in 1989. External grants and contracts support research in all academic disciplines at the university. Those range from environmental science to the humanities. These external grants come largely from federal agencies. The 1990 total doesn't include state contracts and grants for research at the university. Those total an additional $85.7 million. So, if you put it all together, including federal and state sources, the total of research contracts and grants for 1990 was more than $143 million. That's up from the 1989 total of $131 million. More than $11 million in research contracts came from two federal contributors. They were the U.S. Department of Energy and the National Institutes of Health. They were the top federal contributors.

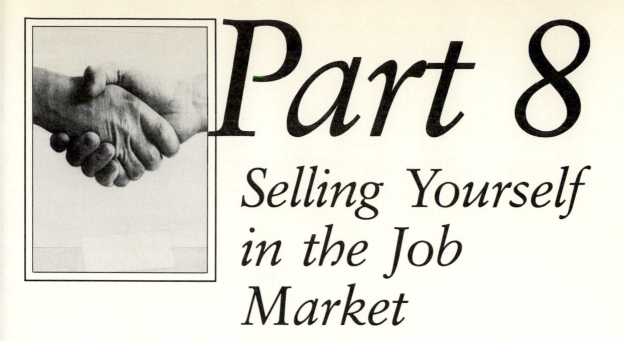

Part 8

Selling Yourself in the Job Market

Get used to the idea: If you want to develop career opportunities in journalism, selling yourself is a big part of what's ahead. Not many editors got up this morning in New York, Chicago, Los Angeles or elsewhere wondering how they can help advance your career. *You* must do that.

To position yourself for career opportunities think deeply about your strengths and weaknesses. You can identify weaknesses with the help of your instructors in this and other courses you take. Then, attack those weaknesses methodically and aggressively. Even the finest of the professionals whose work we studied in this text must engage, throughout their careers, in constant self-examination to identify and correct weaknesses in their reporting and writing.

Of course, if you're a typical student your primary weakness is, simply, lack of experience. The first step toward remedying that is to capture in a résumé whatever strengths you possess and thus sketch a self-portrait that will convince an editor to *invest* in you by helping you gain the experience you need.

Chapter Eighteen

Writing Your Résumé and Making Job Contacts

Your résumé is an important document. Write it with care to reflect your potential, then update it with any relevant course work or hands-on experience that makes you more attractive to editors who can help you stride toward professionalism.

Look at the sample résumé on p. 450 of Robin L. Smith (it's fictitious, of course) and note the categories of information.

PARTS OF THE RÉSUMÉ

Employment Objective

State specifically what you're after—internship, part-time job or whatever. Editors despair if you wander in, vaguely murmuring, "Who am I? . . . What do I want to be?" If *you* don't know, how can *they*? Stating goals precisely doesn't lock you in. You can change your mind—tomorrow, even. Note in the example the sense of enthusiasm in Robin Smith's desire for "exposure to as many dimensions of reporting and newswriting as possible." That shows excitement about learning and willingness to experience all a newsroom has to offer. Editors like that.

State Your Objective Clearly

Career Objective

Here, too, your résumé should show a career pattern at least beginning to develop in your mind. It can be tentative and can be changed as your experience widens. But it gives professionals a general direction to take in discussions with you. In this section of your résumé let your dreams run! If you want eventually to be executive editor of a major metropolitan paper, or a Washington correspondent, say so. Think positively about yourself! If you don't, no one will.

Think Big in Your Résumé

Work Experience

As a beginner, you might not have strong professional credentials for this category. But you probably have more strengths—and appeal—than you think. *Any* reporting, editing or writing experience should be emphasized, of course. And being able to list something like general-assignment reporting, as in the example, is ex-

Robin L. Smith

Home Address
102 Norest Lane
Chicago, Ill. 60616
(312) 666-3333

Campus Address
406 Terrell Hall
University of Michigan
Ann Arbor, Mich. 48106
(313) 676-8989

Employment Objective

Newsroom summer internship, preferably in general-assignment reporting, with exposure to as many dimensions of reporting and newswriting as possible.

Career Objective

National affairs reporting, preferably in Washington.

Work Experience

General-assignment reporting, *Campus Daily,* an independent, student-run daily of 6,000 free circulation for the student body and faculty, 1991–present.

Sports editor, *Argus,* campus quarterly magazine of 3,000 free circulation published by Department of Communication, 1991.

Cashier, two summers, McDonald's, Evanston, Ill., 1989 and 1990.

Playground supervisor, Centre Free School, Evanston, Ill., summer, 1988.

Education

Sophomore and will declare a journalism major next year. Expect to receive an A.B.J., University of Michigan, Department of Communication. Have taken three journalism courses: Introduction to Mass Communication, Introduction to Professional Newswriting, Editing and Layout.

Minor is in political science. Have taken Introduction to American Politics and Political Practices and Procedures.

Scholarships and Awards

Michigan Press Association $1,000 scholarship for Outstanding High School Journalist. Dean's List, two years, U of M.

Organization

Society of Professional Journalists, Media Management Club, Campus Camera Club.

Other

Reported, edited copy and took photos for high school paper, Evanston High School, Evanston, Ill.

Read and speak conversational Spanish.
Backpacked for six weeks in Nepal, senior year in high school, and am an experienced hill climber.

Hobby: Reading 19th-century British novelists.

References

John Jones
General Manager
Campus Daily
116 S. Neefer St.
Ann Arbor, Mich. 48106
(313) 764-3324

Alicia Withers
Professor/*Argus* Adviser
Department of Communication
University of Michigan
Ann Arbor, Mich. 48106

Wilson Wilsen
Manager
McDonald's
908 Hinman Ave.
Evanston, Ill. 60091
(312) 675-9834

Consider All Your Job Experience

tremely important. But note two other entries: Having worked as a cashier means (1) Robin Smith was smart enough to handle money and (2) somebody trusted her to do so. That's important for prospective employers to know. Serving as a playground supervisor means somebody entrusted Smith with scheduling programs and overseeing the work of others—again, important to people trying to judge her potential. Be certain to update this section of your résumé any time you add significant work experience. And, like people who sell apples, put your best items on top. List experience in order of importance, not chronologically. Be certain also to explain fully what your work experience involved. A distant editor won't know what the *Campus Daily* is. Explaining it is an independent, student-run daily of 6,000 free circulation, and that Smith is a general-assignment reporter, fills in the blanks.

Education
List every course taken that supports your contention that you're ready for an internship or job. Even after only a year or so in journalism school you will have some newswriting credentials. Your minor should be listed. It, too, can show serious preparation for a news career.

Scholarships and Awards

How to Handle Grade Point Average

The question often arises: Should I list my grade point average? If it's a perfect 4.0, or 3.5, yes. If 2.5 . . . well, perhaps not. Incidentally, if you've worked to support yourself in school make sure that's mentioned prominently in "Work Experience." It can explain why you don't have a 4.0.

Organizations
Extracurricular activity can show commitment to journalism, as in this example. Join professional organizations early in your school career. Such activities can add extra dimensions to your overall experience. Don't join simply to build "résumé material."

Other

Here is the place to reveal other qualities of the real you. List attributes, interests, hobbies that show your uniqueness. Being a hill climber and a fan of 19th century British novelists sets Smith apart as an interesting individual.

CONTACTING PROFESSIONALS

Opening a dialogue with professionals is an important way to augment your classroom learning. If you find it difficult to push yourself forward to meet them (and many students do), remember that you'll have to push—and push hard—to get news stories as a reporter. Now is the time to learn how to push. Besides, many professionals welcome contacts from students, and you'll find talking with them can be great fun.

Many professionals are within easy reach. They visit campus to lecture, meet with student clubs or interview prospective employees. To learn of visits, stay in touch with professors who regularly invite professionals into their classrooms, watch bulletin boards; contact your school's placement office—build the "awareness factor" that marks all good reporters. Become aware of who has information you need and learn how to tap into it.

It's best to write or telephone in advance to arrange meetings with professionals who will visit campus. Offer to meet for breakfast, before their day's schedule begins or during any free moments they have. Leave your résumé for them at the registration desk of their hotel.

If All Else Fails, "Ambush" Them

If you learn belatedly that a professional is on campus, make contact through the "ambush interview" technique: Walk up, stick out your hand and say hello. You'll get high marks for aggressive enterprise, for having a little of the "brass" that all good reporters must have.

Fashioning an opening conversational gambit is extremely important. What you say will reveal how professional you are and, simply, how interesting you are as a person. Show you are aware of what's happening in the newspaper industry and that you know something about the professionals you're approaching and their newspapers. Giving background information about yourself is easy. (Note in the sidebar on p. 453 one editor's views of what makes beginners attractive.)

THE FOLLOW-UP

Your first goal in contacting professionals and volunteering to cover stories should be to gain hands-on experience through internships or part-time jobs. But with proper follow-up you can create even greater advantage for yourself.

There's a tradition of *mentoring* in the newspaper business—of older professionals "adopting" beginners by critiquing their work and suggesting career moves. Don't be shy about trying to hook onto a mentor. Mentoring also benefits professionals. They get a close look at talent they might want to hire one day, and most newspapers encourage them to spend time developing campus contacts. Besides, many professionals have great fun working with young people.

Hints on developing a relationship:

Get Your Résumé in Their Hands

1. Follow-up even the briefest meeting with a quick letter expressing appreciation for the time you had to talk. Enclose your résumé if you didn't hand it over earlier. Start the process of identifying yourself in the minds of professionals as an alert individual, someone who deeply desires a news career.

A Professional's View:
You, IQ and Energy

What do hiring editors look for when interviewing prospective newswriters for their staffs? John Costa, who has recruited many young staffers for the St. Petersburg (Fla.) Times, *provides a few clues.*

To me, nothing replaces IQ points and energy, followed quickly by breadth of curiosity and an open mind. Whether I'm interviewing a college junior or a very experienced reporter I apply this test: Would I, as a news maker, be comfortable telling my story to this person?

Is this person interested in me? Will he or she treat me fairly, or convert my story narrowly to his or her own ambition? Does the reporter understand what I'm talking about specifically, and in the context of the greater world around us?

I don't know that there is anything a college can do about IQ points and energy, except to make it apparent that journalism is a very competitive world and without these attributes you are not going far.

What I see missing most often is a sense of perspective; a feeling for how the world really works; some real-life scales with which to measure what they've got.

An aspiring journalist can use a university to get a sense of the world. Sample a broad, broad range of material. Languages, economics, politics, history, science are all excellent. When you hit a paper, you are going to have to know what interest groups are all about in our country, what a bank does, how to sift—probably shovel—the hyperbole out of a politician's thoughts.

Critical things to do?

- Read and write until you fall over.
- Get internships. There is no quicker way to understand a paper than to get inside one.
- Develop reporting skills. I know it is fashionable for editors to say good writers always advance. That's true as far as it goes, but you are not going to be a really good writer without really good reporting skills. Getting crucial information, with wonderful detail, and getting it right, remains the standard of professionalism.

John Costa, assistant managing editor/metropolitan, St. Petersburg (Fla.) Times

2. Ask to visit the newspaper. Never pass up a chance to tour a newsroom. Next time you're driving home for a weekend or taking a vacation, pull out a map and plot newspapers you could visit along the way. Write ahead for appointments (*Editor & Publisher International Yearbook* provides names and addresses).

3. Once you begin a relationship with a professional, ask for help with planning your academic program or career. Write, for example, that you plan to be a national affairs reporter (or whatever) and would like an opinion on which courses would best prepare you. Keep the professional advised of new courses you take. When you start publishing, send clips of stories and ask for suggestions on how your writing could be improved.

Develop Industry Awareness

4. You can develop general knowledge of the industry by reading *Editor & Publisher* magazine, *presstime*, the American Society of Newspaper Editor's *Bulletin*, *Advertising Age*, *Quill* and other periodicals available in most libraries. Media coverage in *The New York Times*, *Wall Street Journal* and *Los Angeles Times* is excellent.

5. To background yourself on a professional's newspaper, check *Editor & Publisher International Yearbook*. It lists city and county of publication, populations of both, circulation, news services taken, names of executives and editors and other valuable information. *Circulation* shows where the newspaper circulates, who its competitors are, and describes the market it attempts to dominate. Of course, the best preparation for contacting professionals is to study their newspapers. Note types of stories published, reporting and writing styles, special sections, the bylines of star reporters—all things professionals talk about among themselves.

LEARN TO HANDLE A JOB INTERVIEW

Take Every Possible Interview

Never pass up any opportunity for a formal interview with visiting professionals. Even if only graduating seniors are being interviewed and you're not close to graduation, *get on the interview list*. If necessary, write the professionals well before they arrive on campus and ask to be squeezed in. Explain that you want to introduce yourself, learn something about their newspaper and open a dialogue. Such initiative—call it "gentle pushiness"—is central to success in journalism and editors are looking for people who display it.

Learning to handle yourself in a job interview—to *sell yourself*—takes practice. Start interviewing early in your school career so you'll be proficient when it really counts, just before graduation. A few hints:

Develop an Interview Strategy

First, an interview is much more than an opportunity to answer yes or no. It's a chance to make a statement about yourself. Thus, go into the interview with a *strategy*. Plan to get on the table four or five things that mark you as a person with potential: your deep interest in news, commitment to journalism, willingness to work hard or whatever. Weave those thoughts into the conversation, but if that's not possible you can say, "Before leaving there are a couple of things I want to say about myself. . . ."

Second, *turn the interview around*. Take the initiative by asking questions about the interviewers' newspapers, competitors, news strategy or, even, their own careers. Demonstrate you know what information is important and that you can formulate questions to obtain it. Use interviewing techniques discussed in Chapter 8. Take notes. *Display your reporting skills*.

Third, don't be flustered by off-the-wall questions like, "Do you have a sense of humor?" or "Tell me about your worst weakness." Some interviewers ask such questions to determine how well you handle the unexpected. *Every* question can be turned to your advantage: "It helps to have a sense of humor when you work the long, hard hours we work . . . but I'm very serious about news . . . let me ask your opinion of my career plan . . ." or, "My greatest weakness is lack of professional experience, and that's why I'm here—you can help me remedy that weakness. . . ."

Fourth, substance will sell you, not glib answers or a sense of humor. Discerning editors (the only kind to work for) want you to demonstrate strong academic performance in relevant courses and to have reporting and writing experience. Knight-Ridder Inc., publisher of many excellent newspapers, won't even interview job applicants who don't have experience.

But how do you get experience without having experience? Review Chapter 11—and write for publication.

INTERNSHIPS AND ENTRY-LEVEL JOBS

Strive for internships early in your school years. These involve working in a newsroom, mainly during the summer, and learning by doing. *They are an extremely valuable experience.* Normally, internships are offered students between their junior and senior years. If you've made the right contacts and progressed satisfactorily in campus journalism, you possibly can take one earlier and have two or even three during your school years.

Internships Are Essential

Most schools offer several credits for paid internships, and college placement offices often coordinate arrangements with newspapers. In the early 1990s, many newspapers were paying $220 or so a week for students who could move smoothly into the newsroom as general-assignment or sports reporters.

Entry-level jobs in newspapers are highly competitive. But you're on the right track toward getting one if you major in journalism and get hands-on experience in campus writing.

Of all newsroom employees under age 25 in 1989, 79 percent were journalism graduates, according to an American Society of Newspaper Editors survey.[1] Of those age 26 to 35, 67 percent were journalism grads.

Graduates who work in campus journalism and take internships have better chances of landing full-time jobs in communications than do students who don't, an Ohio State study shows.[2]

Those who landed full-time jobs reported considerable job satisfaction. One-third said they were "very satisfied"; 45 percent were "moderately satisfied."

Job Satisfaction High in Newswriting

Median weekly salaries for beginners in 1988, according to the Ohio State study, were:

Daily newspapers	$310
Weekly newspapers	$275
TV	$325
Radio	$280
Public relations (agency)	$379
Public relations (department)	$346
Advertising	$315

Although low starting salaries are a problem in communications, more attractive salaries are appearing. Among 1988 grads, 23 percent reported earning more than $400 weekly; 8 percent more than $500.

Many newspapers are improving salaries steadily. *Starting weekly minimums* as of April 1, 1990, in selected papers are shown below. Check for one near you.

New York Times	$1,072.30
Washington Post	$ 640.75
Chicago Sun-Times	$ 592.96
Boston Herald	$ 546.17
St. Louis Post-Dispatch	$ 525.00
Philadelphia Inquirer and Daily News	$ 514.72
Detroit Free Press	$ 479.14
Seattle Times	$ 475.25
Denver Rocky Mountain News	$ 463.00

Minneapolis Star Tribune	$ 434.00
Tacoma (Wash.) *News Tribune*	$ 405.60
Sacramento Bee	$ 400.18
Kenosha (Wis.) *News*	$ 396.00
Joliet (Ill.) *Herald-News*	$ 387.50
Pawtucket (R.I.) *Times*	$ 375.82
Stockton (Calif.) *Record*	$ 368.08
York (Pa.) *Dispatch*	$ 354.51
Bellevue (Wash.) *Journal-American*	$ 344.79
Peoria Journal Star	$ 324.00
Lexington (Ky.) *Herald-Leader*	$ 322.00

After you're on the job a few years, salaries generally improve quickly. The Newspaper Guild, an AFL-CIO affiliate, negotiates minimum salaries that reporters are paid after a break-in period of, usually, three or four years. As of April 1, 1990, these were representative weekly minimums: Akron, Ohio, $718; Albany, N.Y., $602.65; Boston, $697.25; Fresno, $654.77; Knoxville, $550.50; Minneapolis, $812; San Jose, $801.04; Yakima, $447.75. Associated Press weekly minimums ranged from $735 weekly to $785. United Press International's minimum was $670 nationwide, Reuters', $840.75.[3]

Note that minimums are just that. Most news organizations provide "merit" increases for staff members who perform well.

Obviously, better salaries are paid those who win promotion and assume greater responsibilities. The best salaries are paid on large papers. Examples below are from a 1989 survey by Inland Daily Press Association.[4]

1989 MEDIAN BASE PAY
(For three circulation categories)

	5,000–10,000	20,001–30,000	100,001–150,000
Publisher	$51,000	$80,000	$140,000
Editor	29,450	46,000	79,274
Managing editor	25,000	36,731	58,182
City editor	19,427	27,870	43,027
Copy desk chief	*	27,820	38,610
Sports editor	16,950	26,520	41,964
Business editor	*	25,480	39,780
Sr. reporter	*	23,894	33,228
Reporter (1–4 years)	15,018	18,356	26,416
Reporter (entry)	13,350	16,055	19,961
Copy editor	18,124	20,700	28,194

*Numbers not listed if fewer than 10 papers responded.

If you're really thinking big about your career, and you should be, very rewarding salaries are paid at large newspapers. The Inland survey found that publishers of papers over 500,000 circulation received median base pay of $290,000 annually. Their editors were at $178,500; sports editors, $83,000; senior reporters, $53,608; entry-level reporters, $27,641.

Naturally, there are factors to consider other than money. Newspaper work at times is difficult and stressful. Long hours with plenty of work at night and on weekends are ahead for beginning reporters. However, surveys of print news majors show they choose the field because of its contribution to society and credibility with the public, and because they like to write. In short, this is a business where young people expect to *make a difference* and be recognized for it.[5]

If you enjoyed reporting and writing in this course and you feel a desire to get involved in the world around you then you're on the right track!

NOTES

1. "The Changing Face of the Newsroom," American Society of Newspaper Editors, P.O. Box 17004, Washington, D.C. 20041.

2. Lee B. Becker and Thomas E. Engleman, "1988 Grads Like First Jobs; Median Salary Increases," *Journalism Educator,* Spring 1990, p. 22.

3. *Collective Bargaining Manual,* The Newspaper Guild, April 1, 1990.

4. Susan Miller, "1989 Pay Raises for Editors Slightly Lag Salary Hikes for Managers in Other Industries," *ASNE Bulletin,* November 1989, p. 16.

5. Becker and Engleman, "1988 Grads Like First Jobs," op. cit.

Exercise 18–1   Writing a Strong Résumé

Using pointers from Chapter 11, write your résumé. Be specific in "employment objective" and "career objective." Remember to list "work experience" in order of importance, not chronologically. Think deeply about attributes, interests and hobbies for the "other" category. Write tightly but use wordage necessary, going to two pages if that's required.

_____

_____

_____

_____

_____

_____

_____

_____

_____

_____

_____

_____

_____

_____

_____

_____

_____

_____

_____

_____

_____

Exercise 18–2   Selling Yourself

Using standard reference works, such as Editor & Publisher International Yearbook *and* Circulation, *research background on a newspaper your instructor will desginate. Study its city and county populations, circulation, market and the names and titles of key editors. Reflect deeply about your strengths and weaknesses as a beginning reporter and write below, in about 250 words, (1) How you would open contact with someone on that paper and (2) how you would describe yourself and your professional attributes in a conversation with that person. In sum, pick a key individual on that paper and describe how you would "sell" yourself. Your essay must be in AP style and free of errors.*

_____

_____

_____

_____

_____

_____

_____

_____

_____

_____

_____

_____

_____

_____

_____

_____

_____

_____

_____

_____

_____

_____

_____

_____

Appendix

*S*elected excerpts from *The Associated Press Stylebook and Libel Manual* are contained in this Appendix. Experience shows that the items set forth below are particularly troublesome to student newswriters and young professionals.

A

Abbreviate recognizable titles before names (Dr., Gov., 1st Lt.). Abbreviate after names of corporate entites: Smith Co.; Wilson Corp.; Frank Inc.; Burrows Ltd. It's A.D. 1992. The time is 6:50 *p.m.* (or *a.m.*) on *Nov.* 19. The address is 116 *S.* Stratford *St.* They live on Stratford *Street* (when address is not listed). Use Ave., Blvd., St., only with numbered addresses. All but Alaska, Hawaii, Idaho, Iowa, Maine, Texas and Utah are abbreviated when used with a city (St. Paul, Minn.).

Acronyms. Use those generally recognizable: FBI, CIA. As in all things journalistic, use judgment: AIDS in first reference, but later work in full name—acquired immune deficiency syndrome. Don't scatter abbreviations or acronyms throughout a story. Use "the bureau" sometimes for FBI, "the disease" for AIDS. A story with 29 acronyms for 13 different agencies quickly becomes incomprehensible.

Accept means to receive, **except** to exclude.

Accused. A person is accused *of* (not with) a crime. Beware *alleged.* Use only if in quote from official source (district attorney, arrest record). Police arrest *on a charge of* (not for committing a crime). A person or corporation is *indicted* on charges *only* in a legal process. Don't use the word otherwise in a legal story.

Admit connotes wrongdoing. He *admitted* breaking the law. But he *acknowledged* (or said) he hadn't run fast.

Affect, as a verb, means to influence: His skill will *affect* the outcome. **Effect,** as a verb, means to cause: His skill will effect change. As a noun, effect means result: The *effect* was victory.

Ages are expressed in figures: A 20-year-old student. The student, 20, has a sister, 5.

Assassins kill with political motivation; *killers* kill with motives of any kind; *murderers* are *only* those convicted on the specific charge of murder.

B

Bankruptcy applies legally only if a court tells an individual or organization to liquidate assets and distribute proceeds to creditors. Use *only* with careful research into precisely what type bankruptcy action is under way.

Bimonthly means every other month. Twice a month is **semimonthly.**

Boy is male under 18.

Brand names are used only if essential to your story, then are capitalized: The Buick Women's Open.

Broccoli is how it's spelled. George Bush doesn't like to eat it.

Burglary, larceny, robbery, and theft have precise legal definitions. Check burglary entry in Stylebook. Remember: A robber gets you on the street; a burglar enters your home.

C

Capital is a city, *capitol* is a building.

Capitalization. AP style is to capitalize as infrequently as possible. Capitalize *proper nouns* (Fred, America) and *common nouns* used as a name (Ford Motor Co.). In *proper names,* capitalize common nouns (Green River) but not when they stand alone (the river). In *plural uses,* don't capitalize common noun elements of names (Clarke and Jackson counties). Capitalize *formal titles* before names (Gov. Fred Smith) but not after names (Fred Smith, the governor). Don't capitalize *in*formal titles before names (dog catcher Smith).

Cents is used under one dollar (15 cents). Over one dollar, it is $1.06.

Chairman and **chairwoman** are capitalized as a formal title before person's name. *Chairperson* is used when it is a formal title.

City is capitalized in proper name (Kansas City) but not when it stands alone (the city).

City council is capitalized in proper name (Athens City Council) and in stand-alone, specific references (the City Council voted . . .).

Communist is capitalized only when referring to the Communist Party. He is a communist.

Compose means to put together: The market is composed of five counties. *Comprise* means to contain: The market comprises five counties.

Confess has specific legal meaning in a crime story. Check before using.

Consensus means general agreement or majority of opinion. *Never:* "consensus of opinion."

Convince. You may be *convinced* studying is worthwhile. You must be *persuaded* to study.

Courtesy titles (Miss, Mr., Mrs., Ms.) aren't used on first reference (Fred Smith) but often are in second references (Mr. Smith). Many newspapers let women state a preference, particularly in use of Ms.

Courts are capitalized when named in full (U.S. Supreme Court) and also without U.S. or state designation (the Supreme Court).

D

Data is plural (The data *are* here).

Days of the week. Capitalize; don't abbreviate in anything but tabular form.

Decades. Use 1990s; also, it's the '90s.

Destroy means demolish and both mean completely, so don't use "totally destroyed."

Derogatory terms (kraut, nigger, honky) are used only in direct quotations and only if essential to the story.

Different from. Never: different *than.*

Dimensions. He is 6 feet 1 inch tall; the 6–foot-1-inch man. The carpet is 6 feet long, 3 feet wide.

Directions. He drove east (compass direction). He was from the south (again, a compass direction, not capitalized). But, the South fought hard. She is a Southern conservative.

Distances. Under 10, spell it out: The river is four miles long. The lake is 13 miles wide.

Dollars. Under a million, it is $5, $30, $600, $2,000, $750,000. Over that, it is $1 million, $145 million. For specific amounts, use a singular verb: They said $485,000 *is* what they want. This is a million: 1,000,000. A U.S. billion: 1,000,000,000.

Drown. If he drowned, he's dead. If he *was* drowned, somebody did it to him.

Drunk (like intoxicated) is legally defined. Don't write he was drunk unless police say so.

Drugs are narcotics; medicine is the stuff that's good for you.

E

Earthquakes. Terrible for damage they cause, horrible for confusion they create among newswriters. Note: The Richter scale is a gauge of energy released, measured by a seismograph. There is no upper limit to the measurement. Highest on record is 8.9. Consult AP Stylebook.

Editor is capitalized only as formal title before a name.

Elderly can get you in trouble with *older* editors. It's not precise enough for use with an individual, but will do in generic phrases (concern for the elderly). Beware of *senior citizens* for same reason.

Embarrass. Twice with "r," twice with "s."

En route is two words.

Ensure means guarantee; *insure* refers to insurance.

Execute is killing with military or judicial order.

F

False titles derived from occupation (dog catcher) aren't capitalized.

Farther is physical distance (He walked farther). *Further* is time or degree (He is further left, politically).

Federal is capitalized in formal name (Federal Trade Commission) but not as an adjective (federal lands).

Felony is a serious crime; *misdemeanor,* a minor offense. Make certain you check local legal/police authority on which to use.

Fewer is for individual items (boxes, coats), less for bulk or quantity (rain, grain).

Firemen fight fires. Women do, too, so use *firefighter.*

Fliers are handbills or pilots; *flyers,* trains or buses.

Forecast takes an "e." Remember that.

Foreign words such as "versus" and "et cetera" are commonly understood. But, if *you* don't understand a foreign word, many of your readers won't either. So explain it.

Fractions. Amounts less than one are spelled out: three-fifths. More than one: 1 3-16, 5 1-3.

G

Gamut is range or extent (The gamut of possibilities). *Gantlet* is a flogging, literal or figurative. *Gauntlet* is a glove and this, not a gamut or gantlet, is what you throw down to start a fight.

Gay and *lesbian* are synonomous with homosexual.

Gentile is a person who isn't a Jew *but also* a person who isn't a Mormon.

Gentleman isn't synonomous with man; *lady* isn't with woman, either.

Ghetto carries baggage, mostly from Nazi World War II collection points for Jews. Don't use loosely for district, slum, area.

Girl is a female under 18.

Gobbledygook is what you write if you don't know style.

Government is an established political administration. A *junta* is a group or council often seated in a coup. *Regime* is synonomous with political system but it carries negative baggage: Too many foreign correspondents use it for governments they don't like.

Guerrilla is an unorthodox soldier. There is only one orthodox spelling, however— twice with "r," twice with "l."

H

Habeas corpus is a writ ordering a person in custody to be brought before a court. It forces authorities to justify detention.

Handicapped, like *disabled,* is avoided unless essential to your story. Define any handicap and describe how it affects physical or mental performance.

Hang, as AP notes, is used when you hang a picture, a criminal, or yourself. In past tense, use hanged when referring to executions or suicides, *hung* for other actions.

Headquarter can be singular or plural (headquarters), but don't use as verb (He headquartered there).

Her is for a female, not a ship or nation.

His presumes maleness. No: An editor uses his reporters. Yes: Editors use their reporters.

Homicide is a slaying or killing. *Murder* is malicious, premeditated. *Manslaughter* is homicide without malice or premeditation. Use with precision.

I

Illegal is used *only* to mean violation of law.

Imply is what writers/speakers do in words they use. You *infer* from what they write/say.

Include is used for a *partial* series: A newspaper staff includes editors and compositors. Use *comprise* when you list all individual elements: A newspaper comprises 43 job categories.

Indict is used *only* for charges brought against an individual or corporation in a legal process.

Initials take periods with no spaces (C.L. Sulzberger). Use middle initials when integral to the person's name.

Innocent is preferred to "not guilty" because "not" can be omitted inadvertently.

Irregardless is a double negative, never to be used regardless of circumstances.

It's is a contraction (it is). *Its* is possessive (The university counted its students).

J

Jargon generally should be avoided, and always explained when used.

Judge is capitalized before the name, not after or in second reference (the judge).

Junior, senior are Jr., Sr. after full names (Fred Smith Sr.). An individual's preference is followed with such as II or 2nd.

Juvenile delinquent is a legal definition in some states. Check locally whether it's legal to publish their names.

K

Kids are goats; children only if informal story context warrants.

Kilometer equals 3,281 feet, or 0.62 of a mile, so 5 kilometers × 0.62 = 3.1 miles.

Knot is one nautical mile (6,076.10 feet) per hour, so "knots per hour" is redundant.

L

Lady is a title or reference to fine manners, not a synonym for woman.

Languages and dialects are capitalized (French, Cajun).

Last implies finality. Don't use for "latest." (The "last time" it snowed really wasn't the last time.)

Lawyer is a member of the bar; an attorney is legally empowered to act for another but isn't always a lawyer.

Lay. Hens lay eggs. Then, eggs lie there.

Leftist is too vague; precisely describe political philosophies.

Legislative titles are abbreviated before names (Sen., Reps.) but not in quotations ("He said Senator Smith was wrong"). Capitalize in title (Assemblyman Smith).

Legislature is capitalized (the Kansas Legislature) when referring to specific body, even when it stands alone (the Legislature).

Like used as a preposition to compare nouns and pronouns requires an object: The president debates like a veteran. *As* is a conjunction introducing clauses: The president debates as a veteran should.

M

Magistrate is capitalized in a title.

Majority is more than half; *plurality,* more than the next highest number.

Marshal is both a verb and noun; Fred Smith is a field marshal. He will marshal his forces.

Media is plural (American media are free).

Meter is the equivalent (rounded off) of 39.5 inches.

Mishaps are minor misfortunes; people aren't killed in them.

Months. Capitalize, abbreviate when using with specific date, spell out when standing alone: September 1932 but Sept. 16, 1932. Don't abbreviate March, April, May, June, July.

N

Names. Use what people want (Muhammad Ali, not Cassius Clay).

Nationalities and races are capitalized (American, Afro-American). White, red, black aren't.

Newspaper names are used as newspapers prefer. That includes capitalizing "The" (*The Athens* (Ga.) *Daily News*).

Nolo contendere means, "I do not wish to contest." Use "no contest" or "no-contest plea" in court stories.

None is singular (None is here), but use plural verbs if the sense is no two or no amount (None of the students have arrived).

Norm means standard, model, pattern for a group.

Numerals. Spell out under 10 (nine horses) but use figure for 10 and over (13 people). When large numbers must be spelled out, hyphenate to connect a word ending in "y" (sixty-five). Don't start sentences with numerals. Spell out in casual use (Thanks a million). Usage examples: The Board voted 5–4. From $12 million to $14 million (not $12 to $14 million). The inflation rate increased to 6 percent from 5 percent. A 2–4 ratio. A 6–5 score.

O

Obscenities are used only in full quotes when essential to your story.

Occur, occurred, occurring, occurrence.

OK, not okay.

On. The meeting was Jan. 20 (not *on* Jan. 20).

Oral communication is spoken.

Over indicates spatial relationships (He towered over her). It also is used with numerals (He is over 30). However: The temperature rose *more than* 10 degrees. Taxes rose *more than* $100.

P

Pardon forgives, *parole* releases on condition of good behavior before sentence expires, *probation* suspends sentence on condition of good behavior.

Party affiliation. Republican Sen. Fred Smith of Georgia. Sen. Fred Smith, D-Ga., explained. . . . Sen. Fred Smith spoke. The Georgia Democrat said. . . . On state level: Rep. Fred Smith, D-Atlanta, said. . . .

Person for an individual (One person voted) but *people* in plural uses (Thousands of people voted).

Percent, one word, takes singular verb when singular word follows *of* construction (About 50 percent of the membership was there). It takes plural verb when plural word follows (About 50 percent of the members were there).

Plead, pleaded, pleading (not *pled*).

Plurals can be tricky, so check Stylebook. But: When significant word comes first, make it *attorneys* general; when it's in the middle, use assistant attorneys general; when last, assistant attorneys.

Possessives. Check Stylebook. For now, note these uses: plural nouns not ending in *s* (women's); plural nouns ending in *s* (companies'); singular common nouns ending in *s* take added *'s* (witness's) *unless* next word begins with *s* (witness' story); joint possession (Fred and Sylvia's apartment); individual possession (Fred's and Sylvia's separately owned books).

Principal means rank, authority, importance, degree (high school principal); *principle* is a truth, law, doctrine, motivating force (The principle of freedom).

Punctuation. Read AP Stylebook carefully on *colon, comma, dash, ellipsis, exclamation mark, hyphen, parentheses, period, question mark, quotation mark, semicolon.* For now: *colon* is used most frequently at end of sentence to introduce lists, tabulations, etc. (The list:); capitalize first word after colon if it is a proper noun or the start of a complete sentence. *Commas* separate elements in a series, but don't use before conjunction in a simple series (The car is powerful, fast and expensive). Use *exclamation* marks sparingly, to express strong surprise or emotion. *Question marks* are used at end of direct question (Are you there?) but *not* with indirect questions (He wondered if he would be late). *Quotation marks* are used to open (") and close (") exact words of a speaker or writer, both with full quotation (He said, "I am late.") and with partial quote (He said he was "terribly sorry" to be late). Place punctuation (periods, commas, quotation marks, etc.) inside quotation marks; see Stylebook for exceptions.

Q

Quotations. Put it in quotes only if it is *precisely* what was said. If you make the slightest change, remove the quotes.

R

Race identification is pertinent in stories on feats/appointments not routinely associated with members of a particular race, when essential in stories on events (demonstrations, for example) involving racial matters. Derogatory terms are used only in direct quotes when essential to the story.

Ratios. Use figures/hyphens (The ratio was 2-to-1. A 2-to-1 ratio.).

Roman numerals are for wars (World War II) and personal sequence for people and animals (Fred Smith III, Native Dancer II). Otherwise, use Arabic numerals.

Russia is the dominant republic in the Soviet Union. Russia and Russians are acceptable synonyms for Soviets and Soviet Union when referring to the *government*. Russia or Russians are not acceptable in referring to all peoples in the Soviet Union (thus, the *Soviet* tour group, not Russian group, visits the United States).

S

Savings and loan associations are *not* banks.

School is capitalized in proper name (Benton Elementary School).

Seasons. Lower case unless in formal name (Dartmouth Winter Festival).

Semiannual means twice a year; biennial means every two years.

Sentences. Capitalize first word of each, *including* quoted statements (He said, "She knows what's wrong").

Shall expresses determination (I shall win).

Sheriff. Note spelling.

Should expresses obligation (You should help her).

(Sic). Indicates error, peculiar usage or spelling in original. Use sparingly after consulting your editor.

Sisters-in-law is plural.

Slang is used only sparingly but sometimes effectively in features, other special circumstances.

Speech titles are capitalized and set, in quotation marks. (His talk was "The Necessity of Learning Style.")

Speeds. Use figures (Winds of 5 to 8 miles an hour).

Spokesman, spokeswoman (not spokesperson).

Stationary is to stand still; *stationery* is writing paper.

T

Teen, teen-ager, teen-age (not teen-aged).

Telecast is a noun; *televise* a verb: They televised the game (not telecast the game).

Temperatures use figures except for zero (The low was minus 10). Note: Temperatures get higher or lower, not warmer or colder.

That and **which** refer to inanimate objects; *who* and *whom* to people and animals with names.

Their is a possessive pronoun (Their house). *There* is an adverb indicating direction (He went there afterward). *They're* is a contraction for *they are*.

Ton. They are short, long, or metric. Look them up.

Truman, Harry S. To learn how custom influences style, read this entry in AP's stylebook.

U

Under way is two words.

Unique is *one* of a kind, so never "nearly unique."

United States is spelled out as a noun; use U.S. only as adjective (The United States is huge; the U.S. forces are large).

V

Vacuum. Note spelling.

Versus is abbreviated (vs.) in all uses.

W

Wall Street is the entire complex of financial institutions.

War is capitalized in names of specific conflicts (the Civil War).

Bullet is fired from barrel; a *cartridge* is casing, primer, propellant and bullet.

Weather terms (blizzard, cyclone) have precise meanings. Look them up.

Whereabouts takes singular verb (His whereabouts is unknown).

Who's is a contraction (who is); *whose* is possessive (Whose coat is it?).

-wide takes no hyphen (citywide, nationwide).

XYZ

X-ray is hyphenated.

Youth covers boys/girls 13–18; man/woman, 18 and older.

ZIP code. Use it for Zone Improvement Program; lowercase code.

Name Index

Subject Index

Editing

The Defense Department said today	indent
it had proposed spending	run in
110 million for a new jet fighter	insert missing $
to be named the "Cobra."	transpose letters
The jet was thought once	transpose words
to be too expensive for the	separate words
Navy but officials said	lower case; no cap
all services, including the navy--	insert dash
would use the plane⊗	insert period (ALSO ⊙)
Over the week end,	join together
one official said, "We have every	insert quotation marks
hope of success.	
He added, "So does the navy."	insert comma
But Senator Fred Smith said	abbreviate
the white house wouldn't comment.	capitalize
For twelve hours, the Defense	use figure 12
Department	
counted 8 separate incidents.	spell out eight
Finally, the sen said he	spell out senator
would ffinally go to the people.	take out f
For him him, that was a tragedy.	take out him
Sen. John Jones joined *STET*	don't make correction
the debate with Wilsen.	spell as written (also use "wilsen (cq)")
Its a certain	insert apostrophe
thing, whether that was	insert semicolon
Anti war groups booed.	insert hyphen

Other symbols:
Story continues MORE
story ends – 30 –
flush left
flush right
center
set uppercase
set lowercase
set in italics
BF set boldface